# LAW, PROPHETS,
# AND WRITINGS

# LAW, PROPHETS, AND WRITINGS

## THE RELIGION
## OF THE BOOKS OF THE
## OLD TESTAMENT

## J. N. SCHOFIELD

*formerly*
*Fellow of University College Cambridge*
*Lecturer in Hebrew and Old Testament Studies*
*in the University of Cambridge*

---

*President of the Society for*
*Old Testament Study, 1969*

LONDON

S·P·C·K

1969

*First published in 1969*
*by S.P.C.K.*
*Holy Trinity Church*
*Marylebone Road*
*London N.W.1*

*Made and printed in Great Britain by*
*The Camelot Press Ltd, London and Southampton*

SBN 281 02287 9

# Contents

# Introduction

For many reasons I was delighted when the S.P.C.K. invited me to write a book on Old Testament religion. Since the publication of my previous book,[1] knowledge has been enriched by extensive archaeological discoveries in Palestine and surrounding lands. There have been great advances in linguistic and semantic study of Hebrew and the Semitic languages, and in particular the recognition that in Old Testament study we are concerned with the meaning of words in their contexts. There has, too, been much new thinking on biblical theology and the philosophy of religion.

Books on Old Testament religion have approached the subject in many ways, and in the main the method of approach has reflected the prevailing philosophy of the scholar's own age.[2] The scholarly approach of the decades round the opening of the twentieth century has been called Critical Orthodoxy. It was influenced by Frazer's work on the general origin of religion, Robertson Smith's on the religion of the Semites, and the Graf-Wellhausen theories of the growth of Old Testament literature and religion, which rearranged the Old Testament chronologically to show a line of progressive revelation from early Semitic beliefs through the epoch-making preaching of the eighth-century prophets, the cultic practices of the exilic age, and the priestly laws of the Pentateuch, to the new prophetic revival in the New Testament.

There has since been what may be called the "Pattern" approach. This made use of the extensive archaeological and linguistic discoveries, in particular those at Ras Shamra in Syria, and traced connections between the Old Testament and a general "myth and ritual pattern" of Near-Eastern religion postulated from these discoveries. Words and ritual practices in the Old Testament were regarded as showing a similar "pattern". My own book, mentioned above, shared this general approach. It was written after long residence in Egypt and

[1] *The Religious Background of the Bible* (1944).
[2] For a short history of the study of Old Testament religion, see O. Procksch, *Theologie des Alten Testaments* (1950); R. C. Dentan, *Preface to Old Testament Theology* (1950).

Palestine, and time spent at archaeological sites and at the American School of Oriental Research at Jerusalem, where Dr W. F. Albright was Director. It attempted not only to use our knowledge of the religion of the Semites but to set the whole Bible in its contemporaneous world as revealed in archaeological remains, and to trace the chronological growth of the religion. But just as "Critical Orthodoxy" was based on a hypothetical reconstruction of the Old Testament, so "Pattern Orthodoxy" began from a reconstruction based on archaeological remains and went on to postulate elaborate annual religious festivals of the New Year and royal enthronement rites in Israel. Acceptance of the hypothetical cult pattern profoundly influenced the interpretation of the whole Old Testament. Even the central fact of Old Testament tradition, the Deliverance from Egypt, has been treated as the putting into an historical form of the myth of the annual death and resurrection of the god of fertility.

Another approach that has influenced the study of Old Testament religion is closer in spirit to "Critical Orthodoxy" in that it stresses the development of the literature. It emphasizes the length of the oral period through which the traditions came to us, the formative and modifying influences of the centuries that handled them, with their successive remintings of the traditions, and points out that it is virtually impossible to recover their original form. It believes that most of the Old Testament as we have it was not written until after the destruction of Jerusalem by the Babylonians in 586 B.C., and that the traditions crystallized round the great religious festivals, Spring/Passover, Autumn/New Year. Here it is rather the formation and growth of the great units of tradition that belong to the sphere of hypothetical reconstruction. It is not yet possible to date them accurately.

These successive theoretical approaches or "Orthodoxies" have brought valuable insights into the background and original meaning of much of the religion conserved in the Old Testament. But the stress is on origins rather than on the difference made to these borrowed words, traditions, and practices when they were adapted or incorporated by Israel. It is always dangerous to assume that similar language and practices have the same meaning in different religious settings.

A method of approach that has to some extent broken away from the stress on origins is associated with the phrase "Salvation history". This regards the Old Testament as written to show God's saving acts, and as having little interest in accurate presentation of actual "pragmatic" events. It sees the selection and order of events with their whole treatment as determined by doctrinal and cultic considerations, and maintains that in the Old Testament the records of history are made subservient to the theme of salvation.

In all this activity, there has been the usual danger that besets biblical scholarship. It has been claimed that no scholar can work profitably on the Bible unless he has faith with which to interpret it. Certainly all of us find it difficult to free ourselves from the subtle, often unrecognized influence of our credal background. But even more evident, especially to those who differ from us, is the way our overall interpretation of the heterogeneous Old Testament material is influenced by the theories we hold true in our critical assumptions. Inevitably, we all tend to notice evidence that supports us, and to miss evidence to the contrary.

There is still much debate about the chronological order in which the books of the Old Testament were originally written or attained their present form, for it is clear that additions have been made to them. Thus any attempt to trace the historical development of the religion must be based on theoretical reconstruction that may be disputed. On the other hand, if we abandon such an attempt and try to abstract ideas and produce a systematic treatment of the religion, the ideas themselves escape us when divorced from the historical or narrative setting which gave them their peculiar meaning. Any system has to be superimposed on the Old Testament.

Wrestling with these difficulties, Procksch began his great *Theologie* with an historical account, which he compared with some justice to a longitudinal section. But when he came to supplement this with a picture of the Old Testament thought-world, the analogy of a cross-section he found to be inappropriate, for any cross-section of growth would have to be on to a "projected" plane—again the hypothetical element would take control (p. 420). After all, in biology a cross-section is made of a selected part, not of a whole organism. Thus he suggested the analogy of water. He chose such great key-words as faith, covenant, righteousness, and considered them as stones flung into pools causing ripples in widening circles. But it has been objected that this method leads to the presentation not of Old Testament religion but of a collection of abstractions.

It therefore seems wiser to take the final form of the Hebrew Old Testament as the basis of our study, and consider the religion as it is presented by the final editors. It also seems best not to attempt to make a cross-section but to take the final stage of growth when, as in the Yarrow, blossoms are carried up to the same plane on stems of varying length from the main axis to form a magnificent flower-head.[1] The analogy of this corymb form is perhaps the more appropriate because it resembles the stylized Jewish emblem of the seven-branched lampstand if the number of lamps were irregular and greatly increased. Sometimes the differing age of the traditions and the date at which they have been used is as clear and incontrovertible as the varying lengths of stems in the flower-head, but we shall not be concerned with the length of stems linking each blossom to the main axis, but with the whole flower. It is not development in history that is our concern, but we shall attempt to appreciate the religious ideas in the contexts in which they were presented by the final editors.

There is a need for a fresh look, as detached as possible, at the Old Testament in its final form, and an attempt in the light of recent advances in biblical sciences to see what is the impact of the whole. It would be presumptuous to lay claim to scholarly detachment, but the wide welcome accorded to my short survey, *Introducing Old Testament Theology* (1964), has encouraged me to hope that a similar approach to Old Testament religion may help. In the present book, Old Testament religion is regarded as limited to the Hebrew canon; the threefold division there into Law, Prophets, and Writings is followed; the given content and order within them is accepted, and an attempt is made to study the religion of each section, remembering that each spans most of the Old Testament period. Each may be thought of as a different aspect of Old Testament religion, and in each may be seen distinctive ideas, so that Law, Prophets, and Writings have been characterized as Priestly, Prophetic, and Wise[2] religion. But, and this is most important, we shall find that these three elements in religion are blended in each of the three sections, as they were in the religious life of Israel. Our chief aim is not to analyse or separate them, but to appreciate them as a whole. In this way we can study the complete flower-head in the form in which the final editors have given it to us, recognize its essential unity, and see the magnificent beauty and fruit-bearing capacity of the Old Testament as a whole.

It then becomes apparent that it is worth looking at for itself, and that we should try to appraise its value in its own right, not treat it as simply a preparation for the New Testament and superseded by its fulfilment there. It has been said that America was not discovered till men explored it for its own sake, not as a stage on the route to some-

---

[1] Cf. the illustration on p. xiii opposite.
[2] "Wise" implies discreet, sound judgement concerning what is true or false, proper or improper, often based on long folk-traditions.

where else. The Old Testament, like the New, contains the revealing word of God. It was the Bible of Jesus of Nazareth, and three world faiths still hear that word from it.

In this book we shall therefore attempt to see the central religious element which for so many centuries has drawn men to use the Old Testament, encountering afresh as they read it the God who confronted the men and women whose experiences are recorded there, and being helped to discern perhaps the outline of his form as it comes to them in their own daily life. We shall not attempt to do what many recent writers have done so well, to state and discuss the various theories formulated to interpret it.

But I cannot adequately express my indebtedness to so many previous writers, in particular to Otto Procksch and two of his illustrious pupils, Walther Eichrodt and Gerhard von Rad, and to Dr H. H. Rowley, whose extensive work contains such valuable and comprehensive reference to the previous contributions of scholars. I wish also to express my gratitude to Professor D. W. Thomas for his ready assistance. The recent work of A. Neher and E. Voegelin I have found helpful and stimulating. My own references here have been kept to a minimum.

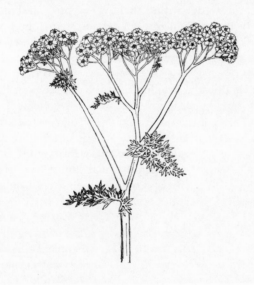

# PART I
# LAW

PART I

# LAW

# 1  The Preface to the Saga

The first section of the Old Testament in its present form is called Torah, translated Law; but a look at its contents shows that the Hebrew word has a far wider meaning than ours. The five books from Genesis to Deuteronomy relate the popular stories of the Patriarchs, whom tradition regarded as the ancestors of the Hebrews, the deliverance of a group from slavery in Egypt, God's revelation of his name and will to them at Sinai, and in Deuteronomy a repetition of the account of that theophany and law-giving as the group was about to enter the land promised them by their God.

But prefacing the patriarchal saga are recounted stories important for understanding the religion of the Old Testament. There is the magnificent frontispiece depicting the Creation, in which everything was made and pronounced good by God; the story of Paradise, the Garden of Eden, lost through human disobedience; of human jealousy and murder; of sin whose corruption spread to both heavenly and human beings; of divine judgement that destroyed the world and then began patiently to regain for man his lost paradise, restoring life to the world from the survivors of the flood. These stories come from different milieux of time, thought, and place. Using the botanical metaphor[1] we may say that the stems bearing the flowers are of different lengths, but the blooms in the final form presented to us in the Pentateuch have much to teach us of the God of Israel.

## Creation Stories

The Old Testament opens with the wonderful picture of God the Creator, whose word formed order from confusion, a universe from chaos. The difficulty of translating the opening sentences of Genesis 1 makes it unwise to dogmatize. The first words may mean "In the beginning God created the heaven and the earth". The stress here would be that at a definite moment history began, the timeless God stepped into time, the spiritual became involved with the material. At that moment God created from nothing the universe, heaven and

[1] Cf. above, pp. xif.

LB

earth as an embryo surrounded by waters. But the grammatical form of the first Hebrew word here, and the opening of the parallel story in Genesis 2.4ff suggest that the first absolute statement is that God said, Let there be light, the first two verses showing the condition prevailing when God spoke: "In the beginning of God's creating (or, when God began to create) the heaven and the earth, when the earth was without form or order and darkness was over the primeval deep and the spirit of God was brooding (hovering) over its waters, then God said. . . ." Here the stress is on the conditions in which God's creative word was first heard, the vivid contrast between the formless chaotic mass and the great Creator: the fact that God outside space and time spoke a word. This translation lends no support to the doctrine of creation from nothing, but the writer does not attempt to explain the origin of the primeval formless chaos, the covering darkness, nor the waters of the vast deep. He strongly suggests that it was not outside God's control, for the wind or spirit of God[1] was fluttering, brooding over it like some watchful bird.

Neither interpretation could be further removed from myth or dualism. God is thought of as utterly separate, distinct from the material universe which he completely transcends. He and it have no common origin: he does not emanate from it, nor is any physical act of his, apart from speaking, necessary to make it. The only concession to underlying cultic myth is the absence of a definite article with *Tehom* —deep—as though recognizing that it was once a proper name. The spirit of God provides the only movement and life in that inanimate desolate waste. There is also no suggestion here, as in the myths of peoples surrounding Israel, of any struggle or fight before God could create.[2] The limitation of primeval darkness and of the waters flows effortlessly from the all-powerful God. He need only speak and the all-enveloping darkness is immediately limited by light, and later is controlled by the heavenly lights. Light and darkness are separated. So also the firmament like an inverted beaten-out metal bowl is inserted as a dam into the watery mass, restraining the waters above and allowing the waters underneath to be gathered together so that dry land can be seen—possibly the seas were thought of as piled up to touch the firmament on the far horizon. Darkness is not presented as negative, the absence of light, but has a positive quality of its own over against light, as have the surrounding waters of chaos in distinc-

---

[1] Possibly the phrase should be treated as a superlative, i.e. a Mighty Wind.

[2] D. W. Thomas (ed.), *Documents from Old Testament Times* (1958).

tion from the dry land and the firmament. It is important to note that here there is no hint that man need fear the return of the darkness and waters of chaos. Light has broken darkness, firmament and dry land have once for all limited the waters. Vegetation is possible, light is controlled and made to alternate with darkness as day and night.

Except in the introductory and concluding verses (1.1; 2.3f) the Hebrew verb "create"—only used of God's activity and always with a sense of wonder—occurs only in v. 21 of making the great sea monsters, fish and birds, and emphatically three times in v. 27[1] of making mankind, as though to stress that humanity owes the wonder of its being directly to God's "creative" action. In more secondary fashion, vegetation and animal life have been brought forth by the earth, itself "created" by God. With man the words of creation end.

Much has been written about the meaning of "Let us make" and "our image" (1.26). The later use of the two words "likeness" and "image" of Adam's begetting Seth (5.3) suggests here a reference to the whole form of man as God-like, perhaps, unlike the beasts, standing erect, and the context stresses a primary reference to man's God-given dominion over all created things. The plural "us", "our", may reflect simply the plural form of God in Hebrew (*Elohim*) and be the natural pronoun to use.[2] If the writer had wished to assert that man's likeness was to heavenly beings around God's throne and so to avoid the idea of any image or likeness of God,[3] he could more easily have used the phrase "sons of God" to express this idea.

The purpose of the account might have been expressed in the words "Lo! I tell you a mystery" (1 Cor. 15.51). What is clearly expressed is the wonder that things exist at all. God, who is a living God, not a philosophical First Cause, stepped into history and creation was the result. This is not in the strict sense Wisdom Literature. It is both science and religion, before there was conflict between them, attempting to answer the question How? Possibly this is the teaching or preaching referred to in Isaiah 40.21: "Have you not known? Have you not heard? Has it not been told you from the beginning? Have you not understood the founding of the earth?"[4] The language shows links with priestly and institutional religion. The purpose of sun, moon, and stars is to separate day from night and to be

---

[1] Note here the chiasmic pattern, created, image/image, created, a favourite device of the writer of Isa. 40—55.

[2] Though the noun is construed, as usual in Hebrew, with a singular verb.

[3] Cf. von Rad, *Old Testament Theology* (E.T. 1962) I, p. 145.

[4] Cf. p. 137 below.

a token to mark the religious festivals; and the climax of all these great creative acts is God's blessing and hallowing of the seventh day as a rest day. There is no act of creation of the Sabbath, nor its institution as obligatory observance. Later, Israel will be commanded to share in hallowing this day's cessation from toil as a weekly memorial, when God's mighty acts of creation and salvation may be celebrated.

The characteristic priestly phrase "These are the generations of" (2.4) has often been regarded as simply the conclusion of this first account; but here as elsewhere the priestly writer uses it when introducing the next development in the story. In this half-verse he briefly recapitulates what has gone before as a preparation for a new phase. For him the second story (2.4bff) is not a parallel story of creation, but goes beyond the mighty act of creating heaven and earth to the story of earth's first human inhabitants. Second-Isaiah stresses the same connection when he says, "He did not create it a chaos, he formed it to be inhabited" (45.18).[1]

In this second story, usually designated J,[2] to the word "God" (*Elohim*) used in chapter 1 is added a second divine name not explained until the account of the age of Moses (Exod. 6.2f). It is a personal name whose pronunciation has been lost, because later Jews regarded it as too sacred to utter, and substituted the Hebrew word for "My Lord".[3] In Genesis 2 and 3 appears the unusual combination of the two terms, the Lord God. God's activity is also differently pictured. Vividness replaces majestic wonder. Not only does he speak, but he makes the rain come, moulds[4] clay like a potter, blows his breath into human nostrils, and plants a garden. Everything is done by God alone; he makes the trees grow out of the ground, and moulds the animals from it, whereas in the first account earth and water are given the power of themselves to bring forth life. Man, however, in both stories is allowed to share in God's labours, replenishing the earth and tilling the soil. Further, the order of creation in Genesis 1 is not followed in the second chapter, where first God moulds man,[5] then plants the garden, and forms animals and finally woman for man's sake.

[1] A similar method is seen in Gen. 5.1ff, where the transition is made from the creation of mankind to the descendants of Adam.

[2] See below, p. 13, n. 1.

[3] *Adonai*, the vowels of which, with phonetic changes necessary when combined with the consonants of the Hebrew sacred name, produced the hybrid English word Jehovah.

[4] Another Hebrew word, not the one translated "create".

[5] In Hebrew there is a play on the words "man" and "ground"—*adam* and *adamah*.

The climax of the first story is that God, having finished creation and made provision for man's needs, rested pleased with all his mighty acts of wonder; it is comparable to the New Testament picture of Jesus, having completed the work of salvation, ascending and sitting at the right hand of God. The climax of the second story is human rather than divine—the happy human pair living together and working for God in his garden (2.25). But their happiness is to be short-lived. On this idyllic picture of paradise with one prohibition (2.17) separating the human from the divine, follows the story of man's grasping at equality with God (cf. Phil. 2.6f), human rebellion and human death.

The very existence of the ordered universe depends on bounds being kept, and man's life too depends on his obeying God's commands and accepting a limitation of freedom. Man has been made in the image and likeness of God, and now he is placed in the garden with the two trees of life and of knowledge. In ancient myths there was a forbidden tree whose fruit, if eaten by man, would make him immortal. The tree of life is here too in the garden (3.22), apparently free to man in his innocent state, and the forbidden tree is one that gives the divine power of awareness of evil as well as of good, the intimate experiential knowledge of the difference between them, from which the Lord God wishes to shield his young creation.

Eating this fruit "opened their eyes". They knew the possibility of evil as well as of good, they were ashamed of their nakedness. Laid on them was the responsibility of choice, of refusing evil and choosing good (Isa. 7.15). God condemned them, for they had disobeyed him, rejected his lordship, an act which broke their fellowship with him and made them hide in fear at his approach. His statement that eating the fruit would bring death probably referred solely to the act of disobedience, and did not imply that all their subsequent choices would be evil. The judgement here is cast in the same solemn form as appears in the legal sentence of death for the breach of divine commands (Heb. emphatic, dying he shall die; cf. Exod. 21.12).

In the first creation story the origin of chaos and darkness is ignored, whereas here the temptation to evil is traced by the writer to the mysterious semi-demonic figure of the serpent. Archaeology shows the serpent cult to have been widespread in the ancient Near East (cf. 2 Kings 18.4), sometimes linked with healing (Num. 21.9), sometimes as here with sex and fertility cults. The problem of how any part of God's good creation could entice to evil and rebellion is ignored in this second story, where the point of interest is not the origin of sin but its nature and consequences, the guilt being man's, because of his disobedience. In Genesis 8.21, another explanation is given, that the mould or formation (RSV, imagination) of a man's personality (heart) is evil from his youth. The implication of this is not quite clear, but the post-biblical Jewish belief that man is born with an evil inclination, and receives a good one when in early youth he becomes a "son of the law", is not suggested by the use of the word "youth" rather than "birth" in 8.21. Possibly there is a recognition that the struggle between the right and wrong use of sex which can so often pervert personality comes at puberty—the fruit is eaten then.

## Sin and its Consequences

After the two creation stories there follow four pictures of sin and its meaning. In the Eden story disobedience did not immediately bring physical death—on a short view the serpent was right. It made man ashamed and afraid in the presence of God. The serpent, through whom the evil impulse had entered the world, was cursed.[1] The woman was punished by pain at childbirth, together with a desire for, and subjection to, her husband that made childbirth inevitable. The assumption is that, before sin entered the world, childbirth was painless, and because there was no need for the man to control the woman, who had not then tempted him to evil, she lived in intimate equality with her husband. Neither man nor woman was directly cursed. The curse fell first on the serpent and then on the ground, and it is from this latter curse that the punishment of the man derives (because of you, Gen. 3.17). Thorns and weeds will grow, but his need for food will force on man the toil of keeping them in check. Before the fall, man's purpose and joy was the cultivation and care of the garden (2.15), and we are not to assume that woman was denied the purpose and joy of motherhood, nor that Paradise was to have been empty of boys and girls. But sin had brought sorrow, and now the happiness of parenthood and man's joy in his work were to be troubled by pain, anxiety, and frustration. For the writer of the story the major consequences were that the tree of life, which would have enabled man to live for ever, and which was not previously forbidden to him, was put beyond his reach, and he was driven out for ever from the garden of God that he had known in his innocence, to spend, toiling on the accursed ground, his limited number of days. On the longer view, sin had brought death; but there is a significant hint of one way in which

[1] Cf. Matt. 18.6 where Jesus pronounced a similar sentence on the tempter.

man's condition will be redeemed. God will put enmity between the woman's seed and the tempter, so that constantly man will fight against sin and loathe it.[1] Though there is no direct reference to this story in any other part of the Old Testament, it would be true to say that it embodies the teaching of the Deuteronomist and the prophets that man has no life apart from fellowship with God. "Loving the Lord your God, obeying his voice, and cleaving to him . . . means life to you and length of days" (Deut. 30.20).

The story of Cain and Abel presents the second picture. Cain like his father tilled the soil, Abel was a shepherd. Cain brought a gift of the fruit of the ground, Abel, in accord with ritual later required, brought firstlings from the flock and fat portions, and God took an interest in Abel's offering but not in Cain's. Was it because God preferred animal to vegetable offerings, or that Cain did not bring firstfruits whereas Abel brought firstlings? God's pleading with the angry, jealous Cain shows that there was no divine caprice, but Cain had not done well and so had not found favour. God's plea is interesting: "Is it not true that if you do well you will be treated with favour, but if not, then at the door Sin [missing-the-mark] is a crouching wild beast; his desire is to get you, but you can bring him into subjection" (Gen. 4.7).[2] One act may lead to another, but there is no inevitable sequence in the rake's progress. Cain chose to allow the beast in, and committed premeditated[3] murder and a cynical rejection of social responsibility. On him fell the curse of the ground which had received his brother's innocent blood. The cry of the blood for vengeance gave him no rest to till the soil. Then God intervened in mercy, not to take away the consequences but to mitigate them. With God's protective mark upon him, Cain was driven out from God's presence. No longer able to till the soil, he became a city-dweller;[4] but his descendants were wandering Kenite smiths with tents, cattle, musical instruments, and metal-working. That they held human life cheap is shown by Lamech's boastful song to his two wives (4.23):

> A man I have slain for wounding me,
> A young man for bruising me.

It seems probable that in the original Cain story it was emphasized that there was no necessary, inevitable heritage of sin. The writer

[1] See below, p. 271.
[2] The same words, desire and subjection, are used of Eve's relationship to Adam (3.16).
[3] Cf. Gen. 4.8, RSV margin.   [4] For Kenite cities cf. 1 Sam. 30.29.

maintains that Cain's son was Enoch, who according to the priestly
writer talked with God and was "taken"[1] to him. A later descendant of
them both was the vengeful Lamech, whose son Noah, however, was
to bring comfort to mitigate the curse on the ground.[2]

The third picture (Gen. 6ff) using highly symbolic language from
ancient myths, presents another aspect of sin. Divine beings were
roaming the earth (Job 1.7) taking wives from the daughters of men,
and there was again danger that the distinction between God and man
might be obliterated, so God limited the length of a human life, the
time that God's spirit would dwell in flesh. But still there were
giants[3] and mighty semi-divine beings, and corruption on earth
increased so that God was distressed[4] as he contemplated what was
happening to his good creation. Evil was to be swept away in the
great Flood and, so that the righteous die not with the wicked (Gen.
18.23), a new beginning was to be made with the one righteous man,
Noah, who, like Enoch, walked with God (6.9). To him God revealed
his plan of destruction, and Noah made no intercession for creation
but obediently co-operated with God's plans. Archaeology has shown
that other forms of flood stories ended with sacrifice to God[5] and our
story ends in a similar way. Here again we are made aware of a keen
interest in religious institutions, like that of the Sabbath already
mentioned. Interest focuses on the meaning of sacrifice, the distinction between clean and unclean animals, and the sacredness of blood.
Judging from the result of Noah's holocaust (8.20), its purpose was
that God should be pleased, forgive man's sin, recognize the impossibility of human perfection, and promise never again to destroy
creation. Probably, too, there was an element of gratitude from Noah.
God's promise became the first covenant between God and man,
made with Noah and through him with all historic humanity, its
visible and perpetual sign being the rainbow. The later religious distinction between clean and unclean animals is recognized by one
writer here, who thinks of seven pairs of the clean and one pair of the
unclean animals being saved in the ark (7.2). Elsewhere in the story all
animals without distinction enter the ark in pairs (6.19). Noah takes
only clean animals for his sacrifice (8.20), but, in contradistinction to

[1] See below, p. 281.

[2] P includes both Enoch and Lamech in the genealogy of Seth (Gen. 5.21,
25).

[3] Hebrew *Nephilim*, suggesting Fallen Ones; cf. Num. 13.33.

[4] The Hebrew word is the same as is used of Eve's sorrow in childbirth
(3.16).

[5] Cf. D. W. Thomas, op. cit., pp. 17ff.

later regulations, all animals are allowable for food (9.3). With the gift of animal food goes a regulation as to blood, which is the life (9.4). No animal blood may be eaten, and man or beast shedding human blood must be slain by man, for in the image of God man was made (9.6). The responsibility for punishing the crime is man's—he is God's representative and must enforce the moral world order.[1]

The fourth picture of sin (11.1–9) appears to arise from the sight of the great tower-like temples of Babylon, and to deride them with verses from a popular song. The tower was thought of as another challenge by man to God's authority, and an effort to gain human independence:

> Come let us make bricks
> And thoroughly bake them,
> Come let us build ourselves a city,
> And a tower with its top in heaven,
> Let us make for ourselves a name
> Lest we be scattered abroad
> Over all the earth.

But God replies:

> Come let us go down
> And confuse there their language (11.7).[2]

Confusion of language in the world was not part of God's original plan, but necessary punishment, perhaps on Babylonian foreigners for rebellious pride.

In the present form of the Old Testament these stories of creation and sin provide the religious and historical setting for the patriarchal saga. The impression left by these introductory stories is that they were an essential part of education in the home (Deut. 6.20–5) and the sanctuary (26.1–11). There they were told in order to win from the hearers a willing acceptance of some law or ritual requirement. In this setting the commands were presented not as arbitrary orders from a capricious God but as reasonable regulations "for our good", and obedience was an act showing loyalty to God (Deut. 6.24f). In the form in which they are retained in Genesis 1—11 we have the simple stories without the moral or the relevance to the particular contemporary situation. This had to be drawn out on each occasion by

[1] von Rad, *Genesis* (1961), ad loc.
[2] Cf. 11.5, where in the prose of the writer who quotes the song God had already gone down.

speakers or hearers. To win acceptance of the sabbath law, the first creation story would lead hearers to a joyful sharing of the sabbath rest with the Creator, and the weekly remembrance of the wonder of creation. Genesis 2 might be used in preparation for marriage (cf. v. 24). The stories of Cain and Lamech might show the necessity for the absolute law of capital punishment for murder (9.6). God's care for Cain protected the murderer from the full consequences of his crime; but after protection came licence, the unlimited shedding of human blood by the braggart Lamech. Perhaps, too, bloodshed was thought to be part of the corruption which led to the Flood, so that a completely new attitude to all bloodshed was willingly accepted at the new beginning of the life of historic humanity.

In all these stories there is a depth of religious experience still relevant to our own age. Creation is seen as very good, sin is presented as active and malignant. It is the refusal to live in humble submission before the Creator, and to accept as good his known will. Its outcome is the disruption of divine order and purpose, the breaking of companionship with God; and among humans the disloyalty that made Adam blame Eve, the violence of Cain to Abel, the disunity that scatters families and peoples.

# 2 The Patriarchal Saga

The introductory stories have ended with a decisive scattering of the nations, and for the first time no mitigation by God of his punishment on sinners. He had made clothes for Adam and Eve, placed a mark on Cain, and saved a remnant from the Flood, but finally mercy comes only after the Babel story is ended. Then God calls an individual, Abraham, makes definite promises to him, and enters into an intimate relationship with him.

The appraisal of the historical worth of these patriarchal stories belongs to books on literature and history. From the religious standpoint, there is little to be gained by trying to penetrate behind them to past events, or to unravel the tangled skein of oral and written traditions.[1] We cannot now be sure whether the stories belonged originally to the history of the invading Israelite people or to the land, being preserved at sanctuaries in Palestine as tales of their founders, and sung to pilgrims on their journey to the great festivals.[2] The patriarchs are presented as semi-nomads, and some of the most important stories (Gen. 17.1ff) are not attached to any locality, but centre on people not places. Others have as setting one of the sanctuaries known to archaeology to have existed from the Bronze Age. Abraham's main centre was at Hebron, but he worshipped also at Shechem, Bethel, and Beersheba. Isaac was connected with Beersheba, though he was buried in the patriarchal grave at Hebron where he had been living with Jacob (35.27), and a later tradition possibly connected him with Bethel (Amos 7.16). To Jacob Bethel was central, although stories are told of his worshipping God at the other three centres and at sanctuaries in Transjordan.

[1] For English readers, the use of the divine names in the RSV gives a rough guide to the extent of the underlying source-documents and traditions differentiated by scholars. J, from the southern kingdom, uses the divine name translated the Lord, and P (priestly) uses God; but God (*Elohim*) is also used in the Pentateuch from the patriarchal stories onward by a northern writer or tradition called E. In the patriarchal stories, analysis is mainly of literary interest, and for the usual analysis of the text a critical commentary should be consulted. See below, p. 27.

[2] See below, p. 24.

Probably the stories had different origins and a very long history before they coalesced as the early story of the Israelite people and received their present form. Ezekiel's reference to the Abraham traditions (33.24) suggests that they were part of the sub-literary heritage of the common people left in Palestine after the upper class had been taken captive by the Babylonians. They said, "Abraham was only one man, yet he got possession of the land; but we are many; the land is surely given us to possess" (cf. Isa. 51.2). If the stories had a long previous history, some details may be due to the set form in which our story-teller received them. Such features as the appearance to Abraham at Mamre near Hebron of three men, of whom one apparently becomes the Lord and the other two become angels (Gen. 18.1ff; cf. 19.1)[1] or Jacob's fight with the man by the river Jabbok (32, 24, 30), were so well known that they had to be retained, and could be only slightly modified[2] to suit an overriding religious purpose.

Many of the details of the stories in their present form are due to the exigencies of story-telling. The presence of Lot may be as a foil to Abraham, to show a generous nature that would risk his heritage by allowing Lot first choice of land (13, 8f), and risk his life to rescue him (14.14ff). Abraham's immoral act in jeopardizing his wife in Pharaoh's harem (12.10ff) is indefensible by modern standards, but the use of the word "plagues" (12.17) and the great wealth won from Pharaoh might carry to Jewish hearers reminiscence of a slavery in which a Jewish wife might be forcibly taken away, and the spoiling of the Egyptians was a punishment from God. The rivalry of the wives for the right to sleep with Jacob, the play on words used in the naming of Jacob's children (30), and the story of the mandrakes may show crude humour and wit, and may have been retained for the entertainment of the audience. The motif of the childless wife in the story of all three patriarchs, and the wonderfully told story of the journey to sacrifice Isaac, are excellent examples of the art of retaining interest by suspense. The meaning of some details can only be conjectured. The placing of Abraham's altar outside Bethel, between it and Ai (12.8), may reflect his nomadic character, his avoidance of a heathen city, or

[1] Notice how, in RV (more accurate here than RSV), plural and singular address alternate (18.2ff).

[2] This story may be a remnant of a primitive cult connected with a river spirit, but here it is aetiological, to explain the name Israel as "a fighter with God" (v. 28), the local name Peniel as "the face of God", and the taboo on using a certain part of an animal as food.

show the bias of the narrator against Bethel, which for many years rivalled Jerusalem as the national sanctuary.

It is only in broad outline that the stories can concern us here. Through them clearly shine valuable religious experiences and beliefs held by the earlier narrators, and accepted by the final editors as part of the religion of the Old Testament. We must attempt to understand the total picture of their religion and the way they tried to express their experience of encounter with God. Procksch, who believed that there was an historical kernel behind the patriarchal stories in all three literary traditions (JEP) wrote, "If Abraham or Moses had to be given up as an historical figure, my faith and with it my Christian position would certainly not be destroyed, but changed in a more or less decisive point. And in the same way it is enriched by a great figure of faith which shows itself in my consciousness."[1]

## The Call of Abraham and God's Promise

For the first time is formulated God's plan for saving the world, the programme of salvation history.[2] With Abraham God makes a new beginning, and again takes the initiative. Abraham is to separate himself from all natural ties of land and kindred so that he and his descendants may become the new centre for all the nations, scattered as a punishment for the Babel rebellion. God's promise is that Abraham will be the founder of a great nation, that he will be blessed, and that in him all nations will be blessed.[3] Later (12.7), after the Lord has appeared to him in Shechem, the gift of the land of Canaan is added to the original promise of progeny. To this dual promise may be traced the beginning of Israel's faith, her claim to the land of Canaan (Ezek. 33.24) and her consciousness of a special destiny as a people through whom God's blessing would enter the world.

This promise of descendants and land is the constant central theme of the patriarchal saga. It is made to each of the three patriarchs and often repeated. It is prepared for by the statements that of all Noah's descendants Abraham and his wife Sarah alone had no children (Gen. 11.30), and that, when the call of God came to Abraham, Abraham's father Terah was already on the move and had travelled from Ur of the Chaldees to Haran in N. Syria (11.31). This movement by Terah appears to be included in the divine plan for Abraham, who is spoken of as brought by the Lord from Ur (15.7).

[1] Op. cit., p. 15.     [2] Gen. 12.1–3; cf. Noth, *Exodus*, (1962), p. 15.
[3] Or possibly "All nations will use his name for blessing".

The call itself is introduced quite suddenly, without any theophany or reference to place or time. Nor is any reason given for God's choice. Apparently it was a completely arbitrary act, utterly unmerited. Noah had been chosen because God saw he was righteous among his contemporaries (7.1), whole, complete in his generations—perhaps with a reference back to his family past—and he walked with God. Of Abraham even after his call it is only said that he trusted the Lord and righteousness was reckoned to him (15.6). The thought clearly expressed in Deuteronomy is here relevant: Not because of your righteousness or the uprightness of your heart (9.5) but because the Lord took a delight in your fathers to love them and to choose their descendants after them (10.15). The people itself, like its ancestor, was not intrinsically sacred.

In the stories of the patriarchs their lack of moral perfection is continually recognized. Abraham deserved the reproof of the Egyptian Pharaoh and of Abimelech (Gen. 12.18; 20.9). On the latter occasion he admitted he had been wrong in fearing that the heathen king's moral standards were lower than his own: I did it because I thought, There is no fear of God at all in this place, and they will kill me because of my wife (20.11). Isaac committed the same crime against Abimelech (26.9). Abraham's treatment of Hagar is hard to justify. Jacob's character clearly earned him the name Deceiver or Twister, and in the remainder of the Old Testament the play on this word seems to suggest that Israel was not proud of all the conduct of this great ancestor, however much they might delight in his shrewd trickery. It is true that he was to suffer for his treatment of his brother Esau over the birthright (25.28ff); his deception of his blind old father was repaid when he was deceived by his own sons over Joseph's coat (37.31ff); and he and his uncle Laban seem both to have been tarred with the same brush.

The message of all the stories seems to be that as God is able to overrule evil intention, so he can use for his purposes imperfect characters. Perhaps the thought is that he has a concern to preserve righteousness wherever it is found and in however small an amount. Noah, the one righteous man in a whole generation, was saved from the destroying Flood, ten righteous men could have saved the whole wicked city of Sodom, and Lot and his family [did not perish. So also, though there may be only a small percentage of righteousness in Jacob, God is able to use it. This character of God fits with his promise to Abraham, that through him blessing will fall on all nations.

## God's Covenant

Very important for religious thought in the Old Testament is the fact that in the patriarchal saga God's promise becomes his covenant with Abraham (15.18). In the present arrangement of the story there is a gradual unfolding of God's purpose and of Abraham's fluctuating response or faith. God repeats the promise of descendants (15.5) to the childless man who has only a slave born in his house to succeed him. Abraham accepts without question this promise, that his seed shall be numberless as the stars. But when God repeats the promise of possession of the land (15.7; cf. 12.7) Abraham asks for a proof or token before he can believe the Lord, his doubt springing naturally from the circumstances accompanying the first occasion: "At that time the Canaanites were in the land" (12.6). God answers Abraham's doubt by making his promise into a solemn covenant.

He had already established a covenant with Noah both before and after the Flood, but his covenant with Abraham was confirmed by a solemn rite.[1] A heifer, a she-goat, and a ram, all three years old, were cut in half and laid with a dove and a pigeon on each side of a path. In a night-vision Abraham heard the Lord foretell the future of his family to the fourth generation, saw a smoking oven and a flaming torch pass between the two halves of the animals, and heard the words of the Lord's covenant: "To your descendants I have given this land." The account of a similar covenant ceremony at the beginning of the sixth century B.C.[2] suggests that the oven and torch represented one participant of the covenant, here the Lord. In the secular form of the covenant rite, both participants passed between the pieces chanting a curse on the one who broke the covenant, that he might be cut in pieces like the animal.[3] The Lord's announcement included a forecast of the Deliverance from Egypt, and it has been suggested that the smoking oven points symbolically forward to the theophany on Mount Sinai, where the smoke that accompanies the Lord's appearance is "like the smoke of a kiln" (Exod. 19.18).[4] Added impressiveness is given to the terms of the covenant (Gen. 15.13ff) by this preview of the long period of waiting before the promised possession of the land is fulfilled—four hundred years of slavery in a foreign

[1] This contrasts with the usual patriarchal lack of interest in cult matters.
[2] Jer. 34.18, "the calf which they cut in two and passed between its parts".
[3] The Hebrew text in Jer. 34.18 omits the word "like" and is even more emphatic (cf. 1 Sam. 11.7).
[4] Cf. O. Procksch, op. cit., p. 522. But a different Hebrew word is used.

land[1] until the Amorites[2] are wicked enough to justify their expulsion. Von Rad[3] describes the prophecy as "a showpiece of Old Testament theology of history" with its characteristic beliefs that God rules world history, judges nations at their allotted time, and has a special plan of history for his people Israel. Seen here also is Israel's constant forward look, the deep underlying hope in the future and trust in the ultimate triumph of God's purpose. This covenant, like that made with Noah, is an act of pure grace from God and is in no sense merited, nor is it a bargain requiring a response from Abraham or his descendants.

When it is repeated (Gen. 17.2, usually regarded as P), it is with new elements. There is a new revelation to Abraham, a new name for the Lord, and Abraham's name is changed from its Hebrew form Abram, used up to this point in the stories, to its Aramaic form Abraham, with a play on the meaning of the word, "Father of a multitude". Still more important is a new hint that the covenant is conditional on Abraham's walking before God and being blameless (whole, 17.1; cf. 6.9). Its outward sign too needs human co-operation. When the covenant was established with Noah, his descendants, and every living creature, the rainbow was set in the clouds as the sign to remind God of his promise. But here instead of the rainbow there is circumcision on the eighth day of every male "throughout your generations, whether born in your house or bought with your money" (17.12), and it is emphasized that an uncircumcised male is no longer a member of God's covenant people—he has broken God's covenant. The new sign is one that requires individual response. Further, as the covenant and possession of the land will be everlasting, so also the sign must be repeated by each succeeding generation. This sign overleaps strict racial barriers, and it is not in any real sense a rite of initiation. To anyone, native or foreigner, who has become part of an Israelite family and so is already part of the covenant people, it is the token of sharing the covenant relationship and being privileged to call the Lord his God (cf. 17.7f).

The expression "covenant", used to sum up God's relationship to Noah, Abraham, and his descendants, became still more important in the account of events at Sinai, but was of primary significance in the religion of Jeremiah and Ezekiel in the sixth century B.C.[4] It is not yet

---

[1] Exod. 12.40 has 430 years; the four generations of Gen. 15.16 agrees with Exod. 6.16–20.

[2] Contrast Canaanites (Gen. 12.6).          [3] *Genesis*, p. 183.

[4] Since Mendenhall's comparison (*Law and Covenant in the Ancient Near East* (1955)) of the Hittite forms of treaty covenants with the patriarchal

possible to be certain of the date when the word first began to be used in Old Testament religious language, but possibly it was deliberately introduced to supplement the concept of God's promise by emphasizing man's response and responsibilities, hinted at in Genesis 17. The original promise appeared to be unconditional, dependent on God alone; the covenant, though thought of as given, established, or even imposed by God as suzerain on vassal, not made between two equal partners, yet contained conditions which man must fulfil unless the covenant were to be broken.

## Testing Faith

God's covenant with Abraham meets his doubt caused by delay in fulfilment of the promise; this continual delay is an outstanding feature of the stories. The motif of the barren wife is repeated in the tales of all three patriarchs as though part of God's test of human trust. The jeopardizing of Sarah in Pharaoh's harem, and of Sarah (and Rebecca) with Abimelech before the birth of the promised son, by heightening suspense speaks directly to the faith of the listeners to the stories and involves them sympathetically in the problems that are raised. Although we are told that Abraham believed in the Lord and his promise (15.6), we find him in the next chapter having a son by Hagar, Sarah's Egyptian handmaid, and asking that the boy shall be recognized as the promised heir almost as though attempting to force God's hand and hasten the fulfilment of his purpose (17.18). When Abraham and Sarah (17.17; 18.12) laugh at the divine promise that they will have a child when both are over ninety, not only is there a play on the name Isaac (he laughs), but there is a challenge to the audience, who are laughing too; listeners to, as well as protagonists in, the story need to be reminded that nothing is too hard for the Lord (18.14).

Tension for the audience and testing of Abraham's faith reach their height when he is commanded to kill as a sacrifice the long-awaited son, now grown to boyhood and still the only possible hope of the fulfilment of the promise. Although the purpose of the story in its original form may have been the abrogation of child-sacrifice[1] by offering an animal substitute (Exod. 22.29; Ezek. 20.31), in its present

---

covenant, there has been a tendency to claim the Hittite treaties as prototypes of Israel's covenant with her God, and hence to assert that the story of Abraham's covenant is of early, even pre-Mosaic date. But compare N. K. Gottwald's highly critical study, *All the Kingdoms of the Earth* (1965).

[1] See below, pp. 57f.

form it is given as a deliberate test of Abraham's faith. Von Rad[1] speaks of the story as showing a God who "once and again withdrew without making good his promise" and who "hid himself to the point of most incomprehensible self-contradiction"; but possibly we must treat it as designed to reveal a truth about God. He does not require the sacrifice of firstborn sons, but he does demand that man should worship him for himself alone—for nought (Job 1.9)—not for any future hopes or fulfilment of promises. God requires that man's life must be God-centred, not centred even on an only son. Had Abraham refused God's test and withheld his son from God, he would have shown that he loved best his son and not God.[2] Whatever the historical tradition used by the writer, the story by taking an extreme example wins support for the same demand as was made in an equally extreme form by Jesus (Luke 14.26).

But there is no hint that the sacrifice of a firstborn son had magical qualities or was a most powerful offering to compel God's response (2 Kings 3.27; Mic. 6.7). Throughout the story are clearly stressed valuable religious beliefs held by the writer and accepted by the final editors as part of the religion of the Old Testament.

## God's Oath

At the end of the story of Abraham's willingness to sacrifice Isaac there is introduced another synonym for promise and covenant, that of an emphatic unchangeable oath sworn by God (Gen. 22.16) as though to give additional confidence and security to Abraham after he had passed God's test of his faith. The oath is a blast of triumph sounded on God's trumpet. Abraham has obeyed, for him the struggle is now over and he returns home in utter reliance on the oath as making the future certain. In the stories of each of the patriarchs (24.7; 26.3; 50.24) the word is used with reference to the gift both of descendants and of land, and it becomes especially frequent in Deuteronomy.[3] As the word "oath" is primarily associated with Abraham's

[1] Von Rad, *Old Testament Theology* I, p. 171.

[2] For an extreme example of the antithesis of Abraham's behaviour, there is a shocking moment in the Capeks' *Insect Play* when the hideous Fly pounces on the harmless Cricket and gives—or sacrifices—it to his hideous young with the words, 'If you want to keep alive, you've got to fight your way. There's your future and there's your family. And then you know there must be a certain amount of ambition."

[3] Sometimes the two words, oath and covenant, are used together (cf. Deut. 29.12; 1 Chron. 16.16f = Ps. 105. 9f).

victorious emergence from the desperate circumstances of his test, to hear it repeated would encourage Israel to place her trust in God alone at a time when she seemed without hope or future.

All three concepts, Promise, Covenant, and Oath, have clearly been transferred from the secular sphere, and all, used in this religious setting, can be regarded as expressing a real relationship, not as highly figurative (like, for example, Rock, Shepherd, Shield). Perhaps the most figurative and also the most significant image of intimate relationship existing between God and man is the metaphor of marriage, vividly expressed by Hosea from his own tragic experience, and frequently used by Jeremiah (3) and Ezekiel (16). But this closest union is also suggested here (Gen. 18.19) by the writer: "I have known (RSV marg.; cf. 4.1) him, that he may charge his children and his household after him to keep the way of the Lord." Amos[1] uses the same word of God's relationship to Israel: "You only have I known of all the families of the earth" (3.2), stressing the obligation of complete human response to God in the whole of life, which this figure of speech particularly contains.

In the same chapter (3.7) Amos expresses the other idea prominent in these verses in Genesis: "Surely the Lord God does nothing without revealing his secret to his servants the prophets." Intimate relationship with God requires human response, so that God can reveal his purpose, making a man into a prophet; Abraham is the first man in the Old Testament to whom the title prophet is applied (Gen. 20.7). It is of considerable interest for understanding Old Testament prophecy that both words, "know" and "prophet", in these stories of Abraham are associated with intercession. Abraham is a prophet because he can intercede successfully for the wife of the innocent Abimelech; and that the Lord waits (18.22f) with Abraham before the destruction of Sodom is a hint that he expects Abraham's intercession for the doomed city.

## The God of the Patriarchs

The experience of a close intimate relationship with God is typical of the religion attributed to the patriarchs. God speaks to each patriarch according to his personal circumstances. Isaac must remain in the land and not go to Egypt, because of God's oath to Abraham (26. 1–5), although Abraham himself had earlier travelled to Egypt. Jacob is promised the presence of God on his wanderings and a return to the

[1] See below, p. 230.

promised land (35.12). God is thought of as sometimes intervening in the ordinary affairs of life, and guiding the patriarchs without any mediation of prophetic word or priestly oracle. As Eve could say of the birth of Cain "I have gotten a man with the help of the Lord" (4.1), so it was God who saw Leah's affliction, opened her womb, and made possible the birth of Reuben (29.31). Rachel's barrenness was God's doing (30.2). He intervened to save Abimelech from sin against Sarah (20.6; cf. 26.8), and to rescue Hagar and her son (21.19). God co-operated in the scheme outlined by Abraham's servant for the choice of the right wife for Isaac (24.11ff) and accepted Jacob's bargain at Bethel (28.20f; cf. 48.15). But especially was God's guidance seen in the story of Joseph. It was God who sent him to Egypt (45.8) and it is God's activity that is summed up in Joseph's words to his brethren, "As for you, you meant evil against me; but God meant it for good" (50.20).

To Jacob as to Abraham God spoke in night-visions and dreams (15.13; 28.13) revealing his control and purpose. Sometimes the vision appears to have been a divine response to a sacrifice (46.1), at others there is a hint that it was associated with human reflection on a particular situation (31.1ff). There is little stress on fear of the deity, though clearly the night-visions bring awe and dread (15.12; 28.17). Some dreams needed no interpretation, but this does not apply in the Joseph stories, where God himself does not speak in the dream (37.5). Joseph was credited with the power to discover the future through other people's dreams, and also had a divining-cup.[1]

Occasionally, when God appeared, it was in a human form indistinguishable from that of men, as at Mamre and at Jabbok.[2] But there is frequently very close association between the Lord and angels, as in the phrase "the angel of the Lord" (22.11, 15) and "his angel" (24.40). God himself appears as the Angel of the Lord (16.7; 22.11; cf. Exod. 3.2). Angels are particularly prominent in the stories of Jacob (especially in the traditions ascribed to E). He saw them at Bethel (Gen. 28.12), they met him as he returned to face Esau (32.1), and in his blessing of Joseph's sons he speaks of "the angel who has redeemed me from all evil" (48.16). The Hebrew word translated "angel" also means "messenger", and the word puts warmth and simplicity into the divine–human encounter. Just as the fear of God is not stressed in

---

[1] Joseph's administrative skill is attributed to the Spirit of God (Gen. 41.38f). This is the first reference to the gifts of the Spirit in the Old Testament.

[2] See above, p. 14.

dreams, so too his angel appears to the patriarchs as a friendly figure. However, in the writer's thought a certain distance between God and man is acknowledged. The intimacy of the earliest stories that tell how Enoch (5.24) and Noah (6.9) walked "with" God is changed, and the patriarchs are spoken of as walking "before" him. A similar sense of distance may also be expressed in spatial symbolism for God's dwelling-place. As he came down "to confound the men of Babel" (11.5), so he came down to see whether the reputation of Sodom and Gomorrah was deserved (18.21), and his angels used a ladder to reach between heaven and earth (28.12).

## Holy Places

As we have seen, some occasions when God appeared or spoke to the patriarchs are not precisely localized. We are not told exactly where Abraham was when he heard the Lord's promise repeated (13.14), or even when the Lord himself appeared to him (17.1). But many patriarchal theophanies occurred at places later sacred in Old Testament traditions. It was at Shechem, later the northern covenant sanctuary, that Abraham built an altar after the Lord had appeared to him and promised him possession of the land of Canaan (12.6f), and he built an altar also between Bethel and Ai (12.8; 13.4). By the oaks of Mamre at Hebron (13.18) he built another, and here he pleaded with God for Sodom (18.1). His association with Hebron became closer when later he purchased a cave there for burial (23.3ff; cf. 25.9; 49. 29f). At Beersheba he planted a tree and worshipped the Lord, the Everlasting God (El 'Olam, 21.33), and there he returned and dwelt after the pilgrimage to sacrifice Isaac (22.19). Mount Moriah (22.2), the place of the sacrifice and of the angel's appearance, is identified in the tradition in 2 Chronicles 3.1 with the Temple mount at Jerusalem. Abraham is apparently connected with Jerusalem also when he gives tithes to the God of Melchizedek, King of Salem (Gen. 14.20; cf. Ps. 76.2). Perhaps this story is related to justify giving tithes there, and to give additional holiness to the Davidic dynastic centre.

Isaac is linked with Beersheba (Gen. 26.23, 33), he dwelt with Jacob at Hebron (35.27), and possibly tradition associated him with Bethel (Amos 7.16). All these places are mentioned in the stories of Jacob. At the oak at Shechem he buried the idols brought by his family from Transjordan, and purified the religion before moving to Bethel (Gen. 35.2ff). At Shechem too he bought a piece of ground on which to erect an altar (33.18f), as Abraham had bought ground at

Hebron for a grave, and as David later was to buy ground for an altar at Jerusalem. At Bethel the Lord first spoke to Jacob, there he made his vow to which the tithe at Bethel may have been traced (28.22), and thither he returned after his long sojourn with Laban (35.14f). It too was a sacred burial place (35.8). At Beersheba he was dwelling when God appeared to reassure him about the journey to Egypt to Joseph (46.3), and at Hebron he was buried (49.30; 50.13). The origin of shrines in Transjordan, Mahanaim (32.2), and Peniel (32.30), was traced to divine appearances to him. Some of these holy places had the three common features of tomb, pillar, and tree.[1] These shrines may have marked stages on pilgrim routes to the great religious centres, and may have been places where pilgrims could rest on their way to festivals. The traditions may thus have sprung from tales told of the history of the shrine.[2]

These stories tell how cultic centres famous for many generations first became authenticated to the Israelites as sacred. God had revealed himself there. As Jacob said of Bethel, The Lord was in the place, and it was the gate of heaven, where there could be communication between God and man. At these places the patriarch had responded by acts of worship—building an altar, anointing a stone, planting a tree, giving a tithe—and later descendants could share this worship of the patriarchal founders, and expect to meet there the same God. The writers had very little interest in particular forms of ritual acts; but despite the long gap of 400 years during which Abraham's descendants were thought of as absent from the land, the stories of the many holy places made all the land God's home, where his children could expect to find him when they returned from the far country. It was the homeland of them and their God. As he had appeared there to the nation's forefathers, so he would appear to them to guide, help, and fulfil his age-old promises.

Constantly, when we read the patriarchal stories, we need to remind ourselves of the small extent of the land of their sojourning, and the closeness of these few traditionally sacred places to one another. From Shechem in the north to Beersheba in the south is less than a hundred miles, and Bethel and Hebron lie near the route between them. Amos and Hosea in the eighth century condemned the inadequacy of worship at these shrines, but in the patriarchal traditions there is a completely different atmosphere. There is no polemic, and no interest in the elaborate ritual mentioned by the prophets. The

---

[1] Cf. E. Dhorme, *L'Évolution religieuse d'Israël* (1937).

[2] J. N. Schofield, *Religious Background of the Bible* (1944), p. 75.

stories may have been drawn from ancient popular traditions handed down through many centuries, and mediate a simple religion before the break between North and South, and between prophet and priest. But their retention in the Old Testament must be due to a deep desire for religious unity, perhaps at the destruction of the northern kingdom or in the reconstruction at the close of the Babylonian exile.

## The Names of God

The same strong desire for unity may perhaps be seen too in the names by which Israel's God is regarded as having revealed himself to the patriarchs. These vary in the different literary traditions, but all are thought of as revealing the same one God. It was the Lord (*Yahweh*) who called Abraham to leave his father's household and gave him the promise of being the founder of a great nation and of divine blessing, and to call on the Lord's name Abraham built altars (12.8; 13.4). The new divine name revealed to Abraham when his own name was changed (17.1, P) was *El Shaddai*—God Almighty. This name was used by Isaac to Jacob (28.3) and by God to Jacob (35.11; cf. 48.3) and by Jacob to his sons (43.14) and in blessing Joseph (49.25). It was the particular name by which the patriarchs were regarded as knowing God (Exod. 6.3, P) and was shared by non-Israelites.[1] Another name used by Abraham was Everlasting God (*El 'Olam*, Gen. 21.33) or God of Eternity.[2] The covenant with Noah, with Abraham, and the possession of the land are all called everlasting, as though originally connected with this divine name, though there is now no story of a theophany at which the name was revealed. In the oath required by Abraham from his servant sent to find a wife for Isaac, Abraham uses the name the Lord, God of Heaven (24.3, 7), which should possibly be connected with the name used of Melchizedek's God whom Abraham identified with the Lord[3] and called God Most High (*El Elyon*), maker of heaven and earth. This name too is clearly regarded as used by non-Israelites.[4] God revealed himself to Jacob as the God of Bethel (31.13; 35.7), and Jacob built an altar at Shechem to God the God of Israel (33.20). Jacob also referred back to the God of Abraham, and the Fear of Isaac (31.42, 53). In his song of

[1] Cf. Balaam (Num. 24.4, 16), Ruth, and very often in Job.
[2] See von Rad, op. cit. I, p. 179, n. 8 for *El Shaddai* and *El 'Olam*.
[3] Gen. 14.22, but not in LXX (Septuagint or Greek Version of the Old Testament).
[4] Balaam (Num. 24.16); cf. Isa. 14.14, and the Psalter.

blessing, his own God is referred to as the Mighty One of Jacob. (49.24. This title is used by the prophets and psalmists.) The distinguishing name for Abraham's God may have been Shield of Abraham (cf. 15.1, "I am your shield; your reward shall be very great").

A. Alt, in an influential article,[1] suggests that the ancient sagas presented the patriarchs as worshipping different gods alongside each other, until they became mingled in the one historic God of Israel. In Greek and Semitic inscriptions gods are mentioned without personal names, but distinguished as gods of individuals, especially when invasive peoples dwelt in one city. The patriarchal gods may also have been called originally by the name of the person to whom each was first revealed—the God of Abraham, the God of Nahor (31.53). Later, the linking of the patriarchal names in one family tree of father, son, and grandson may have emphasized the belief that what had been assumed to be the three separate gods of Abraham, Isaac, and Jacob were in truth successive manifestations of the one God. Thus comprehensiveness and richness were added to the worship of the one national God, the Lord (*Yahweh*), recognized as God of the patriarchs and Deliverer from Egypt. Though the national Yahweh religion reigned supreme, the homely characteristics of the patriarchal God could still make their independent contribution to the whole Israelite theological picture. What the patriarchal God was to the smaller groups, the Lord was to the whole nation. Important was the close relationship between God and individuals, as well as that between God and groups of men. The God who entered by free choice into a relationship with an individual patriarch is the God who chose Israel as a nation.

[1] *Der Gott der Väter*, 1929 (E.T. 1966).

# 3 Mosaic Religion:[1] The Deliverance

That Moses brought the ancestors—or some of the ancestors—of the later Israelites out of Egypt and "afterwards to a mountain where Israel received through him a revelation which was a new departure in the national religion and became the foundation both of the later religion of Israel and of Christianity; that he originated or, more probably, adapted customs and institutions from which the later civil and religious organization of the nation was developed; and that thus Israel owed to Moses both its national existence and, ultimately, its religious character—these, and other facts such as these, cannot be called in question by a reasonable criticism". Written in 1911 by S. R. Driver,[2] this opinion would still be accepted by the majority of Old Testament scholars, except that there might be a greater stress on the imperative from God than on the work of Moses.

## Abraham and Moses

The patriarchal stories show God choosing and becoming involved with individuals, promising them progeny and a land in which to live. When the story of Moses begins, the first promise had been fulfilled, the children of Israel had become a great people (Exod. 1.7) but the land they filled was not their own. The second promise had tested Abraham's faith and caused his request for a special token or confirmation (Gen. 15.8). The repetition of that promise was made in the

[1] The literary analysis follows the more detailed results given in S. R. Driver, *Introduction to the Literature of the Old Testament* (1913). They are not regarded as in any way final, but are useful for our purpose and indicate different traditional sources (cf. above, p. 13, n. 1.) traced by scholars throughout the Pentateuch and even into the Former Prophets. In the Mosaic material these different traditions are relevant to the whole religious structure, and are indicated in the following chapters. The final editors have seldom attempted to resolve differences, but "insert expressly directive passages at important nodal points" (von Rad, op. cit., p. 124).

[2] *Exodus*, xlivf.

great theophany recounted in the story of the burning bush. Again
God intervened, called another individual, Moses, and revealed himself and his purpose (Exod. 3.1–14). That periodically God makes his
presence in history known by some clear token is an essential element
in Old Testament theology.[1] For long periods there is no record of
any definite act or word, but when he acts or speaks again, it is clear
that he has always been present and concerned, has seen what was
happening (2.24f), made his plans, and chosen his agent as long
before he had chosen Noah. The Creator who had begun history in
the opening acts of wonder now reveals himself as the Saviour whose
further acts of wonder rescue the Israelites from slavery in Egypt, in a
special, peculiar sense makes them into his people, bound to him by a
covenant, and brings them into a good and broad land, a land flowing
with milk and honey (3.8).

Later we shall notice hints in the traditions of some rivalry in loyalty
to Israel's great religious ancestors, Abraham, Jacob, Moses, and
David, and it is worth while comparing the more shadowy figure of
Abraham with that of the lawgiver Moses. Both were conscious of an
intimate relationship with God, of being called by him to a special
task. The one obeyed without question or hesitation, the other showed
considerable reluctance (3.11—4.17), met by God's promise that
Aaron would become the prophet of Moses and Moses would be as
God to Aaron. Both were recipients of God's covenant (Gen. 15;
Exod. 34.27, J), but Abraham's covenant was a personal one while the
Mosaic covenant was for Israel as a people. Both were mediators
of the commands of God; the one ordered his sons and household
(Gen. 18.19) to keep the way of the Lord by doing righteousness and
justice, the other is regarded as giving to the whole nation not only
the moral code of the ten words, but the civil laws and religious
institutions for the national future. Both are called prophets, Abraham as the first man to venture into genuine dialogue[2] with God
(18.22ff) and as an intercessor (20.7), Moses as the ideal prophet
whose relationship with God is unique. With other prophets God
speaks in vision or dream, but with Moses mouth to mouth, clearly,
not in dark speech, and he beholds the form of the Lord (Num.
12.6f). He spoke to Moses face to face as a man speaks to his friend.[3]
No prophet like him has arisen in Israel since (Deut. 34.10). Even
the Decalogue is presented as ten "words", as though a prophetic
utterance.

[1] See below, p. 360.         [2] See below, p. 80.
[3] Exod. 33.11, E, but cf. 33.20: No man can see my face and live.

## The Revelation to Moses

In the dominant Old Testament tradition, the Deliverance[1] was the real beginning of the saving acts of Israel's God, Yahweh the Lord.[2] The whole story of the life of Moses reflects a growing apprehension of the character of this God, as expressed by successive writers whose contribution it is not for our purpose profitable to attempt to distinguish or date accurately. The religious theory behind the story is that God had been waiting 400 years or four generations to rescue his enslaved oppressed people (Gen. 15.13, 16) until the sins of the Amorite inhabitants of the promised land had reached the stage when God must drive them out and when Israel was ready to be given possession. God had been watching over his people in slavery and guiding their fortunes. Through two Hebrew midwives who revered him rather than the Pharaoh and through a simple female ruse, the mighty power of Egypt was outwitted and the future agent of Deliverance kept alive and trained for his task. Forced to flee from Egypt, Moses was granted hospitality by Jethro, priest of Midian[3] and led his flocks to the holy mountain of Horeb (Exod. 3.1) where he received his new revelation of God, his call to service, and the token of God's promise. This mountain is equated with Sinai,[4] the mount where Israel met God and became the people of God, the dwelling-place from which in later poetic thought the Lord came to succour her.

The form of the revelation here to Moses is comparable to those we have seen in the patriarchal stories. An angel or messenger appeared to him out of a thorn bush in a flame of fire (3.2, J). The imagery suggests the sudden startling irruption of God into Moses' life in the flaming thorn bush, and God's remaining until his purpose of attracting Moses' attention was achieved—the surprising miracle of a dry, flaming thorn bush that did not immediately become a few ashes. There seems to be a distinction between the angel and the Lord, who is looking on, watching the reaction of Moses, and then speaks. Flame

[1] To avoid ambiguity between the use of the word Exodus to denote the second book of the Pentateuch and exodus as meaning the movement out of Egypt, for the latter sense the word Deliverance will be used throughout—more in keeping with the religious attitude to the event in the Old Testament.

[2] The Hebrew word is translated thus but in capital letters in the RSV; see above, p. 13, n. 1.

[3] So Exod. 3.1; 4.18; 18.1ff. But in 2.18 the priest is Reuel, and in Judges 4.11, Hobab, who is a Kenite; cf. 1.16.

[4] Compare Exod. 19.18, 20, with Deut. 4.15. The E tradition and Deuteronomy speak of Horeb; J and P prefer Sinai.

or fire is frequently regarded as a mode of divine appearance. We saw it in the appearance at night to Abraham (Gen. 15.17) of a smoking oven and a torch of fire, and we shall see it as a basic element in the theophanies at Sinai. Fire represents God's abiding presence as he leads Israel on the journey from Egypt: "The Lord went before them by day in a pillar of cloud to lead them along the way, and by night in a pillar of fire to give them light" (Exod. 13.21). This pillar of cloud or fire is equated with the angel of God (14.19, E and J), a protection as well as a guide to Israel. The metaphor of smoke and flame may derive from the description of an active volcano, although it would appear that any volcano in the Sinai region had been extinct centuries before any possible date for the Deliverance. It is of interest that the metaphor recalls the smoking oven seen by Abraham, a smelting furnace whose fierce fires with smoke and flame are shown by archaeology to have been a familiar sight, from the time of Solomon and probably much earlier, in Transjordan and down to the Gulf of Akabah.

Religiously, the metaphor is more nearly a preparation for the picture of the glory of God (40.34–8), the cloud being thought of as evidence of the presence of his holiness.

Two other features of the character of the God who revealed himself to Moses are prominent—his wonder-working power and his holiness. The God of the Deliverance tradition, like the God of creation, is from the beginning one who performs wonders and miracles beyond man's comprehension, and beyond human experience of the way nature works. Hebrew words are heaped up in an attempt to express this aspect—wonders (3.20), signs or tokens (4.8), miracles (4.21). His messenger was in a fire in a thorn bush which was not burnt out. He enabled Moses and Aaron not only to perform magical acts similar to those of the Egyptian experts with their secret arts (7.11; 8.7) but to surpass their powers (8.18; 9.11). He took Israel safely across the Red Sea by sending a strong east wind to dry a pathway (14.21, J) or by dividing the waters (14.21, P) at a signal from Moses. The bitter waters of Marah were made sweet (15.23 f, E); food was miraculously provided as manna and quails from heaven (16, P and J; Num. 11), and water from the rock (Exod. 17.6, E). This miraculous element in the tradition may have been enhanced in the telling, but it is basic to the story. God's power showed itself greater than that of the dreaded Pharaoh and the famed magicians of Egypt. He fought for Israel, who needed only to be still and trust (14.14). The warrior God who had enabled Abraham to defeat four great kings could destroy the might of Egypt without human aid, and his great majesty is recorded in the poetic hyperbole of the song of Moses and Miriam (15).

The Hebrew word translated "holy" is first introduced into the Old Testament in these stories of the Deliverance, but not as a new concept that needs explaining, rather as an idea long accepted. On the mountain of God, Moses is told to take off his shoes because the ground had been made holy by God's presence, and in the song celebrating God's victory over Pharaoh's host the word is used to describe God: "Who is like thee, majestic in holiness?" (15.11). Etymologically the word contains the two ideas of separation and brightness, and both are prominent in the Old Testament concept of the divine. It must, however, be remembered that this idea of separateness emphasizes that the secular object has been joined to the divine, rather than that the divine is removed from the mundane sphere. When cattle stray into a holy enclosure they become the property of the god—his holiness has entered them, bound them to him, and separated them from secular purposes. In Isaiah's famous phrase, "Holy One of Israel", holiness binds God and Israel together in indissoluble unity as separated from all else.[1]

## The Name of God

The content of the revelation to Moses on the mountain was God's purpose, nature, and name. Moses is assured that God has seen the affliction of his people, heard their cry, known their suffering, and has come down to deliver and lead them to the promised land. Moses, accompanied by God, is to bring them out of Egypt to worship him on that same mountain (3.7ff, J). It is emphatically stated that the God who speaks there to Moses is the same God that his father and the patriarchs had worshipped, the God of the fathers of the generation of Israelites then in Egypt (3.6, 15, E). It is assumed that this God had up to then no personal name, but was called the God of certain individuals who worshipped him. Moses asks him by what name he can be called now he is to become a nation's God. The reply is given in an ambiguous sentence playing on the name which Israel later used to him in worship: "I am what I am" or "I will be what I will be".[2] He tells Moses to use to the people the third person "He is" or "He will be" to assert that the God who is has renewed his age-old promise. Later (6.2f, P) a clear distinction is made between the religion of the

---

[1] Cf. J. N. Schofield, *Introducing Old Testament Theology*, pp. 51f.
[2] See RSV marg. on Exod. 3.14f.

patriarchs and the new religion of Moses. The ambiguous phrase of
Exodus 3.14 (E) by which God avoided revealing his name to Moses is
treated as the revelation of a new name unknown to Israel. The
writer of Genesis 4.26 (J) regarded the worship of the Lord (*Yahweh*)
as beginning in the primeval days of Enosh; Noah is thought of as
calling Yahweh "My God" or "The God of Shem" (the Semites
9.26, J, RSV marg.) and the patriarchal sagas, except that of Joseph,
use the name Yahweh for the God they worshipped. But here (Exod.
6.3) it is categorically stated that a new divine name was being revealed to Moses: "I am the Lord. I appeared to Abraham, to Isaac,
and to Jacob, as God Almighty [Heb. *El Shaddai*] but by my name the
Lord [*Yahweh*] I did not make myself known to them." There is here
clearly a tradition, perhaps a folk memory, of an Israelite group which,
at some definite point of time, adopted the worship of the God
Yahweh, recognized him as identified with their patriarchal God—or
gods—and associated that identification with the work of Moses.

There is no general agreement among scholars concerning the
meaning and origin of the name Yahweh. Even the pronunciation of
the word, written without vowels in Hebrew, is disputed.[1] From the
context in which the name is announced, it appears that the play on
the word emphasizes the fact that God is living, present, and active
now and always. He is the God of the patriarchs in the past, of enslaved Israel in the present, and of the promise of their own land in
the future. The name is intended to give confidence to enslaved
Israel and to be the permanent description of God, to be remembered
through all future generations (3.15, E).

Archaeology and the evidence of personal names suggest that the
name was not peculiar to Israel's religion nor first used to or by
Moses, but that the verbal play in the announcement to Moses is
intended to explain an already familiar name. In P (6.2f) any etymo-
logy of the name is lacking. Here, in the simple statement I [am]
Yahweh, there is no use in Hebrew of the verb to be, and so no play on
the word as in E (3), and it is this use of the personal pronoun "I"
with the proper name Yahweh which is found so often in Leviticus
17—26,[2] Ezekiel, and Second-Isaiah:[3] "I, Yahweh, that is my name"
(Isa. 42.8; 45.18).

There is another revelation of the sacred name in a later theophany
to Moses at Sinai (Exod. 34.6, J). It was prepared for by Moses'

---

[1] For discussion cf. H. H. Rowley, *The Faith of Israel* (1956), p. 53.
[2] Designated the Holiness Code (H) by scholars.
[3] See below, p. 133, n. 5.

request (33.12ff, J) that God would enable him to understand his ways with men, to know him that he might find grace in his sight, and that he would regard Israel as his people, and continue to go with them. God replies that Moses can see his goodness,[1] and hear him proclaiming his name and the arbitrary freedom of his gracious and merciful, character,[2] but, in contradistinction to other statements that Moses saw God face to face, he is not allowed to see the face or full glory of God, but only its reflection when it has passed by. The Hebrew word used to describe the fulfilment of the promise (Exod. 34.5f, J) is ambiguous. It is not clear whether Moses or the Lord proclaimed God's sacred name and character, but from the account of the promise (33.19, J) it seems the intention is to state that God proclaimed his own name in a twice-repeated act of self-revelation: The Lord passed before him, and proclaimed, "The Lord, the Lord, a God merciful and gracious, slow to anger, and abounding in steadfast love and faithfulness" (34.6). The God who from earliest times had been called Yahweh in the J tradition now proclaimed the name himself, as the name by which he was to be known to his covenant people, thus repeating the revelation given to Moses earlier (3.14, E).

Adequate proof is still lacking for the ingenious and elaborate theories that trace the worship of Yahweh back to the levitical ancestors of Moses, or to the Midianite–Kenite religion of his father-in-law Jethro.[3] Though the name of Moses' mother Jochebed (6.20, P), a daughter of Levi (Num. 26.59), probably contains an element from this divine name, there is no slightest suggestion that Yahweh worship was confined to Levites. Moses' father is put alongside the patriarchs and the fathers of all the other enslaved Israelites; all were worshippers of this God. It is not the intention of the writer to link the Lord especially with Levi. The same appears to be true of the religion of Jethro. When Moses led the Israelites back to the mountain of God at Horeb to claim the fulfilment of God's token and promise (Exod. 18.5, E), Jethro came to him there, heard about the Deliverance from Egypt, said "Now I know that Yahweh is greater than all gods",[4] and offered a burnt offering and a sacrificial meal in which Aaron and the elders of Israel joined. But the writer is careful to say that the sacrifices were to

[1] Goodness is godliness or comeliness of the divine appearance, outward beauty as a visible sign of his moral perfection; cf. Hos. 10.11; S. R. Driver, *Exodus*, 362.
[2] Elsewhere "gracious and merciful" appears to be a late usage: Procksch op. cit., pp. 79. 439.
[3] O. Procksch, op. cit., pp. 70ff.
[4] Jethro rejoiced over all the "goodness" of the Lord.

God and were eaten before God—not the Lord. The Mount at Horeb, peculiarly linked with Yahweh religion, is not regarded as Jethro's dwelling-place either here or in Exodus 3, but as the mountain of God. It may have been sacred to Jethro's people among others, but it may be called the mountain of God here because of its connection with the theophanies to Moses. It is true that Jethro is recorded as advising Moses on the discharge of his priestly function of teaching God's will (18.13ff, E).[1] But careful reading of this passage shows that Jethro's influential contribution begins when he advises Moses to delegate authority. There is perhaps a recognition that the organization of one at least of Israel's priestly institutions was influenced by Midianite practice. But the influence was restricted to the idealistic, semi-military organization of the judiciary with "rulers" or "captains" over groups of thousands, hundreds, fifties, and tens, as successive appeal judges leading to Moses himself, perhaps on the lines of the legislation in Deuteronomy (17.8–13). None of the names yet found in Kenite or Midianite genealogies shows any trace of Yahweh worship.

Addressing Pharaoh, Moses refers to Yahweh as the God of the Hebrews (Exod. 5.3). Whatever the origin of the name and its connection with Mount Horeb in the Sinai peninsula or with the patriarchs, the intention of the writers is to assert that the God of Horeb was not a new God, although the revealed name may have been new. For Moses, the theophany was a new meeting with the God of his father, his own God who met him away from tribe and family in the wilderness, free from all but the most basic form of worship, free from cultic places, times, and persons, and yet who required an act of reverence from the one to whom he himself spoke face to face—an act which recognized that the meeting-place had been made holy by the presence of God. By taking off his shoes as though entering a shrine, Moses recognized the distinction between himself as human and God as holy.

If the different accounts of the introduction of the divine name to Israel spring from genuine historical traditions or folk memories rather than from later theological speculation, Moses' finest achievement was that he united in the worship of the one God various

---

[1] "I judge (decide) between a man and his neighbour" is equated with "I make them know the statutes of God and his laws" in response to the people "coming to me to inquire of God". Giving instruction or laws of God (*torah*) is regarded as a priestly function (Deut. 17.11; 24.8; 33.10). Thus Moses here is regarded as a priest.

Hebrew or Israelite groups[1] from Egypt, Sinai, and Palestine who had previously worshipped God under different names.

## The Passover

This festival, like the song of Moses and Miriam (Exod. 15), is rooted in the tradition of the actual Deliverance from Egypt. It must therefore be considered separately from the religious institutions that were regarded as stemming from Sinai.

The origin of Passover, like that of Christmas, is not simple. In both, a much older festival is probably linked with a memorable historic occasion. As Christmas is thought to associate the ancient festivities of the Winter solstice with the birth of Jesus of Nazareth, so Passover may link a pre-Mosaic shepherd rite with God's great delivery of Israel from Egypt. The writers in Exodus mean us to understand that the Passover took its origin from the time of Moses, that Moses' request to Pharaoh was simply in obedience to God's command (4.22, J) and his promise (3.12, E). But the fact of a sacrifice involving the slaughter of a lamb is assumed by both Moses and Pharaoh.[2] Thus some earlier shepherd custom may be presupposed behind the Passover, which is "the oldest example of the historicising of a cultic feast".[3]

The requirements vary in the different traditions. In the concise account of the first Passover and its regulations (12.21–7, J), a lamb or kid for each family must be killed, a bunch of hyssop dipped in its blood must be touched on lintel and doorposts of the house where it is eaten, and from the house no one must go out till morning. The blood on the outside caused God to "pass over" the door and prevent the destroyer from entering to smite the inhabitants. In perpetuity these acts are to be performed annually, and children instructed in their meaning.

[1] Procksch (op. cit., p. 70) thinks of Levi, Israel/Leah, and Jacob/Rachel groups or amphictyonies at Shechem and Hebron. For "amphictyony" see below, pp. 102f; cf. also A. Alt, *Essays on Old Testament History and Religion* (E.T., 1966).

[2] Compare 8.26 with Gen. 46.34ff. Clearly the object to be sacrificed was at the disposal of shepherds.

[3] Procksch, op. cit., p. 546. M. Buber, *Moses* (1946): "Moses transformed a clan feast of shepherds (Matzoth is nomadic bread) into a feast of a nation without its losing its character of a family feast. He did not change an age-old custom to a cult; he did not add any specific sacrificial rite to it, nor make it dependent on any sanctuary, but he consecrated it to Yahweh."

In another more detailed account for observing the first Passover
(12.1–20, P) and regulations observed when it was carried out
(12.43–51, P) the occasion is so important that from henceforth
it is to mark the beginning of the year, and for the first time Israel is
called "the congregation"[1] (12.3) or religious community. According
to their fathers' houses, a male lamb or kid in its first year and without
blemish is to be selected on the tenth day of the month—perhaps, as
commentators say, because the male was superior to the female; but it
must also be remembered that for breeding purposes a male would be
more easily spared. It must be killed on the fourteenth day in the
evening,[2] it must not be seethed in water but roasted whole and eaten
with unleavened bread and bitter herbs, and any left over till morning must be burnt. No bone of it must be broken (12.46; cf. Num.
9.12). Those who eat it must have loins girt, shoes on feet, staff
in hand, and eat in haste. Emphatically it is stated that this shall
be "a night of watching", a vigil through all generations to com-
memorate the Deliverance from Egypt. Sojourners and hired servants, if circumcised (Exod. 12.43ff), may partake, but foreigners
remain excluded.[3]

## The Firstborn

The motif of the firstborn is strong in the Deliverance story, but is not
mentioned in either group of regulations. In the story, when Moses
meets Pharaoh he must say "Thus says the Lord, Israel is my firstborn son and I say to you, 'Let my son go that he may serve me'; if
you refuse to let him go, behold, I will slay your firstborn son"
(Exod. 4.22f), and in the final plague, which was the occasion of the
first Passover night, all Egyptian firstborn, human and animal, were
killed (12.29f, J), while it is clear that the blood on the doorposts
protected the Israelite firstborn. However, just as neither group of

---

[1] "A specially cultic designation" (Eichrodt, op. cit. I, p. 40, n. 2), peculiar
to P, which also uses with other writers a cognate word (e.g. Exod. 27.21,
RSV "meeting"). A more general word, usually translated "assembly"
RSV, is frequently used by the Deuteronomist and the Chronicler; Deuteronomy using "assembly" traces the beginning of Israel as a religious community not to the Deliverance but to Horeb (cf. Deut. 9.10).

[2] 12.6. Hebrew "between the two evenings", a time of the daily burnt
offering (29.39); the time when the lamps in the Tabernacle were lit (30.8);
perhaps between sunset and the time when the new crescent moon appeared.
Deuteronomy says at sunset. Cf. below, p. 39.

[3] Supplementary rules are found in Num. 9.1–14.

regulations requires that the animal killed should be a firstling, so it is possible that the conjectural pre-Mosaic feast also had no specific reference to the firstborn, but was an annual apotropaic festival to protect the flocks.

Both groups of regulations for the Passover are followed by laws concerning the treatment of the firstborn (Exod. 13.1, P; 13.11ff, J). These begin with the categorical statement of the principle that every firstborn that "opens the womb", both human and animal, belongs to God and must be treated as holy. This is modified in Numbers (18.15ff, P) by the command that human firstborn and unclean animal firstlings must be redeemed by a money payment, but those of sheep, goats, and cattle must be sacrificed and their flesh given to the priests. In further legislation (Num. 3.12, P) Levites are accepted as substitutes for the firstborn of Israel, and similarly the cattle of Levites for Israelite cattle (3.41; cf. 3.44ff, P).

In more detailed laws as to the firstborn (Exod. 13.11ff, J) the same phrase "all that opens the womb" is used, but there is a different word for the disposal of all firstlings. These are not "consecrated" (as in P), but "made to pass through to the Lord" (RSV "set apart to the Lord"). This Hebrew word can be used of transferring or handing on an inheritance (Num. 27.7f, P; 2 Sam. 3.10), but it is also the word used for the ritual of making children pass through the fire to the god Molech, a practice condemned by the prophets.[1] The command in Exodus 13.12 is modified by the limitation to males and by the statement that the ass firstling must be redeemed or destroyed, and the human firstborn is to be redeemed. It is clear that the human firstborn was regarded as subject to this law.[2] There is no distinction in the general statement of principle (13.2, P; 12, J). The longer law, "The firstborn of your sons you shall give to me. You shall do likewise with your oxen and with your sheep; seven days it shall be with its mother, on the eighth day you shall give it to me" (Exod. 22.29f, E), also confirms the inclusion of human firstborn, but clearly does not envisage an annual festival at which human firstborn were given to God. The protests in Jeremiah and Ezekiel and the prohibitions in the Law (e.g. Deut. 12.31), together with archaeological evidence, make it almost certain that infant sacrifices actually took place in Palestine, though we do not know how long they continued, nor whether they

---

[1] Cf. 2 Kings 16.3; Jer. 32.35, cf. 7.30f; Ezek. 16.21; 23.37ff.

[2] This is further confirmed by the repeated statement that human firstborn must be redeemed, that Levites are taken as substitutes for them, and by the story of Abraham and Isaac (Gen. 22). Cf. below, p. 57.

derived from ancient bedouin shepherd rites, or, as is more probable, from the fertility religion of agricultural Canaan.[1]

Clearly there is no consistency in the application of the basic principle that the firstling of every animal belongs to God, and this categorical statement, as we have seen, is modified in several ways. An even more drastic limitation may be implied by the regulations for the Passover lamb or kid (Exod. 12.3ff, P), for if this were a firstling then the number of firstlings sacrificed is restricted to the more reasonable proportion of one male lamb or kid without blemish for each household or group of families, as though the practice was to choose the best male firstling of each flock—the flower of the flock. At the Samaritan passover attended by the present writer some years ago, seven lambs were killed for the whole community of 190 persons.[2]

## Unleavened Bread

Finally, the element in the Passover festival as yet unconsidered here is the eating of unleavened cakes (12.8, P; 13.3, J). In the story of the first Passover this fact is not mentioned, but it is recorded that Israel left Egypt in such haste after the Passover night that they had no time to leaven the dough already in the kneading troughs, and at the end of the first day's journey, at Succoth, the dough was made into unleavened cakes (12.39, J). The prohibition against leaven for seven days each year is made into an ordinance (13.6ff, J), and either the seventh day is to be a feast or pilgrimage to the Lord (13.6), or the first and last days are to be a "Holy Convocation" or a religious assembly at the sanctuary (12.15ff, P; Lev. 23.6f, P) when no work must be done except what is necessary to provide food.

This pilgrimage is one of the three annual occasions on which all males must "appear before the Lord" with an offering (Exod. 23.14ff). "Appear before me" is the usual description of a visit to the sanctuary.[3] There is in Exodus 23 no indication which day or days were to be used for this pilgrimage, the last (as in 13.6, J), or first and last (12.16, P), or all seven days. There is confusion too whether the seven

---

[1] See above, p. 19, n. 1; cf. J. N. Schofield, *Religious Background of the Bible*, pp. 50f, 146f.

[2] Cf. *Palestine Exploration Fund Quarterly Statement* (1937), p. 220.

[3] The Hebrew phrase here and 34.20; Isa. 1.12 has apparently been altered; the original would have been translated "see my face" (cf. Ps. 42.2).

days include the Passover (12.18, P), or whether they began on the fifteenth day of the month, after the Passover on the night of the fourteenth (Lev. 23.6f, P). This confusion may possibly disappear when it is remembered that a "day" began at sunset; in the creation story (Gen. 1.5, P) it began in the evening—the evening and the morning were the first day. It is possible that the ambiguous phrase "between the two evenings", used for the time of killing the Passover victim "in the evening" (RSV; Exod. 12.6, P) was a stock Hebrew expression[1] for "during the day", i.e. while there is still daylight, with an emphasis on twilight nearer the beginning of the second of the "two evenings", the one that ended the day. If so, the lamb would be slaughtered before the evening that ended the fourteenth "day", and the period of the unleavened bread, from "the fourteenth day . . . at evening" (Exod. 12.18), would be in Hebrew reckoning the beginning of the fifteenth "day", so not conflicting with Leviticus 23.6. We are to think of the lamb being slaughtered at sunset, at the end of the fourteenth "day", and being eaten some hours later in the night, which of course was in the fifteenth "day".

The Passover is not among the annual pilgrimages (Exod. 23.14f, E) because it was celebrated in the house and not in the sanctuary. Probably the Passover night was spent at home, and the seven days following were regarded as free from work, and were one of the three annual pilgrimages to the sanctuary. Later, other rites were demanded during the week (Lev. 23.6ff, P; 9ff, H), but these will be considered among the religious institutions required at Sinai.[2]

It is possible that the Passover and the feast of unleavened bread were once separate and held at different times of the year, but the writer in Exodus (13.4, J) put both in the spring month of Abib, when, in Palestine, the first grain crop—barley—begins the harvest. Clearly the feast of unleavened bread is agricultural or at least semi-nomadic, probably springing originally from rites concerned with the fertility of the crops. Leaven was produced by keeping a piece of old dough to ferment the new mixture, and if a break was made between the old grain and the newly harvested corn, the new dough would take seven days before it could be used as leaven. The two feasts may thus have been linked as annual festivals: of the firstborn of men and animals, and of the firstfruits of harvest.

---

[1] Perhaps deliberately used by a later writer, though whether the phrase was used because of some confusion in the text or itself gave rise to the confusion, we do not now know. Cf. above, p. 36, n. 2.

[2] See below, p. 58.

## The Song of Moses (*Exodus 15*)

The Passover perpetuates the memory of the Deliverance in family
teaching and festival; this poem perpetuates in memorable words the
character of Israel's God revealed in these wonderful deeds. Here as
elsewhere in the Old Testament the placing alongside each other of
prose and poetic versions of the same event is of value not only for
understanding the growth of the literature and the actual course of
history, but for enriching the religious lessons traditionally drawn
from the great Deliverance. As late as the end of the Babylonian
exile at the close of the sixth century B.C., Second-Isaiah shows
knowledge of the opening verse (Isa. 43.16), and the language and
religion of the rest of the song has much in common with the writings
of this prophet.

The Lord is praised as "my God", "the God of my father", and
"a man of war", who in defence of his people rises gloriously triumphant over his foes. In vivid contrast to Egypt's confident and fatal
pursuit of Israel, God without any human aid piled up the waters
with the blast of his nostrils so that Israel might escape; then, blown
by his wind, the water covered his enemies. Praise culminates in the
statement of the incomparable wonder of God:

> Who is like thee, O Lord, among the gods?
> Who is like thee, majestic in holiness,
> terrible in glorious deeds, doing wonders? (Exod. 15.11)

In words used also by psalmists and prophets—especially Second-
Isaiah[1] in a similar situation of release from exile—God is described
as leading in mercy those to whom he has shown himself to be a near
kinsman (redeemer), gently like a shepherd leading his flock to
watering-places, and finally guiding them to his holy fold or homestead. Neighbouring peoples who have heard of it begin by melting
away in trembling and dismay, then stand, still as a stone, till the
Lord's purchased people pass over to be brought in and planted by
him on his holy hill, his dwelling-place in the promised land. The
poem concludes with the thought of God's eternal kingship, either as
a prayer or a statement of fact.[2]

The hymn of praise for Israel's Deliverance also contains praise for

---

[1] See below, p. 133, n. 5.
[2] Much of the language of the song is found verbatim in Solomon's
dedication of the temple at Jerusalem (1 Kings 8, in the LXX), and there
traced to Israel's national song-book, the Book of Jashar.

the destruction of Pharaoh's host. A later prophet (Hab. 2.4) will move towards the idea that in evil there is a self-destructive power. But in the song and throughout the Old Testament is the firm faith that God himself fights against evil, against all that would destroy his purpose and his people.

This motif is even more clearly expressed in the prose version of God's victory over Pharaoh. Here there is repeated reference to the hardening of Pharaoh's heart.[1] In all three traditions the statement occurs that God hardened Pharaoh's heart.[2] This statement, even more than that of God's destruction of the Egyptians, has caused offence to those who regard it as springing from an unworthy concept of God. But in the first place it must be remembered that to the Hebrews the heart was not the seat of the emotions but an expression for the whole personality, particularly the mind or intellectual faculty. Thus the expression implies, not that Pharaoh was hard-hearted, unfeeling, unsympathetic, but that he was self-willed and perverse in action. Secondly, in the story itself the problem is looked at from different angles. Six times it is stated as a matter of fact that Pharaoh's heart was hard,[3] three times that Pharaoh made heavy his own heart,[4] ten times that God was responsible.[5] But what in 10.1, J is attributed to the Lord is in 11.9 regarded as due to Pharaoh's unwillingness to listen to Moses.

The Hebrews had the same philosophical problem as we have, to explain the problem of evil in a creation whose sole creator is the good God. The initiative must always be with God, whether in rejection or response. But we shall find that the theory of God's absolute sovereignty and grace is modified by the knowledge from experience of man's responsibility and God-given free will. The paradox of the later rabbinical saying that everything is predetermined and man has free will has its roots deep in Old Testament religion. In the early

[1] Cf. S. R. Driver, op. cit., pp. 53f; M. Noth, op. cit., pp. 67ff. Three different words are used to express this concept: was strong (cf. 7.13, P) in the sense of hard, unyielding; heavy (cf. 7.14, J), perhaps stubborn, unresponsive; and a third occurring only once in the story (7.3, P) associated with the idea of being stiff-necked, obstinate. The RSV unfortunately makes no distinction in translation, but the RV marg. shows the difference by an alternative translation.

[2] E three times, J once, P six times.

[3] Strong (9.35, E; 7.13, 22; 8.19 P) and heavy, stubborn (7.14; 9.7, J).

[4] 8.15, 32; 9.34, J.

[5] Made hard, strong (4.21; 10.20, 27, E; 9.12; 11.10; 14.4, 8, 17, P); made heavy (10.1, J); made obstinate (7.3, P).

stories of Genesis we saw one attempt to give it an answer. Here in the Deliverance story the priestly theologians give it another answer, comparable to that of Jesus when faced by the man born blind (John 9.3)—that the works of God might be manifest. The Egyptian hearts were hardened so that God's wonder and power might be revealed (Exod. 7.5). But Hebrew thought recognized the cumulative effect of habit (Jer. 13.23). A man accustomed to evil finds it hard to do good. Every time Pharaoh hardened his heart by refusing to listen, his heart became harder, though it was possible to regard the Creator as responsible for the first refusal as well as for the psychological law that increased the hardness. Repeatedly we shall find this frank acceptance of God's ultimate responsibility for physical and moral evil and suffering, but always it is a responsibility linked with his redemptive purposes. Further, when a later generation applied to themselves the story of the Deliverance and the wanderings, they emphasized the fact that hardening of the heart was something they themselves could be responsible for—a human not a divine act:

> O that today you would hearken to his voice!
> Harden not your hearts. (Ps. 95.7f)

From this study of the Passover and Moses' Song it is clear that the writers believed that God's relentless enmity[1] against evil and his majestic power were made plain when he intervened to save Israel, his own firstborn, and slew the firstborn and hosts of the enemy. The same effect was achieved by a completely different method according to the writer of Isaiah 53. There the kings of the nations watch with speechless astonishment the exaltation of the Servant of the Lord, who, led as a lamb to the slaughter, gave his life "a ransom for many". After many centuries of religious experience, the Festivals of Unleavened Bread and of Passover could be referred to metaphorically:

Cleanse out the old leaven that you may be fresh dough, as you really are unleavened. For Christ, our paschal lamb, has been sacrificed. Let us therefore celebrate the festival, not with the old leaven, the leaven of malice and evil, but with the unleavened bread of sincerity and truth (1 Cor. 5.7–8).

The celebration of God's Deliverance had marked a new beginning in the national life, and annually the festivals marked a break in the year and a new beginning with "fresh dough".

[1] See above, p. 9.

# 4 Mosaic Religion: Sinai

Historical and literary difficulties are presented by the Sinai tradition as by those of the Deliverance. There has been confusion about the name of the mountain, whether Horeb or Sinai, about the order of events, whether Sinai was reached before Jethro's visit to Moses or after,[1] and about the amounts of legislation given at Kadesh and at Sinai.[2] There is even evidence for the drastic suggestion that the whole block of the Sinai story and legislation in Exodus 19—40, Leviticus, and Numbers 1—10 has been inserted into the account of the Deliverance and wilderness wanderings.[3] It is not yet possible to obtain scholarly agreement as to the origin, both in place and time, and the content of an assumed basic Sinai tradition.

In its present form it contains three main sections: theophanies, groups of laws intended for all Israel, and regulations of special

[1] All three traditions (Exod. 19.1, P; 19.2, E; 19.3, J) relate, after the departure of Jethro, the arrival in the wilderness of Sinai, the encamping before the mountain, and the Lord speaking to Moses out of the mountain. But Horeb/Sinai had already been reached before Jethro's visit to Moses at the mountain (17.6; 18.5, E). It is possible that at one stage Jethro's visit was placed at the end of the Sinai events and lawgiving (Num. 10.29ff).

[2] At Marah a statute and an ordinance were made for the people either by the Lord or Moses (Exod. 15.25, E; cf. RSV marg. "he") comparable to those made by Joshua at Shechem (Josh. 24.25). Marah is linked with the oasis of Kadesh, where Israel dwelt for thirty-nine years (Deut. 1.46). Kadesh may have played a much greater part in the whole law-giving tradition (S. A. Cook, Notes on Old Testament History (1907), pp. 62ff). Stories link it with Massah, where Israel sought to prove or test God, and with Meribah, where they strove with Moses or found fault with God (Exod. 17.1–7). Here Meribah is placed at Horeb, but elsewhere (Num. 27.14) it is connected with Kadesh (Procksch (op. cit., pp. 94f) regards Kadesh as a levitical city linked with Moses' family, and so chosen by him as the Israelite objective after the flight from Egypt; from there Moses and the elders made a forty-day visit to the mountain of God at Sinai/Horeb).

[3] God's gift of manna and quails (Exod. 16) and the appointment of helpers for Moses (18.13ff, E) before the arrival at Sinai seem parallel to the stories immediately after the departure from the holy mountain (Num. 11). Neither Sinai nor its legislation is mentioned in the two credal statements (Deut 26.5ff; Josh. 24.16ff).

concern to the priesthood. In all these sections, as in the Deliverance account, the outstanding human figure is Moses, and it appears that the aim of the final editors was to concentrate all Israelite law-giving, civil and religious, at Sinai as the outcome of the great theophanies there, all having equal validity and authority because mediated through Moses to whom God spoke direct. So important and continuing is his authority that it is spoken of as the purpose for which God came and spoke: "And the Lord said to Moses, Lo, I am coming to you in a thick cloud, that the people may hear when I speak with you and may also believe you for ever" (Exod. 19.9).

## The Theophanies

The story of Sinai opens with careful preparation for the coming of God (19.2ff, J and E). Moses is told to remind the people, in the heightened poetic language that recollects deep emotion, of the excitement of their sudden deliverance from the Egyptians—how God had swooped like a powerful eagle, lifted them out of slavery, and borne them in triumph to his holy mountain.[1] He is to tell them that now God is looking forward to the new covenant he is about to make with them, a new relationship with himself, a new destiny for the nation conditional on their obedience, keeping their part of the covenant terms. Israel will be God's special treasure, picked from all peoples, a kingdom in which every member is to be a priest in God's service and the whole nation holy, bound closely to him. The word "nation" seems intentionally to refer back to the earlier promise to Abraham (Gen. 12.2; 17.6) and to develop it.

The Abraham tradition is recalled also in the idea of the covenant (Exod. 19.5). The covenant between God and "historic humanity" (Gen. 6.18; 9.9–16, P), though it follows the command about the sacredness of blood, is completely unilateral and implies an unconditional oath or promise made by God. In the stories of Abraham (15.18, J) similarly God promises without condition the land of Palestine as an inheritance, but later (17.1–10, P) there is a hint of the condition that Abraham shall walk in the presence of God and be blameless. If this condition is fulfilled, God will multiply him exceedingly, make a nation of him, be the God of his descendants for ever, and give them the land of Canaan for an everlasting possession. The continuance of the covenant is promised for Isaac (17.19,21, P).

[1] The metaphor of the eagle is in a developed form in Deut. 32.10f; cf. 1.31, where the Lord "bore you, as a man bears his son".

In the priestly tradition of the Deliverance story, God "remembers" this covenant with Abraham, Isaac, and Jacob when he intervenes for enslaved Israel (Exod. 2.24), and the land promised to them is described as the land where the patriarchs had sojourned (6.4f; cf. Gen. 17.7f).[1] In the main Deliverance tradition God's relationship to Israel is thought of as father–son (Exod. 4.22 and the whole Passover concept) and not as a covenant.[2] In the Sinai–law tradition, however, there is no mention of sonship (contrast Exod. 19.4 with Deut. 1.31). The basis is a covenant relationship in which the requirements made by God from Israel are very fully stated. Possibly at one time there were two distinct traditions, Deliverance–Passover thinking of a sonship relation and Sinai–Law tradition whose basis was covenant. Such an hypothesis would explain the absence of reference to Sinai and a covenant in some creeds, and the absence of the covenant basis of religion in some prophetic writers.[3]

Following on the people's agreement to accept their side of the covenant, come elaborate precautions to shield them from the dangerous physical contagion of God's holiness. They are to be made holy, their garments must be washed, they must avoid sexual intercourse (Exod. 19.10,15, E); the mountain is to be fenced round lest anyone, layman or priest (19.24) or beast, stray on to it or touch it (19.12f, J) before the priestly ram's horn is sounded. If any do touch it, they must not be touched lest the contagion spread, but killed from a distance by stoning or shooting.

A completely new concept of deity is revealed in the theophanies. In the first (19—20) the human, friendly figure of man or angel is replaced by the phenomenon of a violent storm with thick cloud, thunder, lightning, and the exceedingly loud blast of the trumpet that announced war or special occasions. We have seen there is little need to think of volcanic imagery.[4] The imagery used (19.18, J) is that of a smelting furnace, with its cloud of smoke glowing red in the heat of huge fires, and that of the thunderstorm, in which in poetry God

---

[1] Cf. also Lev. 26.42, 44f, H. In Lev. 26.9,15 there is ambiguity as to which covenant is meant.

[2] J. Begrich (*Zeitschrift für die alttestamentliche Wissenschaft* 60 (1944), pp. 1ff) and O. Procksch (op. cit., p. 91) point out that a covenant can be concluded only between those not already bound by natural ties.

[3] For the covenant relationship see Eichrodt, *Theology of the Old Testament* (E.T., 1961), and M. Newman, *The People of the Covenant* (1966).

[4] See p. 30 above. 19.18, the LXX, and nine Hebrew MSS have "the people quaked", not "the mount quaked", and "quaked" is not used elsewhere of inanimate objects.

comes from the south to help his people (Deut. 33.2; Judges 5.5; Hab. 3). The Lord descended on the mountain in fire, and the mountain was covered in smoke. Aaron and Moses alone were allowed to go up the mountain, but for all the people there was the unique experience of hearing the exalted God speak to them. Though he was there on earth, on the mountain top they had been in touch with heaven. Emphatically they are reminded that it was from heaven that they themselves saw that he spoke to them (Exod. 20.22, E).

The second theophany (24.10, JE) was made to Moses and Aaron, Nadab and Abihu with seventy of the elders of Israel. The presence of the elders suggests it may be a parallel account of the consecration of the seventy elders (Num. 11.16f), or they may be the rulers chosen by Moses in Exodus 18.21, E. They worshipped God from a distance and Moses alone went near to him. But all of them "saw God . . . and there was under his feet as it were tiled-work of sapphire stone clear as heaven" (24.10, J). Again there is the exaltation of being in heaven, God's dwelling-place, with him, but they were conscious only that they were standing on the clear, blue-tiled floor of a sanctuary, as though with him enthroned on the blue vault of the sky. With a sense of wonder it is added that they had been close to God, yet the radiation of his holiness had not harmed them. The vivid description is tempered by a later hand that added that "they had a vision of God, and did eat and drink,[1] the words referring to a sacrificial or communal meal, probably confirming a covenant. But still it must be noted that the second theophany, like the first, expresses the experience of being lifted into communion with God more than it emphasizes his coming down to earth.

This second theophany, which ended in the covenant meal on the mountain top, was preceded by sacrifices in which all the people took part. Moses built an altar and erected twelve stone pillars, young men offered burnt offerings and killed the oxen that were to be shared between God and the people in a common meal. Then the covenant act was performed, half the blood being sprinkled on God's altar and the other half on the people, with the words, "Behold the blood of the covenant which the Lord has made with you" (24.8).

Before the third theophany (34.3, J), as before the first, precautions were taken against holiness. The Lord descended in a cloud and proclaimed his name and character. Moses alone was allowed on the

---

[1] A different word is used for "seeing" God, a word often used of prophetic visions (cf. Num. 24.4) and the word used for God suggests a late levitical hand (cf. p. 53, n. 3 below).

mountain, and his appearance was changed (34.29ff, P). His face sent
forth rays (Hebrew horns[1]) so that people were afraid to come near
him till he put a veil over it.[2] The outstanding feature of the third
theophany is God's twice-repeated proclamation of his name, and his
revelation of his character.[3]

It would be difficult or impossible to weld the details of the story
of any one of these theophanies into a consistent whole, mainly
because they are of such central importance to Israel's religion that
they have been often retold. The first and third are concerned with
the giving and acceptance of a decalogue. The second theophany,
with the more formal making of a covenant and laws written on two
tablets called the Book of the Covenant, authenticates the civil and
religious regulations which it was the duty of the rulers of the people
to administer.

## The Decalogues

The best-known decalogue, popularly called the Ten Commandments, is given at the first theophany (Exod. 20). In its present form
this decalogue clearly presupposes a settled urban and agricultural
community, not a nomadic group. There are menservants and maidservants, gates, and personal property which can be stolen or coveted.
Though possibly there was an original short Mosaic form, there is no
conclusive reason to believe that any of the great prophets knew this
whole series of ten words in any form as having been for many centuries the generally accepted moral code for the nation and the basis
of Israel's faith. It seems more probable that it contains the codifica-
tion in Palestine during the exile of the moral demands proclaimed by
the pre-exilic prophets, but, whatever its date and origin,[4] it is presented as an essential part of Old Testament religion.

These ten easily remembered, unconditional statements are called
"words", not laws or instructions, and are thus linked in origin more

---

[1] This Hebrew word, trans. "shone" (RSV), is the denominative verb
from the Hebrew for "horns", and occurs only in this chapter. Perhaps the
story is intended to give the origin of a priestly custom.

[2] The statement is interpreted allegorically by Paul (2 Cor. 3.7–18) as
implying a splendour that, though it faded, needed to be veiled, but "we all,
with unveiled face, beholding (or reflecting) the glory of the Lord, are being
changed to his likeness".

[3] See above, p. 33.

[4] From a literary standpoint, it has been inserted into its present context.
Noth, op. cit., pp. 154f.

closely with prophetic than with priestly religion. The introduction
(20.2) gives the justification for God's demands and his right to claim
Israel's obedience—gratitude for what he had already done.[1] Basic is
the special relationship of Israel to "the Lord your God" and his
saving act in history—the miracle of Deliverance from slavery in
Egypt. The demands that follow deal with the religious, moral, and
social life of the individual Israelite. There are no specifically cultic
requirements in the sense of religious rites performed as a community.
The only possible recognition of a cultus is perhaps found in the
prohibitions against worshipping any other god in the presence of
Yahweh (perhaps in his sanctuary), against using any image in worship, and the command to treat the Sabbath as holy, or set apart from
any work. Thus the unique relationship between Israel and her God is
not in the cultic sphere, but in obedience to the one God, whose
demands pertain to human relationships.[2]

The first word (20.3, E) requires exclusive worship of one God.
"Before me" is ambiguous, perhaps meaning "in my presence", or
with the ambiguity of the English "in front of me", referring either to
physical position or to prominence and priority.

The second absolutely forbids the making or using for worship any
carved or graven image representing human or divine creatures,
animals, birds, or fishes. Such an image would provoke God to
"jealousy" against those who, by making it, showed their complete
defiance of him; but this English translation suggests a character of
God not true to Hebrew thought. The Hebrew word translated
"jealous" (cf. also 34.14) means also "zealous" for his goodness, for
divine values, and for those who love him, and equally zealous
against all who hate him and wish to destroy him and pervert divine
values. Enshrined in this prohibition was the experience that a perverse attitude to God often affected parents, children, and grand-
children, and their fate might be thought of as due to God's zeal
against evil. This would be particularly true if the images referred to
were those kept in the home to represent the family deity, as in the
stories of Rachel (Gen. 31.19) and Jacob (35.2). But the love for God
is much more potent, affecting the lives and destiny of thousands of
generations (Deut. 7.9), an innumerable host.

The third word forbids any insincere use of the divine name. It is
no accident that this follows immediately on the prohibition against
images of deities, for in Hebrew religious thought the "name" of God

---

[1] This verse occurs exactly in Deut. 5.6, and its language is deuteronomic.
[2] Noth, op. cit., p. 167.

replaces a material image as a way of expressing his real presence, especially in Deuteronomy and the deuteronomic writers. The divine name had been revealed, and those who knew it were thought of as having a special power. The name was available for blessing and cursing, but might perhaps be used carelessly or for magical rites. There is no prohibition against using the name, but only against using it in the wrong way.

The fourth word concerns the weekly remembrance of the Sabbath day as set apart from work, in house or field, by servant or cattle. Here, but not in Deuteronomy, the remembrance is linked with the priestly account of creation.[1] As God "ceased" from labour on the seventh day, blessed it, set it apart, so man must cease from labour and set the day apart. There are no cultic rites or pilgrimages to be performed, and so the Sabbath must be kept as a memorial of God's wonderful acts in creation.

When the Sabbath is next mentioned (Exod. 23.12), there is no reference to treating it as holy, but it is to be a day of rest and refreshment, and this ordinance follows the demand that fields, vineyards, and oliveyards cultivated for six successive years shall be fallow in the seventh year, "that the poor of your people may eat; and what they leave the wild beasts may eat". The land must be left untilled and trees unpruned so that landless peasants may take what grows of itself. In Leviticus 25.4ff, H this sabbatical year is part of an agricultural and social system in which debts and slaves are released, and land[2] returned to its original owner, the theological presupposition being that all land and every Israelite belong to God and cannot permanently be alienated from him. It is possible that the sabbatical year may be related to a communal form of land tenure by which all land was redistributed by lot[3] every seven years for six years' use and one fallow year, the use of fertilizers being unknown.

The origin of the seventh-day Sabbath is also obscure.[4] Often we shall find it linked with the new moon (cf. 2 Kings 4.23; Amos 8.5 "new moons and sabbaths", as if denoting the day of the full moon— when the moon "ceased" to grow; but when the phases of the moon were systematized in Hebrew social and religious life into regular

---

[1] Gen. 2.2f, where "rested" (RSV) translates a cognate verb to Sabbath, and means "to keep Sabbath" or "cease". In Exod. 20.11 "rest" translates a different Hebrew verb meaning settle, as the ark on Ararat (Gen. 8.4,) or generally to relax and be refreshed.

[2] Cf. p. 59, n. 1.    [3] Cf. Mic. 2.4f and Ps. 16.6.

[4] Cf. H. J. Kraus, *Worship in Israel* (E.T. 1966), pp. 78ff and literature there cited.

seven-day periods we do not know. Possibly the reason given in Deuteronomy 5.15 for the celebration of the Sabbath suggests that it was a weekly memorial of the Deliverance from Egypt and of the first Passover, which also was a full-moon festival.[1] Such a usage would enable us more easily to understand how in Christian thought the annual Easter Day became a weekly day of remembrance on Sunday.

The fifth command gives an important place to the honouring of parents. It follows immediately the four that require a right attitude to God, and it is interesting to note that both parents, father and mother, are treated in the same way,[2] as though it is recognized that the peace of the family and permanence of national occupation of the soil rest on equal respect for both. In the Holiness Code (Lev. 19.3) this command has an even earlier place, and the mother is mentioned before the father.

The remaining five words are concerned with relationships within the human community. Killing, like "shedding blood" (Gen. 9.6) does not include judicial execution or slaying in warfare, for which other Hebrew words were used. The seventh word, against adultery, which in many MSS. and often in New Testament citations is placed before the prohibition against killing, also carried the death penalty (cf. Lev. 20.10; Deut. 22.22) and its importance is emphasized throughout the Bible. Then as now the reliability of witnesses was vital to the functioning of the law, but then in addition witnesses were executioners (Deut. 17.7) and a proved perjuror was to receive the penalty his false witness would have brought on the one accused (19.19). In both Hosea (4.2) and Jeremiah (7.9) disregard of these four commandments is regarded as a sign of the general decadence that makes God's punishment inevitable. The tenth commandment has been regarded as the only one prohibiting a mental state rather than an overt act; but it must be remembered that in Hebrew thought mental states were judged by their outcome in action, and though the word translated "covet" often in Hebrew simply means "desire", here it must be regarded as meaning "taking steps to obtain".

The date of this decalogue even in a postulated original form cannot be determined, and is not here of great importance. From the religious point of view, it is clear that it was the outcome of prophetic activity, and it has been pointed out that both Abraham and Moses

---

[1] Cf. Procksch, op. cit., p. 87. It is a theological not a social reason; cf. E. Jenni, *Die theologische Begründung des Sabbatgebotes im A.T.* (1956).

[2] For the Old Testament attitude to women, cf. pp. 158, 304 below; to female slaves, p. 178 below.

have been called prophets. In the prophetic literature the standards here asserted are assumed as God's basic requirements from both king and commoners.

The second decalogue (Exod. 34, mainly J) is prepared for by the story of Moses breaking the two stone tablets on which the first decalogue had been written by God (32.19). This second series of ten words (34.28) is presented as written by Moses. It is the basis of God's covenant (34.27), but is not so easily separated into ten requirements. The command to worship one God only (34.14) has been hedged about by other safeguards, against marriage or any covenant with non-Israelite inhabitants of the promised land, and against retaining their altars, stone pillars, and wooden posts. The images forbidden are not graven but metal, as in the Book of the Covenant[1] (34.17; cf. 20.23, E; Lev. 19.4, H). Stone pillars, as we have seen, were used in another way legitimately by Moses (Exod. 24.4, E), when he set up twelve such memorial stones by the altar "according to the twelve tribes of Israel", to represent the whole people in the covenant ceremony.

There are laws concerning the Feast of Unleavened Bread, sacrifice of firstlings with redemption of firstborn sons, the Sabbath, and the Feast of Weeks or Pentecost. Then follow prohibitions against offering blood and leavened bread together, against keeping any of the Passover feast till morning, and against seething a kid in its mother's milk.

Many of these laws appear in almost the same language in the regulations (13.13f) or in the Book of the Covenant (23.12, 15–19), where also we have simple straightforward rules for laymen to observe either at home or when they go to the sanctuary. Whatever their history, here in the second Decalogue they are given as the religious acts to be observed by ordinary Israelites during the whole year in order that the covenant relationship between God and the people may be kept. Moses has prayed the Lord to "take us for thy inheritance"[2] and in reply God emphatically declares that he is now just about to make a covenant by the new and terrible creation (34.10, RSV "wrought", Hebrew "created" as Gen. 1) of an empty land for Israel to occupy. At the end Moses is told, "Write these words; in accordance with these words I have made a covenant with you and with Israel" (34.27). It is noteworthy that this covenant is entirely one-sided. It is given by God, the people do not express their acceptance, nor is there any ceremony of ratification in which both God and people take part.

[1] See below.    [2] 34.9, elsewhere in the Pentateuch only in Deut.

EL

## The Book of the Covenant (*Exodus 20.22—23.33*)

A third group of ordinances, which are intended for the laity, occurs between the two decalogues, and some scholars regard it as containing a series of decalogues, arranged as aids to the memory. It is in the main from the E tradition and contains words and ordinances (24.3), the words being usually short unqualified commands or prohibitions concerned with moral and religious life, while the ordinances are civil and criminal laws, longer and qualified by provisions from actual cases.[1]

The context (20.18ff) clearly implies that the ten words of Exodus 20 were heard by all the people and not mediated through Moses, but the sight and noise of the theophany frightened them, so that they asked that in future Moses might mediate God's words to them. Because of this, Moses wrote "the book of the covenant, and read it in the hearing of the people; and they said . . . we will be obedient" (24.7, contrast 12). It became the basis of the covenant, and could well have been the law administered by the "rulers" (18.21) or "elders" (Num. 11.16; Exod. 24.1). Regulations governing ordinary life under the covenant are here more fully defined than in the ten words, and are also given the authority of God.

Although in later Hebrew thought it was the priest who gave ordinances and taught Israel God's laws, neither here nor anywhere in the Book of the Covenant is there any separation of the priest from ruler, prophet, or layman. Moses built the altar, young men offered the burnt offerings and killed the oxen for the communal meal, and Moses sprinkled the blood on the altar (24.4ff). The instructions to Moses (20.22) follow the usual prophetic formula. The same simplicity, in contrast to the priestly ordinances, is seen in all the religious regulations in these popular codes intended for laymen.

Pride of place goes to the regulation about central features of worship. There is to be a simple earth altar, but no images however costly, because it was from heaven that God's voice was heard by the people (20.22f). In Deuteronomy (4.12) the point is made more clearly: "You heard the sound of words, but saw no form; there was only a voice"—no adequate image could be made. Wherever a man had an experience of the presence of God he must build an altar, as

---

[1] The two types have been distinguished as apodictic or oracle law, and casuistical or case law. A. Alt, *Die Ursprünge des israelitischen Rechts* (1934, E.T. 1966); M. Noth, op. cit., p. 175.

the patriarchs had done, and kill on it his offerings to God, whether burnt offering, an animal wholly consumed by fire for God alone, or peace offering, in which God's portion was burnt and the rest eaten in a sacred meal expressing thanksgiving or petition. God promised to respond by further evidence of his presence and by blessing. If a more permanent memorial or trysting-place were desired, the altar might be built of unhewn natural stone.[1] Probably at one time such an altar was a great stone thought of as a dwelling-place of God (Gen 28.17f), and if it were mutilated by a tool it would cease to be holy. The prohibition (Exod. 20.26) against altar steps was probably to prevent indecent exposure of the person of a man not in priestly attire (28.42).[2]

All the remaining regulations in this code-book were regarded as religious laws, and were placed here because they were based on the covenant relationship between God and Israel. They represent actions and customs necessary within the covenant community, where no real distinction was made between sacred and secular. From our modern standpoint, only a few of them would be regarded as specifically religious. It is, however, well to remind ourselves that "religion" in the Old Testament can be defined as "the right relations between persons", and that "persons" here includes slaves and enemies, the powerful rich and the unprotected poor, as well as God.

For our purpose, we will select those regulations that mention the name of God and regulate conduct at the sanctuary. The released slave who does not want to leave his wife and family in slavery, nor his master's service (21.5), must have his desire for perpetual slavery ratified before God[3] as a safeguard. Similarly the homicide who flees to a city of refuge must be able to show that the killing was un-premeditated—an act of God (21.13). A man who claimed that a deposit had been stolen, but had no proof, must take his case to God (22.8).

The basic prohibition against worshipping any other god is made more specific by the law that sacrifice to any god except the Lord is to be punished by the "ban" (22.20), being set apart or devoted to God

[1] Cf. the great altar at Megiddo, D. W. Thomas (ed.), *Archaeology and Old Testament Study* (1967), pp. 312 f.

[2] There is no evidence that it had sexual reference, cf. Ezek. 44.18, where the offensive smell of sweaty woollen garments is also to be avoided.

[3] Probably the phrase "his master shall bring him to God" was added later to the text. A careful study of the use of *Elohim* (God) with the definite article, as here, suggests that it often indicates the activity of a late levitical writer.

probably by being killed.[1] A stronger threat of God's punishment is made against any who afflict defenceless widows and orphans. God will surely hear their cry (22.23), his wrath will be hot, and the offender will be slain by the sword, so that his wife becomes a widow and his children fatherless. Both God and the one who has been lifted up or made a leader among the people must not be cursed or reviled (22.28). The significance of "leader" (RSV ruler) here is not clear. The word is commonly used by Ezekiel for the one who, in the post-exilic nation, will take the place of the pre-exilic king, and its use by the priestly writers is ambiguous.[2] The present context might suggest that he had some responsibility for seeing that the customary dues were handed over to God; but there is no hint here how this was to be done or how much constituted the dues, only that it must be done without delay. A proportion of wine and oil, and every firstborn of man and beast on the eighth day of its life, must be given to God (22.28f).[3] There is not, as in the second Decalogue, any provision for redemption. Israel, who earlier (19.6, J) are to be a holy nation, are here told they are to be holy men (22.31) and so must not eat of any animal not properly killed, which might presumably contain blood. In Leviticus 17.15 (H) this food is not forbidden, but makes the eater ritually unclean, necessitating washing and ritual separation till the end of the day.

Again, at the beginning of rules about annual pilgrimages, the prohibition against worship of "other gods" (Exod. 23.13; cf. 20.3; 34.14) occurs in a more stringent form forbidding any use of their names. Of the three pilgrimages, the one of unleavened cakes[4] is the only one for which a period of time is prescribed, a fixed date given, and at which an historical occasion is remembered. The other two are clearly agricultural, the wheat harvest and the end of the year's "in-gathering". The harvest is further defined as "the firstfruits of your labour, of what you sow" (23.16). In Exod. 34.22 it is called the Feast of Weeks. To the Feast of Unleavened Bread alone is attached the clause "None shall appear before me empty-handed" (23.15; cf. 34.20); but other gifts are covered by the requirement that the first or

---

[1] Cf. the same word, Josh. 6.17ff.

[2] Often it is used in the plural, cf. Exod. 16.22, Num. 1.16, leaders of the people who report their conduct to Moses. There seems insufficient evidence to assert that "the leader" was the covenant mediator, who led the people at a covenant-renewal ceremony of the twelve-tribe amphictyony, cf. H. J. Kraus, op. cit., pp. 108ff; M. Noth, op. cit., pp. 188f; M. Newman, op. cit.

[3] Cf. above, p. 37.          [4] Cf. above, pp. 38f.

best of firstfruits from the ground must be taken to the sanctuary (23.19; 34.22, 26). The rule of three annual pilgrimages is repeated in 23.17 but limited to males as in 34.23.

Three other ritual laws follow (23.18f), forbidding the use of leaven with animal sacrifice, seething a kid in its mother's milk, and keeping overnight the fat of any pilgrimage sacrifice—not simply the Passover sacrifice as in the parallel passage in 34.25. Evidence is lacking to support the conjecture that the prohibition against seething a kid in its mother's milk was aimed at a powerful magical fertility rite in which such milk was sprinkled over the ground.[1]

The Book of the Covenant concludes with a renewed promise of God's guidance and leadership if the people are obedient. There is no metaphor of cloud or fire, but the exalted figure of an angel or messenger (23.20f) in whom God himself dwells and who must be treated as God, because God's name is in him. He must be obeyed, he has the power to refuse pardon for rebellion. He will drive out the present inhabitants of the promised land. There is repeated stress that the whole conquest will be achieved by God alone, as in the story of Deliverance from Egypt (14.14ff, J); not only is the angel promised, but God's terror and his hornet.

As in the giving of the second Decalogue, there is a curious breaking-in of practical common sense. There (34.24) when all the males are away on the three annual pilgrimages, no one will try to take their land, and here (23.29f) God promises to leave some original inhabitants to guard and cultivate their land until Israel can use it.

The whole Book of the Covenant is set in a framework which gives confidence to Israel. At the beginning is the theophany where God reminds them of his intervention, as an eagle delivering them and bringing them to himself. At the end is his promise of his powerful aid to establish them in the promised land; but the condition is always Israel's full obedience (19.5) which the people promise (24.7). God will choose them as his treasure, they must worship him as their only God, and the worship must be expressed in their whole life.

## The Holiness Code (*Leviticus 17—26*)

A fourth group of regulations, apparently intended for the layman although clearly emanating from a priestly circle, has for many years

---

[1] cf. G. R. Driver, *Canaanite Myths and Legends* (1956), p. 121; C. H. Gordon; *Before the Bible* (1962), p. 173.

been called the Holiness Code,[1] because of its emphasis on God's
holiness and the need for man's holiness.[2] Like the Book of the
Covenant, it opens with rules about sacrifice (cf. Exod. 20.24f) and
ends with an exhortation to obey the laws (cf. Exod. 23.20ff). The
rules are given by the Lord to Moses to be addressed to Aaron, his
sons, and all the children of Israel, priests and laity together.

All killing of animals must take place at the sanctuary, inside the
camp at the door of the "tent of meeting", to ensure that all sacrifices
are offered to the Lord, not to demons or he-goats, and that the blood
and fat are brought to the altar by the priest (Lev. 17.6).[3] This emphasis on the special duties of the priest is a new feature, for in the
patriarchal and Deliverance stories there is no mention of Israelite
priests. They are recognized however in the Sinai accounts, where
Israel, if obedient, is to be a kingdom of priests (Exod. 19.6, J), and
where the priests are different from the people but under the same
prohibition (19.22, 24, J) against access to the holy mountain. In the
Passover regulations it was the elders who put the blood of the victim
on the doorposts (12.22, J), and in the covenant ceremony Moses as
leader, not specifically as a priest, sprinkled it on altar and people
(24.6,8, E). Now the fat too must be burnt by the priest as a pleasing
odour to the Lord.

No reason is given for this treatment of the fat, but of the blood it is
said that "the life [soul] of the flesh is in the blood; and I have given it
to[4] you upon the altar to make atonement for your life [soul]; for it is
the blood that makes atonement, by reason of the life" (Lev. 17.11). It
is the God-ordained way of "erasing" or wiping out an offence.[5]

How the life essence of an animal offered on the altar clears man's

---

[1] A. Klostermann (1877).

[2] Opinions differ as to the date of the Code, but it seems probable that,
whatever earlier or later elements it may contain, some of it was a code used
at the Jerusalem Temple at the end of the monarchy, 586 B.C. Its literary
form and religious content link it with the time of Ezekiel.

[3] Cf. R. de Vaux, *Ancient Israel* (E.T. 1961), p. 356.

[4] The RSV "I have given it *for* you upon the altar" does not bring out the
clear implication of the Hebrew, that the Lord himself has "given it [the
blood] *to* you upon the altar as the means of atonement for your life," cf.
Noth, *Leviticus*, p. 132

[5] G. R. Driver (*Journal of Theological Studies* 34 (1933), pp. 35ff) points
out that the root meaning of the Hebrew word translated *atone* appears to
denote *wiping*, whether wiping clean, smearing, or wiping away. In Accadian
the root is employed in parallelism with a word meaning "to erase", and
in Aramaic is used of erasing writing. Thus it may also be accepted that to
*wipe, cleanse*, or *erase*, underlies the ritual significance of the Hebrew word.

sins is not explained; it is enough that God has ordained that it should be so. It is assumed that for any break between God and man, man's life is forfeit, but God accepts the animal's life in place of man's life. Because God has set blood apart for this special sacred purpose, Israel must not use it in any other way, and in particular must not eat it (cf. Gen. 9.4, P, where, however, it is all mankind, the descendants of Noah, who are forbidden to partake of blood). Here the blood of the animal is thought of as substitute for man's life, whereas in the covenant ceremony (Exod. 24.6ff, E) when sprinkled on altar and people it makes a bond between God and people. If game is killed away from the tent of meeting, the blood must be poured out on the ground and covered with soil (Lev. 17.13). A carcass, presumably not drained of blood, may be eaten if proper ritual precautions are taken.

This code, like the Book of the Covenant, treats all conduct as the concern of religion. Here it is because the Lord is Israel's God that Israel's behaviour in sexual relationships must differ from that of their neighbours in Egypt and Canaan (Lev. 18 and 20.10ff). God's statutes and judgements are clearly known and must be obeyed because he is their God. All other conduct is an abomination (Lev. 18.26ff).[1] Included in these sexual regulations is a prohibition against a custom, already seen[2] in the Book of the Covenant (Exod. 22.29) of "handing over children to Molech". The meaning of this phrase and the extent of the practice are not known.[3] Here (Lev. 18.21) the context suggests "seed" that is the outcome of illicit sexual intercourse, and later (Lev. 20.1–5) where the law and its penalty are more fully described, it is spoken of as committing whoredom with "the Molech", and is part of a chapter also concerned with wrong sexual relationships. "Molech" combines the Hebrew consonants of *Melek* (king) with the vowels of *Bosheth* (shame). It is always used with the definite article, and should be translated "The Shameful One". In Punic inscriptions *molk* is the name of a particular child sacrifice. An Ammonite god is called Milkom (2 Sam. 12.30, RSV marg.). But the Hebrew word translated "to Molech" might equally mean "for, or on behalf of, the king", and might refer to an annual sacrifice of the child

---

[1] Heathen worship and religious customs are forbidden especially in Deuteronomy, the deuteronomic writers, and Ezekiel, as "abominations". Here in the Holiness Code "abomination" is used particularly of wrong sexual relations. That the word has wider application is seen in Gen. 43.32; 46.34; Exod. 8, 26; Deut. 25.13ff. See below, p. 304, n. 4.

[2] Cf. above, p. 37.

[3] Cf. R. de Vaux, op. cit., pp. 444ff; H. H. Rowley, *Worship in Ancient Israel* (1967), pp. 25, 64ff, and literature there cited.

born in the Tammuz month from the autumnal sacred marriage rite, as a substitute for the life of the king. That a rite of child sacrifice was practised at Jerusalem at the end of the seventh century seems clear from Jeremiah (7.31).

The mingling of secular and religious requirements is seen even more clearly in Leviticus 19, where at one end of the scale is the prohibition against sowing two kinds of seed in one field (19.19), and at the other the command "Thou shalt love thy neighbour as thyself" (19.18). This chapter contains many of the ten words (Exod. 20) in a different order and different language, perhaps suggesting that the two writers did not know each other's version. Here and repeatedly throughout the code particular stress is laid on Sabbath observance and the rejection of all idol worship. The motive throughout this excellent compendium of moral duties is "I am the Lord your God". As God is holy, so must the people be; as he has separated them from all peoples to be his own, so must they separate themselves and make clear the distinction between clean and unclean, what God allows and what he forbids (Lev. 20.24ff).

The remaining commands, through Moses, are mainly given to the whole people (23.1; 24.1; 25.1). Some are addressed to Aaron (21.16) or to the priests, the sons of Aaron (21.1; 22.2); but these too are given that all Israel may know (21.24; 22.17). They are concerned with the conduct and physical condition of the High Priest (21.10f) and priests in order to preserve their special sanctity, and with regulations by which sacrifices can be known to be acceptable to God. There are fuller regulations to enable the people properly to keep the Sabbath and the annual festivals; in the first month Passover and Unleavened Bread made with the firstfruits of harvest when grain is ripe (Lev. 23.9ff), and seven weeks later the harvest festival; and all the feasts of the seventh month, including the Day of Atonement and the Feast of Tabernacles or Booths. Only this last feast is linked with the history of the past, the great Deliverance from Egypt (23.43), probably because the use of "branches of palm trees, and boughs of leafy trees, and willows of the brook" came from a Canaanite autumn festival (cf. Judges 21.19ff) and did not fit easily with the Hebrew tradition of wandering through a waterless desert (Deut. 8.15). Clearly a need was felt to establish a connection between these temporary booths and the tents of the wanderings.

Outside the Holiness Code but related to it (Num. 28f, P) there are further regulations concerned with the calendar of sacred feasts and the appropriate offerings. Both festivals and sacrifices are increased, giving evidence of a growing anxiety in priestly circles to remove barriers between Israel and her God.

In the final regulations in the Holiness Code about the Sabbath year and the Jubilee year, is enunciated the clear religious principle to govern Israel's economy, that all the land belongs to God. The people are sojourners in God's land, and no one can acquire any permanent rights over any part of it (Lev. 25.23).[1] Similarly, every Israelite is God's servant, and must not be sold as a slave (25.42).

The code concludes with a promise and a threat. If Israel is obedient, God will dwell among them, walk among them, and be their God, and they will be his people. Disobedience will lead to national destruction and exile, but even in exile, if they humble themselves, God will remember his covenant with the patriarchs and his covenant with those he brought out of Egypt, so that the nation will not be utterly destroyed.

[1] The only exceptions are land in a walled city on which a dwelling-house has been built, and the pastures of the Levites (25.29, 34).

# 5 Mosaic Religion: Institutions

Included in the Sinai legislation are other groups of instructions, found in the priestly traditions in Exodus, Leviticus, and Numbers, and presented as given by the Lord to Moses during his forty days on the mountain. These relate to the construction of a permanent portable shrine, the persons who are to serve in it, and the acts to be performed there. Like a refrain, through the instructions run the phrases "as the Lord commanded Moses" and "according to the pattern I showed thee on the mount". Some of these instructions too are addressed by Moses to the children of Israel (cf. Exod. 25.2, P) as though intended for the laity like the Book of the Covenant and the Holiness Code, and as rejecting any idea that in Israel this priestly lore was secret to priests alone.

The aim of these cultic institutions was the removal of barriers between God and man, so that fellowship with the divine was possible. This was thought of in terms of human community, and the means of achieving it were drawn from human analogies. There were places and times for meeting which became holy; offerings and shared communal meals; and special persons who mediated between God and man.

Already we have seen in the introductory stories to the patriarchal saga in Genesis reference to some of Israel's characteristic religious institutions—the seventh-day Sabbath, animal and cereal offerings, whole burnt offerings, the sacredness of blood, and the difference between clean and unclean animals. In these stories a place where a patriarch experienced the presence of God became holy to him and he built an altar there, planted a tree, or set up and anointed a stone. This natural fixing of holy places continues in regulations at Sinai. The mountain of God where he appeared to Moses is holy, and there he appeared again to the whole people, though it is stressed that it was from heaven that God spoke (Exod. 20.22, E). Later we are told of a tent that Moses used to pitch outside the camp, far off from the camp, and called the tent of meeting or of appointment (33.7, E). There the Lord spoke with Moses, and Joshua was its permanent guardian.

We have seen too in the stories of Sinai that special times as well as places could be used for remembering God's revelations. In one version of the Decalogue (Exod. 20.8f, E) the Sabbath was to be a weekly remembrance of God's wonderful acts of creation and his ceasing those labours; in another version (Deut. 5.15) it was a weekly remembrance of the wonderful Deliverance from Egypt—which was remembered also in the annual Passover and Feast of Unleavened Bread. At two other times in the year—to present the firstfruits of the wheat harvest and at the ingathering in autumn (Exod. 34.22, J)—every male Israelite was to go to the sanctuary to meet God and to present gifts.

Special persons too have stood out as mediators between God and man—Abraham and especially Moses, who at the people's request became one who relayed God's words to them; and in the Holiness Code priests receive the sacrifices at the entrance to the tent of meeting and sprinkle the blood on the altar (Lev. 17.5f). In the religious institutions we are now to consider, all such means of reconciling man to God become more detailed and explicit.

## The Sanctuary

The people are invited (Exod. 25) to bring liberally and freely precious metals, woven material, skins, wood, oil, spices, and precious stones as an offering to God. They are the costliest materials, chosen like the priestly garments (28.2) for glory and beauty. A special word is used to denote these offerings as lifted up (*terumah*) as though specially taken and dedicated to God's service. From them is to be made a shrine too elaborate to be pitched by Moses, a sanctuary or holy place not for divine visits, but where God may dwell or "tabernacle" among his people.[1] The detailed description of the shrine moves outward from its contents to the tent building itself, the courtyard round it, and then to the vestments and consecration of the priests who are to work in it. The focus of worship is to be a portable ark, a wooden box or chest approximately 3 feet 9 inches by 2 feet 3 inches by 2 feet 3 inches coated inside and out with gold, and containing the Decalogue or "testimony" (Exod. 25.16, P). It is to have a lid or covering of pure gold, to which are attached two cherubs facing each other, their wings spread out to cover it. God's voice will come to Moses from above this lid, from between these two cherubs. The

[1] There are also regulations for gifts from the secular head of each tribe when the tabernacle is dedicated (Num. 7).

Hebrew word for the "lid" or "covering" has the same root as that for "atonement for sin" and means the place where propitiation may be made.[1] The cherubs, mythical figures known from Palestinian archaeology, were probably thought of as the spirit of the wind on which God rides (Ps. 18.10). In Ezekiel (1.5ff) they are described in detail as bearing the movable platform on which God is carried from the doomed Jerusalem to join his exiled people in Babylon. Cherub figures are to be woven into the temple veil (Exod. 26.31); they were carved on the walls and doors of Solomon's temple (cf. 1 Kings 6.29).

In the shrine with the ark there is to be a small wooden table (3 feet by 1 foot 6 inches, and 2 feet 3 inches high) also overlaid with gold. On it are to stand deep gold dishes,[2] spoons and cups for incense, flagons or chalices, and bowls for pouring out liquid offerings. Twelve presence-loaves are to be put on the table every Sabbath in two piles, incense is to be burnt over them, and they are to be eaten by the priests.[3] Another name for these loaves, showbread (RSV), literally "the set-out or arranged bread" (1 Chron. 9.32), avoids the idea of the presence of God. Although possibly these loaves had a parallel in Babylonian temple ritual,[4] in the Old Testament they are not thought of as food for the god, but as Israel's continual memorial of God's everlasting covenant, a simple recognition of the source from which come all man's material blessings (Lev. 24.7).

The other furniture of the shrine is to be a golden lampstand having a central stem with three branches on each side, each branch ending in a cup shaped like an almond flower to give a total of seven oil lamps. All is to be made according to the pattern shown by God to Moses on the mount (Exod. 25.31ff).

The tent structure itself is called a holy place or shrine, where God may dwell in the midst of Israel (25.8), or simply "the dwelling" (RSV tabernacle, 26.1). Other names are "the dwelling of the testimony" (38.21), "the dwelling of the Lord" (Num. 16.9), "the tent" (Exod. 26.9)[5] "the tent of meeting" (27.21), and "the tent of the testimony" (Num. 17.8). It is to be forty-five feet long, fifteen feet in height and breadth, with a veil or curtain of linen to shut off the inner or holiest

[1] RSV "mercy seat" was used by Tyndale (1530), and translates Luther's *gnadenstuhl* (1523). In the LXX this is *hilastērion*, the word used in Heb. 9.5.
[2] This word (RSV plates) occurs only in Exod. 37.16 and Num. 4.7.
[3] Lev. 24.5f; cf. 1 Sam. 21.6; 2 Chron. 13.11.
[4] Schrader, *Die Keilinschriften in den A.T.* (3rd edn), p. 600.
[5] The E.V.V. "tabernacle" comes from *tabernaculum*, the word Jerome used to translate the Hebrew for "tent".

place at one end as a perfect cube of fifteen feet.[1] Within this holiest place stands the ark, and outside are the lampstand and the table. The outer room is also to be shut off by an embroidered linen curtain, outside which stands the wooden altar overlaid with bronze, 7 feet 6 inches square and 4 feet 6 inches high (Exod. 27.1ff).

The making of it all is entrusted to Bezaleel, a layman to whom the spirit of God has given the artistic ability and craftsmanship necessary for the task (31.1ff).

## *The Priesthood*

Directions are given for making clothes for the priests and for consecrating Aaron and his sons. Aaron's rich golden robes include precious stones engraved with the names of the twelve tribes (28.21), and the sacred lot, Urim and Thummim (28.30; cf. Num. 27.21). His robe is to be decorated with pomegranates and golden bells, whose ringing as he goes in and out of the holy place will save him from death (Exod. 28.35).[2] Upon his headdress is to be a golden plate engraved "Holy to the Lord", so that wearing it he may take responsibility for any accidental errors made by the people when offering their gifts (28.36ff).

At their consecration Aaron and his sons are to be washed with water, robed in their vestments, and Aaron is to be anointed with oil (29.7).[3] A young bull and two rams are to be brought, and Aaron and his sons are then to lay their hands on the bullock, which after the offering of blood and fat at the altar, is to be burnt outside the camp as a sin offering (29.14). Their hands are also laid on the two rams, and one is burnt on the altar as a pleasing odour to God; the other is a consecration offering, of which part is burnt for God, and, after its blood has been put on the priests' right ears, hands, and feet, and on the altar, and sprinkled on the priestly garments, part is eaten by the priests. This is spoken of as that "with which atonement was made" (29.33), and all these sacrifices are to be made daily for seven days. Further, continually every day morning and evening sacrifices are to be made on the altar at the door of the tent of meeting, so that tent, altar, and priests may be made holy, and God may dwell among his people Israel (29.44f).

[1] S. R. Driver, op. cit., p. 290.

[2] The woven pomegranates perhaps represented rattles. The hard skins containing dried seeds are still used by children for this purpose.

[3] Here only Aaron is to be anointed (cf. Lev. 6.22, the anointed priest), but elsewhere (Exod. 28.41; 30.30; 40.15) all priests are to be anointed.

In the account of the fulfilment of these instructions, at the end of the consecration ceremony, first Aaron lifted up his hands towards the people and blessed them, and then both Moses and Aaron, after a visit to the tent of meeting, blessed the people "and the glory of the Lord appeared to all the people" (Lev. 9.22f). The words to be used in the priestly blessing, "The Lord bless you and keep you, the Lord make his face to shine upon you, and be gracious to you, the Lord lift up the light of his countenance upon you and give you peace", are given in Numbers 6.24ff. Sacrifices are recorded as burnt on the altar before the consecration ceremony, this probably being intended to denote that the fire on the altar was perpetual, burning continually (cf. Lev. 6.13).

Finally, instructions are given for the making of a smaller altar (Exod. 30.1ff) on which only incense is to be offered every morning and evening, and which is to be touched with the blood of the sin offering once a year on the Day of Atonement. A strange survival of primitive belief is seen in the following law that, to prevent plague after a census, every person over twenty years of age must pay half-a-shekel to sanctuary funds as the price of his life. It is stressed that all are treated alike, rich and poor pay the same amount (30.15). There are instructions for making the special anointing-oil and incense. A bronze laver is to stand between tent and altar, where the priests may wash hands and feet when they enter the tent or approach the altar (30.17ff). There has been no hint of appointment of women to any service at the door of the tent, nor any description of their duties, but it is stated (38.8) that the bronze laver was made from the mirrors of the ministering women who ministered at the door of the tent of meeting.[1] The same description is given of the women in the account of the wicked behaviour of Eli's priestly sons (1 Sam. 2.22). Possibly the thought is that religious prostitution ceased in Israel when these women gave up their precious mirrors to make a vessel for the Lord's dwelling.[2]

## Sacrifices and Offerings

The priestly writers who have given instructions for making and furnishing the tent-shrine now give detailed regulations for the acts

[1] The Hebrew word for the RSV "minister" usually refers to the army or host, but may have a wider meaning of "service" (cf. Isa. 40.2, RSV. "warfare".)

[2] Cf. R. Dussaud, *Les Origines cananiennes du Sacrifice israélite* (2nd edn, 1941).

that are to take place in it (Lev. 1ff). According to these writers, no new covenant was made by God at Sinai—that would have been unnecessary because the one already made with the patriarchs was still valid. The new gift at Sinai was a form of worship, a legitimate cultus to maintain the patriarchal covenant between God and people. The theory is that there had been no such cultic acts before, at least, not properly and officially ordained acts. But now these are set out that people and priests may know them, and that the offerings may be acceptable to God (Lev. 1.3). Addressed to the whole people are laws concerning the five principal offerings—burnt offerings, cereal offerings, peace, sin, and guilt offerings—and these are supplemented by a short manual (6.8—7.38) addressed to Aaron and his sons.

As in the Holiness Code, the offerer of the burnt offering kills his sacrificial animal, cuts it in pieces, and washes it, but a priest alone can approach the altar to put on it blood or flesh. Clearly it is the altar, not the blood, which is too holy for lay contact. A new element in the ritual is that before the offerer kills the animal "he shall lay his hand on the head of the burnt offering, and it shall be accepted for him to make an atonement or wiping out for him". The meaning of this rite is not clear. In the Holiness Code, the men who heard blasphemy laid their hands on the blasphemer before he was stoned, as though either accepting responsibility as witnesses for his death, or as purging from themselves the blasphemy they had heard and putting it back upon him (24.14). In the ritual of the Day of Atonement the scapegoat bears upon himself all the iniquities of the children of Israel, but whether these are transferred by Aaron's confession or the laying on of his hands is not stated (16.21f). Here (1.4) the animal is thought of not as from, but for, the offerer, suggesting that in some way it is a substitute for him. The whole animal is to be consumed in smoke as a soothing odour to the Lord (1.9), as placating God, making the offerer acceptable.

The cereal offering is to provide the same soothing smoke, perhaps from the burning incense (2.2). Only a handful is burnt, the remainder being most holy, and to be consumed in the sanctuary by the priests alone (2.3; cf. 6.16, 26). It is difficult to interpret the technical terms used throughout these instructions; but here the meaning seems to be that the priest shall make the altar smoke with its memorial portion (2.2, 9, 16) as a fire offering of pleasing odour to the Lord. How it is to be a memorial is not stated. Possibly, like the loaves of the presence it is to remind the offerer that all his grain is a gift from God (24.7). All cereal offerings must contain salt. Leaven and honey may be brought to the sanctuary and handed over to the priests, but are not to be included in burnt offerings.

The third type of sacrifice is called a peace offering (Lev. 3), but again the meaning of the Hebrew term is doubtful. It may be cognate with *shalom* (peace), so denoting a sacrifice that brings about a right relationship between offerer and God; or it may be linked with a Hebrew word meaning repay or recompense, and so have been thought of as a thank offering to God. In the priestly manual (7.11ff) peace offerings may be for thanksgiving, for vows, or they may be freewill offerings. This offering may be an unblemished male or female from flock or herd. The priest is to burn the fat on the altar "as food offered by fire to the Lord" (3.11), representing God's share in the meal. The "waved" breast and the thigh are for the priests (7.34). As implied in 7.19ff, the remainder is for a meal shared by the offerer and his friends if they are ritually clean. Emphatically it is stated that neither blood nor fat is to be eaten, but as in the Holiness Code no reason is given for the prohibition against the fat.

After the peace offering, sin offerings are considered. All these are for sins committed unwittingly (4.2), and are to be made when the sin is realized or made known to the offender (4.14, 23, 28). By the blood ritual and burning, in the sin offering the priest makes a cleansing for the sinner concerning his sins, or from his sins (4.26), and he will be forgiven. Four successive laws provide for sin by the anointed priest, by the whole community, by a ruler (cf. Exod. 22.28, E; 16.22, P, RSV leader), and by an ordinary layman. If the anointed priest has sinned, he must lay his hand on the head of a bullock and kill it before the Lord, sprinkling blood seven times before the veil separating the sanctuary from the inner holy place (Lev. 4.5f); the incense altar must be touched with blood, and all the remaining blood poured out at the altar of burnt offering, where the fat is burnt. All the rest of the animal must be burned outside the camp on the clean ash-heap.[1] The same offering is made for the sin of the whole community, but here it is the elders who put their hands on the victim. For the ruler, the victim is a male goat, whose blood is brought to the altar and its fat burnt. Nothing is said here about the disposal of the flesh, but in the manual for priests (6.24–30) this is to be eaten in the sanctuary by the priests; the words "every male priest" imply that it is too holy to be partaken of in the households of the priests.[2] Earthenware used for cooking it must be broken and bronze vessels scoured. For a layman

---

[1] Cf. also Num. 19.9, the disposal of the carcase of the red heifer.
[2] Contrast Lev. 10.14, the peace offering.

the offering is usually a female goat or lamb, provision being made for even the poorest to make a suitable offering.

The fifth principal offering, the guilt offering (6.1–7), refers to a deliberate offence against a neighbour in respect of a deposit, bargain, or robbery. Restoration plus a fifth in value must be made, but in addition a ram must be sacrificed to the Lord, whose forgiveness is essential. This offering, unlike the sin offering, does not vary according to the importance of the offender, and all the blood must be dashed against the altar. But, like the flesh of the sin offering, this too is to be treated as most holy, and eaten by male priests in the sanctuary.

Here follows the manual already mentioned (p. 65) designed to help the priests. After this comes an account of how the instructions in Exodus were carried out when Aaron was anointed. It is the priests' duty to make clear the distinction between holy and common, clean and unclean, and to teach the people the Lord's statutes (10.10f). Clean animals have cloven hooves and also chew the cud (11.3), clean fish have fins and scales (11.9). No such principle is enunciated for birds, and among winged insects only four kinds are enumerated as clean. All other "swarming" creatures are unclean, so that they must not be eaten, and if their carcasses are touched uncleanness must be ritually removed.

There is legislation for two unclean states, childbirth and leprosy. After a male birth uncleanness lasts forty days, and eighty days after a female. By a lamb and a young pigeon (again concessions are made to the poor—12.8; cf. Luke 2.22ff) the priest is to make atonement for the mother, and "she shall be cleansed from the flow of her blood"— clearly this like menstruation has caused ritual uncleanness (Lev. 12.7; 15.19ff). For leprosy, two cleansing rites have been combined (14.1–8; 9–20). Neither is regarded as curing the condition but as part of the pronouncing clean of an already cured leper. What were regarded as similar contagious diseases—skin eruptions, moulds on cloth and walls—have different rites and periods of cleansing, and must be reported to the priest, who appears as the repository of biological as well as of legal and religious knowledge. Blood and running water have cleansing power, and a living bird is released, probably to carry away contagion. In addition, the cleansed leper is to make a guilt offering, a sin offering, and a burnt offering, of lesser value if he "is poor and cannot afford so much" (14.21).

The divine purpose behind all the rites of cleansing and for the different periods of uncleanness is clearly stated. The priests have received instruction so that they may "keep the people of Israel separate from their uncleanness, lest they die in their uncleanness by defiling my tabernacle that is in their midst" (15.31). It is because the Lord dwells in their midst that the people are to be separate, and to see to it that shed blood does not pollute the land where they live (Num. 35.33).[1]

## The Day of Atonement

The same sense of the overwhelming holiness of God lies behind the various rites of the annual Day of Atonement (Lev. 16), "the culmination and crown of the sacrificial worship of the Old Testament".[2] Annually on the tenth day of the seventh month Aaron or his successor, having made a sin offering for the priesthood and another for the people, must enter alone the innermost holy place of the sanctuary (Exod. 26.33), dressed in simple linen garments, and God will appear in the cloud above the lid of the ark. This is the one great day in the year when the blood of the sin offering is "brought into the immediate presence of God" within the veil, and sprinkled on the ark. On this day too a living goat bearing the iniquities of the people is released into "a solitary land" (Lev. 16.22). The purpose is summed up in verse 33: the anointed priest "shall make atonement for the sanctuary . . . for the tent of meeting and for the altar . . . for the priests and for all the people of the assembly." Once every year all is purified. Whatever the day of the week, this Day is a Sabbath of solemn rest and fasting. No work may be done, and the people afflict themselves.[3] The historical occasion of instituting this Day is given as the sudden death of Aaron's two sons Nadab and Abihu when they penetrated into the holy place with wrong fire and incense (10.1ff).[4] Rules were made to protect Aaron, and to prevent his entrance into the holiest place except once a year. In the Holiness Code (23.26ff) the Day is one of other special days in the seventh month, and is marked by fasting and Sabbath rest. It is also the day when the Jubilee year is proclaimed by the loud blowing of the trumpet (25.9).

---

[1] A primitive and permanent means of cleansing after contact with a dead body is seen in the use of water in which were put ashes from a specially burnt red heifer (Num. 19.1ff).

[2] A. R. S. Kennedy, *Leviticus*, p. 110.

[3] In another form of the regulations (Num. 29.7ff), the burnt offerings are increased and are to appease the Lord with a pleasing odour.

[4] Cf. Num. 11.1–3 where the same fate befell complaining Israelites.

## The Levites

The last major group of regulations with which we deal is concerned with setting apart the whole tribe of Levi for special sanctuary duties. Already in the story of the flagrant apostasy of making the golden calf, we have been told that sons of Levi responded to Moses' call for those who were on the Lord's side (Exod. 32.26ff, J). Ignoring ties of family and friendship,[1] they had killed 3,000 faithless Israelites, and "ordained"[2] themselves "for the service of the Lord" and for a blessing to be bestowed on them. When the census of the tribes was taken, Levi was not numbered (Num. 1.47, P) but was appointed for service with the tent, to carry it and encamp round about it—it is not to be outside the camp but in the centre, and the Levites are to protect the other tribes from wrath (1.53). Later, a census was taken of all Levites and their duties were carefully defined (3.5ff; cf. 8.5–26; 18.1–7).

They are not themselves to be priests,[3] the priesthood being reserved to Aaron and his sons (3.9f), but are a gift to Aaron on behalf of all Israel instead of Israelite firstborn (3.12). They are treated as an offering "waved" before the Lord, as though a part or token from all Israel to serve in the tent of meeting in attendance on Aaron and his sons (8.13ff), to whom they are given to provide an atonement for the children of Israel, so that no plague will spread through the nation when the people come near the sanctuary.[4]

The Levites are set apart to special service in transporting the tent sanctuary and its furniture; but certain differences distinguish them as of a lower order than the priests. Their period of service is limited, from the age of thirty to fifty.[5] When they are set apart, they are cleansed by washing, shaving, and sin offering (8.6ff) but not, like the priests (Exod. 28.41ff) consecrated by anointing with oil and arraying in new and special garments. Before a journey, everything to do with the sanctuary must be carefully wrapped and put ready by the priests themselves, lest the Levites should see or touch holy things. They camp nearest to the tabernacle on north, south, and west; but the

[1] Cf. Deut. 33.9, where Levi is praised for this.

[2] Cf. Exod. 28.41, where the same phrase "fill your hand" is used. Deut. 10.8 may refer to this occasion.

[3] Cf. below, p. 85.

[4] 8.19, a verse which seems to give the basic meaning of the word "atonement"; cf. p. 56 above.

[5] 4.3; in 8.23ff it is twenty-five to fifty, with lighter duties afterwards; in 1 Chron. 23.27 the age of twenty is mentioned without any upper limit.

priests are nearest to it on the east, where the entrance and altar are. Finally, the Levites must perform all their tasks under priestly direction.

That this situation—the sacral privileges of the Levites and their inferiority to the priesthood—was not fully satisfying to all sections in Israel is seen in the composite story of the rebellion of Korah the Levite, some Reubenites, and 250 leaders of the congregation. Two streams of protest clearly emerge in the story. According to one, the complaint is that Moses and Aaron "have gone too far, for all the congregation[1] is holy, every one of them, and the Lord is among them" (Num. 16.3). According to the other, Moses has to rebuke the sons of Levi: "Is it too small a thing for you that the God of Israel has separated you from the congregation of Israel to bring you near himself . . . and would you seek the priesthood also ?" (16.9f). The matter is put to the test, the Lord's wrath destroys the rebels, and the censers they have used impiously are collected from the ruins to become a plated covering for the altar, "to be a reminder to the people of Israel, so that no one who is not a priest, who is not of the descendants of Aaron, should draw near to burn incense before the Lord" (16.40). In a further test, Aaron and the Levites together are shown to be chosen by God out of all the tribes for service in the sanctuary (17). An almond rod representing each tribe with the tribal name on it was put in the tent overnight. The levitical rod had Aaron's name on it. In the morning Aaron's rod alone had blossomed and borne ripe almonds. By this form of ordeal,[2] God himself had silenced doubts about the special position of Aaron and the Levites. The Levites are "joined" to the priesthood (18.4).[3] In a later chapter (35.6) in contradistinction to the statement that the Levites, though given tithes, should have no landed inheritance (18.24), forty-eight cities, including six cities of refuge for unintentional homicides, are set apart with the pastures around them as a possession of the Levites.

## Nazirites

Not only priests and Levites are dedicated to God, but there are given rules for self-dedication by vow of any ordinary Israelite, man or woman, to permanent or temporary service of the Lord (6). The word "nazirite" used for anyone who had taken such vows really means "devotee". Like the Levite at his dedication, he is to be shaved at the

---

[1] See below, p. 278.  [2] Cf. the suspected wife ordeal, 5.11ff.
[3] The Hebrew word "joined" is cognate with the word "Levi".

beginning of his vow, but afterwards no razor is to come near his head till the period of the vow is complete, when he makes offerings and shaves "his consecrated head" and the hair is burnt in the fire of the peace offering. The priests were forbidden to drink wine when they entered the tent of meeting (Lev. 10.8), but a more stringent command forbids not only wine but fresh and dried grapes to Nazirites (Num. 6.3). Like the Chief Priest (Lev. 21.11), the Nazirite may not go near a dead body, even if it is that of his closest relative. Elsewhere in the Old Testament we shall see examples of individuals who took this Nazirite vow.

## Civil Leaders

As we saw,[1] civil as well as religious law-giving was traced to Sinai and thus had Mosaic authority. The institution of civil leaders is related in three places. In Exodus (18.21ff), on the advice of Jethro, Moses appointed men of substance (RSV able), having religious and moral qualities, as heads over the people and captains (or men in charge, RSV rulers) to be judges and help him. He himself was to be judge of final appeal, who would reveal God's will. In Deuteronomy (1.13ff) the people[2] at Moses' request picked wise, understanding, and "known" (RSV experienced) men according to their tribes, for Moses to appoint as heads over the people and officers (possibly men with scribal ability); and they are apparently equated with judges (1.16).

In Numbers (11.16ff) Moses was told to gather seventy men from the "known" elders of Israel and their officers (the same title as in Deut. 1.15). But here (11.24ff) the number seventy is particularly specified (cf. Exod. 24.9) and the institution of the authority of the seventy is deliberately and explicitly linked with Moses and the Spirit. God, having ordered Moses to gather seventy elders at the tent of meeting, came down in a cloud and took some of the spirit that was on Moses and put it on the elders, who thereupon prophesied. The Hebrew word for "put" seems to mean "reserve", or "keep back", as though some of the spirit usually given to Moses was diverted to the seventy giving them the same power and authority that Moses had. By the prophesying of the seventy at their institution it was clearly manifest that the delegation of legal authority had been commanded by God himself and was associated with his Spirit, and the gift of prophecy remained long enough to establish this point, and no longer.

[1] Above, p. 44.     [2] But contrast LXX.

Further, when Eldad and Medad, two of the "registered" seventy, prophesied though they had not attended the ceremony of institution, the Lord had demonstrated that he himself had chosen the seventy "rulers", just as later in the stories of the Judges and the kingship divine choice is demonstrated by the gift of the spirit. Deriving their authority ultimately from the Lord, the seventy must "not be afraid of the face of man, for the judgement is God's" (Deut. 1.17).

## Attitude to Prophecy

Interesting sidelights on prophecy are given in this story of the institution of the seventy. In the first place, the act of prophesying showed publicly that the Spirit had been given. Just as we are told that Moses took off his shoes at the burning bush but we are not told when reverence for the holy first began, so we are not told when prophecy was first recognized as the gift of the Spirit of the Lord. Secondly, it was made clear, as we have seen, that the gift of the Spirit could not be tied to any rite or ceremonial. Joshua believed that, as Eldad and Medad had not been at the Tent of Meeting, they could not have received God's Spirit, and that Moses must forbid them to prophesy, and so publicly show that they lacked the authority given to the others. But Moses did not recognize any danger in their inspiration: "Are you jealous for my sake? Would that all the Lord's people were prophets, that the Lord would put his spirit upon them" (Num. 11.29). The words put into the mouth of Moses were a reminder of the spirit-filled men who revealed God's character and will, whose inspiration was like that of Moses and the great prophets of Israel, whom the Lord himself took to be prophets without human intervention.

Two other stories show clearly the function of the prophets in the thought of the editors. At his call Moses protested that he was a poor speaker, and God replied that Aaron would be his mouthpiece (Exod. 4.16); Moses would be as God to Aaron. Later (7.1) it is said that Moses would be as God to Pharaoh and Aaron would be his prophet. The words are in complete contrast to the usual priestly view of Aaron as the great High Priest and founder of the true priestly succession; and even in the sequel to the story it is Moses who speaks to Pharaoh (7.16; 8.1). But clearly the writer regarded a prophet as a speaker of divine words, an intermediary between God and people.

The other story (Num 12.1–16) concerns Miriam's jealousy of the special position of her brother Moses as a prophet. She herself is the first woman to be called a prophetess (Exod. 15.20) when, like a later prophetess Deborah (Judges 4.4), she led the women in antiphonal singing of God's mighty acts.[1] To her statement that the Lord had spoken through her as through Moses, the Lord replied, "If there is a prophet among you, I the Lord make myself known to him in a vision,[2] I speak with him in a dream. Not so with my servant Moses; he is entrusted with all my house. With him I speak mouth to mouth, clearly and not in dark speech; and he beholds the form of the Lord."[3] The words imply that God's relationship to Moses was direct and immediate but that there were prophets in Israel whose message came in dreams and visions, so that with them an element of interpretation might give rise to error. A similar distinction is made in Deuteronomy (18.15).[4]

## Conclusion

From the traditions of the forty years' wandering in the wilderness in preparation for entering the promised land, the dominant impression left is of God's guidance and care, and in contrast the complaining, murmuring, and apostasy of his people. This guidance came through the cloud that rested on the tent in the camp, or on the ark as it was carried on the march to the next resting-place for the tribes (Num. 10.33f). In differing forms belief in the guiding fiery cloud is common to all the traditions, and emphasizes the continual presence of God. The murmurings were punished when they occurred, and the punishment ended by the intercession of Moses (cf. 11.1ff). This latter motif is continually found in the traditions (cf. 12.13; 14.19f; 21.7). Though some perish in their sin, Moses' intercession causes the plague or other expression of God's wrath to be stayed, saving the remainder of Israel so that God's purpose of making Israel his chosen people is never completely frustrated. On one occasion, intercession was made by Aaron's ritual act (16.46). To stay the plague, he stood between the living and the dead, and with a cloud of incense made an atonement for the people. This word is not used of the effect of Moses' intercessory prayer, and it must not be assumed that the prayer of Moses

[1] See below, pp. 350f.
[2] Appearance, perhaps reflection as in a mirror (Exod. 38.8).
[3] "form" means "likeness" (Exod. 20.4); cf. "satisfied with thy likeness" (Ps. 17.15).
[4] See below p. 80 for another example of the pre-eminence of Moses.

which obtained God's forgiveness was thought of as working in the same way. In the final story of the people's murmuring, after Moses had interceded he made at the Lord's command a replica of the punishing fiery serpent, and every Israelite who looked at it was healed (21.9)—perhaps suggesting that God's healing power (Exod. 15.26, E) became available when Moses' intercession was supported by the faith of individual Israelites.

But the end of murmurings did not finish the sins of Israel in their wanderings. Before they left Sinai, they had sinned by trying to make an image of the Lord and by worshipping a golden calf (32), but towards the end of their wanderings, before crossing the Jordan, shameless adultery with Moabites and Midianites led to the worship of Baal Peor (Num. 25.3,18). The prompt, zealous action of Phinehas, Aaron's grandson, saved Israel, confirmed for his house the perpetual priesthood (25.10ff), and caused a war of the Lord against Midian (25.17; 31) led by Phinehas the priest "with the vessels of the sanctuary and the trumpets for the alarm in his hand". The whole Midianite tribe apart from young unmarried girls was wiped out without a single Israelite being lost. Though it was "the Lord's vengeance on Midian", after the battle the Israelite soldiers had to purify themselves for seven days before they entered the camp (31.19). So miraculous a victory under priestly leadership would probably have qualified for inclusion in the Book of the Wars of the Lord (21.14).

# 6 Mosaic Religion: Deuteronomy

The last book of the law receives its name from a mistranslation in the LXX, where "a copy of this law" (Deut. 17.18) became "this second lawgiving" (*deuteronomium*). But the title is not inaccurate, for the book retells the story of the law-giving, and presents the law in a new form. It claims to be the final address of Moses to "all Israel" as he "undertook to explain this law" (1.5) at the end of his life. Israel, already in possession of the territory promised to them east of the Jordan, the land of the two Amorite kings Sihon of Heshbon and Og of Bashan (2.30f; 3.12f), stands poised on the banks of Jordan, about to enter Canaan and possess the land stretching to the Lebanon. Moses' request to enter Canaan with them has been finally refused by God (3.23ff), and he has been ordered to climb to the top of Pisgah (3.27; Mt Nebo, 34.1), view the promised land, and die. "All Israel" is presented as the second generation, whose fathers had been brought out of Egypt and had all died in the wilderness (2.14f). But often this stance is abandoned and Israel is addressed as those who had been slaves in Egypt and present at the law-giving on Horeb.

## The Historical Retrospect

Certain key words reveal the standpoint and interests of the writers. Israel is repeatedly told to "remember" and "forget not", usually with reference to historical events in the nation's past and the law-giving. Most often the call is to remember the slavery in Egypt and God's great Deliverance (5.15); the events in Horeb, what their eyes had seen (4.9), the covenant that forbade the making of images and the worship of other gods (4.23; 8.19); or God's guidance and care in the wilderness (8.2ff) and Israel's continual rebellion (9.7; 24.9). It was God who had defeated the two Amorite kings, having first hardened Sihon's spirit and made his heart obstinate.[1] The lesson is emphatically expressed in words that often appear in the teaching of

---

[1] 2.30; cf. God's treatment of Pharaoh, above, pp. 41f. This religious explanation is not in the parallel account (Num. 21.21ff.)

the great prophets: when Israel "believes" in God (1.32), total victory is assured over all foes that oppose his purpose. God's fight against evil is ruthless.[1] When Sihon and all his people come to fight Israel and her God, all his people, men, women, and children, are destroyed (2.34), and it is equally true that the consequences of the unnamed sin of even Moses were not averted (3.26f; 4.21). Israel must not only remember the great experiences and teaching of the past, but treasure equally the commandments, statutes, and ordinances she is receiving in the present (8.11), and in the future must guard against the temptation to forget God in the luxury and prosperity of settlement in the good land of Canaan (8.18).

Another frequently used word is "fathers". God is the Lord God of your/thy fathers, and Moses often reminds the Israel to whom he is speaking of God's relationship with their fathers. Sometimes the reference is clearly to the oath made with the patriarchs Abraham, Isaac, and Jacob, who are specifically mentioned,[2] but many more times the patriarchs must be meant, because the reference is to the oath by which God swore to give the land to Israel. In the creed recited at the presentation of firstfruits (26.5ff) it is probably Jacob who is referred to as a nomadic Aramaean who went down to Egypt, and another mention of the descent into Egypt must also be interpreted as of the patriarchs (10.22).[3] The fathers on whom the Lord set his heart in love, choosing their descendants after them (10.15), are probably the patriarchs too, for in a similar statement (4.37), the Hebrew slips into the singular, "because he loved thy fathers therefore he chose *his* seed after *him*",[4] showing an association of ideas with Abraham, and suggesting that the plural "their descendants" used elsewhere may refer to the descendants of the patriarchs. God's love and choice were continued to the Israel of Moses' day (7.7ff). No reason is given for his favour; but emphatically it is stated that it was granted not because of their number or their righteousness. With Israel God had made a new experiment (4.34). He had entered the world to take a nation for himself by signs, wonders, war, mighty power, and great terrors.

The present love and choice of Israel by God is expressed in the third word used so often in this book—today, or this day. There have

---

[1] See above, p. 9.

[2] Seven times in Deuteronomy and only eighteen times in the remainder of the Old Testament.

[3] Cf. Gen. 46.27, P and Exod. 1.5, P.

[4] LXX, Syr., Targ., and Vulg. have "their".

been noteworthy days in the past. Especially important was the Day of the Assembly (9.10; 10.4; 18.16) at Horeb when, called to the Mount of God, Israel heard God speaking the words delivered to Moses as mediator on the two tablets of the law, and became a congregation or church. The significance of the events at Horeb is carefully expounded. That day must never be forgotten; children in each successive generation must be taught about it (4.9f). It is reiterated that on that day, though God's voice was heard and his fire appeared on earth, no divine form was seen and so no material representation of God may be made, nor may the sun, moon, and stars be worshipped as by other nations. Israel is different, rescued by the Lord from Egypt to be his own people like an inherited possession (4.20; cf. 32.9). Also important were the day they crossed the Ar to pass through Moab and the day when the conquest of Sihon's land began (2.18, 25).

But the great day of Deuteronomy is the day when Israel crosses the Jordan. On this day, again they stand before the Lord as at Horeb (29.10). On this day, represented as the last in the life of Moses, all the past is taken up into the present and made relevant to this great moment in Israel's existence. In the present form of Deuteronomy, this day is prefaced by God's command to Moses to make another covenant with the children of Israel (29.1). The Deliverance from Egypt, the wanderings in the wilderness, and the victories over Sihon and Og are recalled. Then in one wide sweep the whole Israelite community is addressed (29.10ff). Leaders and men, women and children, the protected sojourners and servants, those present, those absent—all are called to enter God's covenant and his oath "which the Lord your God makes with you this day that he may establish you this day as his people and that he may be your God" (29.12f). It is the fulfilment of the oath made to the patriarchs, and it is another covenant beside the one he made at Horeb.

## The Decalogue

The setting in time and place (1.4f) when Israel is reminded of her past, is repeated (4.44ff) when she is reminded of the Decalogue, the terms of that first covenant at Horeb. Two very emphatic statements are now made. The first is that Moses is talking to a second generation of listeners. After all the previous generation who were at Horeb forty years before have perished (2.14), it is this new generation to whom that covenant applies. "The Lord our God made a covenant with us in Horeb. Not with our fathers did the Lord make this covenant, but with us, who are all of us here alive at this day" (5.2–3). The privilege and responsibility of being a covenant people has passed from the fathers to the chosen seed here addressed.

Secondly, it is stated that no other commands except the ten words had been given to Israel at Horeb. "These words the Lord spoke to all your assembly at the mountain out of the midst of the fire, the cloud, and the deep gloom, with a loud voice; and he added no more" (5.22). Almost as though in deliberate contradiction to the stories in Exodus, Numbers, and Leviticus of the actual construction of the tabernacle, the institution of the priesthood with its duties and its garments, the setting apart of feast days with their appropriate offerings, it is stated that none of those statutes and ordinances was known to the children of Israel till the moment when they were about to cross Jordan. All the civil and religious ordinances of the Book of the Covenant and the Holiness Code, as well as the priestly ordinances, had been given to Moses at Horeb for the people to observe "in the land which I give them to possess" (5.31). The idea that all these laws apart from the Decalogue were mediated by Moses to a frightened people is found elsewhere (cf. Exod. 20.19), but that none of them was known or practised by Israel before Canaan was entered, that in the wilderness wanderings the Decalogue alone regulated civil and religious life, is new and startling. But it agrees with the tradition we shall find in Jeremiah: "For in the day that I brought them out of the land of Egypt, I did not speak to your fathers or command them concerning burnt offerings and sacrifices. But this command I gave them, obey my voice, and I will be your God, and you shall be my people" (7.22f; cf. Amos 5.25).

The new law, given to Moses at Horeb and by him imparted to the people in Moab, is in two parts: the commandment, and the statutes and ordinances (Deut. 5.31; cf. 6.1).

## The Commandment

The commandment contains some of the words which for centuries have expressed the basic essential creed of Judaism (6.4ff), an assertion about God and about Israel's duty to him. The Hebrew is terse and not easily translatable: the Lord our God, the Lord one,[1] "and

[1] Cf. RSV, The Lord our God is one Lord, with alternative renderings in the margin: the Lord our God, the Lord is one; the Lord is our God, the Lord is one; the Lord is our God, the Lord alone.

you shall love the Lord your God with all your heart, and with all your soul, and with all your might [or, with your whole being and strength]". So much a part of the ordinary daily life of every Israelite and his family must these words be that they "shall be upon your heart, and you shall teach them diligently to your children, and shall talk of them when you sit in your house, and when you walk by the way, and when you lie down, and when you rise. And you shall bind them for a sign upon your hand, and they shall be for frontlets between your eyes. And you shall write them upon the doorposts of your house, and upon your gates." These injunctions are like those for the Passover (Exod. 13.9, 16, J).

In Deuteronomy, after further exhortation not to forget God amid the comforts of Canaan, a form of words is prescribed in which the great truth of God's Deliverance is to be taught in the family circle (6.20ff). The central importance for Israel's religion of this commandment is seen in the fact that eleven times it is mentioned[1] as given through Moses, and obligatory on Israel because of all God has done and in order to obtain his blessing and help (cf. 11.22f). It has a special place at the conclusion of Moses' address:

> For this commandment which I command you this day is not too hard for you, neither is it far off. It is not in heaven, that you should say, "Who will go up for us to heaven, and bring it to us, that we may hear it and do it?" Neither is it beyond the sea, that you should say, "Who will go over the sea for us, and bring it to us, that we may hear it and do it?" But the word is very near you; it is in your mouth and in your heart, so that you can do it. See, I have set before you this day life and good, death and evil; in that I command you this day to love the Lord your God and to keep his commandment and his statutes and his ordinances (30.11–16).[2]

The exposition of this fundamental commandment (7—11) reveals much of the same religious attitude as is basic to the statutes and ordinances (12—26), and concludes similarly with a statement of blessings and curses to be pronounced on those who obey or disobey (11.26f; 27.11ff). The God whose power enabled Sihon and Og to be destroyed will deliver the great and mighty nations in Canaan to Israel, who must utterly destroy[3] them and all their religious symbols

---

[1] 5.31; 6.1, 25; 7.11; 8.1; 11.8, 22; 15.5; 19.9; 27.1; 30.11. In 31.5 the reference seems to be to 7.2.

[2] The LXX reads in v. 16a, "If thou hearken to the commandment of the Lord thy God which I command thee".

[3] Put to the ban, or devote to God.

—altars, pillars, asherim, and graven images. Further, there must be no intermarriage (cf. Exod. 34.16).

The God of Israel, his people, and his relationship to them are described in terms found elsewhere in the Old Testament; but particular emphasis is laid on the fact that Israel is a holy people, set apart and bound to God, his special, private (peculiar) treasure, loved and chosen by him, bought or ransomed (cf. Exod. 13.13) from slavery. Israel's God is the true God. He is God of gods and Lord of lords (Deut. 10.17), the one who can be trusted; he keeps his covenant and his attitude of "lovingkindness" (gracious mercy, *hesedh*) to those who respond by loving obedience. Such response is expressed in a character like that of God himself, loving the unprotected and needy (10.18f), and fulfils the same requirement as demanded by the prophets: "And now, Israel, what does the Lord your God require of you, but to fear the Lord your God, to walk in all his ways, to love him, to serve the Lord your God with all your heart and with all your soul" (10.12; cf. Mic. 6.8). But the love is austere, and does not hesitate to destroy the unresponsive and disobedient. Earthly blessings are promised to the faithful: fertility of crops, cattle, and children, health, victory, with the dreaded hornet seeking out their enemies. God's personal, fatherly (Deut. 1.31) care, so manifest in the past, will continue, though sometimes, as before, it will be experienced as a father's discipline (8.5; cf. 11.2), the discipline heard in the words at Horeb (4.36) and undergone in the wilderness, when Israel was given the opportunity to prove her loyalty (8.2). This concept of a Father–son relationship between God and people is all the more remarkable against the usual deuteronomic thought, in which disaster is inevitable punishment for sin, not discipline aimed at restoring a family bond.

That there is a living bond between God and his people is clear in the unforgettable dialogue (see p. 28 above) between him and Moses when the people worship the golden calf. In his anger, God is ready to repudiate them as "*your* people whom *you* have brought from Egypt" (9.12), and tells Moses to let him alone that he may destroy them. But Moses in his persistent intercession replies, "they are *thy* people and *thy* heritage, whom *thou* didst bring out by thy great power and by thy stretched-out arm" (9.29). The whole passage vibrates with the writer's veneration for the mighty figure of Moses, whose intervention saved the people at that dread moment. It seems that nothing further could be added to the picture; but yet it is here alone that another story is recounted. Moses intercedes for Aaron, just as in the statutes and ordinances the prophet's figure towers above that of the priest.[1]

## The Statutes and Ordinances (12–26)

The statutes and ordinances (12.1) correspond to the words and ordinances of the Book of the Covenant (Exod. 20f) and the "word" (RSV thing) of the Holiness Code (Lev. 17.2), both of which begin with regulations about the altar. The Book of the Covenant requires that an earthen or unhewn stone altar be erected wherever God has revealed himself, and all sacrifices are to be made on it (Exod. 20.24). The Holiness Code prescribes that all domestic animals must be killed at the one altar at the door of the sanctuary; wild game may be killed anywhere; but there is a strong emphasis on correct disposal of blood, and on the fact that all sacrifices are to be made to the Lord and not to heathen gods (Lev. 17.7). In Deuteronomy as in the Holiness Code there is only one legitimate altar, but it is to be at "the place which the Lord your God will choose", and it is clearly stated that the law of one legitimate altar is a new departure in the nation's life: "You shall not do according to all that we are doing here this day, every man doing whatever is right in his own eyes. . . . But when you go over the Jordan and live in the land which the Lord your God gives you . . . then to the place which the Lord your God will choose, to make his name dwell there, thither shall you bring all that I command you" (Deut. 12.8ff).

The place in Canaan for this first altar of unhewn stones is given as Mount Ebal (27.4f) or Mount Gerizim (Samaritan text), twin mountains on either side of Shechem, the city which is central to all the land. Again it is stressed that all other altars, pillars, asherim, and images are to be destroyed (12.2ff; cf. Exod. 34.13). There is no hint of any tradition that some altars had been erected in Canaan by the patriarchs; all are thought of as heathen. The stance of the Holiness Code is that the tribes are encamped round, or beside, an easily accessible single shrine, where it is possible to take all domestic animals for killing. In Deuteronomy, however, the people are thought of as about to occupy a large territory on both sides of the Jordan (Deut. 11.24), and the permission given to slaughter game away from the altar (Lev. 17.13) here includes all animals not offered as sacrifices (Deut. 12.15, 20ff), blemished firstling males being specially mentioned (15.22). Though no reference is made to the treatment of the

[1] Cf. the relationship between the two in Exod. 7.19; 8.5.

fat so prominent in the priestly code (cf. Lev. 17.6; see also Deut. 32.14, 38), care must be taken about the disposal of the blood because it is the life. There is no injunction to "cover it with soil", but it must be "poured out on the ground as water" (12.16; cf. 15.23).

The blood of animals sacrificed at the altar is to be poured out on the altar (12.27),[1] but it is noteworthy that there is no suggestion in Deuteronomy that the blood has atoning power, nor is it necessary for a priest to present it at the altar, nor are ritual uses of the blood required. Even the blood rite at the Passover, an essential element in the celebration in Exodus, is ignored, although presumably it would have required modification if the feast were to be celebrated not in houses with their doorposts but at the one central sanctuary.

The absence of blood rites suggests a completely different view of the meaning and purpose of sacrifice. Sin offerings and guilt offerings are not mentioned. No sacrificial blood is shed in the rite prescribed for expiation of unsolved murder, to atone for (cleanse) the blood (21.1ff). The elders of the nearest city must take an unused heifer to a running stream in an uncultivated valley and break its neck. In front of "the priests the sons of Levi" and over the carcass they wash their hands, assert their innocence, and pray God to forgive Israel. Though a life has been given to cover the blood shed, the method of killing the heifer avoids further shedding of blood.

Daily and weekly sacrifices, lunar occasions, and the annual ceremonies of the Day of Atonement are not mentioned (though, as we shall see, there are detailed prescriptions for the three annual festivals). But the absence of the idea that sin is removed by sacrifice in no way lessens the recognition of the heinousness of sin, and the fact that its consequences for the people must be removed. In the historical retrospect sin is against the Lord (1.41), it is lack of belief in God or rebellion against him (9.23), stubbornness and wickedness (9.27), making a golden calf and provoking the Lord to anger (9.18). In the statutes and ordinances, sin may be a mean attitude to a needy brother, or oppressing a hired servant, making him cry to the Lord (24.14f; cf. 15.9). It may be false witness or teaching (19.16; 13.5), shameful conduct (22.14), or a wrong marriage relationship that can bring guilt upon the land (24.4). Failure to fulfil a vow to the Lord is sin, though it is no sin to refrain from vowing (23.21f; cf. Eccles.

---

[1] The word "poured out" is used in P for the disposal of the rest of the blood of atoning sacrifices after blood rituals have been performed by the priest (Exod. 29.12; Lev. 4.7, 18, 25).

5.4f). Repeatedly it is stated that evil must be purged out (Hebrew burned out or consumed). Both land and people have been infected by it. The death penalty may be involved, but its purpose is partly that "the rest shall hear, and fear, and shall never again commit any such evil among you" (Deut. 19.20).

But, in contrast to what we find in the other codes, the sense of sin is not explicitly connected with sacrifices. Sacrifice is the expression of gratitude to God for all his gifts, it is to eat before the Lord, to rejoice with others in all the good things from the Lord. Indeed, the exhortation to religious joy[1] is new in the Pentateuch.[2] Typical is the exhortation after the various kinds of offerings required by God have been enumerated: "you shall eat before the Lord your God and you shall rejoice, you and your households, in all that you undertake, in which the Lord your God has blessed you" (12.7). The "households" are further defined as "your sons and your daughters, your menservants and your maidservants, and the Levite that is within your towns" (12.12), to whom are added "the sojourner, the fatherless, and the widow" (16.14). The joy looking to both past and future is to be "in all the good which the Lord your God has given to you" (26.11), and "because the Lord your God will bless you in all your produce and in all the work of your hands so that you will be altogether joyful" (16.15).

## The Festivals

We have already seen in the historical retrospect the stress in Deuteronomy on the family character of daily religious life. The command to love God must be written on the doorposts of houses, worn on the person, continually talked of in the home, and diligently taught to children (4.9f; 6.7ff). Here, in the statutes and ordinances, this family character is made clear in public worship. Although only males are obliged to attend at the central shrine for the three annual festivals (16.16), the constitution of the group who share in the sacrificial feast clearly envisages a full family pilgrimage, and "all Israel" as whole households must gather there every seven years for the renewal of the covenant (31.10ff).

Obligatory annual religious festivals are three, two lasting for seven days (16.3, 15), while for the third no time limit is mentioned.

[1] Cf. below, p. 332, Eccles. 5.19.
[2] Except Lev. 23.40, where the same phrase is used as in Deuteronomy; but on other grounds this is usually regarded as an addition.

GL

The first occasion is the spring Feast of Passover and Unleavened Bread. The Passover must be sacrificed "not . . . within any of your towns which the Lord your God gives you, but at the place which the Lord your God will choose, to make his name dwell in it" (16.5f). In the Book of the Covenant (Exod. 23.14ff; cf. 34.23) Passover is not included in the three annual pilgrimages to "appear before the Lord", presumably because it is a family feast at home. In the Holiness Code (Lev. 23) there are no regulations as to the place of any of the feasts, but, as all animals must be killed at the altar before the tent shrine, and as Passover is simply the first of the "appointed feasts and holy convocations", it may be assumed that it was thought of as celebrated at the sanctuary. But this is not stated explicitly, as it is in Deuteronomy. It is not clear whether in Deuteronomy (as against Lev. 23) the Passover ends the seven days of unleavened bread and the people return to their homes on the day following Passover night, or whether "in the morning you shall turn and go to your tents" (Deut. 16.7) envisages the people encamping after the Passover for seven days around the central shrine.

The second feast is to be held seven weeks after the beginning of the corn harvest, the corresponding calculation in Leviticus (23.15) being seven full weeks after the Sabbath on which the first harvest sheaf is presented. There is no fixed duration nor prescribed offering, but as in all these festivals a freewill offering given "as the Lord your God blesses you". The third feast, of Booths or Tabernacles, is to be celebrated after the corn is threshed and the grapes have been through the wine-press. There is to be joy, nothing but joy, at this feast. The first feast is vaguely dated in the month of Abib, or perhaps more definitely in the new moon of Abib, the other two are variable according to the time of harvest. Passover and the Feast of Weeks are memorials of Deliverance from slavery in Egypt, and every seven years at the set time of the year of release, the law is to be read at the Feast of Booths to all Israel, men, women, children, and resident aliens (Deut. 31.10f).

Though the amounts to be offered at the three obligatory feasts are not prescribed, the usual types of offering are enumerated (12.6). There are burnt offerings and sacrifices, which may include peace offerings (mentioned in 27.6f), but not cereal offerings. Tithes are further defined as of grain, wine, and oil (12.17) and as of "all the yield of your seed, which comes forth from the field year by year" (14.22). They are to be eaten at the central sanctuary, except that every third year they are to be used in the home settlement, "within your towns", as a kind of poor fund, so that the Levite, sojourner, fatherless, and widow may come and eat and be satisfied (14.28), and in this third year a solemn declaration must be made before the Lord that this law has been fulfilled (26.13ff). The heave offering of your hand (RV, 12.6; RSV has "the offering that you present") and free-will offerings are not further explained. Vows are described as "your votive offerings which you vow to the Lord" (12.11) and voluntary (23.23). Such offerings, like the tithe, must be eaten at the central shrine (12.17f).

Firstlings, defined as firstling males born of the herd and flock, must do no work nor be sheared, and must be eaten at the sanctuary by the offerer and his household; a blemished firstling, however, must not be sacrificed, but eaten at home by the ritually clean and unclean alike, as though it were game. The phrase "all that opens the womb"[1] never occurs, and it is clear that only one firstling from each flock and herd, if unblemished, is to be sacrificed. The prohibition against shearing a firstborn lamb or working a firstborn bullock makes it clear that there is no law requiring the animal to be sacrificed on the eighth day, but it is set apart as holy, to be eaten at the sanctuary perhaps on one of the feast days. Evidently neither tithe nor firstling has intrinsic holiness, for a convenient rule permits "it"[2] to be sold and the money value to be used at the sanctuary "for whatever you desire, oxen or sheep or wine or strong drink, whatever your appetite craves" (14.26).

## The Priesthood

Though Deuteronomy occasionally refers simply to the priest,[3] its characteristic phrase is "the priests the Levites",[4] implying that the terms are mutually inclusive—all Levites are priests and all priests Levites.[5] Nowhere in this book are priests called holy. This word, as we have seen, is used of the people (7.6, and often); the camp must be kept holy (or clean) because God walks in it (23.14); heaven is his holy

[1] Cf. above, p. 37.
[2] The RSV has "tithe" for the inclusive Hebrew masculine pronoun.
[3] 10.6; 20.2; 26.3, cf. 19.17.
[4] For discussion of the problem cf. H. H. Rowley, op. cit., p. 96, n. 3, and literature there cited.
[5] The RSV translation "the levitical priests" scarcely makes this clear. As we have seen (pp. 69ff above) in the priestly code Levites are inferior members of the priesthood. Both traditions, that they were inferior and that they were identical with priests, are preserved; see below, pp. 103, 105ff, 213, 255, 349ff, and for discussion p. 353.

habitation (26.15). For their priestly functions the tribe of Levi is not "consecrated" or "hallowed" but "set apart" or "distinguished" (10.8), a word that can mean simply "separated", as in Genesis 1. Elaborate ceremonies of ordination are absent, as is the story of their zeal for the Lord and subsequent ordination (cf. Exod. 32.26ff). Their priestly duties are carrying the simple wooden box or Ark made by Moses to contain the Decalogue (Deut. 10.5),[1] ministering to the Lord (17.12; 18.5),[2] blessing in his name (10.8),[3] keeping the sacred lot Urim and Thummim (33.8),[4] teaching the law,[5] burning incense and burnt offerings on the altar.[6] These instances clearly show that in Deuteronomy all Levites are competent to perform all priestly functions, and are in no way regarded as inferior clergy, assisting Aaron and his sons but excluded from altar service.

Some of these Levites reside at the central shrine performing priestly and legal duties (10.8; 17.8f). Reference to the appointment of officers and judges to assist Moses has been made in the historical retrospect (1.13ff). Now, in the Statutes and Ordinances, Moses will be succeeded at the central court of appeal by the priests the Levites and "the judge who is in office in those days", through whom the people may inquire the Lord's decision (17.8ff; 19.17).

Priests who function at the sanctuary live on "the offerings of the Lord made by fire".[7] They must be paid by dues from every sacrificial animal, the firstfruits of corn, wine, and oil, and the first of the fleece (18.3ff).[8] Other Levites, living away from the sanctuary, may if they wish join the sanctuary staff and receive an equal portion of the dues. Provincial Levites are classed with strangers, widows, and fatherless as guests who must be invited to the sacrificial feasts (cf. 12.12), sharing with the dependent poor in the triennial tithe (14.29; 26.12). All Levites are spoken of as "having no portion or inheritance" (cf. 10.9), but an ambiguous phrase (18.8) suggests that provincial Levites have rights over some saleable "patrimony" when they move to the central shrine.[9]

[1] A duty of Kohathite Levites, (Num. 3.31, P).
[2] Contrast Num. 3.6, where they minister to Aaron the priest.
[3] Cf. the priestly blessing (Lev. 9.22 f; Num. 6.23).
[4] Exod. 28.30, carried by Aaron.
[5] The duty of Aaron (Lev. 10.11).          [6] Cf. Exod. 30.7 and Num. 16.
[7] The phrase is used in the Pentateuch elsewhere only in P.
[8] "First" may be translated "best". The fleece is mentioned only here. Contrast the priestly portion (Lev. 7.31ff; 10.14f; Num. 18.18, 26f).
[9] Cf. Jer. 32, 6–15; 37.12, showing the right to property of Jeremiah, a priest who moved from Anathoth to Jerusalem. See also above, p. 70.

## The Prophetic Office

Prophetic power is controlled by the Lord, but some prophets are permitted by him to function in order to test Israel's allegiance to the great commandment (13.3). These are "prophets or dreamers of dreams" who are able to give tokens and predictions that are fulfilled, but entice men away from the worship of the Lord, and therefore they must be put to death. There is a clear distinction between such a guilty prophet and the one that Israel need not fear, who prophesies in the Lord's name, but his prophecies do not come true (18.22).[1] Israel is warned not only against these two types of prophets but also against "anyone who burns his son or his daughter as an offering,[2] anyone who practises divination, a soothsayer, or an augur, or a sorcerer, or a charmer, or a medium, or a wizard, or a necromancer" (18.10), all of whom will be found in Canaan. In contrast to all these, God will raise up a native Israelite prophet of the mighty stature of Moses, who will mediate between God and people, utter God's word and speak in his name. The Pentateuch closes with the statement that he is still awaited: "there has not arisen a prophet since in Israel like Moses, whom the Lord knew face to face" (34.10).

[1] A clear indication that in the thought of the writer the prophet does not predict a far-distant future, but something within his own lifetime.

[2] See above, p. 19, n. 1.

# Outstanding Features

The religion reflected in the Law books probably spans most of the Old Testament period, from early patriarchal times to the return from Babylonian exile in the sixth and fifth centuries B.C. and perhaps beyond. Popular, priestly, and prophetic traditions are intertwined, different law codes are brought together, and discrepancies are clearly of less importance to the editors than the preservation of ancient material. At the close of the Pentateuch stands Deuteronomy, a reconstruction on a threefold basis: the Decalogue; the command to love the Lord alone, serving him with all one's being and powers; and at the one legitimate sanctuary a greatly modified form of public worship, with a minimum of sacrificial acts performed by a separate priesthood and a strong, distinctive emphasis on joyful family feasts expressing gratitude to God.

In the Law books are found most of the great Hebrew words which in their English translation have for centuries expressed our religious thoughts; we shall find these same words used in the other two sections of the Old Testament—the Prophets and the Writings—and their meaning made more clear. In the Law, some of the expressions used are frankly anthropomorphic, as when God walks in the Garden, is soothed by the smell of burning incense, or has a dwelling-place. Others are less materialistic. His invisible Spirit—wind or breath— can enter men, he appears in a human form as messenger or angel, his presence is known by cloud or fire, and he dwells unseen between the cherubim over the Ark. His glory and his name replace the thought of body or substance.

The term most frequently used in the Law to express the more formal aspect of the relationship between God and Israel is covenant —a solemn pact made mutually between two parties or imposed by the lord on the vassal. A wide difference appears in the use of the word. Sometimes it is parallel to an oath, and is an unconditional everlasting promise, established by God and including a visible token or proof. At other times it is "cut" (RSV made) suggesting confirmation by slaughter of an animal, so giving rise to the phrase "the blood of the covenant". When God remembers his covenant, he comes to the aid of

Israel, and Israel is reminded to keep or obey its conditions, which are written on the two tablets containing the Decalogue, or in the Book of the Covenant. Its basic content is the mutual avowal that the Lord is Israel's God, and Israel is his people. The covenant concept, which became of central importance in Old Testament religion, indicates an actual, living relationship.

The relationship between God and his people is also expressed in language drawn from closest human family ties of marriage and sonship, the trust of a child in a mother, the warm mercy of loving-kinship or kindness. But God's love-choice has an austere side known to the rebellious and stubborn, entailing even the total destruction of all that would entice his people to disloyalty and evil. His treatment is the discipline of father or teacher, his purpose is to redeem and deliver his people. When he has to plan punishment and disaster, he reveals his purpose, as though to invite intercession so that he can mitigate his plan for the sake of the intercessor. When Moses intercedes for Israel, it signifies that one "like themselves" has seen the meaning of God's judgement. No longer does "all Israel" stand before God as guilty. One man stands out as intercessor, yet with him stand the sinners as a corporate unity. That Moses identified himself with sinful Israel is clear from his willingness to die with them rather than alone to survive as founder of a new Israel. From the earliest stories it is clear that "The prayer of a righteous man has great power in its effects" (Jas. 5.16).

There is, however, another way in which punishment can be mitigated and man's broken relationship with God restored. God allows a priesthood, representative of the whole people but separated from them, to be linked closely to himself by the divine quality of holiness. Dressed in lovely and costly robes, separated by clouds of sweet-smelling incense, and bringing man's choicest gifts, the priest may enter God's presence bearing on himself the burden of human sin. Offerings and sacrifices brought with humble reverence are accepted by God as proof of man's repentance, his changed attitude, enabling him to receive God's forgiveness. For man's sake God ordained at Sinai (Lev. 17.11) that blood brought to his altar could atone for (cleanse) human sin. The "blood is the life", and from a human standpoint the offering of blood may be symbolic acknowledgment that sin has made man worthy of death. Behind all the sacrificial ritual of the sanctuary is the recognition of the awful meaning of sin, man's need for forgiveness, and the fact that God alone can remove guilt and restore the broken relationship.

# PART II
# PROPHETS

# Introduction

The second section of the Hebrew Bible is called Prophets. It begins with Former Prophets, comprising Joshua, Judges, Samuel, and Kings, and carrying the story of Israel from the death of Moses through settlement in Canaan to the destruction of Jerusalem in 586 B.C. followed by the release of the captured Judean king in Babylon in 561 B.C. The Former Prophets is usually called the Deuteronomic history, as distinct from the parallel Chronicler's history at the end of the Writings. The language and religious outlook of one of its editors show the influence of the book of Deuteronomy, which may have been intentionally placed as a preface to the section. The Latter Prophets, which we usually think of as prophetic work, consists of four main groups of material—Isaiah, Jeremiah, Ezekiel, and the Book of the Twelve smaller prophetic writings.[1]

The editors intended to offer a chronological arrangement of the books, and no break is suggested between the end of the Law in Deuteronomy and the opening verse in the Former Prophets. Joshua begins with "After the death of Moses", and Judges follows with "After the death of Joshua", who succeeded Moses as God's leader of Israel. These two books are, however, clearly parallel accounts of Israel's conquest of the promised land, written in different circles of thought and perhaps of time and place. The books of Samuel relate stories of the foundation of the monarchy in Israel and tell of the first two kings, Saul and David. In the books of Kings we see the fulfilment of David's hopes and preparations for the building of a new dwelling-place for God, the Temple at Jerusalem. The mingling or synchronizing of the histories of the two kingdoms into which the nation split, and the introduction of the stories of Elijah and Elisha, have confused the chronology, but the arrangement still provides an account of the nation's attitude to the Temple until its destruction by the Babylonians, and a survey of the contemporaneous prophetic

---

[1] Hosea, Joel, Amos, Obadiah, Jonah, Micah, Nahum, Habakkuk, Zephaniah, Haggai, Zechariah, Malachi. In the Hebrew Bible, Ruth and Daniel are placed in the third section, Writings.

movement with interest focused on the relationship between prophets and kings.

Of the fifteen prophets whose names are given to books in the Latter Prophets only two, Jonah and Isaiah, are mentioned in the books of Kings, although twelve are placed by Jewish dating in the period. Isaiah, son of Amoz, apparently prophesied in the second half of the eighth century, from about 740 B.C.; but to the book that bears his name have been added words written centuries later, and especially, from chapter 40, the work of an anonymous prophet whose words could be regarded as fulfilling Isaiah's promises. Jeremiah and his younger contemporary Ezekiel were active in the latter half of the seventh century and over the time of the destruction of Jerusalem in 586 B.C. If the arrangement of the twelve minor prophets in the Hebrew Bible is intended as chronological, then probably the first six, Hosea, Joel, Amos, Obadiah, Jonah, and Micah, were regarded as older and younger contemporaries of Isaiah in the eighth century B.C., Nahum, Habakkuk, and Zephaniah were thought to have been active in the seventh century B.C., and Haggai, Zechariah, and Malachi at the end of the sixth century B.C.

Few scholars would now accept these dates for many of these books in their present form; and in any case it is unlikely that, to the compilers, chronology was of primary importance. The people for whom they were written, their needs and circumstances, can be conjectured only from the contents of the books themselves. It is generally agreed that these have come to us through a succession of editors and preachers who appear, before the text was regarded as sacred and unalterable, freely to have made modifications and additions[1] in response to the needs of a real people for help and guidance in an actual situation. If we believe in the continuing guidance of the spirit of God, we must accept that God may inspire the transmitters as well as original speakers and writers. The original message, taken seriously as a genuine revelation of God in historical circumstances, was limited by speaker, audience, and situation. Those who came later were certain that the same living God was still speaking to them in their own experiences and their own day. The old prophetic message came to them as necessary and urgent as when first delivered. It was—and is—a timeless word from the eternal God, and its timelessness was made clearer as it was released through its later use from its first setting in time and place.

[1] Cf. R. E. Wolfe, *The Editing of the Book of the Twelve, Zeitschrift für die alttestamentliche Wissenschaft* (1935), pp. 90ff.

Here, in our attempt to give an account of the religion of the prophetic books as we have of the Law, we use the books in their present order and form[1] and try to include in our view the religious experience reflected in them. By thus continuing to survey Old Testament religion in the order of the books in the Hebrew canon, we cannot provide a history of its development, but we can perhaps consider different facets of the relationship between Israel and her God. To attempt to write a history of prophetic religion would mean determining the dates of the separate books and of the various additions, tasks which must be left to works on Old Testament history and literature. Here we shall try, with as little use as possible of theories of chronological sequence and literary reconstruction, but assuming assured results of biblical scholarship, to sketch the main features that distinguish these prophetic books and unite them to the other two sections of the Old Testament.

[1] This method of approach must not be taken in any way to imply rejection of assured results from the work of Old Testament scholars during the last century. Readers should consult standard commentaries and introductions to the literature.

# 7 The Former Prophets

## JOSHUA AND JUDGES

### Introduction

By calling the six books from Joshua to Kings "the Former Prophets", Jewish tradition emphasizes that they are primarily religious works concerned with God's dealings with Israel, history related from a prophetic standpoint. We do not know how much of their content is accurate historical record which could be confirmed from other sources and from archaeological discoveries. Clearly the parallel but varying accounts in Joshua and Judges of the conquest of Canaan, and the duplicate stories in the books of Samuel of the foundation of the monarchy and the lives of Samuel, Saul, and David cannot be regarded as "pragmatic" history. Like the Deliverance from Egypt and the wilderness wanderings, these stories have become "paradigm" history[1] demonstrating the saving acts of God to a people who believed in his nearness and interpreted pragmatic (actual) events as examples of his coming with power and intervening in wonder and miracle. Where events in this spiritual history are confirmed by external evidence, the interest of the biblical writers is clearly in Israel's relationship to God as shown in acts of obedience or rebellion to his revealed will.

Often successive rewritings have been made to enrich the "paradigm" and find new moral and spiritual lessons for the writers' own contemporary situations. The religion of the writers is apparent in their interpretation of pragmatic historical events as acts of a transcendent being who has chosen Israel as his own people. They see history as "a society's moving through time on a meaningful course" to a divinely appointed goal,[2] but for them their own present is the centre of interest. Past events are continually related because they have flowed into the present, so that the present generation to whom the

[1] The distinction is taken from E. Voegelin, *Order and History I* (1956), pp. 121ff.
[2] Voegelin, op. cit., pp. 126f.

words are repeated has to face a similar situation. They too are God's chosen people caught up in the same purpose and meeting the same challenge to obey or rebel, to co-operate with or reject the divine will. The promises made by God to Abraham and through Moses are in Joshua and Judges being fulfilled by great acts of wonder. Israel is being given a land to inherit and dwell in, but the same story of sin and disobedience is being repeated.

The Law told how God's acts of wonder in creation were followed by the sin of all humanity, the corruption of the whole earth. From the rescued remnant after the destructive Flood God called Abraham and bound him to himself by call and promise. Abraham's progeny were delivered from the furnace of slavery in Egypt, bound to God by covenant as his people, and through a prophetic leader, Moses, were given civil laws by which to live and priestly ordinances and institutions to maintain their link with God. But again disobedience brought the discipline of God. Murmuring showed lack of trust or faith in him, and all that delivered generation had to perish in the wilderness.

Now again the next generation (Judges 2.10f) after entering the Promised Land, and despite the reaffirmation of the Mosaic covenant and the making of a new covenant under Joshua, failed to obey God. Heathen Canaanites left in the land were allowed to intermarry with Israelites and allured them to apostasy, breaking the covenant, forsaking the Lord, and bowing down to other gods. Discoveries at Ras Shamra in Syria, the ancient Ugarit, make it possible to understand the vehemence of Hebrew prophetic objection to Canaanite worship. There were close resemblances between the description and function of Israel's God, and Baal and El of Canaan, which made popular assimilation easy. But the character of the Canaanite goddesses, the fertility rituals connected with their worship and their outcome in degrading sexual practices, amply justified the condemnation by Hebrew prophets and the attempt to rid the nation of this whole way of life summed up as "playing the harlot after other gods" (Judges 2.17).[1]

Under the Judges, God's discipline took the form of sending foreign neighbouring nations—Moab, Ammon, and Amalek—to invade the promised land (3.12), but always, when after years of oppression Israel cried to God for help, he sent a saviour to deliver them (2.18; 3.9). Through the last of these deliverers, the prophet-judge

[1] Cf. W. F. Albright, *Archaeology and the Religion of Israel* (1953); J. Gray, *The Legacy of Canaan*, (1957).

Samuel, God gave the people more permanent leaders. First Saul, then David was anointed as king, and a new covenant was made with David. Possibly certain pragmatic events in the lives of both these kings have been arranged as paradigm history to illustrate the deuteronomic belief that punishment and disaster always follow sin. Saul's act of disobedience and David's adultery with Bathsheba are treated as preludes to a series of misfortunes,[1] just as the sins of Eli's sons entailed the destruction of Shiloh, God's dwelling-place in the land of Canaan, together with its priesthood, and the capture by the Philistines of the Ark of the Lord.

God gave them a new shrine, the Temple at Jerusalem, where they could meet him, bringing their confessions and cries for help, and gaining his forgiveness (1 Kings 8). But schism arose in the nation. Ten of the twelve tribes deserted the Temple, and these were taken captive by the Assyrians. Then even on the two tribes God's punishment had to fall despite the warnings of a great succession of prophets. Kingdom and Temple were destroyed, and the remnant of the people was sent to another purifying test in exile in Babylon. At last, at the end of the Former Prophets, in the final verses of the books of Kings, we see a tiny gleam of hope. The boy king of Judah, after thirty-seven years of captivity, is graciously freed from prison and given a seat above the seats of the kings who were with him in Babylon. "He put off his prison garments" and dined regularly at the table of the Babylonian king. The gleam of hope does not focus on God's hand in the deliverance, nor does it herald the dawn of a new day for Israel. But the full glory of this new day breaks before the end of the next prophetic book, Isaiah.

## The Wars of the Lord

It has been pointed out that two different religious attitudes to the conquest of Canaan appear in Joshua and Judges. The one sees the conquest as completely God's doing, hence requiring nothing but obedience from Israel. The other, clear in Judges but hinted at sometimes also in Joshua, presents it as difficult, frustrating, and requiring Israel's utmost exertion.

In its present form, the book of Joshua tells a typical story of a "War of the Lord" in which the deuteronomic war laws are obeyed. It seems wiser to retain the Hebrew term, "War of the Lord", rather

---

[1] Cf. S. A. Cook, op. cit., p. 4.

than to import the term "Holy War" from Greek religion.[1] Though the two have much in common, there is a danger that use of the Greek term may prejudice understanding of the phenomenon in the Old Testament. The Wars of the Lord could be either defensive (under the Judges and Saul) or aggressive (the conquest of Canaan) and are not presented as wars to defend or spread Israel's religious faith, thus differing from Moses' fight against Midian (Num. 25.17f; 31.15f, P) which may be understood as the Lord fighting for the religious life of his people against obscene heathen rites. The establishment of a professional army under the monarchy (cf. 1 Sam. 8.12) tended further to displace the concept of a volunteer, spirit-filled force without weapons (Judges 5.8) led by the Lord, even though some features of what may properly be called the War of the Lord remained.

In the records of the book of Joshua, three great campaigns of a united Israel led by Joshua conquered the whole land. In the first there was complete victory at Jericho and Ai in central Canaan (Josh. 8.2). The second equally successful campaign, this time not aggressive, was against a coalition of Canaanite cities which had attacked the Gibeonites, with whom Israel had made a covenant (10). The third, also non-aggressive, was against attack from Jabin, king of Hazor in the north, and his confederates, and afterwards "the land had rest from war" (11.23).

Joshua had been told that if he kept the law of Moses, he need not be afraid, for God would be with him (1.5, 9). The hearts of their enemies melted (5.1), the Lord threw them into a panic before Israel, and cast down great stones from heaven upon them (10.10f). He drove out great nations before Israel (3.10), he fought for Israel (10.14, 42), and total destruction of the enemy and devotion of the spoil to the Lord was the necessary conclusion to the Lord's wars. As though to emphasize that it is God's war, the story begins with Joshua's vision of the commander of the Lord's host, his sword already drawn in his hand (5.13; cf. Num. 22.23), who is fighting neither for Israel nor for her enemies, but for the Lord's cause. For additional stress, there is the story of the total destruction of Achan, his possessions, and all his family because he broke the ban (the devotion of spoil to the Lord). So important was it that evil should be completely wiped out, that Achan's sons and daughters too had to perish, and his name to cease in Israel. The land is to be Israel's

[1] Cf. G. von Rad, *Der Heilige Krieg im Alten Israel* (1961); R. de Vaux. op. cit., p. 465.

HL

promised heritage, but through the ban all incentive to personal
plunder and gain are taken from the people (Josh. 6.18; 1 Sam.
15.18f).[1]

The account of the campaign of Deborah and Barak against
Sisera presents a similar picture to that of the Lord's War (Judges
5).[2] The Lord marched from Edom,[3] the mountains quaked, the
thunderstorm broke, from heaven the stars fought against Sisera.
Though there was no shield or spear among the forty thousand in
Israel, volunteers offered themselves willingly, the people of the Lord
marched down, jeopardized their lives to the death. The enemies of
the Lord perished, swept away by the onrushing torrent of Kishon in
flood. But perhaps the clearest presentation of this kind of war is seen
in the story of Gideon's fight against the invading Midianites (Judges
7). The Israelite army was successively reduced from 22,000 to only
300 men, armed simply with trumpets and jars covering lighted
torches. But as they stood in their places round the enemy camp,
breaking their jars, blowing their trumpets and shouting their
victory cry, the enemy in panic turned their swords against each other
and fled in utter defeat.

Alongside faith in the warrior God, there is in these books a strong
sense of wonder and miracle, the near presence of the living God
whose power knows no limit, just as in the stories of Creation and the
Red Sea the Lord who revealed himself is remembered as the covenant God who works wonders rather than as the God of War.[4] The
Lord who had dried up the waters of the Red Sea was God in heaven
above and earth beneath (Josh. 2.10f). Before Jordan was crossed
the people were told to sanctify themselves because the Lord was
about to do wonders, and when the feet of the priests the Levites
carrying the Ark touched the water, though the river was in flood
(3.15), the flow ceased and the bed dried up for Israel to pass over. At
Gilgal on the other side twelve stones from the Jordan bed were set up
as a visible token by which children of future generations might be
taught that "the hand of the Lord is mighty" (4.24). The commander
of the Lord's host, like the presence of the Lord on Horeb (Exod. 3.5)

---

[1] Cf. de Vaux, op. cit., p. 465.

[2] There are interesting differences between this poetic account and its
prose parallel in Judges 4. See Peake's New Commentary ad loc.

[3] Eichrodt, op. cit. 1, p. 298, points out that the Lord here comes from
Sinai and not from Canaan.

[4] The experiences of the Battle of Mons in 1914, and at Dunkirk in 1939,
show in how short a time such explanations can be accepted as part of the
historical event. Contrast von Rad, *Old Testament Theology* II, p. 379.

made the ground holy. The priests with the Ark, blowing the seven trumpets continually, are more emphasized in the procession round Jericho than the armed men who went in front, and the falling of the walls was remembered as a miracle performed by God through priestly ritual for a people who had re-entered the Abrahamic covenant by the act of circumcision. The unique miracle (Josh. 10.12–15) of the sun and moon standing still in the sky is related from Israel's national poetry book and may be the prose rendering of poetic hyperbole.[1]

But stubborn facts were sometimes not bent by the writers to the viewpoint of the Lord's wars and miracles. Not all was left to God's action and man's faith. Joshua sent out spies, he used the treachery of Rahab, and the military stratagem of ambush against Ai. The conquest of the land was not quick or easy, and "Joshua made war a long time [Hebrew many days] with all those kings" (11.18). At the end he was "old and advanced in years" (13.1; 23.1) and there remained very much of the land to be possessed. Though God promised that he himself would drive out the remaining Canaanites before the people of Israel (13.6), some of this was done by Caleb (14.12), and groups of Canaanites remained in Jerusalem (15.63; cf. Judges 1.21), Gezer (Josh. 16.10; cf. Judges 1.29), and among the sons of Manasseh (Josh. 17.12; cf. Judges 1.27f). In the book of Judges the list of Canaanite groups is longer, and it is significant that, instead of the statement in Joshua that Israel "could not" drive them out, we have "did not", the writer explaining that it was the Lord's doings that they were not given into Joshua's power because Israel had disobeyed the divine commands (cf. Josh. 23.12f) and he wished to test her loyalty (Judges 2.2f).[2] The facts of history, confirmed by archaeological evidence, here too have been translated into a creed. Despite these contrary glimpses, however, the dominant story of the invasion under Joshua ends in confident reaffirmation of the people's choice of the Lord, the making at Shechem of a covenant with statutes and ordinances (Josh. 24.25).

But the book of Judges, which is supposed (Judges 1.1) to carry the story of God and Israel through the next generation after Joshua's death, makes a very different impression. Because the conquest had not been complete and Israel had made covenants with the inhabitants of the land, their gods had become a snare and the curses of the

---

[1] Josh. 10.13b may be the prose version from the poem in verses 12b–13a; cf. Judges 4 and the poem in Judges 5.

[2] Cf. Judges 3.1f where another reason is given.

broken covenant fell on Israel. The Lord's power was against them, and he handed them over to oppressing enemies, until their repentance and cry for help brought his gift of a deliverer. The story ends, however, in the horrible account not of foreign oppression but of the crime of Benjamin, the youngest of Israel's own tribes (Judges 19ff). Words used in the story are paralleled in the story of the corruption that caused the destruction of Sodom and Gomorrah (Gen. 19).

## The Tribal Confederacy

Many theories of the development of the early religion of Israel have been constructed on the basis of this story in Judges and the final chapter in Joshua. As the Greek term "Holy war" has been used of the War of the Lord, so has the Greek term "amphictyony" been applied to the relationship of the Israelite tribes to one another both before and after the long years in Egypt. This title for a league of Greek states defending a common sanctuary denotes a closely bound group with well-defined obligations, and the stories of the various groupings of Israelite tribes round different sanctuaries may have been influenced by a knowledge of this six or twelve-state league. But it would appear wiser[1] to avoid "amphictyony" with its overtones of meaning and use the more general title "covenant confederacy" to describe the situation in Israel before the monarchy. It is possible that a confederacy of six Leah–Israel tribes round Shechem had been driven out long before by Canaanites, and that some of them—perhaps Levi and Simeon—had been destroyed as tribal entities when they broke a circumcision tabu (Gen. 34). It is possible that another such confederacy of Rachel–Jacob tribes were in the south of Palestine, that Moses at Kadesh after the Deliverance from Egypt united the remnant of these twelve tribes in the worship of the one God, and that Joshua bound them together in a new "covenant confederacy" at Shechem (Josh. 24).[2] But it should be remembered that this is tentative, and that this hypothetical reconstruction of Israel's tribal history and the growth of her faith, linked together in the image of the Greek word "amphictyony", is an insufficient foundation to support the complex theoretical erections raised on it by recent writers on Old Testament religion. The tribal traditions are very complex,

[1] With de Vaux, op. cit., p. 93.
[2] M. Noth, *Das System der Zwölf Stämme Israels* (1930), advocated strongly this type of reconstruction; but its conjectural basis must be remembered.

names and numbers varying considerably, as also names of centres where the tribes gathered and worshipped. Lack of effective central control is emphasized by the repeated statement: "In those days there was no king in Israel; every man did what was right in his own eyes" (Judges 17.6; cf. 21.25).

## Religious Institutions

Whereas the background to the narratives of Judges is similar to that of Genesis, the outlook of the book of Joshua is deuteronomic. Joshua had to meditate day and night on this "book of the Law" (Josh. 1.8; 23.6). He left nothing undone of all that the Lord commanded Moses (11.15). When Jordan was crossed and Jericho and Ai captured, the deuteronomic command was obeyed. Outside Shechem near Mount Ebal or Gerizim an altar of unhewn stones was built, sacrifice offered, the law inscribed on stones, and antiphonal blessings and curses were recited (8.34; Deut. 27.12f).[1] Clearly in early tradition Shechem is made to loom large and the one central altar demanded by Deuteronomy was built near there. It must have been this altar which was copied on an enlarged scale (Josh. 22.10, 28) near the Jordan, but designed, in accordance with the deuteronomic law, to be used only as a witness, and not for burnt offerings or sacrifices. There is no record in Joshua of any other altar being built. The first Passover, celebrated at Gilgal in Canaan before the altar was built near Shechem, apparently did not require an altar (5.10). Later, the tribal centre moved from Shechem to Shiloh (21.2), from here war was prepared against the two-and-a-half Transjordan tribes (22.12), and here the tabernacle was set up (18.1; 19.51); but nothing is said of the building of an altar, though the book of Samuel begins by referring to sacrifices at Shiloh. It is also of interest that the Ark is not precisely located in Canaan except at the encampment at Gilgal and near the one altar at Ebal (4.18; 8.33).

In Joshua as in Deuteronomy, Levites[2] were priests and had no heritage with other tribes, but were given forty-eight cities with surrounding pasture land for their portions (21.41). Enslaved Gibeonites were made hewers of wood and drawers of water for the altar of the Lord (9.27; cf. Deut. 29.11). Eleazar, son of Aaron, is the priest (cf. Deut. 10.6) and acts with Joshua in distributing tribal

[1] Eichrodt, op. cit., p. 307, and de Vaux, op. cit., p. 143, apparently identify Josh. 8 with Josh. 24 as inaugurating the covenant of Exod. 21f, and ignore Deut. 27.12f.

[2] See above, p. 85, n. 4.

heritages, but his son Phinehas comes to the fore in the religious dispute with the Reubenites (Josh. 22.13), as earlier he had taken a prominent part in the war against Midian (Num. 31.6, P), and later in Judges Phinehas has succeeded his father and ministers before the Ark at Bethel (Judges 20.28). Neither Eleazar nor Phinehas is called "High Priest", though in the appointment of the cities of refuge the death of the high priest marks an epoch (Josh. 20.6; cf. Num. 35.25, 28, P).

Despite the deuteronomic influence on the book of Joshua, the covenant made by Joshua after the final conquest of the land is given as a completely new beginning, as though now for the first time the people rejected the gods worshipped by their fathers "beyond the River"[1] and in Egypt and chose the Lord. The foreign gods are still among them. The historical retrospect (24.2–13) does not mention previous covenants with Abraham or Moses, it is Joshua who makes (Hebrew "cuts") a covenant, statutes, and ordinances with the people and writes them in the law-book of God (not of Moses), setting up a great stone under the oak tree in the sanctuary of the Lord at Shechem. This stone is not a "pillar" like the twelve set up by Moses (Exod. 24.4), but is, like the twelve stones set up at Gilgal (Josh. 4.3), simply a permanent witness. No reference is made in Joshua 24 to the altar already built near Shechem, nor to sacrifices nor to a covenant meal to ratify the covenant.[2]

A different religious background is presented in Judges. Here, revelation often comes through the Angel of the Lord. He went up from Gilgal to Bochim[3] to admonish Israel (Judges 2.1ff). He told the loyal Israelite tribes to curse Meroz[4] for not joining the Lord's fighting forces (5.23). He came and sat under the oak of Ophrah to speak to Gideon, and became the Lord himself (6.11, 14, 16) to whom Gideon built an altar and offered a bullock. He appeared to the barren wife of Manoah and foretold Samson's birth, and she described him to her husband as "a man of God and his countenance was like the countenance of the angel of God very terrible" (13.6). When challenged for his name, he replied that it was "wonderful", and after Manoah had offered a burnt offering to the wonderful God, the angel

---

[1] Cf. Jacob's action, also at Shechem (Gen. 35.2f).

[2] O. Procksch (op. cit., p. 522) conjectures that "statutes and ordinances" here refer to the Book of the Covenant (Exod. 20.22—23.33).

[3] An unknown place, meaning "weepers". It may be a cryptic reference to the Israelites after their defeat in front of Bethel and Ai (Josh. 7.6). Judges 2.1ff is clearly the remains of a truncated narrative.

[4] Also an unknown place.

ascended in the flame. Altars were built or sacrifices made whenever a theophany occurred, at Bochim, at Ophrah, by Manoah, and at Bethel (21.4), and Jephthah sacrificed his daughter at Mizpah (11.31, 39).

Micah the Ephraimite (17f) had a private shrine in his house with silver images, teraphim,[1] and ephod to which he appointed his son as priest. But he was glad to receive as "father and priest", for ten pieces of silver a year together with a suit of apparel and his living, a young wandering Levite from Bethlehem, of the family of Judah. The Levite could obtain oracles from God. "Then Micah said, Now I know the Lord will prosper me because I have a Levite as priest." But the young Levite went willingly with the Danites, who stole Micah's images and offered him preferment to the priesthood of a tribe. This Levite is identified with Jonathan, grandson of Moses and founder of the levitical priesthood at Dan, which lasted as long as the temple at Shiloh (18.30f). The sarcastic way the story is told shows the teller's contempt for private shrines, images, and particularly for the origin of the levitical priesthood[2] of the northern kingdom. A similar attitude is taken to the shrine at Ophrah for which Gideon made a golden ephod, and to Shechem, in Judges regarded as the home of the Canaanite Baal- or El-Berith, the lord or god of covenant, as well as to Shiloh, which, even though the house of God was there, was regarded as an almost unknown place "north of Bethel, east of the highway that goes up from Bethel to Shechem, and south of Lebonah", where the annual vintage feast to the Lord was held with dances and perhaps fertility rites (21.19ff).

The final story (Judges 19ff), culminating at Shiloh, also concerns a wandering Levite connected with the hill country of Ephraim. There is a strong motif of hostility to Benjamin, Gibeah, and Jabesh Gilead, all of them in the book of Samuel closely linked with Saul the first king, so soon rejected in favour of the Judean David. But the dominant theme is probably the deuteronomic command of hospitality to the landless Levite, who as servant of God must not be forsaken (cf. Deut. 12.19).[3]

In Judges we seem to be in uneasy transition from the wise leadership of Joshua to the stability of the monarchy, from religion that had centred round the temporary altar at Ebal near Shechem to the Temple at Jerusalem with its levitical priesthood.

[1] Cf. Gen. 31.19; 1 Sam. 19.13.      [2] See above, p. 85, n. 5.
[3] Cf. Judges 20.13 with the oft-repeated "purge the evil from the midst of you" of Deut. 13.5; 17.7, 12, etc.

## Instruments of the Spirit

In this turbulent period there is particular stress on spirit-filled persons, as though preparing for the first Hebrew kings, Saul and David, and the bands of spirit-controlled prophets who are prominent in the books of Samuel and Kings. "At the very beginning of Israelite religion we find the charisma, the special individual endowment of a person: and to such an extent is the whole structure based on it, that without it it would be inconceivable. Old Testament religion is a creation of the spirit."[1]

We have already considered some aspects of spirit control in the administrative skill of Joseph, the technical skill of Bezaleel, and the prophesying of the seventy elders to whom, at a special consecration service, God gave spirit from Moses.[2] His gift of spirit enabled them temporarily to prophesy and proved them to be leaders endowed by God. Joshua was chosen to succeed Moses because the spirit was in him. Here an additional act was necessary to make him a recognized leader—Moses had to lay his hands on him to invest him with his authority (Num. 27.18ff). In another reference to this incident (Deut. 34.9) there seems to be some confusion, giving rise to the impression that the gift of the spirit was due to the laying on of Moses' hands; but the words "and the people obeyed him" suggest that this passage too should signify transfer of authority to a person already endowed with the spirit or charisma.

The presence of the spirit in a person seems to have been a clearly discernible phenomenon, manifesting itself in striking ways. Many of the judges sent by God to deliver Israel received the spirit of the Lord for their task. It came upon Othniel, giving him skill to judge Israel so that she defeated her foes (Judges 3.10). It clothed itself with Gideon (RSV took possession of, 6.34) so that he took the initiative and sounded the war-trumpet, though his weak faith still needed to put God to the test (6.36ff; contrast Deut. 6.16). Similarly, spirit-possession did not prevent Jephthah from making his foolish vow (Judges 11.29f). The spirit of the Lord is mentioned most frequently in the story of Samson, whom early in his life it "began to stir" (13.25), and to whom later it gave abnormal strength to tear a lion to pieces and to kill thirty men (14.6, 19; cf. 15.14). In the book of Judges there is keen interest in the manifestation of the "Spirit of the Lord", but "spirit" is used also as a less exalted term: "and when he drank,

---

[1] Eichrodt, op. cit. I, p. 292.  [2] Cf. above, pp. 22, 63, and 71f.

his spirit [life-force] revived" (15.19); so also when "God sent an evil spirit [bad feeling, or a bad relationship] between Abimelech and the men of Shechem" (9.23), they dealt treacherously with him and the blood-feud revived.[1]

We have already seen the association (Num. 11.25) of prophecy with the spirit, and though the connection is not always specially mentioned, the idea persists. Deborah, the judge who inspired Israel to victory, is called prophetess in the prose account (Judges 4.4; in contrast "a mother in Israel" 5.7); and an anonymous prophet was sent by the Lord (6.8) to prepare for the angel's message to Gideon. The term "nazirite"[2] too is associated with spirit-endowment in the mighty figure of Samson. Chosen by God before conception, as was Samuel later, consecrated by his mother's obedient abstinence from alcohol while he was in the womb, he retained his great physical power during the time his long hair, the outward symbol of his vows, remained. But when he told his secret and his locks were shaved, "he did not know that the Lord had left him" (Judges 16.20).

[1] Cf. Num. 5.14, a spirit of jealousy; cf. also 1 Sam. 16.14 below. cf. below, p. 120.

[2] For the laws of Nazirites see above, pp. 70f; for parallelism with prophets cf. Amos 2.11f.

# SAMUEL AND KINGS

## Religion at Shiloh

Like Samson, Samuel was a Nazirite (1 Sam. 1.11), but his inspiration
was the word, not the spirit of the Lord. At a time when the word of
the Lord was rare, there was no frequent vision (3.1) and Samuel
himself did not know the Lord, the Lord appeared to him, revealing
himself by the word (3.21), speaking to him as to Abraham and Moses.
Like them, Samuel gained a reputation for faithfulness (RSV established, 3.20) and for intercession (1 Sam. 7.5; 12.23; Jer. 15.1). He is
presented as belonging to a period when there was no differentiation
between religious leaders as priests, prophets, and judges. He was
part of the temple personnel at Shiloh, wearing a linen ephod (2.18).[1]
He used the sacred lot (10.20f) and offered animal sacrifice when
imploring God's intervention before the successful battle against the
Philistines (7.9). While in the priestly office he was established as a
prophet, but so long as Shiloh remained he stayed at the temple there.
He was able to predict the future and, having clairvoyant powers, to
find lost property (9.5ff). He anointed kings and was leader of a
prophetic community (19.18ff). On annual circuit in central Palestine
he judged Israel (7.15ff) and appointed his sons as judges at Beersheba in the south (8.1f).

At the beginning of the story of Samuel there is a clear self-
authenticating picture of Israelite religion before the foundation of the
monarchy. Its centre was at the temple in Shiloh with the Ark and
the Tent of Meeting[2] under the charge of Eli, who for a generation
had judged Israel (4.18). To Shiloh the Israelites went annually to
worship and sacrifice to the Lord of hosts (1.3); but at the feast Eli
expected immorality and drunkenness (1.12ff). The householder
performed the sacrifice (any man, 2.13, 16) and apportioned the communal meal. Neither altar nor disposal of blood is mentioned, nor is
there a prescribed priestly portion as in the Law. The custom was to

---

[1] In 1 Chr. 6.28 he is a Levite.
[2] The relationship between the temple (3.3) and the tent (2.22) can only be
conjectured.

boil the sacrificed animal, the fat being burned separately, after which the priest's servant, thrusting his three-pronged fork into the boiling cauldron, took as his portion all that came up on it[1] and the family shared what was left. At this time Eli's sons were trying to break the tradition by insisting on raw meat for roasting, and so eager were they for roast that they sent for their meat before it was boiled, hence before the fat was burned to the Lord; by so putting their own claims first, they "treated the offering of the Lord with contempt".[2] The impiety and immorality of Eli's sons are stressed as the cause of the subsequent destruction of Shiloh and the degradation of its priesthood. The Zadokite priesthood, which under Solomon replaced Eli's line,[3] is prophesied as faithful and permanent to serve the anointed for ever (1 Sam. 2.35). So important was this development to a priestly writer[4] that he prefaces the story of Samuel's monitory night vision with an independent account of another warning to Eli by an anonymous man of God (2.27ff).

## The Ark

Of central importance at Shiloh was the Ark, which, as we have seen in the Law, was the symbol or guarantee of the actual presence of Israel's God in the midst of his people, and was their leader in wanderings and war. This symbol of God's immanence was in the temple at Shiloh, which the writer may have regarded as another name for the Tent of Meeting, in the Law the symbol of God's transcendence, for he visited it to meet his people. From the Ark God spoke to Samuel. But there is a significant change in the people's attitude to it. In Joshua, when the people were defeated, the sacred lot was cast to discover what sin had caused God to withdraw his supporting power. Here, without consultation (1 Sam. 4.3f) the Ark was taken into the camp, as a magical object might be, to force God's saving presence to

[1] For an illustration of a three-pronged fork found at Lachish, cf. J. N. Schofield, *The Historical Background of the Bible* (1938).

[2] Perhaps this story also reflects a conflict of traditions within the priesthood itself, as over the Passover (Exod. 12.9, P; Deut. 16.7; and in Ezek. 46.24 the sacrifice is still boiled). At the root of the conflict may lie concern over the command as to blood and fat (Lev. 3.17).

[3] Eli's descent was traced to Ithamar, Aaron's youngest son (cf. 1 Sam. 14.3; 22.9; 1 Chron. 24.3); Zadok's to Eleazar (1 Chron. 6.8).

[4] "Offerings by fire" (1 Sam. 2.28; cf. Josh. 13.14); elsewhere this phrase occurs only in the Law, where it is usually assigned to P.

give victory.[1] The manoeuvre was useless, however. The Ark was captured, Shiloh destroyed for ever, and Israel defeated.

But it retained its power, and the god of the Philistines was impotent before it. It guided the cattle which brought it back to Israelite territory at Bethshemesh, and later was taken to Kirjath-jearim, a non-Israelite, Gibeonite, perhaps a free city (cf. Josh. 9.17f). It terrified the Philistines and slew seventy men at Bethshemesh who disregarded its holy God (1 Sam. 6.19). One tradition speaks of it as present with the army in the days of Saul (14.18) and consulted by him. But the dominant tradition regards it as being ignored for twenty years, during the life of Samuel and until David had captured Jerusalem after Saul's death, presumably because there was no new religious centre for the tribal confederacy where it could be placed, although descendants of Eli are said to have survived (14.3), and the people gathered at three other shrines, Ramah (9.5-21; cf. 7.17), Mizpah (10.17), and Gilgal (11.15) for the important task of choosing the first king.

The Ark had been greeted with burnt offerings when it arrived back at Bethshemesh from the Philistines (6.14f). But although it is recorded that Levites handled it then, no such precautions were taken by the men of Kirjath-jearim when it was transferred to that city. They consecrated as its keeper the son of the house where it remained twenty years (7.1f). When finally David brought it to the tent he had pitched for it at Jerusalem, there was music, shouting, dancing, and sacrifice, but there is no mention of Levites (2 Sam. 6). Then it again went out with the army to battle (2 Sam. 11.11); but David would not allow it to go with him into exile when he was driven out by Absalom's rebellion (2 Sam. 15.24ff). Solomon offered sacrifice before it (1 Kings 3.15), and when the Temple was built the Ark was placed in the holy inner room (6.19) under the cherubim (8.6). In it were only the two stone tablets made by Moses at Horeb (8.9). No further mention is made of it in the books of Kings. As Samuel and David had won military victories without the Ark, so there is no reference to its use in the wars of the monarchy in Judah.

An interesting new divine title appears when the Ark is called "the ark of the covenant of the Lord of hosts, who is enthroned on the cherubim" (1 Sam. 4.4). What precisely does "Lord of hosts" mean here? David was probably thinking of military forces and the Wars of the Lord when he said, "I come to you in the name of the Lord of

[1] Cf. G. van der Leeuw, *Religion in Essence and Manifestation*, (1938), who speaks of it as a fetish (p. 38).

hosts, the God of the armies of Israel, whom you have defied" (17.45); but it is likely that the term might mean more than this, though in the prophetic literature[1] it is never applied to the heavenly hosts. Joshua saw the captain of the Lord's host (Josh. 5.15). Here (1 Sam. 4.4) the connection with the cherubim, symbols of unseen wind on whose wings God flies (Ps. 18.10), may suggest an all-inclusive reference to heavenly powers.[2]

When Shiloh had been destroyed by the Philistines and the Ark captured, sacrifices were made at many places, as in the time of the patriarchs and that of the judges. There is no suggestion of one central shrine. There was sacrifice at Ramah where Samuel built an altar, at Gilgal (10.8), and at Bethlehem where Jesse and his sons were sanctified as special guests (16.5ff) and where there was a yearly new-moon sacrifice by the family (20.6). Absalom offered sacrifices at Hebron in fulfilment of a vow (2 Sam. 15.7ff) and Solomon at the great high place at Gibeon (1 Kings 3.4). At Ramah it was the custom to wait for Samuel's blessing before the sacrifice was eaten (1 Sam. 9.13f); but in what capacity he came—as priest, prophet, judge, chief man, or paterfamilias—there is no hint.[3]

## Prophet and Priest

That some prophets, like Samuel, had close links with shrines is clear from the Old Testament stories, but we should not dogmatize about the relationship nor assume it of all prophets. Every Israelite, like Elkanah, could offer sacrifice, but did not thereby become a cultic figure or part of the sacerdotal staff of a shrine. The same was true of prophets or bands of prophets who visited holy places or lived in towns where there were well-known shrines.[4]

From comparison with other Near-Eastern religions of the period, it has been claimed that the Old Testament prophet with his message should be seen as part of a cultic occasion, and even that the great prophets of Israel were charged with cultic functions. Before

[1] Where it occurs 247 times; cf. Eichrodt, op. cit. I, p. 192.
[2] Cf. de Vaux, op. cit., pp. 259, 304.
[3] Cf. A. R. Johnson, *The Cultic Prophet in Ancient Israel* (1962), p. 16, who suggests more than the evidence allows when he speaks of "a cultic specialist". Jacob's blessing (Gen. 49) did not make Jacob a cultic specialist.
[4] Cf. Eichrodt, op. cit. I, p. 315, against Hölscher, *Die Profeten* (1914), p. 143; A. R. Johnson, op. cit.; A. Haldar, *Associations of Cultic Prophets among the Ancient Semites* (1945).

discussing the problem, it is necessary to define precisely what is meant by the word "cultic". It can be used of any religious action, public or private. A parent's instruction of a child in the home at regular times (Deut. 6.20), and private prayer using well-known forms, are in this sense cultic, and clearly in this sense the prophets were cult figures. But the word may also suggest public religious acts by professional cult specialists attached to a shrine as permanent paid officials. In this sense, there seems ample evidence to justify us in separating prophets from priests. But the evidence is both interesting and conflicting. At the close of the Old Testament period, when true prophecy had ceased, the Chronicler could speak of the levitical choirs as "prophesying", as though in their antiphonal singing they gave to the congregation as response an oracle of God. And on the other hand, at the beginning of the period David could call the priest Zadok a seer (2 Sam. 15.27 RSV marg.). But in the main a priest was bound[1] to fixed times and places, actions, and words, while a prophet intervened when and where the spirit or the word impelled him. Though it is possible for the same one person to be both sacerdotal and charismatic, the two words denote a clear distinction in Old Testament religion.

These bands of prophets were a new feature of this period. From their behaviour and that of Saul, a close link has been seen between Israelite prophecy and that of other nations, where there had arisen bands of so-called "ecstatic" prophets, spirit-controlled, whose emotional enthusiasm was contagious. Now, just as it is rightly recognized that some Hebrew prophets had cultic functions as permanent members of the staff of shrines, so is it rightly recognized that some of them were ecstatics. But here again the excitement of discovery has caused a few scholars to go far beyond the evidence in the Old Testament, and their interpretation of the passages they adduce as proof needs to be carefully scrutinized. Ecstasy, like "amphictyony", is a Greek word which has been imported into Old Testament studies to label a Hebrew experience which has similarities to Greek experiences. It has then been wrongly applied to prophetic experiences which are not similar to, and certainly not identical with, what in Greek studies are described as ecstatic states.

To Hebrew thought, human personality was open to the invasion of spirit forces, and to varying degrees could be controlled by them. But man himself was a body animated by the spirit of God (Gen. 2.7); when it was taken away man died and returned to the dust. In this way of thought, it is not easy to distinguish between God's spirit and

[1] Cf. G. van der Leeuw, op. cit., p. 219.

man's spirit. Thus "ecstatic" and "rational" are not relevant contrasts in Old Testament religion. Just as holiness could be regarded as a quasi-physical, amoral contagion (2 Sam. 6.6ff; Ezek. 44.19), but could also be transformed by man's changing apprehension of the character of the God who is holy (Lev. 11.45; Isa. 5.16), so the power of the spirit of God has all-varying shades of meaning, from the amoral force that rushed on Samson and David to the holy spirit whose possession ensured the divine presence and a God-like character (Ps. 51.11).[1] Possibly it is because of this variation in the means of spirit-invasion that some prophets are described as inspired by the spirit of the Lord, and some by his word, though some even of the word-inspired prophets showed characteristics that might suggest "ecstatic" spirit control. The word was the inspiration of both Samuel and Jeremiah, yet the one is found presiding over a community of prophets whose contagious enthusiasm seized Saul so that he stripped off his clothes and lay naked for hours, and the other spoke of the word as an irresistible force within himself. Ecstasy may have influenced the way in which revelation was received, and these revelatory states oscillated between ecstasy, inspiration, and rational judgement (Jer. 15.19).[2]

Saul, after being anointed by Samuel, met men taking gifts to God at Bethel and a band of prophets coming down from the high place at Gibeah with musical instruments, prophesying as they came (1 Sam. 10.5). When Samuel gave protection to the fugitive David, he took him to Naioth near Ramah (19.18ff) where he presided over a company of prophets; the word Naioth occurs only here, and probably means a temporary encampment such as shepherds might use. References to such prophets indicate that they were well known in Israelite religious life. They may have been roused by zeal for the Wars of the Lord against the Philistine invaders. Their fervour may have been increased by ritual dances[3] or music (2 Kings 3.15f). But they have left us no words of religious value, nor have we any indication that they received the word of the Lord, a fact that is quite clear in the tragic story of Saul, of whom it is never recorded that he received the word. Though they were revered, they might be popularly spoken of as mad (9.11). Some appear to have worn distinctive

---

[1] Cf. Lindblom, *Prophecy in Ancient Israel*, (1962). For discussion of the important problem of ecstasy, cf. H. H. Rowley, op. cit., p. 146.

[2] See below, pp. 169.

[3] So W. O. E. Oesterley, *The Sacred Dance* (1923); W. Eichrodt, op. cit. I, p. 310.

garments of camel-hair cloak and leather girdle, which may have originally been Bedouin attire, conserving, as religious and professional
dress often does today, a link with the secular past which gave rise
to the particular religious phenomenon. Elijah was recognized by his
hairy mantle (1.8), a garment still linked with prophets in the time of
Second-Zechariah (Zech. 13.4), which appears again in the New
Testament period. Some of these prophets had recognizable signs on
head or forehead (1 Kings 20.41), possibly a tonsure (2 Kings 2.23),
or cuttings between the eyes (cf. Deut. 14.1).

Outstanding prophets had disciples or "sons" (1 Sam. 19.20; 2
Kings 2.3, 7, 15) and might be revered as father or leader (2.12).
Sometimes they had wives and children (4.1f). They might live in
temporary Bedouin encampments or in more permanent houses,
which they built for themselves (6.1–7), in or near towns, some of
which had well-known shrines. Their living was sometimes commun-
ally organized (4.38). Some may have lived like Elisha in a private
house (5.9) with a servant (4.12) or travelled to a foreign capital
(8.7). Under the monarchy, at least in the time of Ahab, large bands of
them were at court, supported by, and perhaps subservient to, the
king, but with the duty of obtaining divine guidance for him. Jezebel
had 450 prophets of Baal (1 Kings 18.22), Ahab had 400 prophets to
consult before his fatal battle at Ramoth Gilead (22.6). There were a
hundred of the prophets of the Lord (18.4) who were hidden by
fifties in a cave by a faithful royal chamberlain.

Sometimes a single prophet would stand out, like Micaiah before
Ramoth Gilead or like Elijah, in dangerous opposition to the king's
plans, and possibly those whose names are recorded from the beginning of the monarchy were noted leaders, as Nathan and Gad, men
of independent spirit whose message was written down because it was
of moral and ethical value. The fact, often noticed, that after the
defeat of the Philistine invaders by Samuel, Saul, and David, and
until the menace of the Assyrian empire, less importance is given to
prophetic bands, and interest focuses on lone, individual prophets
opposing their rulers, suggests that, when there was no need for
united, nationalistic religious fervour, the great prophetic figure would
begin to take shape, criticizing rulers who like David or Ahab regarded
themselves as above the ancient moral code of tribal life. Such a
prophet would champion the national God under whose protection
was that moral code, and from here it would be a short step for
prophets such as Isaiah and Amos to arise to condemn the nation as
well as the king, even when there was danger of enemy invasion. Nor

should it be surprising that so great a prophet as Amos disclaimed any connection with the ecstatic, nationalist bands of sons of the prophets (Amos 7.14).[1]

## Ethical Teaching

Like ecstatic prophecy, ethical teaching was found outside Israel, and was shared with other peoples of antiquity. Social conscience developed in individuals and in Egypt long before the time of the Hebrew prophets.[2] Egyptian wisdom writings contain high ethical teaching, which probably influenced Israel's prophets, and on the east of Palestine have been found Accadian psalms whose concept of God resembles that of Hebrew psalms.[3] Not only was there ethical religion outside Israel, but ethics formed part of Israel's religion before the great prophets of the eighth century B.C. There has been a healthy protest against the older orthodox critical view that the prophets were the founders of Israel's religion and that their teaching was later fixed in the Mosaic laws. This view isolates the prophets and credits them with ideas which were of common Israelite stock.[4] Prophet, priest, king, and chief were figures in the contemporaneous social order. All were linked with divine power.

It is clear that both prophet and priest were concerned with ethical instruction and with inculcating a known morality. It is possible that priestly instruction was more concerned than prophetic with sacerdotal rules for ritual purity;[5] but it is clear from the prophetic writings that the teaching of both included a moral code or an accepted way of living, and this too it was the priest's duty to teach. The religion of both prophet and priest sprang from human traditions. The God proclaimed by the prophets from deep personal experience was not an unknown God, but one who had been in living relationship with Israel for centuries, whose requirements had been handed on by priest, prophet, and parent. What distinguished the Hebrew prophets was not the novelty of their teaching, but their clear vivid awareness of the fact of God—his presence, demands, judgement, and saving activity. God had spoken to them and given them a word that was

---

[1] Cf. below, p. 234.     [2] J. H. Breasted, *The Dawn of Conscience* (1939).

[3] G. Widengren, *Literary and Psychological Aspects of the Hebrew Prophets* (1948).

[4] Pedersen, *The Role of Inspired Persons; Studies in O. T. Prophecy*, ed. H. H. Rowley, pp. 127ff.

[5] Cf. Hag. 2.11ff.

applicable to their contemporary situation. Such a word might imply a truth far beyond the present, like the fact of the saving power of vicarious suffering proclaimed by Second-Isaiah (53), but its primary significance was to the prophet's hearers. Those prophets through whom the religion of Israel became the vehicle of the most outstanding spiritual and moral development and a dynamic force in human history were primarily speakers who came with a word that God had spoken directly to them. It had come to them, and they were forced to proclaim it by word and deed.

So they applied age-old truths to their contemporary situations. In differing metaphors they tell how they learned the message of God, and were forced, often unwillingly, to proclaim it. In their personal encounters with God, traditions were stripped of accretions, and essential truths stood clear. Their intimate relationship with God forced them into opposition to kings, priests, and nationalist prophets, and produced what it is fair to call the prophetic religion of the Old Testament.

The ethical teaching of the early prophets is illustrated most clearly in the well-known stories of the opposition of Nathan and Elijah to their kings. Both David and Ahab had flouted the basic community laws codified in the Decalogue as God's requirements from his covenant people. David had coveted Bathsheba, wife of Uriah, one of his absent army officers. Uriah was a Hittite, and as a foreigner sojourning in Israel could claim special protection. Adultery had been committed, and the murder of Uriah arranged after this Hittite had resisted the king's deceitful temptation to flout the laws of the Wars of the Lord (2 Sam. 11.6ff). David's behaviour showed that he "despised the word of the Lord" even more clearly than Saul's lack of obedience to Samuel's command. Ahab coveted the vineyard of his neighbour Naboth, and allowed his foreign wife Jezebel to take steps to obtain the ground and have Naboth killed. Both prophets pronounced God's condemnation of the king (12.7f; 1 Kings 21.19).

## Repentance

But in both instances judgement is changed by the king's repentance (2 Sam. 12.13f; 1 Kings 21.29). As in stories of the doom on Israel in the Mosaic age, it is made clear that God's judgement through the prophet is not irrevocable. God sometimes "repents"[1] and changes his mind if the sinner humbles himself and turns to him confessing his

[1] See below, pp. 173, 188, 232, 237, 338.

sin. The character of the God who revealed himself to Moses as "merciful and gracious, slow to anger and abounding in steadfast love and faithfulness" (Exod. 34.6) is maintained in these prophetic pictures. Sometimes part of the punishment falls, sometimes it is all postponed as if to give further opportunity of a penitent change of attitude. Saul appears to be an exception to this, though Samuel is reported to have saved him once from public judgement (1 Sam. 15.30f). But Samuel incurred God's rebuke for grieving over Saul (16.1), and there is no mitigation or remission of the doom pronounced, emphasizing the last part of the revelation to Moses that he "will by no means clear the guilty".

The whole story brings into sharp relief the paradox of the God who has "repented"[1] (15.11, 35) and the God who "will not lie or repent; for he is not a man, that he should repent" (15.29), a paradox running throughout the Bible. In the Law there is the same paradox: "the Lord repented [RSV was sorry] that he had made man on the earth" (Gen. 6.6), but also:

> God is not man, that he should lie,
> or a son of man, that he should repent (Num. 23.19).

It is particularly evident in the prophets, who insist on the inscrutable element in God's dealings with man, forcibly expressed in the "perhaps" of Amos (5.15), Joel (2.14), and Zephaniah (2.3); and a similar tension is expressed in the Law, in Moses' words "perhaps I can make atonement for your sin" (Exod. 32.30). Though Saul confessed his sin and pleaded for pardon, God did not repent,[2] and consequently man has no right to expect that any action or words of his will force God to change his attitude towards him. In this prophetic emphasis there is no thought of divine caprice or favouritism; it is not God's "freedom" that is being considered, but rather that his thoughts are not our thoughts, and his ways are past finding out. Though he is different from man, he must be thought of as personal, not legal or

---

[1] The Hebrew word translated (RSV) "repent" or "relent" is a passive or reflexive elsewhere translated "be comforted" (Jer. 31.15). In its active form it can be translated "comfort" (Isa. 40.1). Its simple basic meaning appears to have been "pant" or "gasp", so possibly "sob". Perhaps here, as often in Hebrew, stress is on the consequences of an act, so that the thought is not simply of changing one's mind: sobbing issues in emotional relief that brings comfort. Compare the parallelism, "The Lord repented (RSV was sorry) . . . and it grieved him to his heart" (Gen. 6.6).

[2] Cf. Hebrews 12.16f.

abstract. It is maintained that man is being dealt with by a living God, whose abiding purpose is salvation.

Another exception to God's "repenting" seems to be the judgement that is accompanied by a prophetic action or sign. The first of such actions recorded is that of Ahijah, a prophet who lived at Shiloh (1 Kings 11.29f). The punishment on Solomon had been postponed and he was allowed to complete his reign, although like Saul he had tried to kill his God-appointed successor. But when Ahijah tore his new coat into twelve pieces and gave ten to Jeroboam, he was not only instigating revolt but making inevitable the division of the kingdom of Solomon. Similar actions of the dying Elisha against Israel's enemies were regarded as equally effective; but here stress is laid on the limitation of God's action by man's lack of co-operation: "Then the man of God was angry with him and said, You should have struck five or six times; then you would have struck down Syria until you had made an end of it, but now you will strike down Syria only three times" (2 Kings 13.19).

These actions have been called magical symbolism, but neither word is strictly true in Hebrew thought of them. Magic attempts to coerce God to do the magician's will; in these actions the prophet is co-operating with God's will already revealed to him. And they do not symbolize God's purpose. They are much more powerful and dangerous. They actually set the purpose of God irrevocably in motion. God has begun to act. As we saw when considering prophetic intercession, so here too stress lies on the importance of co-operation, whether the prophet's or the king's, with God's will when it is known. These actions, rightly termed "functional prophecy", are regarded as in some way releasing energies to make God's will effective, to accomplish his purpose through human co-operation.

## True and False Prophets

The actions are also interesting as showing that the writers accepted an element of prediction in prophecy. The test of a true prophet in Deuteronomy (18.22)[1] is that he is expected to predict correctly the near future. So Ahijah and Elisha are predicting and beginning events which will be completed within their own generation. But prophecy was not thought of as always confined to events within the lifetime of its audience. The same Ahijah who prophesied the division of Solomon's kingdom is represented as predicting the destruction of the

[1] See above, p. 87; below, p. 172.

dynasty of the rebel Jeroboam when, like Saul, he had failed to justify God's choice, and even the exile of the northern kingdom beyond the Euphrates about two hundred years later (1 Kings 14.10–15; cf. 15.29).

In the curious story of the conflict between the man of God from Judah and the old prophet from Bethel, an even more precise long-distance forecast, covering at least 300 years, is credited to the man of God: "Behold, a son shall be born to the house of David, Josiah by name; and he shall sacrifice upon you [the altar] the priests of the high places who burn incense upon you" (13.2; cf. 2 Kings 23.15f). He gave a confirmatory sign to prove that it was the Lord who spoke through him, and the sign was fulfilled. In Hebrew thought, prophecy had no time limit. The immediate future, as well as the far-distant, hidden (RSV "for ever", "everlasting") future, was within God's purpose and he could reveal it to his servants the prophets. Nathan foretold to David events that happened in a week (2 Sam. 12.15), and the establishment of his dynasty "for ever" (7.13).

The audience who listened to the story were being taught that God is timeless. Looking back from the actions of Josiah, and from 400 years of Davidic rule, they saw the thread of God's revealed purpose running back and forth through history. The view presented is an historical construction which we should not reject as childish nor as wanton forgery, but should rather apprehend as an attempt to depict the salvation which was given to man at the centre of history,[1] God being regarded as the beginning and the end.

This power of foretelling the distant future is quite frankly related as a wonder or miracle, like many of the actions attributed to Elijah and Elisha. "At its deepest roots, belief in miracles declares nothing other than: there is a living God. But real injury is done to belief in miracles as soon as the rarity and amazing element in miracle outweigh its purpose in revealing the character of God. The essence of a miracle is that it contains revelation."[2] No one who believes in God doubts his power to perform "wonders", nor thinks of him as limited by man's formulations of the laws of nature. To the Hebrew, God was power as well as love. Without the sense of wonder at God's power, there can be no religion.

The stories of the conflict between the prophet from Bethel and the man of God from Judah, and that between Micaiah and the 400

[1] Lehmann, *La pensée du Jahviste, Studi e Materiali Storia delle Religioni* (1927), quoted by van der Leeuw, op. cit., p. 581.

[2] G. van der Leeuw, ibid.

prophets of the Lord at Ahab's court (1 Kings 22), give further
interesting sidelights on the difference between true and false
prophets. It was a perennial problem how to be sure that a prophet's
word was the Lord's word. In the Law (Deut. 13 ;18) two clear, simple
criteria were given: (a) a false prophet entices men away from the
worship of the Lord to false gods and false ritual; (b) events predicted
by a false prophet do not happen. The story of Saul's séance
with the woman of Endor speaks of lawful and unlawful ways of
learning the purpose of God and future events; dreams, the sacred
lot, and prophets are contrasted with mediums and wizards (1 Sam.
28.6, 9).

In the story of the conflict at Bethel (1 Kings 13) an unnamed man
of God obeying the word of the Lord travelled, as did Amos later,
from Judah to Bethel and condemned its altar and the schismatic king
Jeroboam, but was then deceived by the old prophet of Bethel into
disobeying the Lord's command.[1] The man of God, having received
direct command from the Lord, owed the supreme prophetic duty of
obedience. He was being tested by the Lord when the lying old northern prophet enticed him. As is stated in Deuteronomy, the true
word of the Lord should have been discernible.

When Saul had disobeyed the word of the Lord through Samuel
(1 Sam. 15.19–22), the spirit of the Lord departed from him and an
evil spirit from the Lord troubled him (16.14) and led him to ruin.
So also, Ahab could be enticed to his death by a lying spirit from the
Lord. Ahab's plan to attack Syria was supported by 400 prophets of
the Lord, whose leader Zedekiah in a functional prophetic action put
on horns of iron to push back the enemy. Ahab's ally, Jehoshaphat of
Judah, suspected that the unanimity meant that a dissentient voice
had been silenced. When Micaiah was fetched and recounted his
threatening vision, the Lord was giving Ahab a last opportunity to
listen and obey. Ahab, true to character, refused. Despite his recognition of the Lord in the names he gave his children, and despite his
personal bravery (1 Kings, 22.35), he was not willing to listen to God's
voice if it opposed his own will. The impression given by both the
Law and the stories, as also in the experience of Jeremiah, is that

---

[1] The story probably comes through a southern writer and reflects the
rivalry between Bethel and Jerusalem, and southern contempt for the
religion of the north, made to sin by Jeroboam, who associated a different
symbol with God—a bull of fertility, not cherubim of the unseen wind—had
a different date for the New Year Feast of Tabernacles, and appointed priests
who were not of true levitical descent (1 Kings 12.25–33).

though it might be impossible to differentiate true from false prophets by their methods and technique, ultimately willingness to obey the will of God as far as it was known provided the key to distinguishing the precious from the vile.

## Prophet and King

Most of the prophets named in the books of Samuel and Kings engaged in political activities, but in politics viewed from the standpoint of the salvation history, concerned with God's dealings through his prophets with his people and with the king whom he had chosen to lead them. In Israelite thought, God never delegated, let alone abrogated, his right to govern his people. The belief that God is king, in contrast to other nations whose king is God, runs through all Old Testament religion.

Long before the people demanded "a king like other nations" there had been movements towards this form of leadership. Gideon had resisted the people's request that he would found an hereditary dynasty, on the ground that God was their king (Judges 8.22). Ahimelech, his son, had no such scruples and allowed himself to be made king at Shechem (9.6). It is of interest that continually an editor of Judges refers the evils of that time to the absence of a king in Israel (17.6; 18.1; 19.1; 21.25). In conformity with this opinion, one tradition of the choice of Saul as king regards kingship as a free gift of God to the nation to save it from the attacks of the Philistines. Saul was chosen by God and anointed to be leader rather than king (1 Sam. 9.16; 10.1, RSV prince), and three signs from God confirmed the choice (10.2ff). In another account Saul was chosen by lot at Mizpah (10.21), and in yet another was elected king by popular acclamation at Gilgal, after the great military victory over the Ammonites (11.15; 12.12). The people's choice of him as king was met by a strong warning from Samuel, confirmed by a miracle from God (12.17f), the unusual natural phenomenon of thunder and heavy rain at wheat harvest. Samuel's warning to king and people was against disobeying the voice of God and rebelling against his commandment, and, as we have seen, it was for two failures in obedience that Saul was rejected by God—the first time being within a week of his election.

His successor, David, was chosen by God alone, much to the surprise of Samuel, who had been sent secretly to anoint one of Jesse's sons and expected one of the fine older sons to be chosen. But again God's choice was confirmed. When Samuel had anointed David, the youngest son, "the spirit of the Lord came mightily [Hebrew, rushed] upon him from that day forward" (16.13).

At David's court was the prophet Gad, David's seer (2 Sam. 24.11). The description is quite precise—Gad was David's seer, but he could be a prophet only of the Lord, not of David. Gad fled with David to their hide-out in the cave of Adullam (1 Sam. 22.5) and was able to give him timely warning that Saul would discover his place of refuge. It was Gad whom God sent to offer David the choice of three punishments to expiate his sin of numbering the people, and who showed him where the altar at Jerusalem should be built to avert the plague from the city (2 Sam. 24.18ff).

Nathan, who had rebuked David for his adultery with Bathsheba, joined in the intrigue that put her son Solomon on the throne instead of his elder brother Adonijah (1 Kings 1.11), and with Zadok the priest was responsible for anointing him as king (1.45). Through Nathan God's promise was made to David and his dynasty. This begins as a promise to David's son of a permanent dynasty and kingdom and a special relationship to God (2 Sam. 7. 12–15), and passes into the promise to David himself (7.16, 18–29) which became of such importance in later Old Testament religious thought.

We have seen how towards the end of Solomon's life the division of his kingdom was prophesied by Ahijah. Otherwise, prophets play little part in Solomon's reign, and his building and dedication of the Temple are of first importance. Subsequently, in the history of the southern kingdom of Judah, until the stories of Isaiah in the reign of Hezekiah (2 Kings 19f) interest is focused on four successive religious reforms and on the importance of the Temple as the only legitimate sanctuary in the land. Attitude to the Temple became the criterion by which kings of both north and south were judged.

## Elijah

Prophetic interest after the division of Solomon's kingdom is centred in the north, in the stories of Elijah and Elisha, which continue to stress the national and moral character of Israel's religion. The book of Judges as well as some of the latter prophets, particularly Hosea and Jeremiah, show the protracted struggle against the indigenous fertility cults of Canaan. In the books of Kings, Elijah is depicted as the first prophet to fight against what is here represented as an invading, foreign religion. Jezebel, Ahab's Phoenician bride, had at court 450 prophets of Baal and 400 of his female consort Astarte (1 Kings

18.19). Probably these simply gave additional impetus to the Canaanite religion which had persisted in the land, the influence of which is clearly seen in the form and decoration of Solomon's Temple, carried out by Phoenician builders. But for Elijah, Jezebel's prophets focused the need for Israel to put a stop to assimilation and to choose between the worship of Baal and the worship of the Lord represented by the traditions of Horeb and Moses. The story of Naboth's vineyard makes it clear that Elijah was as true a prophet of the Lord as Nathan when he told David the parable of the poor man with the one ewe lamb.

As a nationalist, Elijah is represented as believing in a united Israel. He built his altar in the north on Mount Carmel with twelve stones to stand for the whole nation, including the two southern tribes (18.32). He fled through the southern kingdom to Horeb to meet the God of Moses, and according to the Chronicler (2 Chron. 21.12) on one occasion wrote a letter conveying the Lord's rebuke to the king of Judah.

But this is not the heedless nationalism of false prophets. Behind the stories of both Elijah and Elisha stands the prophetic conviction that God controls history and that Israel's yielding to the seduction of the worship of Jezebel's gods will not go unpunished. After the wind, earthquake, and fire when the fugitive Elijah heard the still small voice, the Lord told him to anoint Hazael, Jehu, and Elisha (1 Kings 19.15f) for their divinely appointed tasks. Later the history relates how Elisha wept when he saw Hazael at Damascus, because the Lord had shown him Hazael was to be king over Syria and was to be the scourge of Israel (2 Kings 8.11ff). Repeatedly afterwards sinful Israel is oppressed by Hazael (cf. 13.3). It relates too how Elisha obeyed God's command and incited Jehu to revolt against Joram, and how Jehu carried out the Lord's plan of purging Israel's worship: "When Joram saw Jehu he said, Is it peace, Jehu? He answered, What peace can there be, so long as the harlotries and the sorceries of your mother Jezebel are so many?" (2 Kings 9.22). Finally, the last great prophet in the books of Kings, Isaiah of Jerusalem, is depicted as fighting against the invasion of Assyria and her gods.

## Temple Reforms

The plan of the Temple and of its equipment is similar to the pattern of the Tabernacle in the wilderness as presented in the Law. It was small in comparison with Solomon's royal palace, and like the temple at Bethel (Amos 7.13) was in origin probably a royal shrine. Despite its clear affinities with what we know from archaeology of Phoenician and Canaanite shrines, there were repeated efforts to eliminate these religious contacts. It is of interest that none of these attempts is ascribed to prophetic instigation.

The first reform, under Asa (1 Kings 15.9ff), took place about twenty years after Solomon died; immediately before the story of it comes an idealization of David as perfect and upright except in the matter of Uriah the Hittite, and it is recorded that God had promised to keep a lamp in Jerusalem for David's sake (15.4f). Some eighty years later a second reform (2 Kings 11.17ff) was carried out by Jehoiadah the priest when the boy king Joash was crowned, the queen-mother Athaliah, Ahab's daughter, was slain, and Baal worship, for which she was regarded as responsible, was removed. The basis of this reform was two covenants which Jehoiadah made, one between the Lord, the king, and the people that they should be the Lord's people, and one between the king and the people. But after the reform of Joash, as after that of Asa, it is commented that the native high places were not removed (1 Kings 15.14; 2 Kings 12.3). Sacrifice and incense continued to be offered at them.

The third and the fourth reforms, under Hezekiah (2 Kings 18) and Josiah (2 Kings 22f) are the most fully recounted. Hezekiah removed high places and idols, even breaking the bronze serpent attributed to Moses, because it had become an object of worship, and it is reported that he ordered that all the worship of Judah should be centralized at the altar in Jerusalem. The Chronicler relates Hezekiah's reform in much fuller detail (2 Chron. 29f), and includes the reopening of the closed Temple at Jerusalem and an invitation to the remnant of northern Israel to join there in a united Passover.

Josiah's reform too is given greater prominence by the Chronicler (34f), and what in Kings is related as happening in his eighteenth year is attributed in Chronicles to his eighth, twelfth, and eighteenth years. During repairs to the Temple begun by the king and the high priest "the book of the law" was found there.[1] On the basis of this "book of the covenant" the king made a covenant before the Lord

---

[1] By many scholars identified with Deuteronomy or some part of it. But cf. E. A. Payne (ed.) *Studies in History and Religion* (1942), pp. 44ff and literature there cited. Mowinckel, *Psalms in Israel's Worship*, p. 4, n. 20: "It is recognised that the basis of Josiah's reform cannot have been Deuteronomy, which is most certainly an early post-exilic book." This view has long been maintained by the present writer.

in the presence of elders, people, priests, and prophets "to perform
the words of this covenant that were written in this book". The
account shows the writer's impression of the state of religion in
Jerusalem at the close of the monarchy, and also the deep hostility to
Bethel (2 Kings 23.4, 15ff). Canaanite and Assyrian cult objects in the
Temple were destroyed, priests of the high places, of Baal and of the
cult of the heavenly hosts, who had been appointed by Judah's kings,
were suppressed. Houses by the Temple for fertility cults, and the
horses and chariots for sun-worship there, were destroyed. Altars
built by Ahaz, Manasseh, and other kings of Judah on the roofs of the
Temple building, and all the high places built by Solomon for his
foreign wives were also broken down. The purge was carried out all
through the southern kingdom from Geba to Beersheba, and extended
to Bethel and all the cities of Samaria.

But the reform, though so sweeping, was yet in some way insufficient to appease the fierceness of God's great wrath provoked by the
trail of wickedness left by Manasseh, Josiah's grandfather, and the
final awful doom on Jerusalem and the Temple was pronounced:
"And the Lord said, I will remove Judah also out my sight as I
have removed Israel, and I will cast off this city which I have chosen,
Jerusalem, and the house of which I said, My name shall be there"
(23.27).

# 8 The Latter Prophets

## Introduction

We have seen[1] that the stories from Genesis to Kings are not a critical history of pragmatic events, but an account of Israel's relationship with God, her acts of obedience or disobedience to his revealed will. They are events of paradigm or sacred history in which precision about God's will on a particular occasion is more important than details of time, place, or persons. This religious attitude is focused in the next four books of the Old Testament (Isaiah, Jeremiah, Ezekiel, The Book of the Twelve), where are collected the traditions and teaching that have crystallized around the names of fifteen prophets, who give us insight into the rich religious experience of Israel during four centuries. Though there is considerable doubt as to date, authorship, and original contents of much in these books,[2] yet in their present form in the Old Testament three common features stand out as distinguishing marks.

In the first place, each prophet believes intensely that God is intimately concerned in the events of the prophet's world, that God is alive, contemporary, and involved in what is happening. God in his incomparable majesty is exalted over the whole universe, but is active within his created world and within the national life of his people Israel. In contemporary events his presence is seen by the prophets as overwhelming and inescapable, determining all moral and political relationships. This divine presence, unperceived by others, is a new reality of which they have suddenly been made aware, and often it completely and violently changes the pattern of their lives. They express in different ways their experience of meeting God; but for all of them it is a confrontation, human and divine remaining separate. The I and Thou are not merged, and the distance between God and man is always clearly recognized. They never speak of God as in the depths of the human soul, but as distinct, out there; they

[1] Cf. above, p. 96.
[2] For well-established results of research, see the introductions to Old Testament literature by A. Bentzen and O. Eissfeldt.

speak of what they have seen or heard, or of what God has shown them. The spirit, word, or vision came to them from outside, and God revealed himself *to* them, not *in* them. Their experience may well be expressed in the phrase "The Beyond in our Midst". To all the prophets God is knowable, and the language they use of him is concrete and clear. Sometimes his will and his ways are difficult to understand. His ways and his thoughts are higher than ours (Isa. 55.9) and obscure. Sometimes he hides himself (45.15) and withdraws, man has to live as though there were no God, and even the prophet has to wait hours or days before the divine silence is broken; but it is only the fool who says in his heart, There is no God, for the essence of religion is seeking God.

In the second place, each prophet is sure that God has called him to proclaim a message to his contemporaries. The call may come through a voice or a vision. It may be terrifying as to Amos, like the roar of a lion in open country, it may be a sudden mental vision or hallucination with no objective material reality, like the divine figure on a cherub-borne platform described by Ezekiel, or a voice interpreting in a new way some everyday object such as the boiling cauldron or flowering almond shrub to Jeremiah. The experience may be described as waking from sleep (Zech. 4.1), or come in dreams or night visions. Always its inspiration comes spontaneously as the irruption of something new, and there is no evidence that visions were deliberately induced as Elisha's prophecy was with music. However the prophets express their experience of a call, it means the certainty of becoming a herald or messenger, chosen by God to confront men with the demands that his presence makes on their lives. There has been personal encounter with God himself, a revelation that must be passed on. Not everyone can become a prophet or speak God's word, for not everyone has heard it; but those who have heard must speak it.[1]

To each prophet the word comes with compelling urgency. It brings the conviction that they stand in a time of crisis, a turning-point in history when national existence itself is at stake. Some prophets offer men a choice, as did Joshua (Josh. 24.15) or Elijah (1 Kings 18.21) between good and evil, obedience and destruction, life and death, and there is a "perhaps" in their message. Others are more conscious of inevitable judgement. But whether they emphasize choice or judgement, their keen awareness of the real presence of God in national and individual life, while it makes all prophets begin their

[1] Cf. Barth, *Church Dogmatics* I, p. 491.

preaching with God's absolute moral demands and man's failure, also enables them to look beyond the judgement to the steadfast love of a new covenant.

As the call-vision with its message comes to each prophet direct from God, so the prophet passes it on by word or action without any cultic mediation. It is a personal challenge to individuals from a personal God, and the only adequate response is in personal obedience.

Finally, each prophet knows that he himself is called to become involved. He is not a detached messenger, delivering God's word and then standing aside to watch what God will do, but a watchman who having sounded the alarm goes up into the front line to help man the defences and share the sufferings of the people to whom he belongs.[1] His total life as well as his voice is involved. To use the metaphor of the Servant Songs, he becomes the meeting-place between the holy God and sinful man[2] whom both he and God love and are trying to save from inevitable disaster. As he turns from God to the people, and back again in intercession, the prophet shares the suffering of both, God's anguish at being rejected and man's burden of sin. He is passionately concerned that the will of God be done fully and without compromise.

All these beliefs were the outcome of deep personal experience. The actions and words of each prophet sprang from close contact both with his God and with his people, so that his message was inseparable from his personality and his life in its total setting. His preaching was "truth through personality". It came through a particular person coloured by all his individual characteristics, to a particular people with their needs, at a particular time and place. It must be seen in a setting of history and biography. It had primary relevance to the situation in time in which it was delivered, and was not repeated in exactly the same form even to such contemporary prophets as First-Isaiah and Micah.[3] When Isaiah wrote down his prophecy for a future generation (Isa. 8.16f) because it was rejected by his contemporaries or because it had not found speedy fulfilment, he was breaking this immediate connection of prophecy with the occasion when it was first delivered. Whatever our theory of the stages by which the spoken word became preserved and written, we should

---

[1] See below, p. 203.

[2] As the Lord "made to meet (RSV laid) on him the sin of all of us" (Isa. 53.6) so he himself "made a meeting-place (RSV intercession) for transgressors" (53.12).

[3] Cf. below, pp. 173, 202, 238; also von Rad, op. cit. II, p. 299.

perhaps remember when we speak of "writing" prophets that the prophets themselves recognized that the word of God was timeless. Disciples, editors, and compilers were inspired in the certainty that the same eternal God was speaking to their own generation, and that the old prophetic message was still as urgent, relevant, and necessary as when first uttered.

Both those who wrote the prophetic message for future generations and those who later edited it to make it relevant for a new situation had a characteristic outlook on the meaning of history. Sometimes they used the past as it is used in Deuteronomy to teach lessons to the present, but they were also always conscious that what was past had real significance for the contemporary situation. To them history was a continuous process and there was continuity in divine activity from the past through the present towards a goal. God's struggles with Israel were links in the great chain of time joining the traditions of the past to that present decisive choice for which prophets earnestly pleaded. This intense awareness of divine reality was the crucible in which the traditions of the past were purified and fused with the new experience of the prophets to form the developing religion of Israel. As the new religion of Moses had taken the noblest elements of patriarchal and nomadic religion as God's requirements, so the prophets did not teach a new concept of God nor a new ethic, but a new recognition of the relevance of the traditional, known requirements of God, and a new demand to take God seriously.

Micah (6.8) reminded men of what they had been shown that God required, and Jeremiah (5.5) spoke of "the way of the Lord and the law of their God" as known. Further, the prophets inherited from the past the belief that the Lord revealed himself through external historical events in individual and national life, that there was a special relationship between him and his people Israel, and that he dwelt in their midst, and for some of them his dwelling was especially in the holy place of the Jerusalem Temple. This special relationship they spoke of more often in terms of marriage than of choice or covenant; but neither bond was thought of as unbreakable, though Second-Isaiah[1] emphatically denied that God had divorced Israel, and other prophets spoke of an everlasting covenant. In the traditions of the past, this special relationship was thought of as giving the Lord a special claim on Israel for faithfulness, obedience, and acceptance of the moral demands of the law. Later, there was increasing tension between love and wrath, blessing and judgement.

[1] See below, p. 133 ,n. 5.

Central to the prophetic preaching was the emphasis on the Lord's mighty acts in delivering his people; but there was a new stress that Israel not only had fallen away but was even now being apostate. She had forgotten and was rejecting the Lord her Saviour, and inevitably his righteousness must bring judgement. Denunciation of Israel and pronouncement of disaster and doom was a new feature in prophetic preaching. But doom was never the final prophetic word. Throughout, there still rings the Lord's proclamation to Moses, "The Lord, the Lord, a God merciful and gracious, . . . forgiving iniquity . . . but who will by no means clear the guilty" (Exod. 34.6f).

The first three books of the Latter Prophets bear the names of great figures in Jerusalem's religious life: First-Isaiah in the eighth century, Jeremiah and Ezekiel in the seventh and sixth centuries B.C. They record the revelation of God's will and purpose as apprehended by very different personalities, in similar historical situations but with different religious backgrounds. All three prophets lived through the destruction of part of their nation by the invasion of great outside empires. First-Isaiah watched the destruction of ten of the twelve tribes of Israel, and the capture of many of the cities of the other two tribes in the south; Jeremiah and Ezekiel survived the destruction of the remainder of the land, people, and Temple. First-Isaiah and Ezekiel were closely linked with the Temple, and held that it was in a special way the dwelling-place of Israel's God. Jeremiah, not a native of Jerusalem, was brought up at a provincial sanctuary, and though he was equally involved with the nation and its God, he was much less concerned with national and religious institutions.

Hosea, Amos, and Micah, like First-Isaiah, are definitely dated in the eighth century B.C., a period which marked the political and economic summit of the Israelite kingdoms during the long and prosperous reigns of Jeroboam II in the north and Uzziah in the south. From this height the two nations began to decline in political power. Before this time foreign enemies—Philistines and Syrians—were no greater than themselves, and God's interventions through his prophets were concerned with reforms in internal affairs: Nathan's concern with David's adultery, Ahijah's prophecy that Solomon's despotism would be punished by the division of his kingdom, Elijah's and Elisha's fight against Jezebel's introduction of Syrian gods and tyranny against Naboth. When Assyria first appeared on the horizon, she was unable to defeat the combined forces of the Palestinian states, which included Israel under Ahab. But as she grew stronger, first Jehu in the north and then Ahaz in the south appealed to her for help against the small neighbouring states and voluntarily submitted to her, thus breaking the unity of the Palestinian coalition.

These events marked the beginning of decline in political power for both Israel and Judah, ending in their destructions in 721 and 586 B.C. Against this decline we can trace the growth of the prophetic movement from the eighth to the end of the sixth centuries B.C.[1]

It is not clear whether the prophets had some divine intuition of the future or ordinary foresight, whether they were better informed than the man in the street or possessed moral insight into inevitable political consequences of national behaviour. They certainly believed that the nation needed simple trust in her God, not political intrigue, and they themselves were quite sure that any foresight or insight they had was given them direct from God. He gave them visions, spoke to them his word, or put his spirit on them. Their intense awareness of God's powerful presence and his deep concern for Israel's righteousness made them sure that the coming political disasters were the Lord's doings, acts of a loving father trying to win rebellious children back to their family loyalty, trying to get them to reject evil by showing them its inevitable consequences.

[1] Toynbee, "religions are the products of disintegrating societies", quoted by E. Voegelin, op. cit., p. 20.

# 9 The Latter Prophets: Isaiah

## Introduction

The material collected under the name Isaiah, like that in the Former Prophets, covers a long span of history. The first dated event is the death of Uzziah, king of Judah, *c.* 740 B.C. (Isa. 6.1), and the last is the rise of Cyrus and his spectacular conquests, at least two centuries later; this time span is perhaps recognized by some Hebrew MSS. which place the book after Ezekiel. Of the sixty-six chapters, 1—35 contain prophetic teaching, some of which is attributed to Isaiah son of Amoz[1] "in the days of Uzziah, Jotham, Ahaz, and Hezekiah, kings of Judah"[2] together with autobiography (6, 8, 11) and biography (7.3); chapters 36—39 is an historical narrative which repeats with some slight differences a section of the Former Prophets (cf. 2 Kings 18ff);[3] and the final section, chapters 40—66, where occur the references to Cyrus (44.28; 45.1), consists of prophetic words without narrative or biographical details, and only a few hints of autobiography.[4] As early as the twelfth century A.D. the Jewish scholar Ibn Ezra raised doubts as to the unity of the whole book, in 1775 Döderlein divided it, ascribing chapters 40—66 to the prophet he called Deutero-Isaiah, and in 1892 Duhm made a further division, using the title Trito-Isaiah for 56—66.

Alongside this recognition of a multiple origin is to be set the fact that in the Old Testament the whole is one unit. The text of Isaiah is the best attested of any book of antiquity. The references in Ecclesiasticus (48.22–5) nearly cover the book as a whole; with slight exceptions the whole book is found in the LXX, and, more important, in the material discovered in caves at Qumran near the Dead Sea in A.D. 1947, which includes one complete copy of the whole book.[5]

---

[1] Not Amos.          [2] 1.1; cf. 2.1; 13.1; 20.2; cf. also 14.28.

[3] The analogy of Jer. 52 and 2 Kings 24.18–25, 30 suggests that this historical narrative may have ended the collection of prophecies attributed to Isaiah son of Amoz.

[4] 40.6 LXX; 49.1–6; 50.4–9; 51.4, 7; 61.1.

[5] The balance of archaeological evidence suggests that this was deposited in the cave before A.D. 133, but written much earlier.

There is no indication that 40—66 had been once separate from 1—39, or had been regarded as by a different writer. Verses quoted in the New Testament as from Isaiah range over the whole book; nine quotations in Matthew, Luke, Acts, and Romans from 40—66 are given as from Isaiah.[1] It has been rightly said, "The spiritual sympathy of the two Isaiahs is so close that the canon does not separate them."[2]

From considerations of historical background, literary style, and religious ideas it is abundantly clear that at least two prophets are involved. But it would be over-simplification and indeed falsification to think in an arbitrary way of two Isaiahs. During a long spiritual history men of God have supplemented the words of the eighth-century prophet with promises and hopes to make them relevant to new situations; in particular, 24—27 has been distinguished with the title, The Little Apocalypse,[3] and 34—35 has been ascribed to one anonymous writer. Much of the additional material[4] comes from a great prophet who lived at the end of the sixth century B.C.[5] Thus we must not think of 1—35 as deriving from the eighth century and 40—66 as from the sixth century B.C. Living traditions beginning with eighth-century material have gone through the hands of successive writers both before and after major additions were made in the sixth century, and the whole has been made into one book containing prophecy and fulfilment.

Of the personal life of either First or Second-Isaiah we know little. Many of First-Isaiah's prophecies are linked loosely to historical events as though to make a connection between words and occasion rather than to date the utterances accurately. His initial vision of God is dated in the year that king Uzziah died (6.1),[6] and the death of the great leper king of Judah is clearly contrasted with the prophetic

---

[1] It must be remembered, however, that (a) the state of the text in the Dead Sea Scrolls shows that it was not rigidly fixed before the second century A.D.; (b) a Jewish tradition (Baba Bathra 14 b) ascribes the writing of the book to men of Hezekiah (cf. Prov. 25.1).

[2] A. Neher, L'essence du Prophétisme (1955), p. 243.

[3] Cf. below, pp. 337ff. For dating these sections, cf. O. Eissfeldt, Einleitung in Das Alte Testament (1934), pp. 363ff.

[4] Particularly in 40—55.

[5] Called Second-Isaiah in the following pages. The eighth-century Isaiah, who is often referred to as Isaiah of Jerusalem, is here called First-Isaiah. For literary analyses of the whole book, see standard textbooks.

[6] 2 Chron. 26.22 credits First-Isaiah with writing the life-story of Uzziah. The prophet was still active when the Assyrians besieged Jerusalem in 711 (or perhaps 701 B.C. or even later).

sight of the holy Lord as king. No prophecies are dated in the reign of his successor, Jotham, but *c.* 734, when Syria and the Northern kingdom of Ephraim tried to force Ahaz, Jotham's son, to join them in revolt against Assyria, Isaiah was given a message for Ahaz, and took his son, already named "A remnant will return" to meet the king (7.1ff). An oracle against the Philistines was given in the year that Ahaz died (14.28), and another, in the year that Sargon sent his commander-in-chief to capture Ashdod, was directed against trusting in Egyptian help (20.1; cf. 30.1ff; 31.1ff), and in the historical section (36—39) other sayings are dated in the reign of Hezekiah. Some of First-Isaiah's prophecies were made by actions, so being of the same type as the functional prophecies of Former Prophets. The names of his two sons "A remnant will return" and "Spoil speeds, prey hastens" herald the beginning of both the remnant and the destruction. Walking naked and barefoot over a period of three years[1] was "a sign and portent" of Assyrian conquest of Egypt (20.3).

No personal details are given as to Second-Isaiah; but the prophecy of the imminent fall of Babylon and the mention of the spectacular victories of Cyrus would set some of these chapters in the momentous years between 538 and 536 B.C. Before he began his prophecy, and during and after the lifetime of First-Isaiah, there had been a series of tremendous catastrophes. The Northern kingdom of Israel was destroyed by the Assyrians in 721 B.C., Judah was devastated, and Jerusalem besieged. Great numbers of Israelites were taken captive to Assyria, and other settlers brought in to replace them (2 Kings 17.5f, 24). There followed the final destruction of Jerusalem and Judah by the Babylonians in 586 B.C. and three successive captivities denuded the Southern kingdom.[2] Archaeology reveals that southern Palestine is littered with sites of cities ruined at this time and never again inhabited. Two hundred years of exile from the north, and fifty years from the south before the rise of Second-Isaiah, had brought a new generation of Jewish people in Mesopotamia to hear the prophet's call to return to the homeland, and in the land of Israel to welcome or reject those of the captivity.

[1] Not "lived for three years" as J. B. Phillips, *Four Prophets* (1963), p. 105.
[2] In 597, 586, and 581 B.C. Cf. Jer. 52.28ff.

# FIRST-ISAIAH

## Teaching

The first five chapters of the book, described as "the vision of Isaiah the son of Amoz which he saw concerning Judah and Jerusalem" comprise undated general teaching, apparently outstanding statements made by the prophet on various occasions, not recorded in the chronological order of their delivery. In 1.7 punishment has fallen and the daughter of Zion is left desolate—to use Sennacherib's words, shut up like a bird in a cage—and if the all-powerful Lord of Hosts "had not left us a few survivors", there would have been total destruction as at Sodom and Gomorrah. In 5.26, punishment is about to fall—God will whistle for a nation far off.

Jerusalem is a central theme in these chapters, with alternating pictures of the actual and the ideal city. Doom and hope often follow one another. The picture of the corrupt city in the first chapter is followed by that of Zion exalted in the second, and again in the third chapter there is oppression and extravagance for which the city will be left leaderless and in chaos, while in the fourth Zion is purged. In the fifth chapter, the Song of the Vineyard, the house of Judah and the men of Israel are thoroughly evil and deserve their fate; it is of interest, however, that the reproach to the vineyard is later revoked (27.2),[1] and the Lord is spoken of as protecting it. Throughout this introductory section three protagonists stand out: God, the whole sinful city, and the prophet. There has been a great development in social structure and sophistication since the days of the wilderness and early settlement, and First-Isaiah's grasp of his complex environment is shown by his two images for it in these early chapters: that of the body with its head, heart, and feet (1.5f) and that of the vineyard with hedge, tower, and vat; each image presents a self-contained unit.

### SIN

The first element that stands out in the prophet's teaching is the sinfulness of city and nation. The men of Judah, God's pleasant

[1] Cf. above, p. 133.

planting (5.7), have corrupted themselves like the men destroyed by
the Flood (1.4; cf. Gen. 6.11f) and Isaiah recognizes that a bad
history lies behind them when he calls them "offspring of evildoers".
As the first generation to enter the promised land were punished for
forsaking their own God (Judges 2.13), the "Holy One of Israel",
so now Israel is to be smitten, her land desolated. Both here and in
later chapters First-Isaiah attacks the perennial sins of city life that
prophets always must condemn: insidious foreign temptations, in-
ordinate wealth, and pride (2.6–11), women's vanity, wantonness, and
extravagance (3.16; cf. 32.9). Elders and princes, aided and abetted by
unscrupulous lawyers and scribes (3.13ff; cf. 10.1f), have been grind-
ing the faces of the poor so that numerous small-holdings are being
swallowed up to make one vast concern of a great house surrounded by
fields, and one dwells "alone in the midst of the land" (5.8). Senseless
feasting and drinking all day (5.11ff) make men unable to see any
meaning in life, and priests and prophets, who should be the eyes of
the nation and tell what is right (cf. 29.10; 30.10), are just as drunk,
and join them in jeering at First-Isaiah, quite secure in their minds
that God will leave them alone (5.19; cf. 28.14). They are full of
self-conceit, so that they are committing the unforgivable sin of saying, Evil, be thou my good—they can no longer discern between the
two and are called "a people without discernment" (5.20; cf. 27.11).

Scholars have rightly talked of the Isaianic "school", for this emphasis on discernment and understanding is continuous throughout
the whole book of Isaiah. First-Isaiah spends much of his ministry
combating lack of comprehension among his contemporaries; he
lays stress on teaching the law, and obedience to the counsel and
guidance of God. Priests and other prophets accuse him of treating
them as children who need a spelling lesson[1] (28.10). They are weaned
from the breast and do not need his teaching on the meaning of
"faith".[2] He himself speaks of his pupils or disciples, through whom
the message rejected by his contemporaries will be preserved for the
future and given permanence (8.16; cf. 30.8). The precious teaching,
the revealed understanding of God's purposes, must not be lost.
Hidden among the disciples it waits for better days. These the
prophet is sure will come—a time when the rash will have good
judgement and stammerers speak distinctly (32.4). The lesson will be
properly learned at last, and the outcome of God's spirit will be

---

[1] RSV line upon line—the literal Hebrew is comparable to our "a, t, spells
at, b, a, t, spells bat".
[2] Cf. pp. 149f below.

understanding that rests—abides—on the prince in the happy days to come (11.2).

The same interest in pupils or disciples persists in Second-Isaiah, who speaks of the ear and tongue of the disciple (50.4f, RSV those who are taught). There are still, as in the time of First-Isaiah, men without understanding, worshipping idols they themselves have made (44.18). But the prophet reminds those who listen to him that they have been taught great lessons; "Has it not been told you from the beginning? Have you not understood the founding of the earth?" (40.21: literal translation). At the climax of his teaching, in the final Servant Song, we are told that kings who have had no such advantages as Israel, who have never been taught God's lesson, though they have not heard, will understand (52.15).

First-Isaiah believed that God teaches us his ways (2.3). All instruction comes from him (28.26), and it is the voice of the great Teacher that says, "This is the way, walk in it" (30.20f). This emphasis on understanding, discernment, and the Way, connects these prophets with the Wisdom literature, and reminds us that there is no arbitrary division between prophets and wise men. Both were cognizant of the wider learning of their day: of foreign nations (19.8f) of medical matters (21.3), of natural history (the worm that can crush soil to powder—"thresh mountains"—41.14f). The royal wisdom school of the men of Hezekiah (Prov. 25.1) is evidence of a lively intellectual concern at this time, and First-Isaiah often seems to show a sense of responsibility to make "the way" (Isa. 8.11) of faith in God relevant to the wider knowledge of the most active minds of his day.

## ATTITUDE TO THE CULT

The second element in First-Isaiah's vision of Judah and Jerusalem is his teaching of the complete irrelevance of all sacrificial ritual for dealing with the nation's guilt. From rulers and people like those destroyed in Sodom, multitudes of bloody animal holocausts give no delight to God; he is satiated with the stench of burning fat (1.10f). In a crescendo of rejection of the Temple ritual,[1] the prophet declares emphatically that God has never required such vain offerings, that weekly, monthly, annual festivals are hateful and wearisome to him. Even the ceremonial spreading out of their hands when they pray reveals only the bloodstains on them and makes him hide his face.

The sins of the city First-Isaiah has summed up as ingratitude and

[1] It is of interest that First-Isaiah uses "abomination", a term applied to heathen worship, of burning incense. See above, p. 57, n. 1.

rebellion of sons against a father's love, as the senselessness of animals that do not recognize the stall where they are fed, as corruption demanding the same complete destruction as befell Sodom and Gomorrah. The address of the prophet to "you" is answered by the people and their leaders recognizing "our" guilt and God's saving intervention to deliver a few survivors (1.9). But the prophet simply returns to the attack with an even more devastating condemnation of another aspect of their relationship to their Father and Owner. Nathan and Elijah condemned their kings for practising a despotic Canaanite form of kingship that had no place in the national traditions, and First-Isaiah seems to be condemning in a similar way religious practices that had never been required by the nation's God,[1] but had been grafted on to Israel's simpler worship from Canaanite sources. It is clear from other eighth-century prophets that throughout the whole land, perhaps as a reaction to the disturbed political condition and the threat of foreign devastation, there was a sensational multiplication of altars (Hos. 8.11), pilgrimages (Amos 4.4), and religious ceremonials (Mic. 6.7), perhaps in an attempt to win or force God's favour and help. To First-Isaiah such acts are not only useless but offensive to God. Though the people add year to year and let the feasts run their round, God will yet distress them (Isa. 29.1f); the people draw near with their mouths and honour God with their lips while their hearts are far away (29.13). Though they fear the Lord, this "fear" or worship has been learnt by note; it does not spring from any personal experience of relationship with him.

First-Isaiah's condemnation shows what was actually happening in the eighth century in the Temple at Jerusalem, just as Hosea and Amos reveal the forms of worship of the Lord at other sanctuaries. But it is difficult to know what these prophets regarded as the true traditional forms of Israel's public religious acts. That First-Isaiah knew some of the laws now in the Pentateuch regulating worship seems clear from his use of the same language and terms. The word of the Lord is parallel to the law or teaching of our God (1.10), and the phrase "to appear before me" (1.12)[2] is used in Exodus of the three great annual festivals when all males were required to make pilgrimage and of the Feast of Unleavened Bread, and is repeated in Deuteronomy (16.16), where the joy of religious festivals is so strongly emphasized. He knew also the joy of song "in the night when a holy feast is kept; and gladness of heart, as when one sets out to the sound

---

[1] Cf. Amos 5.25; Jer. 7.21ff.
[2] Probably originally meaning "to see my face", cf. above, p. 38, n. 3.

of the flute to go to the mountain of the Lord, to the Rock of Israel"
(Isa. 30.29; cf. 33.20). The Temple itself he regarded as the dwelling-
place of God (8.18; cf. Exod. 29.45), but it was a live coal from the
altar fire that he regarded as efficacious for cleansing guilt and uncleanness (Isa. 6.6f; cf. 33.14), not the blood of a sacrificed animal on
the altar (Lev. 17.11). The altars themselves can take men's eyes away
from their Maker, the Holy One of Israel (Isa. 17.7f). Altars, asherim,
and incense altars[1] are man-made, and have no importance compared
with God himself. Jacob's guilt will not be expiated nor his sin removed till the stones of the altars are crushed to pieces like chalk-
stones (27.9). It is true that in a future day when conquered Egypt
swears allegiance to the Lord there will be an altar and pillar to the
Lord in Egypt, "and the Egyptians will know the Lord in that day and
worship with sacrifice and burnt offering, and they will make vows to
the Lord and perform them" (19.21); but it is of primary importance
that "it will be a sign and a witness" of their allegiance and God's
promised deliverance. Perhaps the prophet is recalling the altar built
by Reubenites in Transjordan not for burnt offering and sacrifice but
as a witness,[2] and is suggesting that this altar in Egypt is to be a witness binding together Israel, Egypt, and the Lord.

It is possible that the traditional religion known and accepted by
First-Isaiah was nearer to that reflected in Deuteronomy,[3] where
blood, though too sacred to be eaten, had no special sacral power, and
the important element in animal sacrifice was scrupulous care about
the disposal of blood, when life was taken for a joyful communal
feast shared by God and the whole family. It was part of this whole
complex of ideas that the Temple was a place for meeting God in
prayer, judgement, and forgiveness (1 Kings 8.27ff).

The traditional public religious acts observed by Israel, when
compared with God's moral requirements and his demand for absolute obedience, have no more importance for First-Isaiah than for
Samuel (1 Sam. 15.22f), Micah, and Jeremiah. The nation has forsaken and despised the Lord (Isa. 1.4, 28). They have forgotten the
God who delivered them, and vainly worshipped the gods of fertility
to obtain the harvest (17.10f; cf. 1.29; Adonis gardens and tree cults).
They have made gods of silver and gold; but when God arises in all
his terrifying majesty and men take refuge in caves and clefts in the
rocks, these aids to worship will be thrown away (2.18ff; cf. 30.22).

[1] Cf. D. W. Thomas, op. cit., p. 325.
[2] Cf. above, p. 103.
[3] Cf. Whitehouse, *Century Bible*, Isaiah, Vol. I, p. 47.

They consult mediums and wizards, and listen to voices from the grave instead of to the words of God's testimony through the prophet (8.16, 19). Even in their plans for the defence of their city they leave God out of their thoughts, and when he calls to mourning and repentance they turn to joy and feasting (22.9ff). Urgently and emphatically the prophet states that God requires the people to return to him to be forgiven. He pleads with them to change their whole way of life and to listen to God in willing obedience. Let them wash the blood from their hands, remove the evil from their actions, do good, seek justice, defend the widow and orphan. These are the weightier matters of the law (1.16ff; cf. Matt. 23.23). Heaping up the old, well-known divine attributes of power—Lord of Hosts, Mighty One of Jacob—he predicts the purging wrath of God that will treat rebellious sinners as enemies to be destroyed, till Zion is redeemed by justice and her penitent ones by a righteous act (1.27).

In the Law, animal sacrifice and religious occasions could express and make visible a personal surrender to God, and could be the symbol of an existent covenant; they were the way ordained by God to wipe out sin. The prophet picks up phrases from the actual commands of God through Moses in the Law, but makes it plain that multiplication and elaboration of offerings cannot force God's favour. If the nation wants a change of fortune, it needs a change of heart.

HOPE

A third element found throughout First-Isaiah's teaching is his unquenchable hope, his certainty of the future. As in other prophetic books, hope often alternates with condemnation, as though in the thought of the prophet blessing comes only to a purged community and is the aftermath of suffering regarded as necessary punishment. Dross must be smelted away before restoration is possible (1.25f). After this statement, the prophet goes on to quote (2.1ff) a contemporary poem of hope found also in Micah's book (4.1ff). It sings of a new Jerusalem raised by God's miraculous power high above the surrounding hills.[1] Through this centre God will enter the world, his law and word will be accepted by all nations, and a new Zion will be the meeting-place of all peoples, among whom peace will be maintained by their ready acceptance of God's decisions.

After another poetic condemnation (2.6—3.26) there follows a

[1] The poem speaks of the mountain of the Lord, not of God (contrast Exod. 3.1), and of the house of the God of Jacob, cf. house of God (Gen. 28.17).

promise of something new and significant. The prophet declares that the branch of the Lord will be beautiful and glorious (4.2), as the fruitfulness of the land will be the pride of those who have survived its purging. When later he speaks of the one who will be prince over the prosperous land in the coming golden age, he calls him not a branch but a shoot (11.1). But his word "branch", that had summed up the fruitfulness of purged Israel, is the one later chosen to mean the young prince (Jer. 23.5; 33.15; Zech. 3.8; 6.12) perhaps stressing that hope was centred not in an isolated individual, but in one who represented a purged people.

Sometimes First-Isaiah speaks of the future as coming "afterwards" (1.26), but usually announcements of either calamity or happiness begin with the phrase "in that day". Other prophets speak of "the Day of the Lord", and it is possible that this phrase too was born from the lips of First-Isaiah, who uses it occasionally.[1] In the poem of condemnation an emphatic refrain asserts, The Lord alone will be exalted in that day (2.11, 17), while another, equally emphatic, repeats that man will cower "before the terror of the Lord and from the glory of his majesty". (2.19, 21). Sometimes "in that day" Jerusalem and Judah suffer judgement (3.7ff; 4.1) or the land of the house of Jacob is punished (2.6ff; cf. Deut. 31.17 where perhaps there is the thought of a Day of Judgement). At other times "that day" is a day of blessing (4.2) when the remnant will lean on the Holy One of Israel (10.20–7), and when a second time the Lord will bring back his remnant (11.11f; 12.1, 4; 27.12) and Israel will cast away idols. Against Israel's foes the day of the Lord will be cruel with wrath, against Babylon (13. 9, 19), and Egypt, who will turn to worship the Lord with Israel (19.16, 19ff). It will be a day when Zion will be avenged (34.8), when Ephraim will be punished (28.5f). In words similar to those of Second-Isaiah, we are told that the deaf and blind, the meek and poor will rejoice (29.18f), cattle will graze in large pastures, and "the light of the moon will be as the light of the sun, and the light of the sun sevenfold, as the light of seven days, when the Lord binds up the hurt of his people" (30.23–6).

In the Little Apocalypse "that day" is used of the universal punishment of the great ones of the earth (24.21), the Lord's slaughter of the mythical leviathan (27.1), and his salvation for his people (25.9; 26.1; 27.2ff). Clearly the phrase here means a tremendous, far-off day, not a time soon expected, as it obviously is outside this section in the prophecy of the rise and fall of Eliakim (22.20–5).

[1] 2.12; 13.6, 9; cf. Exod. 32.34.

Predominantly throughout First-Isaiah the "day" is to be a day of
blessing for Israel and judgement on its foes, a view which in its
popular specious form, as we shall see, was rejected by Amos. In both
Isaiah and Amos, when the day is one of punishment, it appears
imminent, but as a day of blessing it is further away and will come
after suffering. First-Isaiah teaches that the punishment will mean the
end of most of Israel, for Ephraim will be destroyed and most of
Judah. All his hopes are firmly set on the remnant that is to be saved.

## The Initial Vision of First-Isaiah

From the song of the loved vineyard—the house of Israel and the men
of Judah (5.7), now to be destroyed as a disappointment to its owner—
the prophet turns back (6) to his early youth, the beginning of his
contact with God, and the source of his right and power to stand with
God in condemnation of Israel and the nations. When Uzziah died
First-Isaiah saw the Lord high and lifted up so that the whole Temple
was filled with the ends of his flowing robes. Above him stood
attendant seraphs[1] singing their antiphonal song ascribing holiness to
the all-powerful Lord, whose visible resplendent glory filled the whole
land.[2] In obvious contrast to Uzziah, the Lord is described as the
king, powerful ruler of all the hosts of heaven and earth.[3] At the sight,
the prophet is filled with dismay because of his own and his people's
guilt and uncleanness. "Unclean" translates a Hebrew word used
for ritual impurity, and suggests that the prophet is thinking of the
king's leprosy, and realizing that he himself and the whole people are
guilty of the same sin against the holiness of God as caused Uzziah to
be smitten (2 Chron. 26.16ff). But Isaiah's sin had only to be confessed
to be purged and forgiven. Like Micaiah (1 Kings 22.19) he found
himself in vision standing in the council of God, overheard God ask
for a messenger, and leapt unhesitatingly to offer his service. He was
given a message to which Israel would not listen, a vision at which
they would not look, and a proclamation of destruction.

[1] There may be confusion between the cherubs, symbols of the invisible
wind, whose outspread wings covered the Ark in the inner shrine of the
Temple, and the bronze seraph or fiery serpent made by Moses (Num. 21.9)
and destroyed by Hezekiah (2 Kings 18.4), but not here condemned by
First-Isaiah.

[2] RSV "earth", but the Hebrew may refer specifically to the land of Israel.
Isa. 40.5 removes the ambiguity with "all flesh".

[3] Cf. J. P. Ross *Vetus Testamentum* XVII, 1 (1967), pp. 76 ff, a discussion of
the meaning of "Lord of Hosts".

As we have seen, for Hebrew thought there is only one primary cause, and a result could be regarded as a purpose. Just as the hardening of Pharaoh's heart was spoken of as caused by God,[1] so the fate of Israel is thought of as caused by God. "The Lord has sent a word against Jacob, and it will light on Israel" (Isa. 9.8), and as Pharaoh's rejection of God's word left his heart harder, so recalcitrant Israel will grow less sensitive and less able to respond. But the word whose rejection brings judgement, as certainly brings salvation if accepted. Isaiah believed that God's plan and counsel was salvation (14.24ff), and here too at the close of the vision there is possibly a gleam of hope. There might be sap and vitality in a tree's root when shoot and trunk were cut down, and a purged remnant might persist after cities had been laid waste and people removed far away.[2] As to Abraham and Moses, the first great prophets, God has revealed his purpose to a prophet, but not here apparently that he should intercede for the people but that he should co-operate in God's plan. Later the prophet is able to proclaim the reversal of the judgement. Eyes will not be closed, ears will hearken, and hearts understand (32.3ff).

Because of the vagueness of both the details and the dating of the vision, it is sheer conjecture to try to connect it with any particular festival[3] or even to speak of the prophet as actually in the Temple itself.[4] It is a vision of the ideal Temple whose confined space extends without limits to be the place where the majestic Lord of Hosts can be enthroned. From the vision we see the prophet's belief in the central importance of the Temple and Zion in which it stands, the grandeur and holiness of the divine king of Israel, the doom on a sinful people, and the hope that a remnant, however small, will return to him.

## ZION

This central significance of Zion is the theme of the poem on its wonderful elevation (2.1ff). In Zion is the dwelling-place of God. When the prophet speaks briefly of God as localized in Zion (8.18), basic to his thought is Jerusalem of the vision and of the poem, centre of the whole world to which the nations flow to hear God's guidance. The Lord has founded Zion, so that the afflicted of his people can take

---

[1] Cf. above, p. 41.
[2] Following RSV translation of the difficult Hebrew of 6.13, which is not in LXX.
[3] Cf. I. Engnell, *The Call of Isaiah* (Uppsala Universitet Arskrift, 1949).
[4] M. Buber, *Prophetic Faith* (1949), p. 127.

refuge there (14.32; cf. 27.13). He will protect it (37.35), and though all the nations were to come in tumult against it, they would fall, defeated not by human armies but by the power of the Lord (31.8). A story is told of just such a miraculous deliverance of the city besieged by the mighty force of Sennacherib, the Assyrian king (37.36ff).[1] The fire of the Lord is in Zion and his furnace in Jerusalem (31.9; cf. 10.17).

That First-Isaiah had proclaimed that Israel's God would prevent Assyria capturing the city is implied by the words put into the mouth of the Assyrian commander (37.10), and there is no question but that the prophet believed that the powerful Lord of Hosts could lop the Assyrian boughs with terrifying might (10.32), and save the remnant of Judah.

## GOD AS KING

It is significant that First-Isaiah uses the title "king" of the mighty Lord of Hosts (6.5). He does not employ the phrase, found in Second-Isaiah (52.7) and often linked by scholars with annual enthronement rites, "The Lord is become king". But his absolute title, The King, used in parallelism with the Lord of Hosts, goes beyond Samuel's claim (1 Sam. 12.12) that the Lord is king of Israel. Not the great king, the king of Assyria (Isa. 36.4), nor Ahaz or Hezekiah, but the Lord rules, and his will is paramount over Israel's fortunes. In the vision of the future, above sun and moon and the host of heaven, and above the kings of the earth, it will be the Lord of Hosts who will reign on Mount Zion and in Jerusalem, revealing his glory to his elders (24.23). He has no rival as judge, ruler, king, and saviour (33.22), and the poet who sings of a king who will reign in righteousness (32.1) and who will be seen in his beauty in the background of a land stretching to the far horizon (33.17) probably refers to the divine ruler.

## HOLINESS

Probably the most important quality ascribed to God in the vision is that of holiness. It is a divine attribute we have seen in the Law, which requires safeguards because of its dangers to human contact, made clear in the Former Prophets in the story of Uzzah (2 Sam.

[1] There does not seem to be enough evidence to decide whether it was the experience recounted here that gave rise to the belief in the inviolability of Zion, or whether, as von Rad suggests, this belief goes back to a still earlier tradition of Jerusalem (op. cit. II, pp. 156f).

6.6ff). But it is a divine quality that men can be expected to acquire by obedience to regulations for ritual purity (Lev. 19.2). First-Isaiah lacks nothing of this reverence before the holiness of God, but he has a new concept in which this holiness reveals itself, not in apparently automatic and capricious acts that claim to itself anything or anyone profane who touches a holy object, but in righteous acts that demonstrate God's close link with Israel (Isa. 5.16). Hence he often uses the title Holy One of Israel, as expressing not only God's holiness but his close connection with his people.[1]

## The Promised Son

The prophet's intervention in politics is clearly based on both these attributes of God. National policy must be framed on religious lines to embody God's will, not the king's intrigues, for to First-Isaiah God shows himself concerned not only with men's life within the city, but with the king's conduct of state affairs. A threat from neighbouring kings of Israel (the Northern kingdom) and Syria showed, as the historian in the Former Prophets makes clear (2 Kings 16.7ff), that the king had no trust in the power of Judah's God nor in a unique link between him and his people. The prophet is sent to the king with a demand for trust in God in the face of inevitable disaster. Sometime, perhaps years before this, First-Isaiah had prophesied disaster by naming his son "A remnant will return" (or be converted, cf. Amos 4.6ff). Now he goes to the frightened king with this embodied prophecy, and with the prediction that this feared threat against Judah will fail if the king relies on simple, childlike trust in God; but that a much greater disaster is coming from which only a small remnant will be saved. Four short threats, introduced by the phrase— here ominous—"In that day" speak of Assyrian invasion and a devastated land (Isa. 7.18, 20, 21, 23).

Further, as a warning to the royal house the prophet announces God's "sign", the proof that he has begun to act. A young woman already pregnant will have a son and call his name Immanuel—God is with us (7.14). The warning lies in the "us", in contrast to the house of David which is not willing to obey God—the "us" may well be the converted remnant who trust. The same double message springs from the next dramatic prophetic act of begetting a son by the prophetess. Assyria will hasten, spoil, and plunder, but those who can

[1] 30.11 shows that those who opposed him were tired of his reiteration of the phrase.

m God is with us, those to whom God is a sanctuary, not a stone stumbling (8.14), will see the foreign invaders broken in pieces (0.8ff). The name Immanuel, and the thought it expresses—"the Beyond in our midst"—seems original to First-Isaiah,[1] and is the first of a series of promises concerning the future that cluster round a baby or a "little child" (11.6).[2]

Another prophecy speaks of a son (9.6f) whose birth marks a great change from the gloom and anguish of part of the Northern kingdom, in the former times, to its honour in the latter time (9.1).[3] The armed might of the oppressor has been broken, and the new prince on whose shoulder government rests is given four names, Wonderful Counsellor, Godlike Warrior, Eternal Father, Prince of Peace. There is to be no end to the increase of his peaceful government over the Davidic throne and kingdom to confirm it with justice and righteousness, the two qualities which the prophet teaches will redeem Zion (1.27).

The next great promise (11.1–9) comes after other prophecies whose climax is the sudden intervention of the Lord of Hosts, lopping the mighty Assyrian empire like an overgrown cedar of Lebanon. But in contrast to the lopped Assyrian stock, a new shoot will grow from the stump of Jesse. The spirit of the Lord will rest on the new shoot, endowing him with the sixfold gifts of the spirit, of which two—counsel and might—are possessed by the prince with four names (9.6). Righteousness too is stressed as one of his characteristics, and his peace extends to all creation, animal and human, for by his judgement all the wicked are slain; he will have no need of military force, (11.4), for his mouth will be like a sharp sword (cf. 49.2), and with the breath of his lips he will slay the wicked. A similar picture of an ideal ruler, here as in 32.1ff no longer necessarily a child, recurs in the oracles against Moab (16.5).

All these passages express the prophet's concept of the ideal ruler, which is the basis of the messianic faith. It is significant that he is not called "king" (except 32.1–8), for the Lord alone is king. Further, these prophecies are in terms of a new beginning, perhaps because the prophet regards the present monarchy as so corrupt that unbroken succession is unthinkable, and a return must be made to the primitive

[1] Amos 5.14 and Mic. 3.11 apparently warn leaders and people against basing a false security on misunderstanding of this assertion of God's presence.

[2] For a discussion of this section of Isaiah, cf. J. Lindblom, *A Study on the Immanuel Section of Isa. 7.1—9.6* (1958); Bentzen, op. cit. II. p. 108; N. K. Gottwald, *Vetus Testamentum* (1958), pp. 36ff.

[3] This contrast between former and latter times is frequent in Isa. 40ff.

simplicity of Jesse before the splendours of David and Solomon. Although, as we should expect after the Davidic dynasty had continued in Judah for so many centuries, the prophet speaks of David's throne and tent (16.5), "tent" too suggests simplicity, and implies drastic modification of any religious tradition of an exalted Davidic figure. The contemporary prophet Micah (5.2) also looks back to the shepherd's home in Bethlehem, not to the palace in Jerusalem. As Samuel's choice of David from Jesse's family had been surprising, so a new shoot from Jesse's stump will be chosen not as king but as prince, and on this prince will be poured the full glory of the Lord's favour. First-Isaiah's pictures of this gifted ruler are painted on a canvas of suffering. It was the end of the Assyrian oppression that made way for the Lord's empire, and it was a purged remnant (cf. 4.3f) left in Zion and Jerusalem who returned to trust in God (30.19).

Two points are of particular interest in these prophecies—the stress on the child or baby, and the belief that his coming is present and contemporary. Idealism clustering round the figure of a leader, later so important in the hopes of a Messiah,[1] as formulated in First-Isaiah is clearly concerned with a child who has been born (9.6), or is expected in the future (11.1) and is there linked with prophecies of the day of the Lord's blessing (11.10f).[2] He is a political as well as a religious figure, but one who is endowed with the supernatural power of God's spirit. Associated with this picture of a spirit-filled child is that of the little child who leads the wild beasts tamed.

The stress on a little child or a new-born leader may, as we have seen, express the prophet's belief in the necessity of a completely new start. On the other hand, it may spring naturally from the complex of his ideas on faith, and be comparable to the New Testament saying, "Unless you turn and become like children, you will never enter the kingdom of heaven" (Matt. 18.3).[3]

The second matter of interest is the emphasis on the contemporary character of the leader and the change. It has been said that Isaiah was the first Christian prophet, because to him the Messiah was a contemporary.[4] The birth of the Messiah to him is a present

[1] Cf. Mic. 5.2; Jer. 23.5f; 33.15f; Isa. 61.1f; Zech. 9.9f.

[2] It is wrong to import the idea of "end of Time", or eschatological hopes. This is a hope for the near future, and will bring conditions thought of as wonderful or miraculous.

[3] In either case it seems difficult to find such a close dependence on a David and Jerusalem tradition as is postulated by von Rad.

[4] A. Neher, op. cit.

experience. Immanuel is already conceived, so in nine months God's presence will be realized by some of Israel. The wonder-child is born and is called by the four names.[1] If we accept the historical setting of the Immanuel passage, it must be a prediction made *c.* 734 B.C.; other passages are undated, and many scholars regard them as later additions to the eighth-century book. However this may be, possibly they were uttered after the "remnant" of Israel had become a reality through the Assyrian destruction of the north and much of the south[2] and express the prophetic vision of the future imminent after the suffering of war and invasion. Certainly through them gleams the prophet's faith and belief in the miraculous power of God.

Not only is the leader contemporary, but the remnant too is really present, so that the fall and return of Israel, catastrophe and salvation are both actual in the present, salvation being itself within the catastrophe, as the new shoot is within the complex of stump and root. A similar concept may be discerned in the story of the destruction at the time of Moses, when some died and some lived through (Exod. 32.33ff). God's saving intervention is not simply a future expected event, nor is it for all the people. Jerusalem and the remnant have been saved from the Assyrians. But there is a sense in which salvation has to be appropriated to be effectual. The teaching has to be written on a tablet and inscribed in a book for a rebellious people (Isa. 30.8). God is waiting to be gracious (30.18) till they repent and rest, finding their strength in quietness and trust. The message was the same to Ahaz. Unless he trusted, he could not be nourished and grow strong (7.9), and the prophet had to bind up the testimony among his disciples, waiting for the Lord "who is hiding his face from Jacob" (8.16f).

Religiously, the concept of a God who waits and hides is extremely important. His character is the same as that dramatically revealed to Moses (Exod. 34.6), merciful, gracious, patient; but man's lack of quiet, restful trust inhibits God's exercise of this character even to the righteous remnant. The God who hides his eyes from looking at blood-stained hands (Isa. 1.15) will hide his face so that Israel cannot see him, and even the righteous prophet can only wait in hope (8.16), till, though they have the bread of adversity and water of affliction, their eyes again see their Teacher and they hear his guiding voice

---

[1] Scholars' interpretation of the verbs as future—or prophetic—perfects seems to spring from theological reasons rather than from syntax.

[2] 11.1 follows upon the prophecy of the destruction of Assyria; 11.12 may suggest the period of Second-Isaiah.

(30.20). Perhaps it is in such a time of alone-ness that the prophet cries, "Look away from me . . . do not labour to comfort me for the destruction of . . . my people" (22.4; cf. 1.4–9), and likens his suffering to that of a woman in childbirth who writhes and cries out in her pangs (26.17f). But in the main this prophet, unlike Jeremiah, does not seem to resent the hurt of his destroyed people, but accepts its necessity, and stands with the saved remnant. First-Isaiah never seems to be baffled by God, but throughout shows the implicit trust he demands from his fellow men. His whole life and teaching is God-centred, and faith means leaving room for the miraculous power of God to act[1] and waiting for the working out of God's plan and purpose (14.24ff).

## Trust

The most important contribution to Old Testament religion made by First-Isaiah sprang from his concept of faith or trust. We have seen this quality in the character attributed to Abraham.[2] The root word in Hebrew is in the English word Amen, used in the sense of true, reliable. It can also be used of pillars that give support to a building. But its most interesting usage is of a mother who supports, nourishes, and nurses a child, and it is this simple meaning that appears to be natural to First-Isaiah. His hopes were expressed in the birth of a baby; he was taunted for the elementary teaching which his opponents claimed they had outgrown. Most clearly the meaning of faith as a baby's relationship to a nursing mother is seen in the encounter between the prophet and King Ahaz, and as so often elsewhere in the prophets, it is highlighted by a play on words. When the Lord's message concludes with: "If you will not believe, surely you shall not be established" (7.9), the English translation obscures the religious significance and insight of the message. Only one Hebrew verb is used (instead of the two in the translation) and there is a play on its causative and passive forms. Its simple form can mean to suckle or nurse; the causative form can mean to suck, and so to cause a mother to suckle or nurse; the passive means to be suckled or nourished. A literal translation would be: "If you won't suck, you can't be suckled."

As a troublesome baby that draws back from the breast cannot be fed by his mother, so the king and his kingdom cannot be supported and strengthened except by reliance on God. God desires the king to be in a living relationship to himself, and the analogy is that of an

[1] 5.12; cf. von Rad, op. cit. II, p. 160.          [2] See above, pp. 19f.

infant contentedly and peacefully taking food at its mother's breast in absolute reliance. The prophet's strong, simple faith brings the message that whatever the opposing might of Syria or Assyria, the king must be as a little child in his relationship to God, for man's hope lies in trust. Later the prophet speaks of the state of security and confident assurance which in the RSV is translated "trust":

> "In returning and rest you will be saved,
> In quietness and trust will be your strength". (30.15)

Just as righteousness[1] and trust are linked together in the Abraham story (Gen. 15.6), so are they complementary in Isaiah's thought: "The effect of righteousness will be peace, and the result of righteousness, quietness and trust" (Isa. 32.17).

[1] Cf. J. N. Schofield, *Introducing Old Testament Theology* (1964), p. 41.

# SECOND-ISAIAH[1]

## Call-vision

Without any introduction that might show time, place, or author, or indicate that about 150 momentous years have elapsed since Hezekiah made his ambivalent comment (Isa. 39.8), we hear that God is bidding the prophet tell those around him to take comfort to a discouraged city (40.1). There is to be a new beginning for a sinful people, who are given the assurance of God's forgiveness. Probably at first this prophet lived in Syria;[2] but after chapter 48 his keen interest in Jerusalem and insight into the thought and suffering of her people suggest that he moved there, perhaps with the first group of exiles who availed themselves of Cyrus' edict (c. 536 B.C.). Cyrus is hailed in glowing terms as the anointed agent of the Lord, his Messiah on on whom his spirit rests, whom he has girded and who will perform his purpose (48.14) for Israel's sake. But abruptly Cyrus ceases to be mentioned, in the same way as another outstanding figure, the Servant of the Lord, disappears.[3] The refrain "There is no peace . . . for the wicked" (48.22; 57.21) divides 40—66 into three parts. Scholars have detected a growing disillusionment culminating in internal strife (63.16; 65.1ff, 13ff) although joy and blessing continue to ring out from a rescued people (55.12ff; 62f).

It is God's own voice that is first heard by Second-Isaiah, persistently (40.1, Hebrew "keeps saying", as 1.11) pleading for messengers to carry comfort to the desolate remnant around the still ruined Jerusalem. Reminiscences from the past echo through the prophet's words. "My people, your God" emphasizes the old covenant relationship (Deut. 26.16ff; Hos. 2.23; Jer. 7.23; cf. Isa. 1.3), "comfort" reverses the "No one comforts her" at the opening of the great lament over Jerusalem in 586 B.C. (Lam. 1.2), the "double" payment implies that Jeremiah's prediction (Jer. 16.18) is fulfilled and finished with.

---

[1] Cf. above, pp. 133f.
[2] Cf. the metaphors of forests, mountains, sea, snow, and rain-fertility.
[3] The plural "servants" appears consistently after 53.

The voice reveals a new prophetic attitude to the inhabitants left round Jerusalem after 597 and 586 B.C. Jeremiah (24.8ff; 29.15ff) had pronounced God's curse on them and prophesied their utter destruction. Ezekiel (33.24ff; cf. 11.15f) had also condemned them and refused to accept their interpretation of the Abraham tradition. Second-Isaiah reverses this attitude of Ezekiel by accepting their claim to descent from Abraham and linking it with the Lord's comfort of Zion (Isa. 51.2f). In the great spiritual height of the book (52.13–53) the people who had been left in the land of Israel are called by their own name for themselves, the "many" (52.14; 53.11f).

A second voice proclaims the building of a straight, level royal road for God's return to the homeland, and the sudden revelation to all flesh of the glory that proves his presence—a wider vision of the glory than that seen by First-Isaiah around the Temple (Isa. 6), or pictured by Ezekiel returning to the rebuilt Temple (Ezek. 43.2ff; 44.4).

The third voice gives the prophet a basic element in his lifelong message: amid all that is temporary and transient, the revealed purpose of God, his word, endures for ever (cf. 55.11; 59.21).[1] In bold progressive imagery the voice declares that all created things, however lovely and precious, are transient as grass; the most faithful human "steadfast love" (RSV its beauty, 40.6) becomes a fragrant memory; and further, even the chosen nation is not an end in itself, but has its place only as fulfilling God's purpose.[2] Excitedly the prophet calls for heralds to proclaim the vision he sees of God himself approaching Jerusalem as a powerful victorious warrior (cf. also 42.13) surrounded by his freed people, and as a shepherd caring for his flock, bringing them back as whole families (40.11).

The vision and voices of Second-Isaiah mark a new era in prophetic preaching. First-Isaiah's ministry had begun with a vision of the glory of the enthroned holy God; but his hopes were mingled with doom, blessing would come only after judgement had fallen. Now, judgement is past, blessing is in the imminent future. Old prophecies have been fulfilled, new events are happening, already happening. Jerusalem is to be rebuilt and the exiled remnant return. Even more important is the fact that God himself is returning with comfort and strength (40.10; 52.7ff). But the central significance of the prophet's message is

---

[1] "And I said," (40.6, RSV following LXX) suggests that these words were part of the autobiography of a call-experience, other possible references being 49.1ff; 50.4ff; 61.1; cf. Lindblom op. cit., p. 192.

[2] Second-Isaiah is very careful in his choice of words, and "my people" (40.1) and "the people" (40.7) refer to the same folk.

that the purpose of the return is the salvation of the world (49.6), that the deliverance may be known to all nations. The God who had been the light of Israel (10.17) will now make restored Israel a light to the Gentiles, a people who are his covenant binding the Gentiles to himself.

## The Concept of God

To Second-Isaiah it is very important that Hebrew religion will become the world religion (56.2–7). The poem in First-Isaiah (2.2ff) reveals a kindred spirit, but Second-Isaiah is the first prophet to teach that God's purpose in restoring Israel is the salvation of the world, and to issue the wide invitation, "Turn to me, and be saved, all the ends of the earth! For I am God, and there is no other" (45.22), an invitation which, as its context shows, sweeps out beyond the dispersed of Israel to the Gentiles. The prophet, however, has not surmounted all nationalism. As in First-Isaiah Jerusalem was to be the centre to which all nations flowed, so in Second-Isaiah Israel will be God's light to the Gentiles and from Israel will go out God's law and instruction for which the Gentiles wait (42.4). Foreigners will rebuild the walls of Jerusalem and their kings will serve Israel (60.10). They will be shepherds and farm-workers so that Israel can become priests and ministers of God for them (61.5f). This world religion is not unqualified universal salvation nor a blessed future for the wicked and rebellious (47.3; 66.4). But whereas for Israel the test is seeking and serving the Lord, for the nations and their leaders it is sometimes spoken of as serving Israel (60.12; but contrast 56.6ff).

As with First-Isaiah, the whole atmosphere of Second-Isaiah is saturated with miracle. There are new roads through the desert, springs and pools of water, trees springing full grown to give shade (41.18f). Second-Isaiah finds evidence of wonder in all Israel's past history, which he links with the creation of heaven and earth: "God created . . . and gives breath to the people upon it" (42.5).[1] When Abraham was childless, God made him many (51.2). The slavery in Egypt (51.9, Rahab; cf. 30.7) was ended by the Lord's miraculous power drying up the sea as a way for "those treated as kinsmen" (51.10). He looks forward to the time when the new spiritual community, founded on Zion, will stand as a shining miracle before the world "and the glory of the Lord shall be your rearguard" (58.8). Their light will shine before men, who will glorify the Father in heaven

[1] "People" takes the place of "man" (Gen. 2.7). For the significance of "people" as used by Second-Isaiah, see below, p. 161.

(cf. Matt. 5.16). Equally wonderful to the prophet is God's control of present history, of other nations, their princes and their gods. First-Isaiah had not been impressed by the world-conquering might of Assyria. It was "the rod of God's anger", to be used for his purpose and broken when it vaunted itself against him. Second-Isaiah too, as against the usual Semitic view that the gods of conquerors were the most powerful gods, teaches that Israel's defeat and exile were caused by God's wrath (54.8) and were not a sign that his power was insufficient nor that he had turned against Israel. To Second-Isaiah the next generation of mighty nations to conquer Israel, Babylon and the Medes and Persians, are completely controlled by God. Nations are like the last drop hanging from the rim of an upturned empty bucket, as breath on a scale-pan, as a speck of dust whirled up by the wind. God sees them as of the same proportions as if he were enthroned on the lofty arch of the sky, as mere grasshoppers, just as in the old tradition Israel had thought of herself when about to enter Canaan (40.22; cf. Num. 13.33). The prophet likens the nations to the formless chaos over which the spirit of God hovered before creation began (40.17, RSV emptiness; cf. Gen. 1.2, void). Their princes are no more to be feared than those whom God defeated before Deborah.[1] God blows on them (40.24) as on the Egyptians when the sea covered them (Exod. 15.10). Cyrus, whose swift victories were causing panic among the nations, had been called by God from the east like Abraham. God had anointed him as his chosen, his Messiah, to deliver Israel and rebuild Jerusalem. He was an unconscious agent of the Lord, who had girded him for battle.

Heathen gods cannot be compared with Israel's Lord. Heaping up word-pictures, Second-Isaiah describes the Lord's activity as warrior, ruler, shepherd, as one whose power to grasp every detail of his vast universe passes human comprehension. He knows the measurements of heaven, earth, and seas in spans, quart-vessels full of dust, and handfuls of water, he knows the weight in a balance of mountains and hills. In complete contrast, heathen idols are just lumps of wood or metal skilfully carved and overlaid with gold, highly expensive and quite useless, needing silver chains to hold them in place and stop them tottering (Isa. 40.18ff; 41.7). Sarcastically the prophet pictures the joy of the smith when he finds his nails and solder hold, and says, like the great Creator, It is good (Gen. 1.10). Sometimes these gods are bits of wood left over from domestic fire roughly carved, stuck into the ground and worshipped (Isa. 44.9ff). The prophet uses all his

[1] 40.23; cf. the same unusual Hebrew word, princes, in Judges 5.3.

powers of persuasion, humour, and ridicule to win his fellow-Israelites from attraction to image worship.

First-Isaiah spoke of the Lord as hiding his face from Jacob, and Second-Isaiah's condemnation of Gentile gods suggests that he may be answering a taunt that Israel's God could neither be seen nor portrayed as an image. When foreigners come making supplication to Israel because they realize that God is in her alone, declaration is openly made that Israel's God and Saviour is a God who hides himself (45.14ff). Here the prophet is not thinking like First-Isaiah (1.15) of God hiding his eyes from bloodstained hands lifted to him in prayer, an idea found in a later chapter (59.2f). Certainly the man who seeks God[1] must turn from his wickedness, and Second-Isaiah (55.6f) is deliberately lifting "seeking" completely into a moral context. But at the same time clearly Israel's God is One who hides himself, a God of whom no image can be made, and who must be sought "while he lets himself be found". This concept of the hidden God is still heard in the cry of the small righteous group in the returned community who complain of God's silence and long for him to show himself in a new theophany, rending the heavens again and coming down (64.1, 12). It is doubtful whether there is any suggestion of a God who withdraws from his creation so that men must learn to live as though there were no God; but it is clear that the tension here is not resolved between the God whose aim is to reveal his glory and purpose to Israel and the nations, and the God who hides his saving power. The tension appears starkly in the juxtaposition of titles, "a God who hidest thyself, O God of Israel, Saviour". This tension is firmly resolved in the words of Deuteronomy (29.29): "The secret things belong to the Lord our God; but the things that are revealed belong to us . . . that we may do all the words of this law." Second-Isaiah emphasizes that God, who reveals his secret to his servants the prophets (cf. Amos 3.7), created the world from chaos before he put Israel in it to seek him and hear the truth. From the beginning he has not spoken in secret (Isa. 45.19; 46.10; 48.16). He expresses the same attitude in striking imagery (55.10ff). God's ways and thoughts compared with man's are high as heaven is above earth, but from heaven rain comes down to make earth bring forth and sprout. Similarly, God is far above man's comprehension, but from him the revealing word comes through the prophet for a specific purpose. Revelation always has an aim, and man must not only accept the revelation but

[1] The word "seeks" is used in the Law of ritual inquiry (cf. Exod. 18.15; Deut. 17.9).

seek to discover its purpose. "It is the glory of God to conceal things, but the glory of kings is to search things out" (Prov. 25.2). Much of Second-Isaiah's account of this unobtrusive God ascribes to him ceaseless activity in the present.[1]

The Lord's control of nations is matched in the prophet's thought by his miraculous power over nature, a power unlimited by any natural laws formulated by human observers, and exercised directly without any human mediation. The Lord of the hosts of heaven and earth created the stars, knows their names and number, and by his great might keeps each one on course (40.26). He is still creating, (41.20), he creates new heavens and a new earth (65.17). He creates light and darkness, peace and evil (45.7); and salvation and righteousness are both his creation.

The prophet delights to think of God as creating, and, in one of his most startling statements on God's whole plan for his universe, links the old religious lesson taught to youth of God's founding the earth (40.21, cf. above, p. 5) with the thought of God's choosing Israel—two acts of equal significance: "stretching out the heavens, and laying the foundations of the earth, and saying to Zion, 'You are my people' " (51.16). All three verbs[2] for "create" found in the two creation stories in Genesis Second-Isaiah hears God apply to Israel—sons and daughters whom I created for my glory, whom I formed and made (43.7).

First-Isaiah had been a statesman, challenging kings and rulers and carrying his faith in the majestic divine king into national politics. Second-Isaiah is a poet using his great gifts of language and imagination to proclaim that the Holy One of Israel is creator and sustainer of the whole universe, controller of human affairs and of nature. It is often claimed that he was the first prophet to proclaim an explicit monotheism; it might be more accurate to say that no other prophet proclaims monotheism so often or in such striking terms. There is a clear statement that the Lord is the only God and beside him there are no other gods (43.10; 45.5f, 18, and often), and the ascription of creation to him leaves no room for others. Persistently the Lord challenges other nations to prove the real existence of their gods by showing their power to predict the future and to interpret the past (41.21, etc.). But Second-Isaiah is here only making explicit what had

---

[1] RSV frequently translates the prophet's present participles as present indicatives—cf. 40.22, "who sits", "who stretches", "who spreads", for "sitting", "stretching", "spreading"—and thus does not, like the prophet, suggest continuous and inclusive activity.

[2] "Create", "mould", "make"; cf. pp. 5f.

been implicit in the teaching of earlier prophets. In the book of Amos the Lord is spoken of as controlling the heavens and the underworld (9.2f). First-Isaiah used the Canaanite phrase "rider on the cloud" (Isa. 19.1), regarded him as controlling Assyria, and called other gods by an ambiguous word that means "little gods" or "worthless things".

It is true that there is no more stirring presentation of God as creator than is proclaimed by Second-Isaiah, but his serene, confident monotheism does not begin with awareness of the Creator whom he equates with Israel's God. Rather, he recognizes in Israel's God universal and timeless significance. God is free from time, as both beginning and outcome (44.6). The title Holy One of Israel, used by First-Isaiah, Second-Isaiah treats as a well-loved proper name (40.25) for him who created the host of heaven, who is Creator of Israel and their king (43.15). He encourages a despondent people with the thought that the never-failing strength of the great Creator is available to them, they are not hidden from the one who created the far ends of the earth. Second-Isaiah closely links creation with salvation, and just as God is continually creating, so he is continually delivering; thus the Deliverance of Israel from Egypt long ago is of the same kind as her deliverance now from exile. At the beginning, the voice told the prophet that amid all the transience of earthly things "the word of our God will stand for ever" (40.8), and this perception is central to his message. He declares to Israel the promise of the compassionate Lord, that, though mountains depart, his steadfast love will not depart from them (54.10). The Lord proclaims that earth will wear out like a garment, but his salvation is for ever (51.6; cf. 45.17; 55.3), an everlasting salvation. This salvation is more important than all created things.

The comfort the prophet brings to his people is enhanced by the most startling name he uses for God, the name Next-of-kin.[1] When he calls the Holy One of Israel her Next-of-kin (41.14; 54.5) he emphasizes again the bond between Israel and God. As in holiness the Lord binds Israel to himself, so does he bind her in kinship. She is to be redeemed—made next-of-kin—by the Holy One and called a holy people (62.12). It is Second-Isaiah's most characteristic appellation for God, occurring thirteen times in 40—66 and only once elsewhere in the prophetic literature (Jer. 50.34), and the cognate verb he uses almost as frequently of the Lord's action on behalf of Israel. Basically it is like "father", a word denoting a family relationship, but with greater stress on the duty of a kinsman to assist his less

[1] RSV Redeemer. The title is applied to Boaz as near kinsman of Ruth.

fortunate relatives.[1] When in the patriarchal narrative Jacob blesses
Joseph's sons, he recalls that God through his angel has treated him
as next-of-kin in all his adversity (Gen. 48.16, E).

The word is used of the Lord's Deliverance of Israel from Egypt in
the song of Miriam (Exod. 15.13) and in the theophany to Moses
(6.6, P). Second-Isaiah uses it with the same nuance, reminding
Israel, whether in exile or in poverty around ruined Jerusalem, that
the Lord has pledged himself to rescue them from all their distress.
The linking of the implications of this word with the law-court and
with any thought of a purchase-price being paid is quite secondary
(cf. Isa. 43.3). Primarily it belongs to the family circle, and the story of
Ruth and Boaz (Ruth 4.6ff) shows that the kinsman's duty[2] was not
legally enforceable. More than "Father and son", it expresses God's
gracious, voluntary acceptance of a relationship. It is his unconditional promise of help (Isa. 41.14), and carries with it forgiveness of sins,
blotting them out or dispersing them as the sun disperses thick cloud,
so that man can return to him who is his Nearest Kinsman (44.22).
Once the title is used in parallelism with the marriage relationship
found so clearly in Hosea and Jeremiah, "For your Maker is your
husband, the Lord of hosts is his name; and the Holy One of Israel is
your Redeemer, the God of the whole earth he is called" (54.5).

The more usual imagery from family life Second-Isaiah also uses to
express the relationship between God and Israel. There is marriage
and divorce (50.1), the picture of God calling his sons and daughters[3]
from the end of the earth (43.6), and the analogy of the mother who
cannot forget the child she is suckling (49.15), a mother who comforts
her child (66.13). When he speaks of the nursing mother, the prophet
is very close to First-Isaiah's complex of thought on faith (66.11ff).[4]

## Attitude to the Cult

First-Isaiah believed that God dwelt in the Temple at Jerusalem and
would defend it against foreign foes, but scathingly rejected its
sacrifices and festivals. Jeremiah explicitly stated that animal sacrifice
and child sacrifice had never been commanded by the Lord, and that
though God had a special relationship with Jerusalem—his name

[1] Cf. O. Procksch, *Theologisches Wörterbuch zum Neuen Testament* IV,
p. 381.
[2] See below, p. 326.
[3] Given equal status with sons; cf. above, p. 50, n. 2
[4] Cf. above, pp. 149f, and van der Leeuw, op. cit., p. 99.

dwelt there—now he was about to destroy it. Ezekiel also believed that God had caused the destruction of Jerusalem and its Temple, but he accepted as God-ordained its institutions and sacrificial ritual, and prophesied the return of God to a rebuilt Temple and its institutional life. Second-Isaiah seems to look towards a religious unity that makes this conflict of ideas outmoded. His is not a delicately balanced compromise after long discussion and intricate give and take, but religion on such a different level that much that was disputed has become irrelevant. It was the suffering of Israel that had as its outcome God's forgiveness, not animal blood on an altar (40.1f; cf. 44.22f). The God worshipped by the prophet was so great that not all the trees and beasts of Lebanon could provide a worthy sacrifice (40.16). He says that, though the sacrifices condemned by First-Isaiah had ceased, Israel's sins had continued, yet without reference to altar or sacrifice God had blotted them out for his own sake (43.23ff). At the end of the book there is the strongest statement of the irrelevance of Temple and sacrifice found anywhere in the Old Testament, "What is the house you would build for me? . . . All these things my hand has made. . . . This is the man to whom I will look, he that is humble and contrite in spirit. . . . He who slaughters an ox is like him who kills a man; . . . they did what was evil in my eyes and chose that in which I did not delight" (66.1–4). This negative attitude to the whole cultus is not found elsewhere in the post-exilic Old Testament literature, and represents a complete break with a certain part of the past.

Such wholesale condemnation, however, is not the only voice heard. There was bound to be increasing stress on institutionalism as the returned community became established, and many words of warning and advice show the prophetic attempt to resolve the tension between an ideal holy people in direct relationship with the Holy One, and an actual human society struggling with obstinate problems. Even apart from this, right from the first a clean break with the past is certainly not consistently envisaged. Zion, the holy city, is to be rebuilt (54.11; cf. 44.28), and no uncircumcised shall enter there (52.1). Ritual purity is essential for those who carry the vessels of the Lord (52.11; cf. 66.20). Keeping the Sabbath is in parallelism with keeping the hand from evil and with holding fast God's covenant (56.2, 4). But warnings are extended to those over-zealous for religious rites. Fasting is not an end in itself (58.6). Similarly, there are right and wrong ways of keeping the Sabbath (58.13; cf. 66.23, where Sabbaths and new moons still appear associated together). The whole book of Isaiah closes with a picture of Israelites brought back from exile,

taken irrespective of their family descent as priests and Levites to lead
the worship of all flesh. Month by month, and Sabbath by Sabbath as
they come to worship, all will be reminded of the fate of those who
rebel against God, and perhaps go away saying, There but for the
grace of God go I.

As we have seen, this book looks toward unity. In an all-inclusive
prophetic vision, the Temple is called "a house of prayer for all
peoples" (56.7). All who do justice and righteousness and join themselves to the Lord, whether Israelites, foreigners, or those who have
been ritually excluded (56.4ff; contrast Deut. 23.1ff) God will bring
to his holy mountain, make them joyful in his house of prayer, and
their burnt offerings and sacrifices will be accepted on his altar.

## The Servant of the Lord [1]

From Second-Isaiah is missing any reference to the child or young
prince and ideal ruler. It is the people who are to be born. The barren
wife is surrounded by children (54.1ff) and Zion, torn by internal
hatred in the post-exilic period, will miraculously bring forth a male
(66.8) like a land born in a day or a nation at one time. Similarly, the
focus shifts from the individual to the community [2] when the promise
of the sure mercies to David as God's witness, leader, and commander
for the peoples is transferred to all the new inhabitants of Jerusalem
(55.3). The "remnant" of First-Isaiah has also gone except when God
pictures himself as a midwife or everlasting father, taking the house of
Jacob and all the remnant [3] of Israel from birth and always supporting
them down to old age (46.3); to whom this "remnant" refers here is
not clear.

At least four main groups contemporary with the prophet could
lay claim to the title "remnant of Israel", for the two great historical
disasters had split both northern and southern kingdoms into two
parts. There were the descendants of exiles from the northern kingdom, and of those who had been left in the land in 721; and there were
the descendants of exiles from the southern kingdom, and of those left
in Judah after 586 B.C. Second-Isaiah seems to use Jacob/Israel for all

---

[1] For literature and full discussion of the whole problem, see C. R. North,
*The Suffering Servant in Deutero-Isaiah*, and H. H. Rowley, *The Servant of
the Lord.*

[2] Perhaps stressing again the original significance of "Branch", see above,
p. 141.

[3] Here the word is a derived form of the Hebrew word found in First-
Isaiah.

or any of these groups, as though to him ideally Israel is one unit. But in the early chapters at least he seems to make a main distinction between those outside the land of Israel and those within it. For those left in the land he uses the word Jerusalem/Zion and "my people". For those in exile outside the land he uses a plural address. Such a distinction is clear in the opening verse (40.1), where "my people", in parallelism with Jerusalem, is a concept in the singular, and the imperative "comfort" is in the plural.

Instead of the anointed young leader and the remnant, Second-Isaiah speaks of the Servant. In the Old Testament this word is often used as a title of honour, denoting someone chosen by God or the king, and specially trusted—just as today a position of responsibility is implied by the phrase "a public servant". First-Isaiah uses it once of David as the Lord's servant for whose sake he will defend Jerusalem (37.35), and once it is used of the prophet himself (20.3). Second-Isaiah uses the word often, frequently in parallelism with "chosen". Until the eighteenth century, the Christian Church treated the term simply as equivalent to Messiah or Christ; but when scholars separated 40—66 from First-Isaiah, Christian scholars tended towards the view in Judaism, that Israel, whether actual or ideal, is meant. Since Duhm it has been generally agreed that there are four particularly outstanding poems or Servant Songs, "a connected cycle of poems". Opinion is not unanimous as to the number of songs[1] or as to their extent, but they are usually cited as 42.1–4; 49.1–6; 50.4–9; 52.13—53.12.

It has been rightly said that no statistical word analysis has been able to dispel the impression of a stylistic unity in the songs themselves, or to suggest that they do not derive from Second-Isaiah himself. No other prophet displays throughout the same power over language, nor the same interest in ways of making his meaning clear to his contemporaries. He shows knowledge of all the traditions of Israel's past—creation, patriarchs, Deliverance, David and Zion—as well as of her rich liturgical forms. He may also have pondered the meanings haltingly expressed through the cruder rituals of Babylon or Syria—the idea of the dying and rising god in the Tammuz fertility cults, and the humiliation of the king at the New Year festival. All this has been taken up into his attempt to understand God's purpose in the suffering of Israel. It is reasonable to think that a poet who always regarded his gifts of the disciple's tongue and ear (50.4f) as God-given, and believed that God had made his mouth like a sharp

[1] O. Procksch, following Delitzsch, adds a fifth song, 61.1–3.

sword (49.2) should, while continuing to meditate on his favourite concept "Servant", have filled it with the deeper spiritual meaning that age and experience gave. In the Songs some of the diffuseness of expression is gone; he says less, and means more.

Scholars are not agreed whether the usage of the term "Servant" is consistent throughout 40—55; nor whether it refers to the community as a collective figure, either Israel or a part of it, or suggests an individual identified with a great figure of the past or from mythology, with the prophet himself or a royal figure in the present, or with the ideal Messiah of the future. Much of the difficulty is solved if we remember the fluidity of both Hebrew and modern thought, and the ease with which groups can be given personal names, and persons looked on as typical of groups. The individual and the community in Second-Isaiah's thought are often inseparable.

Though it is of course possible that there have been later alterations of the original text, we start here from the belief that the prophet used the word "Servant" with his customary verbal skill, that the ambiguity is deliberate and rises from a blending of features from many sources. He is making an appeal to all the groups of divided Israel with their peculiar traditions and loyalties. Clearly, elements in the composite figure have associations with the life-story and teaching of Jeremiah and Ezekiel; and traditions of great figures of the past, Abraham, Jacob, Moses, the Davidic monarchy, modified through contemporary thought, show themselves as living and significant in the concept of the Servant.

He is first introduced (41.8) as "Israel my servant, Jacob whom I have chosen, the offspring of Abraham my friend". In contrast to the Gentile nations panic-striken at the victories of Cyrus, he is in a special relationship to God, who upholds him. They have no prophets nor do they worship the living God, but only cling to vain delusions and useless idols (41.28f). At this point appears the first Song, where God presents his Servant[1] who is chosen and endowed with his spirit to reveal, quietly and unobtrusively, true religion to the waiting Gentile world. God, the only creator and sustainer, defines his Servant's task as bringing light to the whole world, and being the covenant bond which binds them to Israel's Lord (42.1–9). A paean of praise from Jew and Gentile breaks out at the Lord's gracious announcement (42.10–17).

From this ecstasy of praise, the prophet turns to the actual Servant and describes him in terms associated with First-Isaiah's reproach to

[1] The LXX in 42.1 adds Jacob and Israel.

Israel. He is blind and deaf (42.18; cf. 43.8ff) and does not u
stand his mission as God's witness to the world. He is, howevₑ,
repeatedly assured of God's special favour ,and that the conquests of
Cyrus have been planned for his sake (43.14; 45.4).

In the second song the Servant himself speaks, describing his call,
in phrases similar to those of Jeremiah (1), as being called from the
womb "to raise up the tribes of Jacob and restore the preserved of
Israel" (49.6). Like Jeremiah, he feels he has laboured in vain, only to
find that he too like Jeremiah (Jer. 12.5)[1] is given a greater task, to
bring God's salvation to the ends of the earth.

Personal experience expressed as autobiography is continued in the
third song.[2] He has faithfully used the prophetic gifts with which God
has endowed him, the disciple's tongue and ear, and God had promised to confirm his Servant's word (cf. Isa. 44.26). But he has met only
suffering and rejection, and he appeals to those who fear the Lord and
obey the voice of his Servant. This experience of deep personal suffering persists into the fourth song.

The setting of this final song in its context is highly significant. The
Lord has made his momentous announcement that puts the choice of
Zion as his people into the framework of creation (51.16). Immediately, Zion is called on to rouse herself and put on festal garments, ready to receive the herald who speeds to tell her that her God
has become king and is returning to Zion. All the ends of the earth
will see his salvation. Those still in exile are given their final urgent
summons to return, purified and bearing the vessels of the Lord.

In confident unhasting procession (52.12) they are to stream towards Zion, the Lord himself leading them and being their rearguard. Suddenly he points to his Servant, hailing him in royal terms,
in language which Jeremiah (23.5) and Ezekiel (34.24) had used for
the promised Davidic leader. He is about to be exalted from the
deeply despised, abhorred position (Isa. 49.7) to the astonishment of
nations and kings (52.13ff). In words used by Ezekiel (17.22f)[3] to
prophesy the survival of the Davidic dynasty, the Servant is likened to
a suckling springing from parched ground, unattractive and despised,
but suddenly recognized as the one who had vicariously borne the
punishment for the nation's sins. By his death the righteous one
brings righteousness to the "many" who had been appalled at his fate,

[1] Cf. below, p. 184.
[2] The word "servant" is not used in 50.4-9, but occurs in 50.10.
[3] RSV "twigs"; cf. Isa. 53.2, "young plant", which is the same Hebrew
word in a masculine form.

and among whom he is to be allotted a portion. The "many" has associations with those survivors left in Jerusalem and its surroundings after 597 B.C., who used the word of themselves (Ezek. 33.23f). In this final poem the contrast between the Servant and the "many" (the Jews in Palestine after 597 B.C.) and the royal metaphor suggest that the Servant was the returning exiles portrayed under the figure of a young innocent Davidic prince who had borne the shame and suffering of long captivity because of the sins of the pre-exile Jerusalem.

But it is impossible to unravel the many threads from the traditions of the past and from contemporary events which the prophet wove to make the pattern of God's Servant, who fulfilled the purpose God wished to achieve through Israel. In the earlier chapters (40—52) God offered his free forgiveness to all groups in Israel, acting as their near kinsman. The dark cloud of their rebellion he has wiped out (43.25; 44.22). It is the Father's welcome to his prodigal son. Zion has sinned and suffered and been forgiven. Now in the final song the prophet moves to a deeper concept of sin and the cost of forgiveness, perhaps indeed moving forward from an idea he had begun to grasp earlier (43.3f). Ezekiel had said that even a righteous man could not intervene to bear the wickedness of the wicked (Ezek. 18.20; cf. 14.14). The Law had no idea of one person bearing away another's guilt (Lev. 19.8; cf. Deut. 24.16) and, as we have seen,[1] sin was not transferred to a sacrificed animal. But in the rituals of the Day of Atonement the sin of the community could be laid on the scapegoat and so borne away into the desert (Lev. 16.21ff). In the same way the Servant is pictured as one who has borne our griefs and carried our sorrows.

To Second-Isaiah as he meditated on the unmerited sufferings of God's righteous Servant came the revelation that it was possible for a Righteous One to suffer willingly, and thus bear the sins of many. God had allowed the life-blood of an animal as the most precious offering from a sinner, to wipe out guilt, and had graciously graded the offering in accord with the sinner's ability to offer. Now the prophet thinks of the Servant as offering not the life of an animal for his own sin, but his own life as the most precious sacrifice for the sin of God's people. Because God accepts his life as a guilt offering, the Servant can become the place where sinners meet with God (53.6, 12).[2] In the New Testament the same pattern of the saving activity of God is woven in the life, death, and resurrection of Jesus of Nazareth, who again reminded men that God is our near kinsman—Father—and who bore in his own body our sins, giving his life a ransom for many.

[1] See pp. 56f, 65 above.          [2] Cf. above, p. 128, n. 2.

# 10 The Latter Prophets: Jeremiah

Jeremiah, whose name is given to the next collection of writings, prophesied for nearly forty-five years, from 626 to 581 B.C.[1] He was a
member of the priestly family at Anathoth, about four miles north of
Jerusalem, in the border country of Benjamin between the kingdoms
of Israel in the north and Judah in the south. His family probably
descended from the Eli priests of Shiloh through Abiathar, who was
High Priest under David but was banished there when Solomon put
Zadok in his place (1 Kings 2.26f). Jeremiah's link with the north
explains his interest in the ancient ruins at Shiloh, in the traditions of
Moses and Samuel as Israel's two great intercessors (Jer. 15.1), and
why his outlook and teaching owe so much to the influence of Hosea,
who had prophesied in the north 150 years earlier. His rural background is clear in many of his prophecies. The difference between
living spring water and that collected in cisterns (2.13), his concern for
the showers and spring rain (3.3), the singing of birds that ceases
when devastation comes to the land (4.25), the wonder of migratory
birds that know unerringly the time when they must depart (8.7), the
neighing of horses (5.8), and the breeding of cattle (2.24) all illustrate
and enrich his religious thinking.

His book, which comes to us probably through the hand of his
friend and secretary Baruch, has three main sections. The first (1—25)
is autobiography, the second (264—5) is biographical narrative in
which some chapters (30—33) contain visions of hope and restoration,
and the third section comprises prophecies against foreign nations.
These final prophecies, which in the Greek version are in a different
place and order, include some written after the fall of Jerusalem in
586 B.C., and some, reflecting the language and thought of Second-
Isaiah, written after the fall of Babylon in 536 B.C. Some parts of these
last two sections, with their emphasis on God's covenant with the
house of David and the renewal of the sacrificial cult, may derive
from another line of predictions and not from Jeremiah.[2]

[1] The murder of Gedaliah (41.2), which seems to close Jeremiah's ministry
in Israel, is not dated, but a third exile in 581 B.C., referred to in 52.30,
seems to have been a punitive purge by Nebuchadrezzar after the murder.

[2] 33.14–26 is not in LXX, but cf. 23.5.

No other Old Testament figure is known to us so intimately as Jeremiah. The first twenty-five chapters of this long book reveal the deep inner conflicts of a tragic, sensitive, lonely soul, who at some time in Josiah's reign was probably uprooted from his native rural home and transplanted in the capital city of Jerusalem, where he always felt himself a stranger. First-Isaiah had condemned the sins of the city against the background of a glowing vision of idealism. To him it was a city set on a hill crowned by the lovely Temple, where God dwelt and from which his glory filled the whole land. To Jeremiah, it had replaced Shiloh, near Anathoth, whose ruins were known to him from boyhood visits. Now Jerusalem was ripe for the same fate. He talks of its streets and squares full of people, he is very conscious that there is a ruling class—princes, priests, prophets, wise men, they all appear in close association with each other (2.8). He accepts the tradition of Zion as the place where God dwells (8.19). But we look in vain for First-Isaiah's realization of the city as a complex unified society where each part makes its own contribution to the life of the whole. What he is aware of is that among the crowds on the streets there is not one man who does not swear falsely (5.2), and that kings, priests, prophets, all the inhabitants of Jerusalem worship sun, moon, and stars and are filled with evil (8.1f; 13.13).

In every street there were altars to shameful deities on which incense was burnt to gods as numerous as the cities that surrounded Jerusalem (11.12f). The streets were full of worshippers not of Israel's Lord but of the Queen of Heaven, probably the Canaanite deity Anath after whom his native town Anathoth was named. It was a family religion, for which children gathered wood, fathers lit fires, and mothers made the flat round cakes (7.18) comparable to clay models which archaeologists have found in the temple at Bethshan.[1] From the near-by Valley of Hinnom went up smoke from fires where infants were being sacrificed (7.30ff). Over all towered the Temple, which since its miraculous deliverance in the days of First-Isaiah had become a magic talisman to the dwellers in the city.[2] Burnt offerings and sacrifices were being offered, communal feasts were being held by people whose lives were full of iniquities, oppression, shedding innocent blood, stealing, adultery, and the open worship of other deities. In all Jerusalem no man could trust his brother or his neighbour, for all of them refused to know the Lord (9.4). Jerusalem to Jeremiah was

[1] Cf. J. N. Schofield, *Religious Background of the Bible*, p. 56.
[2] 7.4; cf. chap. 26, which relates the occasion when the Temple Sermon in 7 was preached.

the city where he was tried for his life (26), put in the pillory (20.1ff),
and where it has been calculated that he spent twenty of his forty-five
years' ministry in prison.[1]

## The Call of Jeremiah

His call came through the word of the Lord in the thirteenth year of
Josiah, king of Judah, 626 B.C. At this time Jeremiah was still a youth
of about the same age as Josiah (1.6; cf. 2 Chron. 34.3) and he may
have been stirred by the reforms of the young king, who the previous
year at the age of twenty had carried out a thorough purge of the
religious life of Judah, Jerusalem, and the northern kingdom as far
north as Naphtali, which would include Anathoth.[2] According to the
Chronicler's story, the altar, stone and wooden images, and the place
of worship at Anathoth would have been destroyed at the time of
Josiah's reform, though the priests themselves were not killed.[3] If the
reformation was so forceful, it would have impressed the priestly
youth, whose family may possibly have moved to Jerusalem at this
time.[4] There is, however, no clear picture in Jeremiah's preaching
of any drastic change in religious life in the land (Jer. 44.4f). Incense is
still burnt to other gods, idols are worshipped (1.16), and fertility
cults are practised on the high places and under green, shady trees
(2.20; 3.2, 6). The only hint of any such reform is found in his final
prophecies, where the women of Jerusalem complain that ceasing to
worship the Queen of Heaven has brought all the disaster upon the
nation (44.18). It is possible that we should accept the later date, 621
B.C., for the reforms of Josiah, and regard the early chapters of Jeremiah as part of the preaching that prepared the way for Josiah's
actions.

Like Samson and Samuel, Jeremiah was marked out for service
before he was conceived, and set apart by God before he was born
(1.5). The poetry here expresses the Hebrew belief that God shares
in all human birth, and especially in the conception of those who later
manifest outstanding spiritual powers—a belief that would find
nothing impossible in stories of the virgin birth of Jesus. The call of
this prophet is told in language intended to link him with traditions of

[1] A. Neher, op. cit.

[2] 2 Chron. 34.2ff; contrast 2 Kings 22f where all Josiah's reforms are con-
centrated in one year, 621 B.C., and regarded as six years later than Jeremiah's
call.

[3] Contrast 2 Kings 23.20, where the priests were killed in 621 B.C.

[4] 2 Kings 23.8, but contrast 23.9.

the great prophet Moses, who also was reluctant to accept God's call because he lacked eloquence. With both men we hear the dialogue between God and the prophet, the prophet regarding his choice as a mistake, and for both, God put his words in his mouth (Jer. 1.9; cf. Deut, 18.18). From the time of his call Jeremiah is concerned not only with Israel but with the nations of the world, and God gives him authority over them, both to destroy and to build up. It is in line with this that later he hears the Lord call Nebuchadrezzar "my servant", whom he has sent against Judah, and announce that seventy years afterwards he will punish Babylon too for overstepping his mark in arrogance (Jer. 25.9, 12).

To Jeremiah, God's word comes through ordinary, everyday objects, without the element of wonder and miracle that lies in Moses' burning bush. Unlike First-Isaiah, he received no splendid vision; but the chance sight of a familiar object suddenly revealed a new truth. Often he had seen the early-flowering almond in the valley bring the promise of spring, and the familiar cooking pot standing on blazing sticks fanned by the north wind (1.11ff). There was no wonder in the object itself, but only in the voice that made it the vehicle of revelation. The name of the shooting almond branch, *shaqed*, calls to his mind the Hebrew participle, *shoqed*, watching, and conveys the message that God is watching over his word to fulfil it—a message emphasized later by Second-Isaiah (40.8; 55.11). Perhaps there is a deliberate association with the message to Moses that the Lord had seen the affliction of his people, for later (31.28), the Lord promises that he will "watch over" the house of Israel.

The second time the Lord asked Jeremiah what he saw, he replied "a boiling pot, facing away from the north"—about to boil over and spread its devastation southward. The message now was that from the north, whence had come so many destructive invasions, God was about to bring new and terrible foes. These enemies from the north are not precisely named; but evidently what is threatened is a great irresistible flood of cruel barbarians, who spare neither sex nor age. These will act as God's judges against Jerusalem and the cities of Judah for their religious sins, forsaking him, sacrificing to other gods, and worshipping idols. But the dominant note is God's presence and power. Like Joshua entering Canaan, the prophet must not be afraid or dismayed, for the Lord will be with him (Deut. 31.8; Josh. 1.9). As a fortified city (Jer. 1.18), he will withstand all assaults when he delivers God's message against the whole land, king, princes, priests, and people.

But the image of the fenced city suggests not only strength but the isolation that is to be the experience of the prophet. His loneliness is shown in his trouble with his own kinsmen at Anathoth (11.21; 12.6), in the fact that he regarded himself as forbidden by God to marry (16.2), and when, because the hand of the Lord was on him, he was separated from the merrymakers and sat apart (15.17). He called himself a man of strife and contention to the whole land (15.10), and felt he was a laughing-stock mocked by everyone, an object of derision and reproach (20.7). In spite of his loneliness, however, Jeremiah was not completely without friends who loyally used their power and influence in his time of need—Shaphan, Gedaliah, and the Ethiopian slave who saved him from death in the dungeon (26.24; 38.7ff; 39.14).

Jeremiah calls the vehicle of his revelation the word, not the spirit, of God. On one occasion he uses the word spirit (*ruach*) of false prophets who "become wind" because the word is not in them (5.13). But the emotional, violent, and almost irrational force linked with spirit possession in the Former Prophets is the continual impetus behind the word of God to him. The metaphorical language he uses of his call might equally express the consciousness of being filled with the spirit. First, the Lord puts forth his hand and puts his words in his mouth, and then, in phrases that might be used by a great king at the installation of an overseer or deputy, he entrusts the prophet with supreme power over nations and kingdoms (1.10). The word is quite irresistible, burning like a fire in his bones (20.9) so that he cannot forbear to proclaim it. Like a hammer it breaks rocks in pieces (23.29). It comes with all the violence of a seducer who is so strong that he prevails (20.7ff). Like food he has eaten, it enters Jeremiah's inmost being—such a metaphor links its action with that of the spirit—and tastes sweet to him (15.16; cf. Ezek. 3.3).[1] It breaks his heart within him, shakes all his bones, and makes him like a drunken man (Jer. 23.9). Through all this turmoil there is one urgent, inescapable message the prophet is bound to make known. God is about to act finally and decisively for the destruction of people, land, and Temple. Only one last chance remains for them, to turn radically from their whole way of life, back to the God who revealed himself when they came out of Egypt.

---

[1] But the LXX does not support the Hebrew metaphor of eating. There, Jeremiah asks that his enemies may be consumed and the word may be to him a joy.

## False Prophets and True[1]

The tragic dilemma of Jeremiah's task becomes clear when we try to contrast his inspiration with that of other contemporary prophets (23.9–40). In the prophets of the north there is folly, they prophesy by Baal and lead astray God's people Israel. The prophets of Jerusalem are worse. They lead evil lives, help evil-doers, and both prophets and people are as wicked as men of Sodom and Gomorrah. They proclaim a vision of their own, not one interpreted by the word of the Lord. They prophesy peace, not judgement, whereas Jeremiah believed that all the true prophets of the past prophesied disaster concerning many countries and great kingdoms (28.8). Continually the Lord had sent his servants the prophets to warn sinful man of the outcome of his way of life (7.25; cf. 25.4ff). Now these popular prophets were trying to heal superficially the wounds of the nation by proclaiming peace (8.11), which was what the people wanted (5.31). Jeremiah had to suffer rejection. Nobody wished to hear a prophecy of doom.

But God has not sent those prophets, nor spoken to them, nor commanded them (14.14), nor have they, like Isaiah, stood in the council of God and overheard him speaking. They preface their message with "I have dreamed" and not "Thus saith the Lord", and their hearers forget the Lord. Falsely they use two characteristic phrases to describe their utterance. They say, "It is an oracle", "It is the burden of the Lord". Emphatically Jeremiah declares that false prophets have no right to claim that they are slaves of the Lord, carrying the weighty burden of his word, when all they have are their own lying dreams and empty boastings. He too on at least one occasion has a dream of joy and hope, but in complete integrity he calls it a dream (31.26).

It was the content of Jeremiah's prophecies, and not his way of delivering them, that distinguished him from his contemporaries. Like the popular prophets and like First-Isaiah, he often expressed his prophecies and made them effective by functional acts. He bought a new linen loin-cloth, wore it to the Wadi Farah outside Jerusalem.[2] There he took it off and buried it in the rocky bank for many days, and when he dug it up it was spoiled and ruined. Israel too, as close to God as the loin-cloth to its wearer, had gone to ruin through the worship of false gods (13.1ff). On another occasion, having bought a potter's vessel, he led a procession of elders and priests to the Valley of Hin-

[1] See above, pp. 118ff.        [2] RSV Euphrates is the same Hebrew word.

nom, scene of child sacrifice (19.1ff). There he smashed the vessel
with the words, "Thus says the Lord of hosts: So will I break this
people and this city, as one breaks a potter's vessel, so that it can never
be mended". He was punished by being beaten and put in the stocks
for the night. When a deputation from the neighbouring kingdoms of
Edom, Moab, Ammon, Tyre, and Zidon tried to persuade Judah's
king to revolt against Babylonia, Jeremiah wore a wooden yoke round
his neck and told the king to submit to the yoke of Babylonia to save
the city and himself (27.2ff). When the official prophet Hananiah
broke the yoke (28.10) Jeremiah was told by God that the wooden
yoke would be replaced by iron. During the final siege of Jerusalem,
when the prophet had been imprisoned by king Zedekiah, a cousin
came to Jerusalem asking him to buy a piece of family land in Anathoth. He "knew this was the word of the Lord", and bought it
because "houses, fields and vineyards shall again be bought in this
land" (32.8, 15). When Zedekiah was summoned to Babylon and took
Baruch's brother with him, Jeremiah sent by him a book concerning
Babylon, to be read and sunk in the Euphrates with the words, "Thus
shall Babylon sink to rise no more, because of the evil I am bringing
upon her" (51.64). And finally, in the sight of the Jews who had fled
and taken him to Egypt, he built a symbolic throne on which Nebuchadrezzar could judge Egypt when he had captured it (43.9f).

Sometimes we watch Jeremiah waiting for long periods before he
received a message from God. When Hananiah challenged his functional prophecy with active opposition, breaking the yoke, Jeremiah
expressed the hope that Hananiah might be proved right, and we hear
him giving a reasoned, rather than an inspired opinion, based on the
history of prophecy. It was "sometime after" (28.12) that he was sent
back with God's reply to Hananiah. On another occasion he had to
wait ten days for God's reply to the loyal Jews who were fearful of
Nebuchadrezzar's vengeance when Gedaliah was murdered (42.7).
Clearly he had no mechanical means of obtaining an oracle, nor was he
able this time to give a reasoned "human" answer, even though the
long, anxious wait made his questioners lose their faith in his integrity
and prophetic power (43.2). From Jeremiah's experience it is clear
that nothing from man's side, not even the prophet's agonized humble
seeking God in prayer, necessarily ensures God's answer. To us, as we
look back on it, it is this silence of God that gives us confidence in the
validity of the prophet's experience. However urgent the issue at
stake, Jeremiah too was silent until God answered him (contrast 1
Sam. 28.6). The popular prophets were always ready to prophesy

peace, and no peace came. Jeremiah was prepared to let events prove
that it was God's word that he had spoken (cf. Deut. 18.22).

## The Teaching of Jeremiah

In spite of all the opposition it brought, this prophet was certain that
he, like true prophets before him, must prophesy doom and disaster,
and so faithfully did he obey the Lord's command that his name has
been proverbial for gloom. Catastrophe could scarcely be more
variously suggested. In vision he hears the noise of horseman and
archer (Jer. 4.29), sword, fire, deportation, and death recur relentlessly,
and he remained in the ruined city till taken out in chains as a captive.
But surprisingly often joy breaks through. There is not a stereotyped
alternation of doom with promise, such as is characteristic of some
prophetic works, but a general impression as if, after visions of hope
recorded in what has been called the Little Book of Comfort (30—
33), the prophet goes back and threads a strand of joy through the
whole pattern.

Scattered throughout are many expressions of joy and the certainty
of salvation, often introduced by the phrase "Behold the days are
coming", and Jeremiah regards his dream of the future as a token to
be later fulfilled.[1] There had been threatening implications behind the
messages he had received at the time of his call, but in these future
days the Lord will be seen as more personal, watching over his people,
not over his word. He will build and plant (31.27f), and Jeremiah
perhaps with a countryman's interest carries the reconstruction back a
stage further, and, like Hosea, talks of the Lord's sowing the land with
man and beast.

The brightest visions of hope and joy within the Book of Comfort
may have sprung from one of his few prophecies of peace made in a
time of deep distress, and so exemplify how with Jeremiah joy comes
through sorrow, and there is a continual movement through conflict,
failure, and suffering into a new creation. He was in prison. The story
stresses that the Babylonian army was besieging the city and the final
assault was about to begin (32.2, 24). It was at this point that he
bought the field in his home town, and foresaw the period of reconstruction which came to pass under Gedaliah, the Jewish noble whom
Nebuchadrezzar made governor after Jerusalem had been destroyed.
Under a new leader, in a new capital at Mizpah, and with the old
sanctuary at Bethel as the new holy place (Zech. 7.2), Jeremiah seems

[1] 31.26; cf. the same Hebrew in Gen. 44.32 (RSV surety).

to have spent five happy years in rebuilding. Probably from this time comes his teaching about the new king, the new covenant, and the miraculous power of God.

This probable background of the Book of Comfort illustrates one of the difficulties in understanding the book of Jeremiah—all his teaching is so closely linked with particular situations and events in his life that to obtain a systematic doctrine this vital link would have to be broken and much of the cogency of the teaching lost. It has been well said that there is no such thing as prophetic doctrine, but lessons are given as history flies on. Sometimes they may appear contradictory.[1] They cannot even be properly called "lessons", for they arise in the excitement of the prophet's experience, and become for him commands to be obeyed, not doctrine to be discussed. There is a constant danger in studying prophetic literature of producing a systematic theology to meet the needs of modern experience, and to answer modern problems that were not the concern of the prophetic age. During Jeremiah's prophetic career many significant moments became the channel for the revelation of the nature and will of God. But while this needs to be stated, and sometimes there seems to be contradiction in the prophet's thought, it must also be recognized that he always speaks from a coherent set of religious ideas built up by a people through centuries of experience, and probably learnt in his youth at home. First-Isaiah's belief that the Temple was inviolable because God dwelt in it is not really contradicted by Jeremiah's agreement with Micah and Ezekiel that when the Temple was defiled by the sin of its worshippers God would leave it, and then its protection and sanctity, like that of the old temple at Shiloh, would go too.[2] The prophets did not attribute to God that foolish consistency which is the hobgoblin of little minds. Though the Lord's thoughts towards Israel were always thoughts of salvation and peace, his ways of working the purpose out were changeable and fluid. It is a constant prophetic idea that sometimes God "repents"[3] and changes his mind.

Most of Jeremiah's teaching concerns the relationship of God and Israel expressed through the metaphors of marriage and covenant, which raise in their turn the difficult problem of the possibility of human repentance, and of vindicating the justice of God's treatment of both the righteous and the wicked. But in order to obtain a whole picture, before we consider these major themes, other aspects of his teaching must be presented.

[1] A. Neher. op. cit., p. 305.     [2] See above, p. 128.
[3] See above, pp. 116f.

In the Book of Comfort there is a picture of the ideal prince, perhaps portraying Gedaliah (Jer. 30.21; cf. Deut. 17.15). He is called a mighty one (RSV prince) or a ruler, and is to be one of themselves; but his main function will be to draw near to God, and God himself will enable him to do this, for otherwise neither he nor any man would risk his life to approach. On another occasion the prophet's hope of a future king arose from his condemnation of the last kings of Judah's royal line (Jer. 22). During his lifetime Jeremiah watched five successive kings disappear in death or catastrophe. Josiah the pious had died in battle, Jehoahaz was deported to Egypt, Jehoiachim may have been slain by the Babylonians, the young prince Jehoiachin (Coniah, 22.24) was taken captive to Babylon with his mother, and Zedekiah too later died there, a blinded captive. We listen to the prophet's estimate of their characters, his dirges over their captivity and death, and his prophecies of exile. But he concludes his condemnation with a prophecy of hope, that God will gather the remnant of his flock and set shepherds over them (23.3ff). Repeating Isaiah's word "Branch", the Lord promises to raise a true legitimate[1] Branch, a rightful heir who will reign as king and act wisely and justly. The new king's name will be The Lord is our Righteousness, or our Loyalty—a name in which appear the two elements in "Zedekiah" (*Zedek, Yahweh*). This new name lights up the startling contrast between him and the present faithless ruler. Zedekiah, brother of the wicked king Jehoiachim, was originally called Mattaniah, and Nebuchadrezzar gave him the name Zedekiah probably to remind him of the need for loyalty and righteousness, a quality of which he later showed himself completely devoid. Just as he broke the covenant with his enslaved fellow-Hebrews (34.16), so he broke his oath to his overlord, bringing down fearful vengeance upon himself and his nation.

As Jeremiah prophesied doom on the monarchy, so he declared that the State in its present form would be destroyed. God had put city and land into the power of Nebuchadrezzar, and he would burn it with fire. First-Isaiah had thought of Assyria as the rod of God's anger, to be used to chastise Israel, but to be lopped down like a mighty cedar before it could harm city or people.[2] Now the Babylonian king as God's agent, his servant, for seventy years would hold the nation in captivity. Israel must accept this situation, "Build houses . . . plant gardens. . . . Take wives and have sons", and found families; "but seek the welfare of the city where I have sent you into exile" (29.5ff). Jeremiah sent this message from the Lord in his letter rebuk-

---

[1] RSV "righteous".                    [2] Cf. above, p. 144.

ing the prophets among the exiles for raising false hopes. The true promises of God are stated in clear contrast.[1] When they call he will listen, when they seek him with their whole heart he will be found by them, and he will bring them back. Reversing the doom Amos[2] pronounced on the virgin Israel, Jeremiah says she will again take part in the merry dance, vineyards will be planted on the hills of Samaria (31.4f), and both Israel and Judah will go to the Lord at Zion. This means that God's dwelling will again be in what had been the Southern kingdom; but it is important to notice that Ephraim in the north will be regarded as God's first-born with all the rights of the eldest son (cf. 1 Chron. 5.1). There will be a new unity in the people, for God will give them one heart and one way. As we saw, Jeremiah has the countryman's simpler view of society with little interest in the city, and though there is to be a ruler or king there is no promise of a new State. What he looks forward to is a reunited people in a replanted land.

Jeremiah shows a countryman's appreciation of the value of ground round a homestead, and the concept "land" is a vital element in his religion. It is plentiful with fruit and goodness, pleasant and given to them as a heritage most beauteous of all nations (3.19), compared with the land of Egypt out of which God brought them and the unsown wilderness where they travelled with him. But the land is ruined and like a desert because they have broken God's law (9.12f), it is withered and mourns for the wickedness of its inhabitants, and nobody minds (12.4, 11). It is the land to which the wretched Coniah and his mother, representing the tragic reigning Davidic dynasty, will never return, and the prophet, answering his own question as to why these things should be, utters the heartbroken threefold cry, "O land, land, land, hear the word of the Lord!" (22.29). The promised land has become barred to Israel until the long weary years of exile have passed.

## The Marriage Metaphor

In the early chapters, the prophet is keenly aware of the promised land as the first home to which God brought his bride from the unsown wilderness. This picture, which is not found in the traditions of the Law, owes much to the earlier teaching of the other northern prophet Hosea,[3] who from his own unhappy experience had applied to the relationship between Israel and her Lord the metaphor of the marriage bond, and though Jeremiah himself was forbidden by God

[1] I know—I have—the I is emphatic, 29.11.
[2] Cf. below, p. 231.     [3] See below, p. 219.

to marry, it is through this picture that he expresses his early teaching. Israel in the wilderness was the youthful, loving bride of God, bound to him with deep and gracious links, keeping herself only to him as firstfruits belonging to him alone (2.2f).

Israel here denotes the prophetic idea of a primitive united people at the beginning of its golden age with the Lord. Later, after the disastrous schism following the death of Solomon, there were two nations, Israel and Judah. In the time of Jeremiah, Israel had been punished for her sins by Assyrian invasion and exile, but there were many survivors still, called by him Israel (e.g. 3.6), an entity distinct from Judah, her sister in the south, who was to suffer a similar fate at the hands of Babylon. But Jeremiah is always looking towards an undivided nation, and sometimes here is using "Israel" to express the full concept of one reunited people.

The blissful early relationship in the wilderness has been changed in a way that neither husband nor wife seems to understand. Like a bride who forgets her wedding-day, gown, and ornaments, Israel has forgotten God days without number (2.32). He pleads with her to explain why she has forgotten even to ask where he is (2.6), why she has forsaken him. Like a slave who does not want to be free, she turns back as in the days of Isaiah to cruel Egypt, not to the Lord for help. In language recalling Isaiah's love-song of the choice vine (Isa. 5; Jer. 2.21ff) that became wild and degenerate, the Lord accuses his nation of utter corruption. With the abandon of an animal on heat, she has chased lovers till her shoes dropped off her feet and her throat is parched with thirst. Ashamed like a thief caught red-handed, she laments that there is no hope for her, that she cannot break her addiction to the fertility cults of Canaan. There seems no possibility of reconciliation. Israel is unnatural and brazen as a proverbial harlot, and will not admit that her conduct is wrong.

But God, her husband, is willing to go to unheard-of lengths to win her back. Proverbially it was said that it was a scandalous thing for a husband to return to his faithless wife who went and lived with another man (3.1ff)—a proverb that is brought into sharp relief against the memory of Hosea's return to his faithless wife. But God is willing to forgive the past and take her back in mercy (3.12). Yet even the example of the fate of her sister Israel in the north brings only a feigned and insincere return.

At this point, Jeremiah turns to the northern remnant in his homeland, whom the Lord addresses as backsliding children and promises that he will bring back to Zion. Using the famous poem quoted by

Isaiah and Micah, Jeremiah pictures all nations gathering to God's throne at Jerusalem (3.17; Isa. 2; Mic. 4) and Judah going to meet the returning remnant of Israel, so that they can come there together. No material representation of God's presence will be necessary (Jer. 3.16, the Ark) for God himself will be enthroned over Jerusalem. Children will come back and call him Father, and however treacherous Israel has been as a wife, and however hopeless it may seem that she will repent, yet, if truly she returns, the promise made generations ago to Abraham will be renewed. Nations will bless themselves by Israel's name (4.2). The conjugal word *baal*, or husband, forbidden by Hosea, is used again here by Jeremiah (3.14, RSV master). For him, as for Hosea, this conjugal relationship means an intimate experience of knowing God. The symbolism of the condemned fertility cults is transformed by the prophets. For individuals as well as for nations life can be a great conjugal adventure.[1] God is not an abstract idea, but Israel's controlling partner, and religion is an experience she shares with him.

## The Covenant Relationship

Though in earlier teaching Jeremiah uses the metaphor of marriage to express the relationship between God and Israel, later he speaks of it more frequently as covenant. Perhaps the thought of Israel as God's bride, deriving from Hosea's experience, came naturally to this prophet from the north. But it is possible that the concept of covenant in this connection was more readily understood and more usual in the south. Certainly the story of the contemporaneous discovery of a book of the law (2 Kings 22.8), called the book of the covenant when formally accepted by king and people in a covenant ceremony (23.2ff), and the formal covenant on behalf of Hebrew slaves made by Zedekiah and all his people with the Lord (Jer. 34.8) show that "covenant" was a contemporary idiom to express the bond between God and people, and in that milieu would be an appropriate one for Jeremiah to use.

Jeremiah was ordered to proclaim "all the words of this covenant" to the men (or cities) of Judah and to the inhabitants of Jerusalem (11.2, 6), and it is clear that it was an age-old covenant that had been broken by their worship of other gods (11.10; 22.9). We have seen this concept constantly in the books of Exodus and Deuteronomy, though it is almost absent from the pre-exilic prophets apart from Jeremiah. It is of interest that on the one occasion when it occurs in

[1] A. Neher, op. cit.

the book of Hosea (8.1) it is in close association with war and disaster, just as we find in the southern kingdom in the time of Jeremiah. Hosea proclaims: "Set the trumpet to your lips, for a vulture is over the house of the Lord, because they have broken my covenant and transgressed my law." Jeremiah is more explicit than Hosea in that he refers apparently to the Sinai/Horeb covenant which God "commanded your fathers when I brought them out of Egypt" (11.4; 31.32; 34.13).

It is usually emphasized that the sudden order to Jeremiah to proclaim an age-old covenant is connected with Josiah's discovery of a law-book attributed to Moses,[1] though it is not explained why it was necessary for Jeremiah to exhort the people after such decisive action, reported in Kings, was carried out by Josiah. To meet this difficulty, it has been suggested that Jeremiah heard God's order to commend the covenant when, at Josiah's death in 608 B.C., Jehoiachim abandoned the reform.

Another historical covenant was of great concern to Jeremiah. When Nebuchadrezzar was besieging Jerusalem, Zedekiah made a covenant before the Lord with the solemn ritual of cutting a calf in two and passing between the parts,[2] while proclaiming liberty to all Hebrew slaves, male and female, in accordance with "a covenant with your fathers when I brought them out of the land of Egypt . . . saying, 'At the end of six years each of you must set free the fellow Hebrew who has been sold to you and has served you six years'" (34.13f). But when the siege was raised, all the slaves were brought back into slavery. The form of this covenant law as Jeremiah cites it includes elements from the Book of the Covenant (Exod. 21.2) and from the code of Deuteronomy (15.12); but the citation follows Exodus in not including female slaves. It was perhaps with an eye to wider appeal to all enslaved persons in a time of siege that these were included in Zedekiah's covenant (Jer. 34.9f), and in any case what actually happened under Zedekiah is what is now laid down in Deuteronomy.

Usually it is held that Josiah's law-book of Moses was some part of Deuteronomy rather than of the Book of the Covenant, and that when Jeremiah speaks of a covenant he means the deuteronomic code; but this in any case is a literary problem. From the religious standpoint, which is here our concern, we notice that the prophet stresses

[1] Often identified with the book of Deuteronomy, but cf. above, p. 124, n. 1.

[2] See above, p. 17.

many requirements like those contained in the Decalogue, particularly that of hallowing the Sabbath (17.19ff)[1] and worshipping no other gods, and emphasizes as do the law codes the blessings and curses that follow acceptance or rejection of God's law, and the necessity for obedience, illustrated by the faithfulness of the Rechabites to their founder (35.18). What emerges from the story of Zedekiah's breach of faith is that Jeremiah regarded all covenants made before the Lord as dangerously binding, and the great covenant made at Sinai/Horeb as containing the law of God and requiring Israel's absolute obedience.

## Attitude to the Cult

There are however cogent reasons against believing that any one pentateuchal law code in its present form represents what Jeremiah meant by "a covenant with your fathers when I brought them out of the land of Egypt" (34.13). The most important of these reasons is the prophet's vehement repudiation of any form of animal sacrifice. First-Isaiah had asked a rhetorical question, "Who required this at your hands?", clearly expecting the reply that animal sacrifice had not been required by God.[2] Jeremiah sarcastically tells the Temple crowds that, if they want a good communal meal of meat, they can add the burnt offering—which should be offered wholly to God—to their sacrificial feasts and eat them both. Clearly and emphatically he states in God's name, "For in the day that I brought them out of the land of Egypt, I did not speak to your fathers or command them concerning burnt offerings and sacrifices" (7.21f; cf. 14.12) and speaks similarly of the burning of children (7.31; cf. 19.5). God's command at the Deliverance was, "Obey my voice, and I will be your God, and you shall be my people" (7.23), the aim of the command being that this relationship should be established: "do all I command you—so shall you be my people, and I will be your God" (11.4). This agrees with the emphatic statement in Deuteronomy that only the Decalogue was commanded at Horeb (Deut. 5.22), but repudiates the sacrificial laws of Deuteronomy, as it also repudiates the law of child sacrifice apparently demanded in the Book of the Covenant.[3]

That the life-blood of an animal could legitimately be used to seal a covenant is clear from the story of Zedekiah's action; but this is not the same as the sacrificial meals legislated for in the law codes.

---

[1] These verses are often denied to Jeremiah, but may reflect his rural outlook already noticed.

[2] See above, p. 137.  [3] See above, p. 37.

Jeremiah's unqualified rejection of animal sacrifices as part of God's requirements from Israel becomes all the more significant when we recognize that he knew of incense offered to the Lord (Jer. 6.20) as well as to Baal (11.13), and of sacrifices and burnt offerings, and of sacrificial flesh (11.15).[1] Burnt offerings are not acceptable to God nor sacrifices pleasing to him. To Jeremiah as to First-Isaiah the sacrificial ritual was not part of the pure primitive worship of the Lord.

## The New Covenant

Of all Jeremiah's prophecies, perhaps the best-known and most influential is that of the New Covenant (31.31ff). In his introduction to this theme he uses again, as in 3.14, the word *baal* for husband (cf. Hos. 2.16). Though God had been a husband to Israel, she had broken his covenant. In this statement the two ways of presenting Israel's relationship to God, marriage and covenant, are combined. Despite the faithless marriage and the broken covenant, God will make reconciliation. There is no divorce nor repudiation of the sinful nation. The steadfast love (2.2, RSV devotion) Israel showed to God centuries before when she was his bride in the wilderness, he shows to her, but with a significant distinction. On his part it is everlasting love, and steadfast love (31.3, RSV faithfulness) that continues.

This New Covenant also will be with the whole people, the House of Israel and the House of Judah. Its purpose is still the binding together of people and God (31.33) and it is still God's law. But it is to be written not on tablets of stone but on men's hearts and put within them. No longer will it be an external law forced on Israel from outside, but it will be willingly accepted so that God's law becomes their way of behaviour. As we have seen, to Jeremiah God's law was of the utmost importance. He seems to use the term here in its most inclusive reference, to sum up all God's guidance for daily life, however mediated, and the way elsewhere he associates covenant law with blessings and curses (cf. 11.3) suggests that he himself acquired knowledge of it at least partly from hearing it recited in home and Temple. This assumption becomes more credible when it is noticed that immediately upon the proclamation of the New Covenant follow verses of a hymn (31.35ff) celebrating the creation[2] and linking creation with God's relationship to Israel.

[1] This obscure question is more intelligible in LXX: "Shall vows and holy flesh cause thy evil to depart from thee?"

[2] Other verses of a similar hymn occur in Amos, see below, p. 232.

Priests regarded the law as belonging to them, just as counsel to the wise and the word to the prophet, and though they did not know God, they grasped at the right to teach the law.[1] When it was reduced to writing, scribes falsified it (8.8), the people had rejected and forsaken it (6.19; 9.13), and all this had caused the destruction of the Temple (26.4ff). When God himself writes on men's hearts, all these blunders will be past and done with. In the days that are coming, the New Covenant proclaims that there will be no need even for oral repetition of the law, for every man great or small will know God (31.34). The barriers of sin will be broken down by his gracious forgiveness, he will give men one mind, and in unity of spirit they will keep the New Covenant. "They shall be my people, and I will be their God. I will give them one heart and one way, that they may fear me for ever, for their own good and the good of their children after them. I will make with them an everlasting covenant" (32.38ff).

## Suffering

The final prophecy, ending this section that contains Jeremiah's future hopes, and in the Greek version concluding all the prophet's words,[2] contains a message that to our own day has rebuked the ambitions and inspired in his frustrations more than one great religious leader. It is the prophet's word from God to his faithful friend Baruch (45) who was probably taken with him into exile in Egypt. It is dated in the fourth year of Jehoiakim, the year when the great scroll bearing all Jeremiah's prophecies against Jerusalem, Judah, and all the nations, written by Baruch at Jeremiah's dictation, was later read publicly and destroyed by the king (36.23). In that same year the map of the Near East was transformed by the defeat of the Egyptians at Carchemish by Nebuchadrezzar, who later was crowned king of Babylon (25.1).

It appeared then to both Jeremiah and Baruch that all the warnings and preaching of the previous twenty-three years were to find their fulfilment. As Second-Isaiah later welcomed Cyrus as the Lord's anointed deliverer (Isa. 45.1), so Jeremiah welcomed the young Babylonian prince with the amazing title "Servant of the Lord" (Jer. 25.9), through whom God would bring the final doom on his people: "This whole land shall become a ruin and a waste, and these nations

---

[1] 2.8 (RSV handle the law). The Hebrew verb is a strong one, meaning to arrest or lay hold of.
[2] In LXX the prophecies about foreign nations, 46—51, follow 25.13.

shall serve the king of Babylon seventy years" (25.11). Jeremiah's command to Baruch to take the book to the Temple and there read it openly seemed to seal the nation's fate. It caused Baruch pain and sorrow, but at the same time he saw the possibility of great things for himself, and probably for his master as acknowledged leader of the nation and vindicated by God.[1]

But Baruch is reminded by the prophet of God's first commission to pluck up and break down kingdoms and nations. Now God himself is experiencing the much greater sorrow of breaking down and plucking up his own whole land that he has built and planted[2] through so many years. Baruch is promised that he himself will survive—his life will remain his own as a spoil of war, but his service of God and of the prophet is lifted completely above any thought of reward. In that service he must not seek great things for himself. No thrones either here or hereafter are promised to disciples of the Lord.

During a long lifetime, Jeremiah was being taught the same lesson. From the way the story of his call is told, it is clear that he had then felt himself treated as a "prophet like Moses" (1.7ff; Exod. 7.2; Deut. 18.18). He is to be God's deputy (1.10, RSV set) over the fate of nations to watch their conquest of Judah and Jerusalem, and will know the opposition of king, priests, and people though he himself will be defended and preserved by God (1.17). He is to be consecrated by God (1.5) not as a priest[3] but as God's own possession. He is a true prophet in whose mouth God has put his word. But the language of the call-story suggests that the prophet in his call-experience felt himself raised to even greater heights. Words are applied to him that other prophets, as well as Jeremiah himself at other times, heard God use of Israel. He is known (1.5; cf. Amos 3.2), made holy (Jer. 1.5; cf. 2.3), and feels himself called by God's name (15.16; cf. 14.9). Just as Moses (Exod. 32.10) was invited by God to become the founder of a new people of God when the old would have been destroyed, so Jeremiah felt that the peculiar relationship which had formerly existed between God and Israel was now being focused in himself as the new chosen community of God.[4]

This intimacy with God is the outstanding feature in his experiences recorded by Baruch. It appears in his dialogues with God, his

---

[1] Cf. 43.3, and its impression of Baruch's forceful personality.

[2] Cf. the fuller working out of this metaphor, 12.14; cf. also 1.10; Isa. 5.7.

[3] A different form of the verb is used.

[4] Cf. O. Procksch *Theologie des Alten Testaments*, p. 269; E. Voegelin, op cit., p. 470.

complaints and confessions, prayers and intercessions, and his deep
insight into the workings of God's justice.

Often the prophet's cries of distress follow his own prophecies of
doom. It is as though the blast of the enemy's war trumpet is piercing
his own heart when he warns Jerusalem of approaching siege (Jer.
4.18; cf. 19). He sees a sudden vision of the whole creation reversed,
all gone back again to primeval chaos before light was formed, before
there was man or birds or vegetation (4.23ff). The snorting of enemy
war-horses invading from the north makes him cry out with sorrow as
he hears the cry of the daughter of his people, throughout the wide-
stretching land, asking why God does not help (8.19). He exclaims,
"O that my head were waters, and my eyes a fountain of tears, that I
might weep day and night for the slain of the daughter of my people!"
(9.1; cf. 13.17). He is torn between sorrow for his distressed nation
and a longing to escape from their treachery and unfaithfulness.
When the siege of the city has begun and it is clear that God is about
to sling the inhabitants out of the land, the prophet seems to accept
his pain (10.19ff).

After this acceptance, comes the first recorded prayer of Jeremiah,
the recognition that neither he nor any man can choose his way, yet
he has chosen wrongly and he pleads with God to treat him as a loving
father would correct his child, but not in anger (10.23f). Though he
feels the prophetic duty to intercede (15.11), often he is forbidden to
intercede for Israel, or when he does, God rejects his plea (14.11). At
the time of the great drought (14.1f), the prophet stands in prayer
with the people confessing their common iniquity. God is addressed
as Hope of Israel, her Saviour in trouble, but reproached for acting
like a passing stranger uncommitted to her, like a mighty warrior with
power to save but fast asleep,[1] whereas really he is in their midst,
Israel is his possession. The prophet pleads with God: "Do not spurn
us for thy name's sake; do not dishonour thy glorious throne;
remember, and do not break thy covenant with us" (14.21). Again
God completely rejects his intercession and states that, though Moses
and Samuel, the two greatest intercessors in Israel's history, stood
pleading before him, he would not listen (15.1ff). Reliance on God's
mercy and longsuffering, which for centuries had been the support of
sinful Israel and her prophets, is ruthlessly taken away: "I have taken
away my peace from this people, says the Lord, my steadfast love and
mercy. Both great and small shall die in the land" (16.5f).

Jeremiah's deep inner struggle, his experience of bitter persecution

[1] So LXX, cf. Ps. 44.23.

from even his own family, and his strange outspoken dialogue with God, show him struggling with the same problem as is laid before us more systematically and philosophically in the book of Job. They both begin with the basic assumption that God is righteous and knows all about the human heart, its innermost thoughts and purposes, which are evil from man's youth (17.9). Both ask why, in his power and righteousness, he allows the wicked to prosper and the righteous to suffer (12.1). But the personal situations of the two men are quite different. Jeremiah had been given a message of doom to proclaim, and it was not unusual for messengers of bad news to receive bad treatment. In addition, he had been shocked to discover a secret conspiracy against his life by his own family at Anathoth. Though he had not realized it, they were leading him like a gentle lamb to slaughter. Without Job's patience and forbearance, he cries to God for vengeance and is told that God will punish them, they will perish in war (11.21f). Throughout his life this is the solution for which the prophet looks. He prays for vengeance (cf. 18.19f), and never abandons the popular belief—sometimes vindicated by God—that the righteous will be rewarded and their wicked enemies destroyed by an avenging God.

Apparently not fully satisfied by God's reply, the prophet continues to attack the central problem, of vindicating God's justice in allowing evil to cause so much suffering to man, beast, and land in the world he has made and controls. This time God's reply is that suffering is inevitable for a righteous man in a wicked world, and Jeremiah's present suffering is small compared with what is bound to come. If he is wearied by infantry, how will he compete with cavalry? If he cannot stand on his own feet amid his kinsmen, how will he hold on his course among strangers? (12.5). His suffering is infinitesimal compared with God's suffering as he gives his beloved into the hands of her enemies (12.7). The problem has been lifted completely out of the context of requital, whether punishments or rewards, on to a plane where issues are raised that are deeper and more significant, and where answers are not easily made.

The problem is pursued even further by the prophet's experience when again he calls for God's vengeance on his persecutors (15.15ff). Forbidden to intercede, isolated from normal friendship because God's hand with its dread message is laid on him, as though in perpetual pain from a running sore that cannot be healed, he begins to doubt the validity of what he had thought to be God's word. He had gone to living water for help (cf. 2.13), but God's help had failed like the water in a stream that dries up in summer when it is most needed. This time God's answer comes in a clear divine oracle, "Thus says the Lord", and the prophet's obedience can be the only response. God demands repentance. "If you will come back, I will bring you back into my service. You will gain the power to differentiate between true and false and become my mouthpiece, and people will listen to you, not you to them." The prophet must become God-centred, not thinking of vengeance on persecutors nor centring his thoughts even on the people for whom he has been interceding.

It is only partially true to say that the oracle means that God's word will come to the prophet through his own moral judgement; rather, his return to God will enable him to think like God and not like man, and his word will express God's thought. Continually Jeremiah had seen that becoming God-centred was the supreme need of the people, and had told them that, if they returned, it must be to God alone (4.1). Now God clearly tells him that this is the only way of salvation for him too. His pain like God's will continue. He is not to know the comfort of wife or friends (16.2, 9f). But if he turns to God alone, God's message that he proclaims will go forth in power, "for I am with you to save and deliver you, says the Lord" (15.20).

There is a third significant occasion when the same problem is raised. Further persecution (18.18f) makes the prophet again call for God's recompense for himself, and terrible vengeance on his enemies. God's answer is to bid Jeremiah set the vengeance in motion by publicly breaking the bottle in the Valley of Hinnom and uttering God's doom; "Behold, I am bringing such evil upon this place that the ears of everyone who hears of it will tingle" (19.3; cf. 1 Sam. 3.11; 2 Kings 21.12). The action is punished by the prophet's being arrested, beaten, and locked for a night in the stocks for public ridicule, a sentence brought about by the Temple official Pashhur. In the morning Jeremiah turns on Pashhur and prophesies death to both him and his friends. But he makes his strongest outburst against God. Using the metaphor of violent seduction (20.7)[1] he accuses God of compelling his submission, forcing himself into the prophet's life. It was as though an outside power or spirit had taken control of him against his will, forcing him to utter words that brought on him infamy and misery. Like Job he curses the day of his birth, and the man who brought joyful news of the birth of a son. This time there is no oracle from God. But the prophet becomes aware of the Lord's

[1] The Hebrew word "deceived" means seduced, and has no association with the word translated "deceitful" (15.18, of the brook, R.S.V.)

presence and power: "The Lord is with me as a dread warrior; therefore my persecutors will stumble, they will not overcome me" (20.11).

Jeremiah's life ends tragically in Egypt, as he still proclaims the unacceptable word of the Lord, and that those who survive for a second exodus from Egypt to the land of Judah will be "few in number" (44.28), a phrase used elsewhere to express the idea of a very small remnant.[1]

## Evil and God's Purpose

Evil seems triumphant in the last tragic picture of Jeremiah in Egypt. The people reject his word and the worship of the Lord, and put in their place their own word and the worship of the Queen of Heaven. The prophet has no way of convincing them and can only claim that future events will prove him right. The points in dispute are the same as when he was a young man. Now he is old, but quite unshaken, a fortified tower still. Equally sure is his belief that evil will be punished in the end, and only a very small remnant will remain. But a remnant there will be, even from these refugees in Egypt. Destruction will not be total—the message is still the same.

It is not the first time that this has happened, and that the tide of evil and disaster has welled round the rock of his faith. The first twenty years of his prophesying had been under the sympathetic régime of Josiah, whose ordinary life of eating and drinking was marked by justice and righteousness (22.15f). There was much then to deplore in the life of the community; but looking back on it Jeremiah felt it was a time when things were well. Certainly the death of this good king in battle in the prime of life was a blow to the faith of the nation. For the next twenty years there were the evil puppet-rulers, Jehoiachim, greedy and unjust, and Zedekiah, whose treachery we have already seen. Jehoiachim had Jeremiah put on trial for his life, and the prophet Uriah executed. His cynical sacrilege in deliberately cutting up and burning Jeremiah's scroll containing the prophetic word of God was followed by the first Babylonian invasion and the fall of Jerusalem. The city itself was spared, but the flower of the nation was carried into captivity. These were what Jeremiah called good figs (24)—the eye of the Lord was on them for good, and from their descendants a remnant would eventually return. Zedekiah was appointed king over Judah, and he and the people of Jerusalem who

[1] Cf. Gen. 34.30; Deut. 4.27; 33.6; 1 Chron. 16.19 = Ps. 105.12.

were left are characterized by the prophet as bad figs, very bad. His deliberate breaking of covenant and oath caused the second more terrible and punitive invasion, with the destruction of people, land, and Temple, the last a final shock to the faith of the nation. We have seen how Jeremiah constantly foretold this outcome as inevitable unless there were a complete change of heart, and how he interpreted these disasters as the acts of God.

Jeremiah's brief respite from foretelling doom ended similarly in disaster with the murder of Gedaliah (41.2). In his book, his prophecies are not arranged in chronological order, but must be seen in this general framework of the nation's experience, and though the teaching is not co-ordinated, the same attitude to God and the nation persists throughout. God is working throughout the history in the same way, and the nation's lack of response remains constant. God's demands are well known and always the same, whether from the nation as a whole or from individuals great or small—obedience and true worship. "Let him who glories glory in this, that he understands and knows me, that I am the Lord who practise kindness, justice, and righteousness in the earth. For in these things I delight, says the Lord" (9.24). If even one such righteous man could be found in Jerusalem, the city would be spared for his sake (5.1). Here the prophet is emphasizing the forgiving mercy of the Lord, for, in the story of the Flood, the righteous Noah could save only his own family, and Abraham in his intercession for Sodom did not base his pleading on a lower number than ten righteous men.

It was his visit to the potter's workshop that enabled Jeremiah to understand something of God's way of working with the nation. There he saw the potter working at the wheel with a lump of clay, to mould the best vessel which the nature of the clay made possible. When the clay vessel was spoiled[1] in the potter's hand, he reworked it into another vessel, as seemed good to him (18.4), until with infinite patience he got the best vessel out of the clay of which it was capable.[2] It is clear to the prophet that just as the potter's purpose is to get the best possible result from the clay, so God's purpose of peace and good remains constant, but like the potter he changes his plan as to what he will do with his people. These plans are not rigid or pre-ordained,

[1] This word is translated "corrupt", Gen. 6.11, RSV.

[2] Paul uses this illustration differently, to show that God has the absolute right to do what he wants with the clay, making from the same lump one vessel for honour and another for common use (Rom. 9.21), an application found also in the Wisdom of Solomon (15.7).

but fluid and continually open to alteration. It is because God may "repent"[1] concerning the nation, that Jeremiah feels it a constant prophetic duty to intercede for them (cf. Jer. 7.16; 11.14; 14.11) and when God refuses to listen to his intercession, this to him is the measure of their utter corruption.

Jeremiah is sent back from the potter's shop to warn the men of Judah and Jerusalem once more that because of their wickedness God is shaping evil against them. If they want him to change his plan, they must return everyone from his evil way. God's change of plan is a response to human change, and here, as continually elsewhere, the prophet pleads for men to return.

This "returning from their evil way" is Jeremiah's favourite expression when he speaks of repentance. He tells the people, "Stand by the roads and look, and ask for the ancient paths, where the good way is; and walk in it" (6.16). There is a known way of life, trodden for a long time by those who followed God's leading. It is the highway and men should keep to it. But stubbornly they have stumbled into the bypaths (18.15) and wandered away from God, and their only hope lies in return, in retracing their steps to the ancient highway (8.4ff).

Often both the prophet and the people seem to regard such a return as impossible. The good vine has become degenerate (2.21). They say "There is no hope! (RV) for we will follow our own plans, and will every one act according to the stubbornness of his evil heart" (18.12; cf. 2.25), and the prophet recognizes that even what appears to be "return" is feigned and not whole-hearted (3.10). He knows that "the heart is deceitful above all things and desperately corrupt" (17.9). As the Ethiopian cannot change the colour of his skin nor the leopard his spots, so neither king nor people can do good because they have become accustomed, or taught, to do evil (13.23). This same stubbornness amounting to a refusal to change is seen in the story of the refugees in Egypt who turned back to apostasy and the worship of the Queen of Heaven (44.17). Like First-Isaiah, the prophet recognizes the power in the present of the evil traditions in which that generation was brought up and schooled. "Your fathers have forsaken me, says the Lord . . . and you have done worse than your fathers" (16.11f).

Alongside his clear perception of the force of evil, the prophet has complete faith in God's supreme and creative power. "It is thou who made the heavens and the earth. . . . Nothing is too hard for thee!"

[1] Cf. above, pp. 116f.

32.17; cf. 27). On the anvil of his own experience Jeremiah is trying to hammer out an answer to the problem of holding together these two perceptions, of the persistent power of evil and the almighty power of God. It is in the cry of Ephraim, the northern kingdom, that there is a real contribution to religious thought here. "I am continually hearing Ephraim bemoaning . . . cause me to come back that I may come back, for thou art the Lord my God. For after my turning I repented, and after I realized [was made to know] I smote upon my thigh. I was ashamed for I carried [as a burden] the disgrace of my youth" (31.18ff). Suffering has made Ephraim realize that he is out of God's favour. He laments the painful discipline that God has had to use in training him and pleads with God to bring him back, because he can only be turned back if God does the turning. After his "turning"[1] he repents, and God responds to his "dear son" with fatherly love and compassion.

Complete surrender to God breaks the power of evil and restores Ephraim to the Father's love. To the "good figs" that he will bring back from exile, God promises that he will give "a heart to know that I am the Lord; and they shall be my people and I will be their God, for they shall return to me with their whole heart" (24.7). The broken relationship is restored.

This seems to be the only miraculous intervention that the prophet expects from God. The whole atmosphere of this book is in complete contrast to that of Isaiah. As there was no wonderful, extraordinary vision recorded at his call, so Jeremiah did not expect divine power to protect him at his trial: "I am in your hands. Do with me as seems good and right to you" (26.14), and the only sanction he used was the matter-of-fact statement that God avenged innocent blood. When messengers from Zedekiah came in the final siege of Jerusalem suggesting that he should intercede with God to obtain a miraculous deliverance for the city, as in the time of First-Isaiah, the prophet rejected the plea and said that the divine power was on the enemy's side (21.2ff). There was no wonderful act of God to save Gedaliah and the prophet, nor to restrain the evil intentions of the murderous Davidic prince who brought back chaos to the land.

In Jeremiah's thought, evil must be allowed to go a certain distance, to have a limited freedom, before its true nature is revealed, and then like Assyria, Babylon (51), and Jerusalem it is destroyed. But there follow rebuilding, resowing, re-forming the clay that remains. God's miraculous power gives a new heart to the surviving remnant. It is

---

[1] RSV "away"; v. 19, is intrusive; cf. RV.

God who makes the New Covenant, who gives the people one heart and writes his law on it. Throughout his life Jeremiah retained the faith given to him at his call, that the miraculous power of God is seen in this double action of plucking up and pulling down evil, and planting and rebuilding the righteous remnant that has been saved. Four times he is told by the Lord to write his prophecies in a book (25.13; 30.1; 36.2; 51.60). Perhaps his obedient putting them into a permanent form, like First-Isaiah's writing and sealing his teaching among his disciples, expresses Jeremiah's confidence in the eventual triumph of good and God.

# 11  The Latter Prophets: Ezekiel

Like the books of Isaiah and Jeremiah, that of Ezekiel is divided into three main sections. In the first section (1—24) there are call-visions and experiences, prophecies in word and deed of the coming destruction of Jerusalem and Judah, statements of the sins that have made this necessary, and a few promises of hope. In the second (25—32) there is condemnation of foreign nations, the small neighbouring ones of Ammon, Moab, Edom, Philistia, and the larger ones of Tyre and Zidon, and Egypt. All are judged according to their treatment of Israel and their attitude to Israel's God. Most of the condemnation is directed against Tyre for pride and self-deification (26—28), and against Egypt for the way she has continually seduced Israel away from the Lord (29—32). These judgements are a prelude to the third section (33—48), which relates the cleansing of the land and people, and the vision of the rebuilt city and Temple, to which the glory of the Lord will return.

Much of the book has the form of long, extended allegories and parables that need and receive detailed explanation, and visions much of whose imagery later becomes characteristic of the apocalyptic[1] literature that succeeded the prophetic. Once, Ezekiel laments his reputation as a maker of allegories (20.49), and there is a constant interplay between God and prophet, and between prophet and people, so that the necessary explanations come to them from God himself (21.7; 24.19ff). An impression is given of a man with a lively mind, not working in seclusion, but in contact with what was being thought and said around him, and with the wisdom of his day. Possibly in his allegories and parables he uses traditional ideas and poetry, some from the folk-lore of his own people and some perhaps from Canaanite sources. The theme of the foundling, for instance, is well known, and he uses this theme in his story of the foundling Jerusalem (16). The proverb quoted by Jeremiah (31.29) is also quoted by Ezekiel (18.2), and becomes the spring-board for some of his teaching which is directed against a similar saying of the people,

[1] See below, pp. 337f.

Our sins have caught up with us, and we waste away (33.10). He cites the proverb "Like mother, like daughter", to bring home to Jerusalem her sinfulness (16.44). Like Habakkuk (2.3), Ezekiel combats the proverb, popularly used to discredit him, that tomorrow never comes: "The days grow long, and every vision comes to naught" (12.22). Two other current sayings that he hears provide him with ways of entry into his subject: "The way of the Lord is not just" (18.25) and "Our bones are dried up, our hope is lost, we are clean cut off" (37.11). He makes use of the traditional saying, referred to by Second-Isaiah (Isa. 51.2; cf. p. 164 above), of the people left in Judea after 597: "Abraham was only one man, yet he got possession of the land, but we are many. The land is surely given us to possess" (33.24). Ezekiel's tradition was that the land had been given to Jacob (28.25; 37.25).

The prophet also uses myths that may be seen in a different form behind the early chapters of Genesis. The king of Tyre, who claimed to be "wise as a god" had been created and placed in the garden of God. With (or like) an anointed cherub he was set on the holy mountain, but he was cast out because of his pride in his wisdom, claiming equality with God (28.2ff; cf. Gen. 3.5). Possibly Ezekiel drew on Phoenician mythology here in order that he might condemn Tyre "out of her own mouth". The cedars in the garden of God (Ezek. 31.8; cf. 36.35) and the life-giving stream (47.1) may also derive from the Paradise myth, and there are pictures of the after-life in Sheol which seem to have a mythological basis (32.27).

The book of Ezekiel is written almost entirely in the form of autobiography. Two exceptions are a second account of his call (1.2f; cf. 1.1), and words suddenly interjected as part of the Lord's word through the prophet after his wife died: "Thus shall Ezekiel be to you a sign; according to all he has done you shall do. When this comes, then you will know that I am the Lord God." (24.24). No other prophetic book shows such clear signs of planning on a chronological basis. Thirteen consecutive dates[1] are given to different sections, ranging from July 592 (1.1f), five years after the first siege of Jerusalem and Zedekiah's appointment to the throne of Judah, till April 572 (40.1), a much shorter span than is covered by the books of Isaiah or Jeremiah, and even so most of the action of the book is confined to the two years immediately before and after the great fall of Jerusalem in 586 B.C.

---

[1] LXX differs in seven of these dates. 29.17 is dated as April 570 and is out of order, presumably to bring together the prophecies about Egypt.

## *His Call*

Despite its autobiographical form, one early Jewish tradition says that the book was written by "Men of the Great Synagogue", and, although there is a clear impression of unity throughout and the feeling of a single strong personality, problems are raised by the first three verses. In the first verse, the prophet's call is dated in the thirtieth year in the fourth month and the fifth day, and is described in a way unique in the Old Testament: "the heavens were opened and I saw visions of God" (1.1). In the next two verses the call is related as biography, in the fifth year after the captivity of the young king Jehoiachin (that is, 592 B.C.), and Ezekiel is called son of Buzi the priest—"priest" here may refer to either Ezekiel or his father. It is interesting that here nothing is said of visions, but the call-experience is described in more usual terms as feeling the pressure of God's hand upon him, an experience recounted often in the autobiography (3.14, 22; 8.1; 33.22; 37.1; 40.1). Both accounts of the call may refer to the same experience. As Ezekiel belonged to a priestly family, "the thirtieth year" may indicate his age at his call, the age at which he would normally have become ordained to the priesthood (Num. 4.3).

A similar problem is raised as to where Ezekiel was when he was told to go to the exiles (Ezek. 3.11). In both opening accounts, he received the call in Babylonia by the river Chebar, and there saw his vision of the glory of the Lord, as he himself affirms (3.23). But the command to go to the exiles must have been given to him when he was elsewhere than with them, and we are told of a "spirit" journey to them (3.12; cf. Jesus, Matt. 4.1. and Philip, Acts 8.39f), though there is no explicit reference to his presence at this time in Jerusalem. This has led some scholars to suggest that there were at least two stages in his call. In the first (Ezek. 2.1–3, 11), after the spirit has entered him, he is told that he is being sent to the rebellious people or house of Israel, and is made to eat the scroll of lamentation; this stage is completed by his obedient journey to Telabib (3.15). It is possible that the biographical account[1] originally introduced this first stage of the call, dating it in 592 B.C., but the month is no longer stated. The second stage would then comprise the vision of God by the river Chebar (1.4–28), the commission to become a watchman received after seven days in Babylon, and the second vision of the glory of the Lord received in the plain (3.23). The autobiographical account (1.1), which mentions

---

[1] 1.2f, without the words "in the land of the Chaldeans by the river Chebar".

the heavens opening and the visions of God, would suitably introduce this second stage as taking place in the fourth month of the thirtieth year.

If this reconstruction of the stages of his call is correct, we may assume that he had been allowed to remain in Jerusalem after its surrender in 597 B.C., just as later Jeremiah remained after its final fall in 586 B.C. But four or five years afterwards Ezekiel felt the pressure of God's hand (1.3; 3.14) urging him to go and minister to the exiles. Clearly he does not share Jeremiah's early view of them as "good figs". They are a rebellious house. This seems to reflect the situation when letters against Jeremiah came from rebellious prophets among the exiles to the Temple authorities in Jerusalem (Jer. 29.25). Ezekiel does not seem to have wanted to go, for he is told, "But you—be not rebellious like that rebellious house" (Ezek. 2.8), and when he is taken, it is in bitterness and heat of spirit (3.14). But he is plainly told he is not to fear the exiles (2.6), nor to think that his mission is to peoples of foreign speech (3.5). Israel is not likely to listen to him. They will make the prophet suffer as though dragged through thorns and stung by scorpions; but if he goes in obedience to God's command they will know there is a prophet among them (2.5). This stage appears to be paralleled in the call of other great prophets. Ezekiel is given the word of God that he has to speak, Jeremiah had felt the touch of God's hand on his mouth, putting his word in it. To Ezekiel God is more removed; but a hand gives him a scroll written on both sides, which was unusual (cf. Rev. 5.1), full of lamentation, mourning, and woe. When he had read it a voice told him to eat it, and like Jeremiah who found the scroll a joy and delight, so Ezekiel found it tasted like honey for sweetness (Ezek. 3.3). But the call made him, like Jeremiah, a prophet primarily of doom, who would know rejection and suffering.

## Ezekiel and Jeremiah

Like Jeremiah too, he had to face the challenge of prophets who came with a message of peace, a message not from the Lord. He condemned them not simply because they misled the nation, but because they were not willing to share the suffering of maintaining the standards of goodness. Like foxes that make gaps in hedges and do not make good the fences, so these prophets did not stand with God in the fight for righteousness. When moral and religious traditions were breached, they would not risk unpopularity by condemning what were perhaps

new perverted practices (13.17ff). Like dishonest builders covering a
cracked and tottering wall with plaster, they whitewashed crumbling
morals for the sake of peace (13.10ff). Willing to compromise with
evil, they did not demand that wicked men should cease from all that
was meant by idolatry and false worship, before offering to them the
guidance of God (14.3).

A very obvious difference as compared with Jeremiah is that so far
as Ezekiel is concerned there are practically no details of his life, and
it is true that his book consists almost entirely of his prophetical
teaching. But some concrete details appear. He is represented as
having a house in Babylonia where he can shut himself up (3.24) and
we see elders of Judah coming to his house (8.1). On another occasion
they come to inquire God's will from him (14.1); but he is not allowed
to give them any message from God because they are still worshipping
their idols. Among those who live around, he has gained a reputation
as a speaker of considerable skill, so that they are only too willing to
make up an audience for him: "Your people who talk together about
you by the walls and at the doors of houses say, . . . 'Come, hear what
the word is that comes forth from the Lord.' And they come to you as
people come, and they sit before you as my people, and they hear what
you say but they will not do it; . . . Lo, you are to them like one who
sings love songs with a beautiful voice and plays well on an instru-
ment" (33.30ff). Perhaps the most vivid sidelight of all is afforded by
the account of his dumb distress at the death of his wife, "the delight
of his eyes" (24.15). There is a Jewish tradition that like Jeremiah he
met his death in exile, and that he was killed by a prince of Israel
whom he had rebuked for idolatry.

Though these two great prophets were contemporary, neither
mentions the other. If Jeremiah came from a priestly family at
Anathoth with little intimate relationship with the Jerusalem priesthood, and if Ezekiel was a member of the priestly family at Jerusalem
about thirty years his junior, who went to Babylon as a young man,
there is no reason why Jeremiah should have known him. There are
considerable differences between them. Both were priests, but
Ezekiel makes us much more aware of this background, with his
emphasis on the need to maintain the distinction between the holy and
the profane, ritually clean and unclean, his stress on hallowing the
Sabbaths and his intimate knowledge of Temple institutions and
ritual. It is clear that they live and move in the same atmosphere of sin,
destruction, and repentance. Both preach the new covenant and the
gift of the spirit, regarding religion as primarily an individual

OL

relationship to God. To Jeremiah no material objects had any intrinsic holiness, and no particular preparation was necessary before the destruction of the Temple. God had never commanded burnt offerings nor sacrifice nor the burning of children (Jer. 7.22, 31; contrast Ezek. 20.26),[1] and Temple officials to teach the law were not essential. Continually he was opposed by priests, and he claimed that the false pen of scribes had made the law into a lie. To Ezekiel, the Temple was where the glory of God dwelt, and it was extremely important that all sacrificial ritual and public worship be reinstituted. The individual relationship with God needed to be expressed and conserved in religious institutions and corporate acts. Ezekiel clearly would not have approved of the whole of Jeremiah's teaching; but each of these two great prophets has his own individual emphasis, and they complement each other.

## The Spirit

At the beginning of the book the inspiration from the Lord that comes to the prophet is called "the word" (1.3), as frequently throughout, and even more than in other prophetic works his dependence on this "word" is repeatedly stressed. We are also often told that the hand of the Lord was upon him. But more than other classical prophets he likes to speak of the activity of the spirit of the Lord. The spirit entered into him, enabling him to stand in the presence of the glory of God (2.2; 3.24; cf. 43.5), and it fell on him, bidding him tell God's message (11.5). He proclaimed that God would put his spirit into Israel, enabling them to walk in God's ways (36.27) and live (37.14), and that God would pour out his spirit on the house of Israel (39.29; cf. Joel 2.28). So too God promises that he will take from Israel their heart of stone and replace it with a heart of flesh and a new spirit (Ezek. 11.19; 36.26), and this hope is so urgent that once Israel is exhorted to get themselves a new heart and a new spirit (18.31). Probably both meanings of the one Hebrew word, spirit and breath, are suggested when God causes the life-giving force to enter the dry bones (37.5). False prophets are not inspired by God's spirit, but prophesy out of their own minds (Hebrew heart) and follow their own spirit (13.3).

An outstanding feature of the spirit's activity is seen in Ezekiel's spirit journeys. Reference has already been made to the first of these, when he first went to Babylon. In the following year, as he was sitting

[1] See above, p. 179.

in his house with the elders of Judah, he felt again the pressure of God's hand, saw again the vision of God, was lifted by the spirit between earth and heaven, and brought in visions of God to Jerusalem (8.1ff). He was led round various places in the Temple, and after he had seen the glory of God move out from the Temple to the Mount of Olives, the spirit brought him back to Babylon to tell the exiles what he had seen in his vision. The next time, twenty years after his call, when he is brought in the visions of God into the land of Israel (40.1f), his journey is described more briefly as caused by the hand of the Lord.

While there is no insuperable objection to regarding these "spirit" journeys as actual physical movement, for, as we see from Jeremiah, there was communication between Babylon and Judah during the eleven years 597–86 B.C., and we know from the contemporary Lachish letters that prophets were used as messengers,[1] the book, as we have it, clearly presents Ezekiel as spending the whole of his prophetic life in Babylon. The whole story of the prophet suggests that he had what today would be called extraordinary psychic gifts, and in line with this is the statement that he had immediate knowledge of the beginning of the siege of Jerusalem (24.1f) although he was apparently hundreds of miles away in Babylon. It must be remembered, however, that, when the city actually fell, it was a long time before he knew (33.21).[2] Some scholars therefore have suggested another explanation of these facts, involving a very different reconstruction of his early ministry. They suggest that he remained near Jerusalem till the final siege began, and that the functional prophecy of moving his furniture out by night (12.1ff) marked his actual movement first to a village outside Jerusalem and later to Babylonia, as related in 11.24. Though this could explain certain facts, it alters the order of events as given in chapters 11 and 12.

## Functional Mimes

Following the call comes his first functional prophecy (4—7), which begins in the form of an extended mime. It is typical of this prophet that the whole dramatic act is much more fully worked out, and contains a more extensive meaning, than, for instance, First-Isaiah's act when he walked barefoot, or Jeremiah's when he broke the pitcher

[1] Or messengers could be called prophets.

[2] Eighteen months, but some Hebrew MSS. and the Syriac version read eleventh not twelfth year, and so reduce the time to six months.

at Hinnom. The mime is bringing about the destruction of Jerusalem, and so of Judah. On a soft tile or brick he drew a plan of Jerusalem, and in mime laid siege to it, pressing the siege ever more relentlessly against it to present its hopeless situation. Still following God's command, he then lay bound for long periods. First he lay on his left side facing the northern kingdom, as bearing the punishment for its sin, and with his back to the besieged city. Then for a shorter period he lay on his right side, facing the southern kingdom and Jerusalem. Here we see the prophet not simply in a detached way revealing God's plan or even simply co-operating to make it be realized. But he is also, as he says, taking on himself the token consequence of the people's iniquity, he is suffering acutely for their sin.

There is no need to think of him as smitten by a paralytic disease, any more than we should think of Isaiah as walking naked and barefoot unceasingly for the whole of three years—he may have carried out his prophetic acts at certain times. The number of years represented by Ezekiel's mime is 390 for the north, perhaps reckoning from the division of the kingdom after Solomon and including the forty years of exile that he prophesied.[1] There follows the highly unpleasant mime of siege scarcity and loathsomeness of food (4.9–17), at which his clean young priestly soul revolted like Peter's when God told him to eat pork (Acts 10.14). Lastly comes the mime concerning the fate of the population—shaving his head, he divided the hair carefully by weight into three equal parts, burned a part, as in the midst of the city, cut up the second part with a sword, as outside the city, and scattered the last part to the wind, having from this last part retained a few hairs and bound them in his garment as if to preserve a remnant. Even some of these he pulled out and burnt (5.4). It is only a very small remnant that will survive in exile (6.8).

After the account of the mimes, we are given the words that explained and perhaps accompanied his actions of lying on his side, but in the reverse order, first concerning Jerusalem (5.5), then the mountains of Samaria (6.2), and finally the whole house of Israel (7.2). Emphatically pointing to the tile he says, This is Jerusalem, whom God set like a gem in the midst of nations and lands, gave her laws and statutes to help her. But she has rejected them and turned them into wicked deeds, and defiled his holy place with loathsome acts and images. For all these things judgement is about to come.

[1] Cf. 29.12f, in reference to Egypt. Forty years indicates the period of Babylonian supremacy. Or possibly, as so often in the Old Testament, it means a full period or a whole generation.

Then, turning as to the northern kingdom, he condemns the popular Canaanite religion which for two hundred years had persisted despite all the recorded reformation, condemned as it was by the eighth-century prophets, and still being condemned by Ezekiel's contemporary, Jeremiah. There are still hill-top sanctuaries and river wadis with their groves of shady trees where fertility cults are practised with their altars, sun pillars, and idols (6.13). His contempt for idols is seen in his characteristic word for them.[1] The people's lives are moulded by their worship of false, loathsome deities, and God himself has been broken (6.9; RSV marg.) by their whorish, wanton hearts and eyes.

Then, speaking to the land of Israel, he includes the whole people, both north and south, and reiterates relentlessly a word that had been given new significance by Amos (8.2). An end, the end is coming. Now the end is upon you. An evil, an evil. Look, it is coming! An end is coming—coming is the end—it has wakened toward you—Look, it is coming—The dawn is coming toward you, the time is coming, the day is near. Look, the day! Look, it is coming—the dawn has broken (Ezek. 7.2–10). It is a day of complete and utter ruin on people and land, against which there is no defence. Those in the fields will die by the sword, those in the city by famine and pestilence. Neither silver nor gold, on which they have relied, will help them, nor the lovely things they have made into foul images. Even God's precious place will be profaned. Prophets will have no vision, nor priests guidance, nor elders advice.

Another functional mime "concerns the prince in Jerusalem and all the house of Israel who are in it" (12.10). It foretells the abortive flight of King Zedekiah, his capture and blinding by the Babylonians. The prophet at night makes a hole in the mudbrick wall of his house, and in the twilight with his face covered so that he cannot see, carries his belongings through the hole as though going into captivity. This act he is commanded to perform so that the "rebellious house" around him may know it is the Lord who will cause Zedekiah, blinded and with his surviving followers, to be taken to Babylon, there to confess both their own evil-doing (12.16; cf. 17.19, breaking the covenant with Nebuchadrezzar) and the absolute supremacy of the Lord.

Ezekiel's final functional prophecy comes after his vision of the

---

[1] *Gillulim* (round things, with a play on the meaning, pieces of dung). This word is used thirty-six times by Ezekiel and only nine times elsewhere in the Old Testament.

resurrection of the whole house of Israel, and consideration of it here
may serve to remind us that behind even the terrible destruction of
the first extended mime, ground for hope still persists in the tiny
remnant. Two sticks, on one of which is written Judah and the
children of Israel, and on the other Joseph (or Ephraim) and all the
house of Israel, are bound tightly together to make one stick "that
they may become one in your hand" (37.17). The living remnant of
both southern and northern kingdoms are to become one nation with
a Davidic ruler. Both these elements often recur in the prophet's
thought of the future. The Davidic ruler is sometimes called a king,
but more often a "leader" (37.24f, RSV prince; one who is lifted up),
and the unity of the whole people of Israel is clear both in Ezekiel's
hope for the future and in his condemnations of his two contemporary
groups, the people left in the land of Israel and the exiles in Babylonia. This thought of corporate unity, implying shared responsibility
of the exiles and of the people left in the land, makes it very difficult
to know what were the actual religious conditions prevalent among
the exiles.

## His Visions

Pervading the whole of this prophetic book is the influence of the
vision Ezekiel received at the opening of his ministry. His vision of
God came to him in the traditional thunderstorm of turbulent wind,
great cloud, and flashing lightning. Instead of two winged seraphs as
in First-Isaiah's vision, there were four cherubs with wings, each
having four faces, human, lion, ox, and eagle,[1] and the movable
throne (or firmament, 1.22f) which they carried could go in any
direction without turning. On the ground, similar movement was
made possible by its "wheels within wheels". Ezekiel also heard a
voice like that of the seraphs saying, Blessed be the glory of the Lord
from its place (3.12, RV). The whole cherub-borne chariot flashed
like lightning and was alive with eyes. To Ezekiel, God was enthroned
above the sapphire firmament,[2] and it was from above the firmament
that the voice spoke. The prophet carefully avoids anthropomor-
phism, and indicates that the majestic wonder of the transcendent
God cannot be described in human language. There is the "likeness"

[1] 1.10, clearly symbolic, and providing symbolism for later apocalyptic
figures.
[2] Gen. 1.7; Exod. 24.10; cf. Ezek. 1.26, and Isa. 40.22, enthroned above
the circle of the earth. See above, p. 46.

of a throne above the firmament, and the enthroned figure, though "a likeness as it were of human form", has the translucence of amber and the appearance of fire, while round the whole is the brightness of the rainbow. This is the appearance of the likeness of the glory of the Lord to the prophet. Though essentially here is the pillar of fire that proved the presence of the glory of God over the tabernacle and the Ark, and indicates again the priestly interest of the prophet, yet there is an indication of an enthroned figure within the flame, as though the prophet is being granted a vision of something more personal than fire. This vision he later often refers to as "the glory of the Lord" (cf. 3.23).

The imagery is worked out in considerable detail and is more fantastic than that of First-Isaiah; but it is pregnant with meaning, expressing not only majestic transcendence but the mobility of God. It is important that Ezekiel saw this vision for the first time not at Jerusalem but in Babylonia by the river Chebar among the exiles, to whom he had gone at God's command. He saw it again in the plain. Next year in his house (8.1) he beheld the glorious figure again, from the loins down as fire, and upward with brightness of amber.[1] The spirit took him to Jerusalem, and the prophet vividly describes what was happening in the Temple to show why it must be destroyed.

At the northern gate by which the people enter and where the altar for sacrifices is (Lev. 1.11) stands an image, probably of the female deity Ashera.[2] In utter repudiation, Ezekiel exclaims, "Look, there it stands, and yet the glory of the God of Israel is here, like the vision that I saw in the plain!" (Ezek. 8.4). Further within the Temple is a secret room where seventy elders of Israel led by Jaazaniah son of Shaphan[3] burn incense in worship to animal figurines on the wall. The elders have turned to secret superstitious rites, as the women to the worship of the Queen of Heaven (Jer. 44.17) when disaster fell, thinking that the Lord has gone away, he no longer sees them (Ezek. 8.12; 9.9). As Blake put it, God is no more. At another place in the Temple women sit wailing for Tammuz, and elsewhere a group of men are worshipping the sun, for which according to archaeology[4] the axis of the Temple was orientated. The descriptions may suggest

---

[1] Not "bronze", RSV. Cf. below, p. 212.

[2] 2 Kings 21.7. Put there by Manasseh but supposed to have been destroyed by Josiah (2 Kings 23.6).

[3] For Shaphan cf. 2 Kings 22.10, and for two of his sons cf. Jer. 36.10; 39.14.

[4] F. J. Hollis, *The Archaeology of Herod's Temple* (1934). Cf. 2 Kings 23.11, the horses and chariots of the sun.

that the whole nation, king, elders, women, and men have turned from Israel's God to heathen superstitions even in the building where his glory still dwelt.

In further clear vision, Ezekiel prophesies the destruction of the inhabitants of the city by God's six armed executioners, after "a man clothed in linen with a writing-case at his side" has gone through the city placing a cross on the foreheads of the few who "sighed and groaned" over the evils committed in Jerusalem (9.4). As the prophetic vision of the nation's wickedness moved inward to its climax in the Temple itself, so the slaughter moves outward, beginning in God's sanctuary. At God's command the man in linen is given live coals to scatter over the city.

Now the glory of the Lord moves out from over the cherub in the inner sanctuary to the threshold of the Temple, filling house and court with its brightness (10.4). Thence it moves on to the cherub-borne platform and is flown to the eastern gate (10.19). Again it moves out of the city over the valley to the Mount of Olives on the east side (11.23) preparatory to going to Babylon to join God's exiled people, but this final step is not described; when in the final vision the glory returns to the rebuilt Temple it comes simply from the east, through the east door which evermore must remain closed (43.4; 44.2). The prophet himself is now lifted up by the spirit and taken back to rejoin the captives (11.24).

God had removed his protective presence from the doomed Temple and city. Both Isaiah's statement that it was inviolable, for God dwelt in it, and Jeremiah's statement that God would destroy it as he had destroyed Shiloh were justified.[1] Ezekiel returned to Babylon to restore by his vision the exiles' faith in the living power of their God, to refute the charge that God had left them, or, as Second-Isaiah heard them saying, My life is hidden from the Lord and he has no interest in my needs (Isa. 40.27). It was God himself, not Babylon who had commanded the destruction of people and city, and God was in control. Within Ezekiel's vision of the religious defilement of the Temple there occurs a picture that seems much more secular (Ezek. 11.1–21). Twenty-five leaders, unaware of the coming doom, are using the Temple for their political intrigue. Confident that the city is strong enough to withstand attack, they encourage resistance to Babylon and self-righteousness among the people. They despise the exiles as wicked people punished by God, and already are claiming as their own the land and possessions the exiles have been forced to

---

[1] See above, p. 173.

leave (11.15; cf. 33.24). God's anger is against them as much as against those who defile his house with their idolatry, and he commands Ezekiel to prophesy their doom.

Throughout all his ministry, the prophet was vividly conscious of the presence of the glorious God who had come to him in the loneliness of exile in a foreign land. Coming as to the great leaders of the past in the terrifying phenomena of the thunderstorm, God had revealed himself intimately not as a nature force but as responsive personality, who talked to him and could be spoken to. The great gulf between him and the wonderful transcendent God was emphasized by the title God used to him, "Son of man" (human being); but the gulf was bridged by the fact that dialogue could take place between them. This relationship of transcendence and intimacy overarches the whole book.

## The Watchman

As we have seen, Ezekiel uses long allegories and parables, which are not always easy to distinguish from functional prophecies and visions. At the time of his call-experience he is not, like Jeremiah, given authority over nations to destroy and rebuild, but the task of a watchman warning his fellow men of the danger of wickedness, responsible with his own life if he fails to warn them (3.17). Later (33.2ff) he is told by God to explain to his people that he is in the same position as a man on guard whose duty it is to blow the warning trumpet if the enemy is about to attack. This heavy responsibility of watchman, shepherd, or pastor is a unique conception in the prophets. It expresses Ezekiel's inescapable link with his community. If he sees danger and does not warn, his life is forfeit, he shares the fate of the unwarned man. The responsibility would be too heavy to bear if it were not for the fact that a simple warning enables him completely to discharge his responsibility. But nothing relieves him of the dread responsibility of utterance, of passing on to his fellows the message whenever he hears a word from God's mouth (3.17). It is of interest that with his priestly background Ezekiel stresses the solemnity of the proclaiming of the word. Jeremiah spoke of it as a hammer and as fire, to Ezekiel it had something of the sanctity of altar or sacrifice. He was forbidden to give God's word to inquirers who were still defiled with their idols, and he objected to being merely a means of entertainment.

In both "watchman" passages a leading motif appears, characteristic of Ezekiel. Each man has an absolute choice between good and

evil, loyalty (righteousness) or disloyalty (wickedness), and his choice
is immediately effective. Twice the prophet enlarges on this theme
(18.21ff; 33.12ff). As in Deuteronomy (30.15ff), man is thought of as
always at the cross-roads, and as at each moment he chooses, so he
can change completely the direction of his life. Thus a wicked man at
any moment may repent, and none of his previous wickedness is
remembered against him. Similarly, a righteous man may commit a
wrong act and none of his previous righteousness is remembered. It is
consistent with this view that Ezekiel seldom speaks of the quality of
righteousness, and does not recognize the cumulative effect of actions
in formation of character. His emphasis is on right or wrong deeds.
To a people who are conscious of their guilt and have lost heart, he
stresses the possibility of repentance. God has no pleasure in the death
of the wicked, but that the wicked turn back and live. But the scales
seem loaded against the righteous. The wicked man who repents lives,
but the righteous man who sins will die, apparently without an
opportunity of repenting however long the record of his righteous
deeds. Unexpressed, behind this may lie the idea that a righteous man
who sins commits apostasy, his sin is more heinous because he has
been close to God.

To the people's complaint that in this matter God is not just, the
prophet implicitly replies that they are all sinners and can repent. The
fate of the righteous is not relevant to their situation (Ezek. 18.30).

## The Power of Evil

When this problem of the power of evil and possibility of choice is
raised by the people using the proverb, "The fathers have eaten sour
grapes and the children's teeth are set on edge" (18.2), Ezekiel rejects
the proverb. They believed they were hopelessly bound by the consequences of the evil past of the nation. The roads of life had been
made, and they must tread them. They were the helpless slaves of a
past that had moulded their present and future. Ezekiel knew that
there was something wrong with their philosophy of life, their faith in
God, if it led them to such an impasse. He swung over in this context,
speaking to men in this situation, to the opposite extreme. There were
no chains from the past that could not be broken if honestly they
wanted it. The past, good or bad, had no power over them. He met the
statement of the second commandment with blank denial. God did
not visit the sins of the fathers upon the children. Children did not
die for the sins of parents, nor could they be saved by the goodness of

their fathers. Ezekiel declared that there were no unbreakable bonds from the past. Within the narrow circle of the ever rapidly passing present, they were free to do what was lawful and right or to do evil, to live or to die.

When rewards and punishments were thought of as removed to a future life, this teaching of Ezekiel gave rise to the belief that "as a tree falls, so shall it lie", the belief that a man is saved or damned for eternity by his final act, on the view that all possibility of change ends at death. But the prophet's own answer to the whole problem is completely different. Though he urges Israel to get a new heart and a new spirit, elsewhere he makes it clear that these are gifts of God (11.19; 36.26) and we hear God's cry to them, "Turn back, turn back from your evil ways; for why will you die, O house of Israel?" (33.11).

Jeremiah was told that the two great intercessors, Moses and Samuel, would be ineffective in pleading for the doomed city (Jer. 15.1). Ezekiel's intercession was unsuccessful (Ezek. 9.8ff). He was implicitly told that the form in which Abraham had interceded for Sodom would not be effective for Israel; though the three men most famous in history for their righteous acts, Noah, Daniel, and Job, were in the city, by their righteous acts they could save only their own lives, but not even that of son or daughter (14.14, 20). As righteousness is not considered as a quality, so it is not a benefit that can be transferred to others.

Ezekiel's belief in the possibility of the repentance of individual Israelites is often absent from his picture of the nation. A wicked remnant will even be preserved by God as a museum piece, justifying by their wickedness his destruction of land and people (14.22f; cf. 12.16). The disease of the nation is so malignant that, if any life is to be preserved, drastic surgery is imperative. As in the days of Noah no remnant of righteousness could be saved without the ruthless destruction of corruption, so now the prophet believed that God's very nature—his name—and his close relationship to Israel meant that the spreading growth of evil must be cut away. False prophets with their soothing talk of peace, their plaster disguising a crumbling wall, only made things worse (13.10ff). God had chosen to cultivate a vine—Israel—because of its grapes (Isa. 5.4). It was useless for timber or any other purpose, and when its grapes proved wild, it had to be cut right back (Ezek. 15).

Now with new allegories presenting the history of Israel, the prophet attempts to make the exiles understand why it was necessary

for God to destroy city and nation, Jerusalem and Judah (16.2). He
calls Jerusalem a new-born baby daughter of an Amorite father and a
Hittite mother. She was put out on a rubbish-heap in Canaan, rescued
and surrounded by love, given the legal security of a covenant bond.
After years of happy marriage she broke out in complete and utter
perversion, killing sons and daughters, insatiably giving herself to
every male she could find; worse than prostitutes who had to hire
themselves out, she even paid hated Egyptians and Assyrians to feed
her lusts. She had watched with self-righteous pride the destruction
of her younger sister Sodom (16.56) and seen the punishment of her
elder sister Samaria for crimes that were not half so bad (16.51), now
nothing can save her from the death sentence that must be passed on
all adulteresses. But afterwards God's unbreakable love will triumph,
the broken covenant will be replaced by an everlasting covenant.
Sodom and Samaria will be restored, and Jerusalem, ashamed and
changed, will receive them back, not simply as sisters but with all the
responsibility of a mother for a daughter.

Using the names Oholah for Samaria and Oholibah for Jerusalem
(23.4) the prophet returns to this allegory, but omits the younger
sister Sodom and omits all hope for the future. His analogies of gross
immorality of Samaria with Egypt and Assyria, and of Jerusalem with
Egypt and Babylon, suggest primarily political intrigue. To Ezekiel as
to First-Isaiah, foreign alliances showed lack of trust in Israel's God.
But this political intrigue is associated with religious disloyalty,
breaking covenant and oath (cf. 16.59), worshipping idols, immoral
fertility cults, bloodstained hands, sacrifice of children, profaning of
Sabbaths. The people of Jerusalem have carried their lewdness into
the Temple, profaning it and misusing God's holy incense and consecrated oil (23.39, 41). Loyal or righteous men will judge them.[1]

To make his teaching quite plain, and perhaps to meet an objection
that he always speaks in parables (20.49), Ezekiel is commanded to
give the elders of Judah God's version of Israel's early history (20.4).
In Egypt God chose Israel,[2] but Israel had been worshipping
Egyptian idols and was not willing to forsake them. It is of interest
that Ezekiel knows a different tradition of Israel's sojourn in Egypt
from the one preserved in the Pentateuch, just as he (and Jeremiah)

---

[1] Jesus seems to substitute "he who is without sin" for righteous men
(John 8.7).
[2] This word "choose" is used only here (20.5) by Ezekiel of God's relationship to Israel, and once in Jer. 33.24, a passage not in LXX. But it is
commonly used by Second-Isaiah.

allows the analogy of marriage to two sisters, which is forbidden by pentateuchal law (cf. Lev. 18.18). For his name's sake God gave them Deliverance from Egypt, and in the wilderness gave them statutes and ordinances to regulate national life, and Sabbaths as a sign of its consecration to God.

Again they rebelled, and God had to exclude that generation from the promised land. The next generation, despite his warning, were as bad as their fathers, so God gave them new statutes and ordinances to make them desolate, including the horrifying demand that they should sacrifice their first-born (Ezek. 20.25f; cf. Exod. 22.29).[1] Yet even in Canaan heathen worship persisted. With this climax of degradation the historical survey closes, and the prophet sternly warns the Israel of his own generation of the danger of repeating their fathers' crimes. With wrath God will take action, asserting his power as king and ruler over Israel. He will take Israel again into the wilderness to plead with her (RSV enter into judgement, Ezek. 20.35), and purge out all rebels. Afterwards he will gather the whole purged people to his land, and on the holy mountain height of Israel accept their offerings, firstfruits, and all their holy gifts. There God's restoration will cause them true repentance (20.43). But first the fire of the Lord will devour both green tree and dry, and his avenging sword in the hand of Nebuchadrezzar will slay righteous and wicked (21.4, 19).

It is noteworthy that the duodecalogue of crimes in Deuteronomy (27.15ff) rather than the Decalogue lies at the basis of Ezekiel's denunciation of Israel, interspersed with crimes he regards as specially abhorrent, connected with holy things, Sabbaths, and shedding of blood. There is idol worship (Ezek. 22.4; Deut. 27.15), dishonouring parents (22.7; Deut. 27.16), sexual sin (a father's wife, 22.10; Deut. 27.20; against a sister, 22.11; Deut. 27.22). To Ezekiel, the ritual of institutional religion is the fitting and ordained accompaniment and expression of a moral life. Ceremonial regulations about clean and unclean and hallowing of Sabbaths (20.12; 22.8, 26) are mingled with moral and social sins (cf. 18.6ff; 45.9ff). This juxtaposition later tended to blur the distinction between moral sins and outward observances.

## The Davidic House

Within this extended context of the sin of the whole people of Israel, the prophet twice turns to consider the sins and catastrophes of the

---

[1] See above, p. 37.

Davidic house. He sings a funeral dirge over the evildoing and fate of Jehoahaz and Jehoiachim,[1] inseparably linked with the withering of the vine Israel in the wilderness (19). But even more momentous in the contemporary situation is the behaviour of the puppet-king Zedekiah, whose treachery towards his overlord is as flagrant as Israel's towards her God (17). Ezekiel's allegory of the cedar and the great eagle is, as we have seen, a factor to be considered when trying to understand the identity of the Servant of the Lord in Second-Isaiah.[2] But religiously, as the prophet applies it here, it is another revealing picture of the basic attitude that has culminated in the final downfall of the nation—lack of loyalty and righteousness. When Nebuchadrezzar, the great eagle, came and took away to Babylon the young king Jehoiachin, highest of the young twigs (RSV) of the Israelite cedar, he replaced him by Zedekiah, seed of the Israelite vine[3] in fertile soil with plenty of water (17.5). Zedekiah bound himself to Babylon, as Israel was bound to God, by oath and covenant (17.13) but soon intrigued with Egypt, another great eagle (17.7). First the roots of this newly planted vine curved underground towards Egypt, then the treachery became apparent as suddenly the vine shot forth a branch in that direction. Possibly some of the exiles too believed that salvation would come through an Egyptian defeat of Babylonia,[4] and Ezekiel is warning them that the thriving of the vine depends on the great eagle that had first set it out in Israelite soil. Now a wrathful east wind from Babylon would wither it. Egypt would not be able to save Zedekiah, because it was the Lord, the God of loyalty to oath and covenant, whom he had despised (17.19). But the Lord who will restore Israel will also restore the Davidic house. He, not Nebuchadrezzar (17.22, emphatic I), the Lord will take a new tender shoot (cf. Isa. 53.2) from the top of the cedar, plant it on a high mountain (Ezek. 40.2), and make it flourish so that all the birds may nest among its branches.

## The Fall of Jerusalem

As the terrible fall of Jerusalem draws nearer, the prophet gives urgent warnings of her fate. He compares the punishment to the

[1] 2 Chron. 36.5f. But contrast 2 Kings 24.6.
[2] See above, p. 163.
[3] The cedar appears to stand for the direct Davidic line. Zedekiah was Jehoiachin's uncle.
[4] Noth, *Revue d'Histoire et de Philosophie réligeuses* (1953), 2, p. 86.

purification of metals in a furnace (22.18ff), and takes up again the metaphor of the iron cauldron which the rebels in Jerusalem had claimed would, like the city's armoury and defences, be strong enough to protect them from fiery siege (11.3f). At random they will be taken out piece by piece, and their bones burned in the fire. Then the emptied cauldron will be set on the fierce fire to cleanse it, by making it red hot (24.6ff). This allegorical prophecy is dated (24.1; cf. 2 Kings 25.1; Jer. 52.4) when the final siege of Jerusalem began. At that time the Lord warned Ezekiel that his wife, delight of his eyes, was about to die, but he was to make no outward sign of mourning. It was a sign to Israel of the imminent fall of the Temple, delight of Israel's eyes, and the Jews in exile must bear their sorrow in silence (24.16ff).

This prophecy marked the end of the first phase of the prophet's activity, and for him the fall of Jerusalem marked the end of an epoch, as did the Cross in Christianity. It was the vindication of that law which was the necessary basis of a God-controlled universe, nation, or individual life. Sin and evil were destroyed in the death of Jerusalem. Order had triumphed over chaos, and was shown to be strong and stable. New creation became possible, and we watch the prophet drawing his picture of the restoration of the land, the resurrection of Israel, and the rebuilding of religious life.

## The Road to Restoration

The order of chapters leading to the final vision of reconstruction reveals the necessary steps that, in the thought of the one who arranged the book, precede it. As we saw, the first twenty-four chapters lead up to the beginning of Nebuchadrezzar's last siege of Jerusalem. The next eight chapters (25—32) contain God's judgement on the seven surrounding nations, leading to the doom on Edom (35), and on Babylon under the code name Magog (38f).[1] Enmity against Edom had grown strongly after the first Babylonian capture of Jerusalem, because she allied herself with the enemy and treacherously occupied some of Israel's territory. She must be driven out by God. Magog symbolized all the foreign domination of God's land, characterized as an unprovoked attack on a peaceful, unarmed people (38.11; cf. Judges 18.27). After a great battle they will all be

[1] As if in English we wrote instead of BBL (Babylon), MGG (Magog) using the next letter in the Hebrew alphabet and inverting the order. Cf. Jer. 25.26, *Sheshak*, also code for Babylon where BBL is YYO, using letters counted from the other end of the alphabet.

defeated and—the practical priest becomes apparent again—for seven years their weapons will provide fuel for Israel (39.9), and for seven months the burial of bodies will provide employment. The aim of God's judgement is partly that he may be known among the nations as well as to Israel, and partly to cleanse the land from foreign defilment. Even the self-righteous remnant of Israel in the land will be destroyed, and an empty land will await the landless exiles (33.27f). The prophet's vision of Sheol, the after-world, however, shows that he regarded national and ritual distinctions as permanent and persistent. Even there, men are separated into national enclaves, and the uncircumcised and those slain by the sword (presumably with the defilement of uncovered blood) are separated from other inmates (cf.32.26ff).

As the prophet proceeds to his vision of the new restored community living close to God, a new side of his nature appears. He had been passionate in invective and condemnation. Now he shows his care for his people and brings them a message of comfort. It is interesting that for the first time the phrase "our exile" (33.21) occurs, perhaps showing how much he has become one with his fellows.

Israel like a flock of sheep had been scattered because her shepherds—her kings—had been wicked. Now God himself has become the Good Shepherd (34.11). He will search for his lost sheep, seek them out and bring them back to their own lush pastures. He will protect the weaker sheep from those that eat their fill, tread down the rest of the grass, and foul the drinking-water. In Ezekiel's picture God judges not between sheep and goats, but between strong beasts, whether he-goats or rams, on the one side, and weaker beasts needing protection, on the other (34.17). Evil wild beasts will cease in the land, and there will be showers of blessing (34.26). God will make a new covenant of peace and welfare, and the idyllic days under the shepherd prince, God's servant David, will return.[1]

There is to be regeneration of individual Israelites by water and the spirit (36.25f). Religious or ceremonial defilement by filthiness and idolatry will be removed by sprinkling with pure water, and the house of Israel will be changed by the gift of a new heart and a new spirit. God will put his own spirit within them, enabling them to keep his statutes and judgements. This initial act of God in restoring them, changing them, and giving them new prosperity, will make Israel remember how evil she had been, and feel shame and loathing for herself.

---

[1] 34.23f. It is not clear whether Ezekiel expected a resurrection of David or of the Davidic house, cf. 17.22.

Neither "pardon" nor "steadfast love" (or "loving-kindness") is used by Ezekiel, but he makes use of the cultic idea of making atonement when he speaks of putting the blood of the sin offering on the horns of the altar (43.20, 26) and on the door posts of the Temple, to make atonement with blood for the sinners of Israel (45.19f; cf. 45.15, 17). There seems to be a new stress here on the necessity and efficacy of sin offerings and guilt offerings of animals, and the use of their blood in the Temple for cleansing or atonement. Ezekiel had already used the idea of atonement when he spoke of the Lord's action in restoring Judah after her exile (16.53–63, which ends with "when I forgive you all you have done" RSV). In this passage that closes the allegory of the foundling, the stages of restoration are clearly seen as springing from God's initiative. God turns to Israel, he changes the fortunes (turns a turning) of her and of her sisters Sodom and Samaria, restoring them to their former estate. When Judah has borne the consequences of her own wickedness, she will change her self-righteous contempt for her sisters. God will remember the covenant he made with her in her youth, and will make an everlasting covenant with her. Then she will remember her ways and be ashamed, and receive back from God her sisters, who will be given to her as daughters. The change in her will remain when God makes atonement for all she has done. It is a picture of changed human relationship and conversion, springing from the prophet's deep religious experience.

The prophet again describes the process of restoring the relationship between God and Israel (39.25ff). There has been the same strong statement of God's punishment on Judah for her trespasses and wickedness, resulting in God's hiding his face from her. But here for the only time in Ezekiel we are told of God's mercy. By bringing them back from exile he will vindicate through them his holy name. They will still "bear their shame" (RV). It is possible, however, that the defectively written Hebrew for "bear" (39.26) might be read as "forget"[1] (RSV), and, if so, this would theologically be a great leap forward in Ezekiel's concept of God's forgiveness as completely wiping out Israel's memory of her sinful past. This would agree with the mention of "mercy" of God, and of his promise "I will not hide my face any more from them when I pour out my Spirit upon the house of Israel" (39.29); perhaps this is a deliberate reversal of the

---

[1] It must be emphasized, however, that "forget" (RSV) here is based on a conjectural reading of the Hebrew text, unsupported by any other passage in Ezekiel or by the versions.

prophet's frequent repetition of the threat, "I will pour out my wrath".

In vision, Ezekiel sees the nation itself brought back to life. Using words that link this vision (37) with his spirit journey back to Jerusalem (8), the prophet feels the hand of the Lord upon him, is carried by the Spirit, and set down in the plain (cf. 3.22), a charnel-house of heaps of dry, human bones. At the prophetic word, the sound of an earthquake (RSV rattling, 37.7; cf. 3.12) and the blowing of the wind or Spirit of God, the bones become an exceeding great disciplined host upon its feet. Life and hope have returned to Israel, and Israel's graves have opened. This renewing of life and hope for Israel is presented as God's act of wonder or miracle, and clearly the thought of bodily resurrection is not far away. Israel has arisen, filled with God's Spirit, ready to be placed in her own land. Northern and southern kingdoms are to be reunited (37.15ff) in the restored Davidic kingdom with an everlasting covenant of peace. God's dwelling will be in their midst again—he will be their God and they his people.

## The New Jerusalem

The final section of the book (40—48) presents the concept of a religious community devoted to the worship of God. The centre of this community is to be the Temple where God dwells, and from which his glory fills the whole land. It is difficult to understand why some of the details and measurements are given; but, as in Ezekiel's functional prophecies and his first great vision, all these details had significance. Much can be learned from them for the history of the development of the religion of the Old Testament, but this development is not our concern. It must be remembered that this is a vision, and blends the practical with the ideal.

The evidence that salvation has been realized is to be the rebuilding of the Temple and the reinstituting of communication in worship between God and Israel. Again the hand of the Lord was upon Ezekiel, bringing him to a very high mountain in the land of Israel. The one who appeared to him (40.3) and was the intermediary between him and God is clearly differentiated from the divine figure of his opening vision. This is a man who gleams like bronze, whereas that was "a likeness as of a human form . . . gleaming like amber".[1] He showed the prophet the framework of the new Jerusalem on a very

[1] RSV uses "bronze" to translate two different Hebrew words, and this to English readers might suggest a similar divine appearance.

high mountain (cf. Isa. 2; Mic. 4) in Israel, probably pictured as much more central to the land than the pre-exilic Jerusalem (but cf. Ezek. 20.40; Zech. 14.10). That the distinction between clean and unclean, holy and profane may be clear, God's dwelling-place in the Holy of Holies is the centre of many concentric circles of diminishing holiness. Courts and a great wall, the dwellings of priests and tribes, shut it off. Approach is carefully graduated through priests, Levites, prince, and people. Into the new Temple the glory of the Lord enters through the east gate, now to be kept shut (Ezek. 43.4; 44.2), and fills the whole building. The altar in the inner court is to be built and consecrated, purged from sin by the sprinkling of animal blood. Only Levites descended from Zadok,[1] whom Solomon installed as priest in the Temple, are to be allowed to enter the Holy of Holies (44.15). They must wear special linen garments so that in God's presence no sweaty wool may cause uncleanness, and these linen garments must be worn only in the inner court lest the dangerous contagion of their holiness infect the people (44.17ff).

When the land is redivided by lot, a special portion must be assigned for dwelling, for priests, Levites, and prince, around the Temple. North of the Temple complex, seven tribes are to have their allotment, and five on the south, Judah and Benjamin being nearest to the holy domain. Offerings necessary for each of the festivals are carefully enumerated, and the festivals themselves accurately dated (45; 46). The year is divided into two parts, and in each there is a Day of Atonement (45.18, 25); the prophet shows the same sense of symmetry in the division of time as in that of space. From under the holiest eastern part of the Temple will flow a stream rapidly deepening to a great river, carrying life and healing to the whole land, even to the saltness of the Dead Sea valley, though with his characteristic mingling of the practical and the ideal, the prophet allows some salty stretches to remain to provide salt for the nation! (47.11).

This mingling of the ideal and the real is most clearly expressed in the new name for the new city with which this prophetic book ends— The Lord There—Yahweh Shamah. The Lord is really present in an earthly dwelling-place in a real land and among a real people Israel, and his presence is the guarantee of their continued holiness and life. In the opening chapters the prophet was most conscious of God, the radiance of his bright burning glory as he moved in from the Beyond, from the north, on his cherub-borne, sapphire throne, above the

---

[1] Other Levites are inferior (44.10, 13). See above, p. 85, n. 5, and below, p. 353.

firmament, into the midst of his exiled people and later to his Temple and land to destroy its evil and perverted corruption. He was still above it all, not bound to it, he could and did withdraw from it.

Now, triumphant and glorious, he has returned and is the centre of all national life. There is no dividing line between Temple and State, no High Priest to challenge the authority of the secular prince, who is God's shepherd and brings to him through the priests the offerings of the people. Hidden from human eye but in the midst, giving security from sin and defilement, pervading and purifying the whole land, is God's glory. Cultus and culture have become one, not in some far-off final, eschatological Kingdom of God, but built in the prophet's green and pleasant homeland and inhabited by human children of Israel reunited into one earthly kingdom.

# 12 The Latter Prophets: The Book of the Twelve

## Introduction

Towards the end of the old Testament period, perhaps as late as the third century B.C., scribes, believing that prophecy as a living force was extinguished and that its witness must be preserved, probably gathered together all extant prophecies into a final collection. The formula with which the whole concludes (Mal. 4.4–6) significantly links this Book of the Twelve with the Law of Moses and the stories of the Former Prophets, as this latest prophet of Israel commands obedience to Moses and looks for the return of Elijah. What the scribes finally produced was a collection that had been growing for about five hundred years, from the time of Hosea and Amos till the whole was canonized, accepted as authoritative, perhaps at the end of the third century B.C. The Dead Sea Scrolls discovered at Qumran in 1947 amply illustrate how such a long process of editing could modify earlier prophetic writings. Successive religious leaders through this long period found strength in these writings, unified and wove together these twelve separate prophetic books, and gathered them into one scroll as a literary unit. As early as the beginning of the second century B.C., its unity in diversity was recognized by the title, The Book of the Twelve, known to Ben Sirach (Ecclus. 49.10). During all these centuries Israel suffered and rejoiced, experienced disaster and times of revival, put forward programmes of action or withdrew to views of a heavenly kingdom, and in her changing situation these words of God were brought to her with different emphases, but always as a message from God to an actual living people.

The northern kingdom had been destroyed (c. 721 B.C.) because of its idolatry and treachery, its worship of idols and at the Canaanite high places. But Judah learned little from Hosea and Amos, despite the command not only to be rid of the abominations but to destroy the high places themselves.

The terrible disaster of the Babylonian exile followed (c. 586 B.C.).

When prophecy is heard again it brings a message of hope, and we
hear it in the Book of the Twelve sounding the same note of joy as in
Ezekiel (37), and Second-Isaiah whose prophecies probably bring us
down to the end of the sixth century B.C. The Lord himself has come
to reign.

But hopes were not realized, and hatred grew up against surrounding nations for their treatment of Israel in her time of distress. We get
reflected in this Book the nationalistic cry for vengeance. This bitterness does not dominate the whole scene—hopes spring again, and
faith that God will intervene and ultimately triumph. He will send his
anointed leader. The terrible Day of the Lord will come, purging
Israel, bringing destruction on the enemies of God and his people.
The hopes for "that Day" become coloured by the belief that when it
shines forth in full glory, and purged humanity is right with God, all
created things will dwell together in everlasting harmony. Through
these long years Israel's faith was expressed also in psalms and hymns,
and some of these, rescued perhaps only in fragments, still sing to us
from the Book of the Twelve, denying reality to idols or any other
gods, and praising the name of the Lord of Hosts.[1]

For understanding the later developments in religion, the secondary writers in this Book are as important as, if not more important
than, the twelve primary prophets.

Some of the twelve are clearly dated. Hosea, Amos, and Micah are
placed in the reigns of kings of Judah and Israel in the eighth century. Zephaniah prophesied in the days of Josiah at the end of the
seventh century. Haggai is precisely placed in 520, the first day of the
sixth month of the second year of Darius, and Zechariah two months
later in the same year. It is possible to gain some idea of the personalities of these six prophets and the historical events in which they prophesied.

But most of the other six prophets, whose books are not dated, are
shadowy figures whose personality and background have to be sur-
mised from their words. Some of them have been regarded as cultic,
Temple prophets whose utterances were made at cultic festivals.[2]
Jonah is intended to be the prophet mentioned in the reign of Jeroboam II (2 Kings 14.25) as prophesying that the king would restore
the borders of Israel from the entrance of Hamath in the north to the

---

[1] Cf. the careful analysis of strata in the Book of the Twelve by R. E.
Wolfe, *Zeitschrift für die alttestamentliche Wissenschaft* 12 (1935/6), pp. 90ff.

[2] Humbert, *Problème du Livre d'Habbacuc* (1944). Mowinckel regarded
Joel as well as Habakkuk as cultic and Haldar added Nahum.

Dead Sea in the south. Nahum refers to the fall of Nineveh (612 B.C.).

The consensus of modern scholarship would definitely date Joel and Jonah in their present form much later than their position in the Book of the Twelve would indicate. It is probable that the compilers' interest was not in dating, but in questions that were vital and contemporary to them—On whom was doom pronounced, was it Israel or foreign nations or all the earth? Was the particular doom fulfilled, or had the Lord "repented" and changed his plan? Such interests may be reflected in their arrangement of the books.

## Hosea

The Book of Hosea contains the prophecy of the last northern prophet, the only northern prophet whose written records we have. It consists of two accounts of his marriage with Gomer (1—3), and some loosely connected sayings and poems without any discernible chronological or logical order, except that the first group (4.1—9.9) appears concerned with contemporary idolatry and political wrong-doing. The second group (9.10—14.9) derives the sin from the past. From the literary and religious standpoint, a striking and interesting feature of arrangement is the way hope alternates with despair, promise with doom. So great are the contrasts that many scholars think that the hopeful verses have been added by a southern redactor after the southern exile of 586. But it must be remembered that there was a northern exile in 721, and possibly Hosea, like Jeremiah in the south but unlike Jesus, survived disaster and tried to help in the rebuilding. The hopeful element may derive from Hosea after 721 B.C., just as Ezekiel's reconstruction is after the southern disaster of 586 B.C.

Interest has centred on the relationship between the two accounts of his marriage, and there is little general agreement whether the two accounts describe the same event, being linked by an editor's insertion (in 3.1) of the word "still" or "again" or whether either the biographical or the autobiographical account is a sequel, one to the other. It is noteworthy that there is no mention of children of the marriage in the autobiography of chapter 3, which perhaps represents the beginning of the story.

If we take the story as we have it, Hosea was told by God to marry a prostitute, a functional prophecy which, like Isaiah's intercourse with the official and respectable prophetess in Jerusalem (Isa. 8) would have shocked his contemporaries. The word used in Hosea is not the one for a religious prostitute attached to a temple and consecrated to a god,[1] and it is plainly stated that her three children are children of whoredom and shamefully conceived (Hos. 2.4f). The prophet threatens that, if she does not repent, he will bring on her the punishment of a harlot (2.3). But before we speculate about the status of Gomer, we must remember that she is an analogy for Israel. God's people had fallen a victim to syncretism, the worship of other gods. The evil must have penetrated right into Israelite homes and families, dividing one against the other. Perhaps Hosea found himself "unequally yoked with an unbeliever" (2 Cor. 6.14), experiencing in his own home life the tragedy of the religious disloyalty within Israel (Hos. 4.12ff). It seems a genuine part of the analogy that, just as throughout the prophecy doom and hope alternate, so in his relationship with Gomer there is an alternation of negative with positive, of Not-pitied with Pitied, of faith shattered and faith restored. But in any case, through the fact that he found himself unable to reject his wife, that his love was stronger than her sinfulness, he came to understand better God's love for his foolish, ungrateful people. Though the legal covenant between then was shattered, God's love remained. As Hosea struggles to preserve his married life, so despite Israel's religious disloyalty God attempts to prevent her harlotry and gain her return.

Basic to Hosea's prophecy is this marriage metaphor, which he is the first to work out fully,[2] probably from his own unhappy experience. God will not tolerate Israel's behaviour, he will take away his gift of her grain and punish her for the feast days of the Baals. Picking up Hosea's threat to Gomer (2.3) that he will make her desolate, like a wilderness, God suddenly promises that when Israel has lost everything, it is then that God himself is just about to allure—seduce—her back to the wilderness and speak persuasively to her (cf. Isa. 40.2), starting married life all over again with her. She will forget false gods; paradisal peace will reign between animals and men, and there will be a new relationship of everlasting betrothal described by a great heaping up of all the words valid in true marriage—loyalty, justice, loving-kindness, mercy, faithfulness (Hos. 2.19f). The old relationship of My people, Your God, will be restored. Then (3.1) Hosea is told to go again and love as the Lord loves Israel. When Jeremiah (3.1f) later talks of the wonder of God's love as the scandalous act of taking back a divorced wife who is living with another man, he is clearly thinking of Hosea's treatment of Gomer. Here in this picture of Hosea's return in love to Gomer we have the deep truth, clearly worked out in the prophet's teaching, that when Israel "filled with the spirit of whore-

---

[1] Contrast von Rad, op. cit. II, p. 141.    [2] See above, pp. 175ff.

dom" finds it impossible to turn or return to God, he himself turns (RSV recoils, Hos. 11.8f) to her, and goes back in love to his people.

Out of the background of a broken and mended marriage comes Hosea's belief in the return of Israel to her God and the reuniting of the two kingdoms under the Davidic monarchy in the future. As so often in the prophetic books, his prophetic call contains the epitome of all his teaching. The daring with which, as he talks of the marriage relationship, he takes words and metaphors from the contemporary fertility cults and myths (2.8f) means that he is deliberately rescuing God's marriage with Israel—a relationship based on sober faithfulness one to the other—from all association with Canaanite sexual cults. The Lord has triumphed over Baal, and Israel has learned that it is he, who brought her out of Egypt, who gave her corn and wine and oil. Hosea links marriage with full family life, using the word "son" of "my people Israel", following the early Mosaic tradition (Exod. 4.22), and enriching it with the very human picture of a father patiently teaching his son to walk (Hos. 11.3). We hear God, the divine father, cry to his stubborn rebellious son who deserved stoning (Deut. 21.20f), How can I deliver you up? How can I hand you over? My heart recoils within me, my compassion grows warm and tender (Hos. 11.8).

Hosea uses the ambiguous name "I am" by which the Lord revealed himself to Moses (Exod. 3.14) when, at the birth of the second son, "Not my people", the Lord declares, I will not be "I am" to them (Hos. 1.9). The threat is terrible and tragic for Israel. God's revelation has been taken away as the family ties between God and Israel are broken. The door of God's home is shut on Israel; he no longer recognizes her as related to him, as his people. But the terrible threat is immediately met by a renewal of the promise made to Abraham of numberless progeny (Gen. 22.17), a united kingdom, and new life from seed that God has sown (Hos. 2.23). Perhaps there is a hint of the resurrection seen later by Ezekiel, that leaps beyond death and the grave (6.1f), and expresses the joy of marital reconciliation and love restored. The door of the home is open again; but before Israel can enter she must make the long journey through the desert (2.15; cf. 3.4f). It is in line with this that Hosea, like Elijah, was not willing to accept as final the rupture in the Davidic kingdom.

In this picture of God the all-important element is the initiative in his love, unconditional on any response from Israel, a love freely given (14.4)—a real truth that the prophet has distilled from the traditions of the past. Over against this is the incredibly stupid behaviour of Israel as bride or as son. Even at birth, when the process was to be straightforward and easy, he suddenly turned and caused all the trouble and difficulty of breach birth (13.13; cf. 12.3 and Gen. 25.26).

Other pictures of God, apart from Bridegroom and Father, are Healer or Doctor who, the people know, can be relied on to heal them whenever they go to him (Hos. 6.1). God is grieved that, when he wants to heal them, he discovers only more disease (7.1). Before they were conscious of his healing, he had been their doctor (11.3); and, if now they return to him, it is he and not their idols or the Canaanite god of health who will cure them and love them freely (14.4).

But it is the sudden images of God contained in a word or phrase that are so striking. God will be the bird-catcher who traps the silly dove Ephraim, calling to Egypt and fluttering to Assyria (7.11f). He will be like a lion to Ephraim, like a young lion that tears and goes away, or carries off without anyone being able to deliver—so God will punish and withdraw till they seek him in sincerity (5.14f). From being their Deliverer who brought them out of Egypt and who knew them in the wilderness, God will become to them a devouring lion because of their pride (13.6ff), fierce as a bear deprived of her cubs, cunning as a leopard suddenly springing on them. Curiously Hosea speaks of God as a moth or dry rot which destroys in secret till it is too late to check it (5.12). And there is another more constructive picture from the realm of nature. He is reliable as the dawn (6.3), as refreshing as the early rain, as satisfying as the heavy autumn rain. He is like the gentle refreshing dew (14.5ff). The prophet even speaks of God in terms of flowers and trees. God gives the beauty of the lily, the strong deep roots of the trees of Lebanon, the spreading, fruitful branches of the olive, and from him goes out all the fragrant scent of Lebanon. But God himself is like a green cypress tree—Israel dwells under his shade—and from him comes all the fruitfulness of tree and field. Clearly the prophet is claiming for the Lord all the fertilizing power ascribed to Baal by his worshippers; but it is the actual historic Israel who is God's partner, and not some goddess of love and war. The godhead remains a unity and is not sexually divided.

All these pictures have in common the fact that they express *activity*. God is the living God (1.10) and is known in all his varied actions. These flashing word-pictures are each one meant to convey one thought, one way in which Hosea experienced God; but all of them are living images in stark contrast to the dead, lifeless images made by idol worshippers, which Hosea is the first prophet to condemn. All of them suggest God who is saving Israel from the degrada-

tion of fertility cults that are eating into all personal and family life
and into the national and political order.

The prophet also uses striking metaphors and pictures to describe
Israel and his sins—Ephraim is a cake not turned, or half-baked (7.8).
He has no consistency—he mixes himself with heathen peoples, dis-
sipates his strength with them, and is getting old. Grey hairs are
coming and he does not notice. He is like a silly dove fluttering round
and achieving nothing. Israel is like a stubborn heifer (4.16), this
simile being loaded with meaning, for the Canaanite Asherah was the
goddess heifer with whom Baal mated. Israel does not cry to God in
her heart, but howls like a child into her bed (7.14), or when they do
cry to him they are utterly self-deceived. Like the Jews of the first
century A.D. who cried Lord, Lord, (Matt. 7.21f) they cry "My God,
we Israel know thee" (Hos. 8.2). There is no sincerity. They are "like
the morning mist, or like the dew that goes early away, like the chaff
that swirls from the threshing floor, or like the smoke from a window"
(13.3). They sow wind and reap whirlwind and there is no standing
corn with full ear for food (8.7).

Though the story of Hosea's marriage refers to something in the
past, the teaching of the book shows the prophet facing a crisis in the
actual present. A characteristic word he uses is Now (4.16; 5.3, 7;
7.2; 8.8, 10, 13; 10.2, 3; cf. 13.13). There is moral anarchy in the
nation's contemporary life, and now God is calling Israel to account
in a legal trial (4.1ff). Lack of truth, mercy, knowledge of God
expresses itself in swearing, lying, killing, stealing, and committing
adultery. There are no limits; murder follows murder. No one dare
reprove, though the prophet suddenly breaks out, "I am a rebuker of
them all" (5.2). Greedy, adulterous, quarrelsome priests have forgotten the law that they should have been teaching (4.4ff). They had
not taught the people the knowledge of God, and so the people were
destroyed for lack of knowledge, and Israel was unaware that it was
the Lord who had given her grain (2.8). She had credited it to Baal.[1]
But the people are like the priests, and though the laws might be
written for them in tens of thousands, they would regard them as
strange, alien to their life (8.12). Prophet and priest stumble together;
the royal house, the civil rulers are as bad. Playing on the word he
declares "Rulers are unruly" or "Princes unprincipled" (9.15). They
should be responsible for justice, yet it is they who plot and murder
(5.2), rejoice in lies and wickedness, and make themselves sick as they
inflame themselves with wine (7.4f). God has had no hand in their

[1] Note that the priest was sent to Bethel to teach (2 Kings 17.27).

coronation (8.4) or their assassination of their predecessors, and like a chip of wood carried away on water they will perish (10.7).

The religious life and festivals (4.13f) are described with all the intensity of a reformer who is himself emotionally involved, and it is possible that some of the difficulties of the Hebrew text reflect passionate emotion that ignores grammar and syntax. An Israelite might know what it meant for his own bride to commit adultery under shady oaks and terebinths and for her to be amazed when he called these syncretistic religious acts whoredom—acts which she merely regarded as customs of the land commanded by the God of Israel. Further, he might know from his own experience that it was the men, the priests, who were at fault, and she was caught up in a system from which she could not free herself. Hosea's experience made him condemn the whole system. It is this whoredom that produces ritual impurity (5.3; 6.10). The golden bulls of Samaria at Dan and Bethel,[1] emblems of the presence of the Lord like the Ark at Jerusalem, are contemptuously called man-made calves. "It is not God", says Hosea (8.6). The multiplication of altars and lovely stone pillars have increased sin and God will smite them (10.1f). People bring animal sacrifices (5.6), offer them, and join in sacrificial meals; but God does not accept them (8.13). They are polluted like the bread of mourners; and in the poured out wine offering he has no pleasure (9.4). The prophet cries, Take with you *words* instead of bullocks and return to the Lord (14.2). God says, "I desire steadfast love and not sacrifice, the knowledge of God rather than burnt offerings" (6.6).

The prophet's emphasis on the present sins of Israel is reinforced in the final section of the book by reference to the nation's past, in which he highlights events that began the present corruption. Already in the first chapter the first child had been named Jezreel, Sown by God—a reference to the fertility cults (2.22f)—but the name is also linked with the place where Jehu massacred all the remnant of the house of Ahab (2 Kings 10.11).[2] When Hosea began this prophecy a hundred years later, this act is about to be avenged by the Lord on the reigning dynasty, founded by Jehu (Hos. 1.4). In Hosea's view of history, the blood of Jezreel is the seed of the present corrupt and unstable monarchy (5.7f; 8.4). But the moral decadence of the monarchy is traced back beyond Jehu to the first king, Saul, whose first act of disobedience that caused his rejection took place at Gilgal (9.15). It was there that princes became unprincipled and rulers unruly, as he

---

[1] House of God, called by Hosea Bethaven, House of Iniquity (10.5).
[2] An act praised in the Book of Kings (10.30).

bitingly declares. Israel had asked for king and princes, and God had given them in his anger and removed them in his wrath.[1] At Gilgal Saul was condemned by Samuel for putting sacrificial ritual before obedient listening to God (1 Sam. 15.22). Gilgal, too, was the first camping-place of Israel when they entered Canaan. There Achan's sin of selfish sacrilege had to be drastically wiped out (Josh. 7.24f); but an obedient Israel will find the valley of Achor[2] a door of hope (Hos. 2.15).

When Israel settled in Canaan, perversion showed itself in Benjamin's conduct at Gibeah, where nearly a whole tribe had to be wiped out at a terrific cost of life to attackers and attacked (Judges 19.16; Hos. 9.9). This time it will be foreign peoples who will smite them (10.9f). Perhaps here too Hosea is thinking of the beginning of the monarchy now so corrupt, for Gibeah was Saul's home town.

Going still further back, it was at Baal Peor (9.10) at the end of the wilderness journey that the beginning of Baal worship in all its loathsome folly was first seen in Israel (Num. 25.3ff). This was a day to which other religious leaders pointed (Deut. 4.3; Ps. 106.28), a day at the beginning of Israel's life with God, who had found her in the wilderness, when he picked her like the first ripe figs in their season. It was then she consecrated herself to the "shameful thing" and became as abominable as the thing she loved.

Yet this is the God who has delivered her from Egypt (Hos. 2.15), called his son from there (11.1), sent a prophet, Moses, to lead her out (12.13). Again he must remind her of it by making her dwell once more in tents as then, and as in the solemn Feast of Tabernacles (12.9) she will know that he is her Saviour and none other (13.4). He is the Holy One in her midst (11.9) but has come not to destroy (cf. 6.1). He will bring peace through all creation when she turns to him in love.

## Joel

Between the books of Hosea and Amos is the undated book Joel.[3] It has much in common with Amos, and both speak of a locust plague and burning drought. Both know the idea of the Day of the Lord, and Joel also uses the verse with which the book of Amos opens (Joel 3.16: Amos 1.2). These affinities may have influenced the placing of the book next to Amos.

[1] 1 Sam. 11.15. See above, p. 121.
[2] Achor in Hebrew means "trouble".
[3] LXX and Baba Bathra place it after Micah.

There is no setting in history, and indeed no detail as to place, time, or the life of the writer. The prophecy arises from the great locust plagues that year after year devastated the land, and it regards these as sent by God (2.25). In one particular year the plague was more severe than in any within the memory of the old men or their fathers. It had stripped bark from all the trees and left the whole country bare, as though fire had devoured pastures or a flame the trees (1.19). Before the locusts came the land was like the Garden of Eden, but afterwards a desolate wilderness (2.3). In vivid language they are described as a great nation and mighty invading army, climbing city walls, advancing in serried ranks, entering windows of houses. Like great thick clouds they darken the light of sun, moon, and stars. More terrible still, daily sacrifices and the Temple ritual have ceased (1.9, 13). The prophet calls priests, elders, and people to a great day of mourning, a fast and solemn assembly at the house of the Lord (1.13f; 2.15ff).[1] Repentance is spoken of in ritual terms. The priests will stand and weep between the outer court and the altar (2.17) and the words of their prayer are prescribed. The blessings too are to be ritual.

The prophet believes that because God's host is exceeding great and his power wonderful (2.11), if the people return to him with all their heart, with fasting, weeping, rending their hearts and not their garments, he will still remove their distress. He describes God in the words used in the theophany to Moses (Exod. 34.6; cf. Jonah 4.2) as gracious and merciful, slow to anger and abounding in steadfast love. As we shall see in the book of Amos, a vital possibility remains open. Perhaps[2] (RSV who knows) the Lord may turn, change his mind, and leave behind a blessing, a harvest that can be used for cereal and drink offerings to himself (Joel 2.14). Priests and people are again urged to join in pleading with God to spare his people. Then suddenly the Lord responds (2.18).

It is the turning-point in the whole prophecy. The enemy—here called Northerners[3]—will be driven out, fertility revived for man and beast, and the years that the locusts have eaten will be restored. The idyllic picture of the future, characteristic of the prophets, is clearly an event of wonder never again to be reversed (2.26f) and the miracle will prove that the Lord is in their midst, that he alone is their God.

This restoration of fertility is to be the prelude to the pouring out of

---

[1] The priests are called by a late title, ministers of the Lord and altar. "Weapon" in 2.8 is also a late word.

[2] See below, pp. 232f. Amos. 5.15.

[3] This may be a reference to Jer. 1.14; Ezek. 38.6, 15.

God's spirit (2.28). It is interesting that the primary association of spirit with wind or breath as an unseen force here, as in Ezekiel (39.29), gives way to the idea of a fluid that can be poured, as though the association is with sacrificial blood poured out (Lev. 4.7), or with the sacred oil with which prophet, priest, and king were anointed. The same imagery is used elsewhere of the pouring out of the spirit of grace and supplication on the house of David and the inhabitants of Jerusalem (Zech. 12.10). The word is often used of God's pouring out of his wrath, and perhaps the pouring out of the spirit makes a deliberate contrast to this.[1]

The spirit is to be poured out on "all flesh" (cf. Isa. 40.5). As Jeremiah saw that the new covenant would do away with the need for priests to teach the knowledge of God, so Joel foretells the end of prophets as a separate class. All will have the spirit of prophecy, young and old, sons and daughters of Israel, servants and hand-maidens.

It is important that the plague is likened to the Day of the Lord expected by priests and people. In words found in the book of Isaiah (13.6) the prophet cries (Joel 1.15),

> Alas for the Day! For the Day of the Lord is near,
> and as destruction from the Almighty it comes.

The Day is described in terms of the darkness of the locust clouds. It is great and very terrible (2.11). There will be portents in the heaven, war on earth, sun eclipsed,[2] and the moon turned blood-red, imagery used by later apocalyptists such as Zechariah and Daniel. These signs will announce the Day of the Lord, and the deliverance of all who worship him (2.30ff). The fortunes of Judah and Jerusalem will be restored.

Unlike Amos, Joel looks for the final Day of the Lord as a day of vengeance on other nations, a day bringing the return of scattered Israel. The nations will be gathered in the valley of Jehoshaphat (3.2–12)[3] and cut down like a ripe harvest. They will have to hand back scattered, captured Israelites, sold as slaves by Tyre, Zidon, and Philistia to the Greeks (3.6).[4] Ironically the prophet depicts the enemy nations, in contradiction to the promise of Isaiah (2.4) and Micah (4.3)

---

[1] See above, p. 211.  [2] Another link with Amos.

[3] The word means "The Lord has judged". The valley is unknown in Palestine until the time of Eusebius. In 3.14 it is called the valley of decision.

[4] W. F. Albright, *From Stone Age to Christianity* (1940), p. 259, says Greeks appear in the Near East in the eighth century B.C.

beating agricultural tools into weapons of war (Joel 3.10). But it will be in vain. The Lord will roar from Zion; dwelling in Zion he will be a refuge for his people. Judah and Jerusalem will abide for ever (3.20).

Thirty of the seventy-five verses in this book are duplicated in other prophetic books. The language is vivid and symbolic, and apocalyptic writers were very familiar with it.

Possibly the whole account of the locust plague is an extended allegory of foreign oppression. Throughout sounds the comfort of a nationalist prophet. There are no specific indictments of the people for idolatry and false worship, nor for social and moral crimes. But they are called to acts of penitence in the Temple. As in Ezekiel and post-exilic prophets, stress lies on the importance of corporate Temple worship.[1]

## Amos

The real successor of the uncompromising Elijah, who had come from Transjordan to confront the northern kingdom with his stern "either ... or ...", was Amos, who, in the eighth century B.C., came to them from even further afield, from the wild Judaean hills of Tekoa, south of Bethlehem. Only about forty years had elapsed after the death of Elisha before Amos appeared at Bethel, the royal shrine in the northern kingdom, and was driven out by the high priest as a dangerous revolutionary. Elisha had championed Israel as her "chariots and horsemen" against the invading Syrians (2 Kings 13.14). That threat had passed, and during the long prosperous reigns of Jeroboam II in the north, and Uzziah who loved husbandry (2 Chron. 26.10) in the south, a generation had grown up without experience of war and devastation.

A false sense of security had brought wealth and prosperity and a note of joyous optimism, but with these came self-confidence and indifference to the needs of others. Goodness and God had gone out of the nation's life and had been replaced by oppression and injustice, luxury and ostentation in secular and religious life. Expansion of Mediterranean trade had put into the hands of individual merchants wealth that was squandered in senseless indulgence (Amos. 4.1; 5.11), emphasizing the gap between rich and poor. The upper classes had built great houses for themselves in imitation of the royal palace at Samaria with its beautiful inlaid ivory (3.15; 6.4; cf. 1 Kings 22.39), examples of which have been found during excavations. Feasting was

[1] J. A. S. Kapelrud, *Joel Studies* (1948).

habitual and the custom of half-reclining on a couch at table had been introduced (Amos 3.12, RV).

Prosperity was bringing with it far-reaching economic dangers. The small farmer who owned his own land and was the backbone of the nation was disappearing; a bad year meant mortgages at exorbitant rates of interest paid to the new rich class, who were engaged in trade and not restrained by the traditional loyalties of the family and tribal system. Documents found at Nuzi[1] show how a wealthy family won its lawsuit because it could afford to keep documents and employ the best advocates, and judges were almost powerless.

A selfish cruelty was encouraged by the leading ladies of the land, sleek cows of Bashan feeding on Samaria's hills, careless of the fact that the wine with which their husbands kept them supplied was obtained at the cost of crushing the needy (4.1). The masters in Zion and Samaria behaved in the same way:

> Lying on ivory beds, sprawling on couches,
> Eating lambs from the flock and calves from the stall,
> Singing wanton songs to harps such as David contrived,
> Drinking wine by the pailful, soothed with fine lotions,
> They feel no smart though their nation be broken! (6.4ff.)

So rampant is evil that the prudent man keeps silent (5.13).

Equally dangerous for national life was religious ostentation. The great sanctuaries at Bethel, Gilgal, and Beersheba were crowded by throngs who, Amos suggests, would willingly bring their annual sacrifices every morning and their triennial tithes every three days, and who would let everyone know how generous were their freewill offerings by seeing that their names appeared prominently in published subscription lists (4.4f). From the shrines flowed the noise of songs and the melody of guitars (5.23),[2] instead of justice and righteousness which should have flowed like a never-failing stream. It was the festival at the sanctuary men were seeking, not the life-giving God whose presence they so glibly boasted of (5.4f, 14).

Into this situation Amos was forced by the God who had seized him as he followed the flock over the hills of Judah (7.15). His call was a dramatic and frightening experience. Not only does he use the violent word "arrest" or "seize" of God's action, but he likens his own reaction to the fear that inevitably comes when the alarm of war is

---

[1] Cf. *Expository Times* (July 1955), pp. 315ff.

[2] The prophet has here chosen a word with a similar sound to the Hebrew word for "folly".

sounded or the lion roars (3.6ff). There is a terrifying imperative in God's call:

> The Lord from Zion roars, and from Jerusalem utters his voice.
> The shepherds' bowers mourn, the top of Carmel withers (1.2).

The man who hears knows that the Lord God has spoken, and he must prophesy. The knowledge brought to Amos new certainty of the real presence of God and of his intimate concern for his people, whom he was trying to save from imminent self-destruction. God was actively judging nations and individuals by known moral standards, not to condemn them but to win their repentance.

In the opening verses of the book, Amos is described as a keeper of small highland sheep famous for their wool.[1] He described himself as a herdsman[2] and one who tended sycamore (a type of fig) trees. Tekoa was the centre of the grazing-grounds for the highland sheep, but was too high and dry for fig trees, which flourished in the Jordan valley, on the western slopes of the Judaean hills, and in Samaria. His self-description suggests that, like many dwellers in Tekoa since, he was a seasonal labourer, eking out a living on the hills in lambing and shearing time and then leaving his home for the seasonal occupation of tending and gathering the fig crops.[3] His home town of Tekoa was famous for its wisdom (2 Sam. 14.2). Amos' book has many contacts with Wisdom literature, and it has been suggested that his teaching reflects the traditional wisdom of home and people rather than the Temple cultus.[4]

His activity is dated in the eighth century, in the reigns of Uzziah of Judah and Jeroboam of Israel, "two years before the earthquake" (1.1), which is referred to again by Second-Zechariah (14.5) as an experience comparable to the dread Day of the Lord's coming. Much of Amos' imagery suggests earthquake experiences. He foretells that the great altar at Bethel and the luxurious houses—winter houses, summer houses, ivory houses, all the great houses—will perish (3.15).

---

[1] Like Mesha king of Moab (2 Kings 3.4).

[2] In Hebrew herdsman and shepherd are words that could be confused.

[3] This seems more likely than that "shepherd" denotes a cultic official at the sanctuary, contrast A. R. Haldar, op. cit. There is no evidence that "herdsman" or "one who tends fig trees" were cultic designations. Against the suggestion that he must have been an important owner of flocks and fig trees because his language shows considerable skill, it must be noted that his father's name is not mentioned, that the uneducated Caedmon looked after the cows for the community, and that Bunyan was "a tinker oft in quod".

[4] H. W. Wolff, *Amos' Geistige Heimat* (1964).

Houses great and small will be smitten with cracks and breaches (6.11). The land will tremble, rising like a flood and falling as though drowned (8.8). In vision he sees Israel as a wall tested by a plumb-line and found to be so dangerously out of true that it will have to be demolished (7.7f). In his final vision of destruction and annihilation, he sees the Lord standing by the altar, calling for the smiting of the pillars of the temple, the shaking of the threshold and the crash of the roof on the heads of the doomed congregation (9.1f). Once he seems to look back to an earthquake and to explain that God had sent it as a warning, rescuing a few as a brand plucked from the burning, "yet you did not return to me, says the Lord" (4.11).

Probably the writer wants us to know how amazingly accurate were the prophet's predictions, made two years before the earthquake actually came. The God who roared from Zion, who did nothing without revealing his secret to his servants the prophets (3.7), had faithfully fulfilled the predictions proclaimed by his servant with such assurance as the word of the Lord.

The prophet's first task (chapters 1 and 2), to which he was impelled when the roar of God's voice resounded from Zion to Carmel in the north and the shepherds' pastures in the south, was to make it known that God was still deeply concerned with all the ancient realm once promised as an everlasting kingdom to the Davidic dynasty. All the small neighbouring peoples of Syria, Philistia, Phoenicia, Edom, Ammon, and Moab, together with Judah and Israel had in the prophet's view constituted that kingdom, and so once knew God's rule and moral demands. It was God's purpose to restore that kingdom, purged of sinners who denied that there would ever be a moral reckoning (9.10f). All these now separated peoples were still under God's judgement, introduced to each one with ,"Thus saith the Lord", and ending with, "The Lord has spoken". Each sentence of doom begins with a numerical formula implying an indefinite number (1.3; cf. Jer. 36.23): "For three or four transgressions, I will not hinder doom." There follows the same punishment for each one: "I will send a fire . . . and it shall devour" (cf. Hos. 8.14; Jer. 17.27, for similar threats against Israel and Judah). Each of the small neighbouring peoples has committed a crime against humanity, Judah has rejected the instruction and statutes of the Lord and worshipped idols (Amos 2.4).

So far the message has probably won the approval of the prophet's audience; but now he dramatically rounds on Israel, the northern kingdom, with a searching indictment. The crimes are moral and within Israel herself; community loyalty has been replaced by self-seeking, cruelty, oppression of the innocent by corrupt judges, selling men into slavery for a debt as trifling as a pair of sandals, trampling on the poor, and perverting the cause of the humble. There is religious prostitution, which was part of the fertility cults of Canaan—the Mesha stone,[1] dated about 830 B.C., records that seven thousand of these male and female prostitutes were taken captive from the Israelite (*Yahweh*) temple on Mount Nebo. As Hosea was concerned with the effect on the family, so Amos condemns the sheer indecency of it, that a father and a son should have intercourse with the same young girl.[2] There is the sin of making religion an excuse to cover inhuman conduct. The Law (Exod. 22.26; Deut. 24.12f) required garments taken as pledge for debt to be returned at night. But unjust creditors retained them, spreading them round altars when, at feasts, they drank wine which had been seized for debt. Amos, thinking of these altars, draws a sarcastic contrast between what he calls "the house of their God" (Amos 2.8) and the Lord, who had defeated their foes and led them into the promised land. He had raised up prophets, but they had forbidden them to prophesy. He had raised up Nazirites to give them the ideal of a consecrated life, but they had made them break their vow and drink wine (2.11f).

The prophet's condemnation was chiefly directed against Israel, the northern kingdom, but through him God has reminded them that they are part of Greater Israel, the whole clan involved in the Deliverance (2.10; cf. 3.1). It is fitting therefore that Amos' second task (chapter 3) is to call together for judgement the whole family, Israel as meaning all the twelve tribes that God brought up from Egypt. The great words covenant, choice, my people, which we find frequently in the Law and in Jeremiah and Ezekiel, are missing from the startling quatrain with which the prophet begins, and instead we have the word for the marriage relationship that occurs, as we saw, in the story of Abraham (Gen. 18.19. RSV marg.):

Only you have I known[3] (been intimate with) from all earth's families,
Therefore I will visit on you all your sins.

Basic to both popular and prophetic religion in both kingdoms was the belief that there was a unique relationship between the people of

---

[1] S. R. Driver, *Notes on the Hebrew Text of the Books of Samuel*, (1913), pp. lxxxvif.

[2] "To profane my holy name" (2.7) is a phrase found in Ezekiel and the Holiness Code, and may be late.

[3] See above, p. 21.

Israel and her God. It seems that here Amos, like Jeremiah and Ezekiel after him, but unlike the editors of the books of Kings, regards the schismatic north as still sharing that special relationship.

As though to answer a protest from those who objected to his unwelcome message, Amos explains why, when God speaks, any man who hears has no choice but to prophesy; it is the inevitable outcome of the close bond between God and his prophets. Seven examples show that every effect has a cause—that there is never smoke without fire:

Two people walking out in the desert must have made an appointment.
A lion roars—he has taken prey.
A young lion cries in his den—he has taken something.
If a bird was snared—there was a trap.
If a trap springs—it was touched.
If a trumpet was blown in a city—someone had been frightened and seen reason to blow it.
If evil happens to a city—God caused it.

Then he argues not from the effect back to its cause, but from the Great Cause onward to its inevitable effect:

> Surely the Lord God does nothing
> without revealing his secret
> to his servants the prophets.
> The lion has roared;
> who will not fear?
> The Lord God has spoken;
> who can but prophesy? (3.7f)

The end of this part of Amos' prophecy raises a question which affects the whole interpretation of his book. Did he see any hope for the future Israel of the north? As often in the prophetic literature foreign nations[1] are called to execute God's judgement, leaving only a useless remnant like a couple of chewed legs or a bit of a lamb's ear rescued from a lion's mouth. Palaces, altars, and homes will all perish. In a later prophecy introduced by the dirge:

> Fallen, no more to rise,
> The virgin of Israel,
> Spread out on her land,
> None raise her up (5.2),

[1] Here Hebrew has Ashdod and Egypt, but LXX, followed by RSV, has Assyria instead of Ashdod (3.9).

he speaks of a tenth remaining. He announces that the day to which they all look forward with joy, when the Lord will come in power, will be a day of mourning and lamentation, of darkness and not light (5.16ff). The wine-drinking, gluttonous leaders will be the first to go into captivity (6.7), and though ten men survive in a house they shall all die. The vivid visions shown by the Lord to the prophet and presented as part of his preaching at Bethel (7ff) describe destruction so absolute that the prophet cries out to God to forgive, to stop the locust plague and the terrible drought that devoured the land as though a great fire raged beneath it. Twice God responds to his intercession.[1] But after this Amos does not intercede and there is no mitigation of the doom pronounced by God. The wall must be demolished. God will not again come to Israel (7.8; 8.2). The basket of summer fruit presages the end of harvest, and the end of Israel and God's special relationship to her.

That Amos twice makes intercession is however highly significant of the relationship between God and the prophet. The human personality and mental powers are not superseded as Amos remonstrates with God and even suceeds in winning him to modify the divine decree (7.3, 6).

To return to the question as to whether Amos was allowed to offer Israel any hope for the future, it must be pointed out that we get glimpses of another picture, faint at first but so boldly outlined at the end (9.11ff) that many scholars have regarded it as added later. Yet it is consistent with the power and purpose of Amos' God. The prophet's task had been not only to pronounce judgement and doom, but to intercede with God and to win the people to repentance. We listen to his interpretation of history as revealing God's persistent patience (4.6ff). Famine, drought, blight, plague, war, and earthquake have been sent by God: "Yet have you not returned to me, says the Lord." Now final doom would come, God himself would confront them, and the prophet cries, "Prepare to meet your God!" As though to emphasize the awe of meeting the great Creator of the world, verses of a hymn of praise[2] are quoted here (4.13; also 5.8f; 9.6) by the prophet or an editor.

But all the suffering and punishment, and God's imminent appearance, spring from his desire and purpose to save. One of the most significant words of Amos and integral to his message is "Perhaps"[3] (RSV "may be" 5.15):

[1] He "repents" and stops the punishment.     [2] See above, p. 180.
[3] See above, pp. 116f and below, p. 247.

Hate evil, love good, and establish justice in the gate;
perhaps the Lord God of Hosts will be gracious to the remnant of
Joseph.

So the problem may be answered by saying that ultimately the prophet believed simply that Israel's future lay in God's hands.

The "perhaps" emphasizes that salvation comes to man not because
of his own behaviour but because of God's free grace. It is independent of human effort and depends on God. The prophet's whole
teaching is theocentric. Even if the people reform, that will not have
efficacy that forces God to grant political rescue. It is a startling doctrine, but consistent with Amos' rejection of the maintenance of the
institutional and sacrificial cult as an enjoyable religious safety pre-
caution. He stands out clearly in the line of Israel's reforming prophets.

Amos' attitude to the sacrificial cult of temples and shrines is still a
matter of considerable controversy, which today reflects the ecumenical temper of the past decades. It used to be suggested without
further qualification that he had carried to its logical conclusion
Samuel's contrast between sacrifice and obedience, and proclaimed
that, though God spoke to men from Jerusalem or Zion, yet all altars,
ritual, festivals, and feasts had no place in the true worship of Israel's
God, nor in her early traditions before they were contaminated by
Canaanite cults; in line with this it was urged that he repudiated any
links with professional ecstatic and cultic prophets. But clearly he did
not condemn all religious institutions, and God had established Nazirites and prophets in Israel's religion (2.11). To them God revealed
his secret with irresistible urgency, and when they heard him speak
they had to prophesy.

Today it is asked whether Amos' condemnation of sacrifice is to
be understood as poetic hyperbole. It is suggested that it would have
been impossible for him to envisage any religion without the public
acts of animal sacrifices, feasts, and festivals, and it is concluded that
he condemned only the misuse of the sacrificial cult, sacrifice without righteousness.

Certainly, when he makes his startling appeal to the Mosaic tradition and asks the rhetorical question, "Did you bring to me sacrifices
and offerings the forty years in the wilderness, O house of Israel?"
(5.25), the answer expected is No; and that there was such a tradition
of the early Israelite religion without sacrifice, known and accepted by
prophets, seems confirmed by Jeremiah's even more emphatic statement later (7.21ff) that God commanded obedience, not sacrifice, and

that if a meat meal was what was wanted, men could eat God's portion as well. So Amos sarcastically calls them to relish their sacrifices better by eating them with leavened bread, although the Law forbids it (Amos 4.5; cf. Lev. 2.11). His explicit contrast between seeking God and seeking Bethel, Gilgal, or Beersheba, the famous traditional pilgrimage shrines (Amos 5.4f), puns on the sound of these names in a way showing scant respect for their holiness. God's rejection of pilgrim festivals and sacred assemblies could scarcely be expressed in stronger language (5.21; cf. Isa. 1.13):

> I hate, I despise your feast days,
> I will not participate in your sacred assemblies.
> Though you offer me burnt offerings with your meal offerings
> I will not accept them.
> Neither will I pay heed to the peace offerings of your fat beasts.

There does not appear to be the slightest hint anywhere in the prophecy that the Lord had commanded or desired animal sacrifices, and in the closing prophecy of the restoration of the Davidic kingdom (Amos 9.11–15) it is the cities that are to be rebuilt; but temples are not mentioned. We know nothing of any ritual way of seeking God approved by Amos.

The position of Amos himself as a prophet is also a matter of current debate. Amaziah addresses him as Seer or Visionary (7.12) and tells him to go back to Judah if he wants to earn his bread in that way (cf. Mic. 3.5). Amos retorts:

> No prophet I. No son of a prophet I.
> Surely a herdsman I, a dresser of sycamore fig trees.
> It was the Lord seized me as I followed the sheep, and sent me to prophesy.

It is idiomatic Hebrew to dispense with the verb "to be" in such a sentence, which may mean I *was* no professional prophet till the Lord told me to prophesy *or* I *am* no professional prophet (RSV and RV marg.), even though the Lord sent me to prophesy—I have not become a professional prophet, I am still a herdsman used by God as a prophet and sent to Israel with a message. It is certainly not possible to dogmatize as to the meaning of the Hebrew.[1] But the natural interpretation seems to be that while Amos had a high regard for prophets as servants and messengers of God (3.7ff), he made no claim to be a professional prophet. From his own experience he knew that God

---

[1] Cf. G. R. Driver, *Expository Times* (December 1955), p. 91.

could and did choose any man. He himself had been taken from his ordinary lay occupation and sent with a special message to Israel. We know nothing more of his life; but it seems a fair assumption that having delivered his message he returned to the flocks.

No miracle and wonder stories are related of him, nor any signs or prophetic, functional acts. His visions were not induced by music or the contagion of group ecstasy. He seems to have done his preaching under strong compulsion from what we may call true spiritual enlightenment. Two streams of religion unite in him, one from Wisdom and one from Prophecy, and he bequeathed to Israel great spiritual truth in his teaching, that privilege implies responsibility and failure to meet responsibility brings inevitable punishment. Men and nations must live, and are judged, by the light they have. Religious ritual, however delightful and elaborate, cannot replace the seeking of God and goodness, nor be a substitute for just and righteous conduct.

Another great truth shines out from his life. God chooses whom he wills to speak for him. In the long line of workmen faithfully following their ordinary daily task whom God has surprised with his call, Amos was a leading figure.

## Obadiah

Like Joel, Obadiah is given no setting in history, and as with Amos we know nothing of his family, not even his father's name. He is placed in the Hebrew Bible after Amos probably because Amos prophesied against Edom (9.12), a prophecy evidently regarded in the book of Obadiah as fulfilled. This shortest book in the Bible, of which nearly a third occurs in Jeremiah (49), breathes a nationalist spirit, like Joel, Nahum, and Zephaniah. Edom had done violence to Jacob or Jerusalem when foreigners invaded—they had looted it. Now Edom's own confederates will be used by the Lord to destroy her from her rock-hewn fortress of Petra.

In verses 12ff the verb, which has been in the past, suddenly changes to the imperative, as though an opportunity is coming to Edom to do as she had done before: "Do not gloat [RSV, you should not have gloated] over the day of your brother in the day of his misfortune . . . in the day of their ruin—the day of distress . . . the day of his calamity." Finally, Edom is not to stand at the cross-roads to cut off fugitives and deliver them up in the day of their distress. This constant reiteration of "in the day" suggests a prophetic formula that could be used, as here, for retrospect of the past, or presentation of contemporary circumstances, for blessing or cursing, a framework that could be adapted to current needs.

The phrase "set thy nest" (v. 4; cf. Jer. 49.16) here used of Edom in its high, rocky cleft of Petra, and exaggerated to the picture of an eagle nesting among the stars, is used by Balaam (Num. 24.21) with a play on the Hebrew words "Kenite" and "nest", a fact which suggests that professional prophets had their set forms of words which they could use on the hills, in the gateway, or at the shrine, wherever men gathered, just as priests used their liturgies in Temple services. If the often misused, and sometimes overworked, word "cultic"[1] is applied to such set formulas, it must not be taken to mean that the prophet, like the priest, was always part of the Temple personnel. Obadiah, like Balaam, may have been a prophet who knew, and here uses, traditional forms and phrases of the prophetic guilds.

This strong emphasis on "the day" when Jerusalem was destroyed is followed (v. 15) by a prophecy of the coming Day of the Lord, which, as in Joel, will be a day of the Lord's vengeance on the nations. Edom will be treated as she treated Jerusalem; Israel and Judah restored to their own land will combine to destroy her, and God's kingdom will come.

Edom's treachery to Judah when Nebuchadrezzar captured Jerusalem and the subsequent Edomite invasion of southern Palestine that produced the Idumaea of the New Testament, left a legacy of bitter hatred reflected in Old Testament post-exilic literature. Edom becomes almost a symbolic name for the forces of evil that seek to destroy God's people and purposes, so that when Edom is conquered, the kingdom of God will be established.

A note that rings out in the prophet's message to Edom is, "As you have done, it shall be done to you (v. 15)—a message that is taken up in the warning of Jesus, but applied to Israel herself: "Whatever you wish that men would do to you, do so to them; for this is the law and the prophets" (Matt. 7.12).

## Jonah

Unlike the other prophetic books, the book of Jonah is not prophetic words, but a story about Jonah son of Amittai, an eighth-century prophet known to us from 2 Kings 14.25, living in a town in Northern Palestine not far from Nazareth (Josh. 19.13). This historic Jonah lived in the reign of Jeroboam II and proclaimed that the Lord was

[1] See above, p. 216, and below, p. 265.

enabling Israel to extend her borders to the limits of the old Davidic kingdom. At that time Assyria was involved in war with Urartu in the north, and was threatening Syria, so that Israel was free to regain lost territory; but later Assyria destroyed Israel with great cruelty, and it is possible that the historic Jonah lived to see this calamity.

In this book, the story tells how Jonah tried to avoid fulfilling God's call to go and cry against the cruel Assyrian conquerors of his country, was met by God's storm, picked up from the sea by God's great fish,[1] and obeyed God's second order to go to Nineveh "and proclaim to it the message that I tell you". His preaching was so successful that the king put on sackcloth, sat in ashes (3.6), and decreed, "Let neither man nor beast, herd nor flock, taste anything; let them not feed, or drink water, but let man and beast be covered with sackcloth and let them cry mightily to God; . . . When God saw . . . how they turned from their evil way, God repented"[2] and changed his mind about their destruction. God responded immediately, in accordance with the teaching of Ezekiel and Joel. But Jonah, who had hoped for the city's destruction, was angry because of God's gracious mercy. A very humane, humorous God by a simple act—very annoying to Jonah— then taught the prophet something of the divine compassion for "that great city, in which there are more than a hundred and twenty thousand persons who do not know their right hand from their left, and also much cattle" (4.11).

Some think the story is allegorical, treating Assyria in a way diametrically opposed to Jeremiah's prophecy against Babylon (51.34ff). There Babylon is likened to a great monster that swallowed Israel and "filled its belly with his delicacies". God will take vengeance, Babylon will become a heap of ruins. That is what Jonah expected God to do to Nineveh, capital of the Assyrian empire.

Perhaps this story is a form of what Jewish writers call Midrash,[3] and is an imaginative development of a biblical subject to teach a religious lesson, comparable to some of the parables of Jesus. However this may be, and whatever its origin, it makes a great leap forward in Hebrew religious thought. It contains one of the loftiest pictures in the Old Testament of the God who has no pleasure in the

---

[1] The sea monster from which, in the legend, Perseus rescued Andromeda was thought of as living near Joppa.

[2] See above, pp. 116f.

[3] The Hebrew word occurs in 2 Chron. 13.22; 24.27 (RSV "story", "Commentary"). It means "search" and in later Jewish literature is used of exposition resulting from search into the meaning of an Old Testament text.

death of anyone, not even foreigners, not even the cruel conquerors of his own people. It teaches the folly and impossibility of escaping from the purpose of God, who can use all nature to achieve his will. It shows God's love to all men—he responds to the prayer of heathen sailors (1.14ff) and is willing to "repent" at the first sign that sinners —even heathen ruler and people—are turning to him. And there is implicit a rueful confession by a prophetic writer, that even the prophet himself, that beloved and admired figure in Old Testament religion, is lagging behind, more concerned with his own reputation than with his God-given task of saving the world.

## Micah

In the preface to his book, Micah is dated as a younger contemporary of Amos, who is set in the reign of Uzziah only, and of Hosea, whose activity covered the longer period from Uzziah to Hezekiah. Micah's span excludes Uzziah and covers the next three southern kings, Jotham, Ahaz, and Hezekiah. He is also regarded as a younger contemporary of First-Isaiah, whose dating is the same as Hosea's. It is Micah's relationship to First-Isaiah that is most important.[1] Both were prophets in the southern kingdom within a few miles of each other— one in Jerusalem, the other in the Judaean foothills to the west; and on at least one important issue their messages were in complete contradiction to each other. Micah proclaimed, "Therefore because of you Zion shall be ploughed as a field, Jerusalem shall become a heap of ruins" (3.12). First-Isaiah stated equally emphatically:

> Therefore thus says the Lord to the king of Assyria: He shall not come into this city, or shoot an arrow there, or come before it with a shield, or cast up a siege mound against it. By the way that he came, by the same he shall return, and he shall not come into this city, says the Lord. For I will defend this city to save it for my own sake, and for the sake of my servant David. (37.33ff)

By the criterion of Deuteronomy (18.22) Isaiah's word was the one the Lord had spoken. But from Jeremiah (26.19) it is clear that Micah's prophecy caused Hezekiah's repentance, and so was not fulfilled at that time. The Lord's purpose was flexible,[2] and after Hezekiah's entreaty God "repented" of the evil he had pronounced.

---

[1] See above, p. 128.
[2] See above, pp. 116f. Interest in this concept, shared by the books of Micah and Jonah, may partly account for their position next to each other.

It is interesting that it is for his prophecy of the destruction of Jerusalem that Micah is remembered a century later—the only Old Testament prophet whose name is recorded, and whose words are explicitly quoted, by another prophetic book. When Jeremiah was being tried for his life before the princes of Judah, priests and prophets, accusing him of prophesying against the city and Temple, demanded the death penalty—that he be given over to the people to be put to death (26.24). But the elders quoted the precedent of the similar trial of Micah, who was acquitted because the king recognized the word as from God and repented.

Even this dangerous episode in Micah's life, however, is not recorded in the book that bears his name. There is no biography. The third chapter is regarded as autobiography (3.1,8) and contains the words "Zion shall be ploughed as a field", which are quoted in Jeremiah. But as we read the book in the light of our knowledge that Micah was tried for his life, we understand it more clearly. The opening poem pictures God coming out of his holy Temple as a king from his palace, to bear witness against his nation before the whole earth and its peoples. Especially is there contemporary relevance in the trial scene, which Micah uses as the setting for his famous prophecy of God's requirements, calling on the enduring mountains and hills of the earth to hear the Lord's legal case against his people (6.1ff). It is not surprising that Micah was arrested, and that people and rulers could not endure his fierce denunciation of their injustice and social crimes, a denunciation more outspoken than that of any other Old Testament prophet.

Using Israel to mean the whole people, Jacob for the north, and Judah for the south (1.5), and with all a countryman's distrust of capital cities, Micah condemns Samaria and Jerusalem. Samaria with her idols and all the prostitution practised there will be utterly destroyed, and as First-Isaiah for three years (20.2) took off his mourning sackcloth and went naked and barefoot, so Micah goes stripped naked in lamentation for Samaria. Devastation had reached the gates of Jerusalem, and as First-Isaiah (10.28ff) vividly depicted Assyria's rapid march on the city from the north, Micah with unforgettable play on words named the villages through which the foe would approach from the south (1.10ff). Once Micah seems to hint that he thinks of himself as standing after the final threat of Amos. Using Amos' word for harvest—summer fruit—he likens himself to one living at the end of harvest, when no clusters of grapes are left (7.1–7). The godly man who shows loyal steadfast love has perished from the land, and as for the upright, no such individual man exists. There is no trust among neighbours, nor confidence among friends. Even within the family a wife betrays her husband, a son treats his father with contempt, a daughter rises up against her mother, and a man's enemies are in his own household. Micah is the first prophet to make it explicit that if the family disintegrates, if it has lost its loyalty and piety, then the whole nation falls apart.

Those with power plan evil at night and fulfil it in the morning, coveting and seizing houses, driving out women and children from their homes. Traders give scant measure and carry their bags of deceitful weights. The prophet is forbidden to preach of disaster, and scornfully exclaims that if, filled with wind and lies, he were to preach of wine and strong drink, he would be the preacher they wanted (2.11). The heads of the North and rulers of all Israel, who should know justice, love good, and hate evil, are acting like savage cannibals. They "tear the skin from off my people, their flesh from their bones, flay their skin from them, break their bones in pieces, chop them up like meat in a kettle, like flesh in a cauldron" (3.3). Prophets proclaim peace when well paid, but declare a holy war on those who do not give them enough food (3.5; cf. Amos 7.12). Prophet, sage, and diviner will all be ashamed because God will give no answer.

In emphatic contrast, the prophet who has been saying (Mic. 3.1) all these words claims that he indeed is "filled with power, with the Spirit of the Lord, and with justice and might, to declare to Jacob his transgression, and to Israel his sin" (3.8). It seems probable that this was the defence he successfully used to justify his words at his trial before Hezekiah. The Lord, calling Israel "my people", reminds them of all his redemptive acts—the Deliverance from Egypt, their leaders Moses, Aaron, and Miriam whom he had sent, his help through all the wilderness journey till it ended at Gilgal. Then, in terms as definite as those of First-Isaiah, Hosea, and Amos, Micah proclaims obedience to the demands of God as showing itself in moral, not ritual, acts. Not burnt offerings or yearling calves, not sacrificial offerings though carried to an impossible extent—thousands of rams, ten thousand rivers of oil, and the burning of firstborn children to expiate mortal sin—but acts of justice, an attitude of loyal love, and living daily life humbly in the presence of God (6.8). Where religion is the right relationship with men and God, temple ritual is unnecessary, irrelevant, and useless. It is interesting that Micah stresses not the national and corporate, but the personal and individual element in religion and worship by his address, not to Israel, but to man, "adam". It is the universal yet individual human being who has been "showed what is good".

It is not clear what any of these eighth-century prophets and Jeremiah regarded as necessary and useful corporate religious acts[1]—or even private religious acts. Amos may have believed that the Lord roared from Zion, and First-Isaiah that he dwelt in Zion. Hosea thought that after many days without king or princes, sacrifice, pillars, priestly oracle or "teraphim", Israel would return, seek the Lord and David, and come in fear to God and his goodness. Amos, having condemned worship at the known sanctuaries, substituted seeking God and good, and doing justice. Micah does not include in God's requirements any act that would normally be called cultic, and certainly none that is a corporate religious act. By the well near Mount Gerizim Jesus is reported to have said, "Neither on this mountain nor in Jerusalem will you worship the Father. . . . God is spirit, and those who worship him must worship in spirit and truth" (John 4.21, 24). Though it has been repeatedly asserted that no Old Testament prophet had any such concept of worship and religion, one cannot avoid a suspicion that, if we accept the plain meaning of the prophetic word in the Old Testament, we may conclude that Jesus stood in the succession of the eighth-century prophets.

As in the book of Hosea, so in that of Micah there are words of hope and promise alternating with threat and condemnation. Using the word for survivors of a military conquest, the prophet promises that the Lord will gather the remnant of Israel as sheep into a fold (2.12). Their king will lead them as they break out of the beleaguered city, and the Lord will be at their head. Again, immediately following the renowned prophecy of the utter destruction of Jerusalem, there is the lovely poem breathing the countryman's desire for peace, the vision of the hill where the Lord's house is built, exalted to the tops of the mountains. All nations flow to it to learn the way of the Lord, and to hear the word of the Lord, his law coming from Zion (4.1ff; cf. Isa. 2). Here there follows a reference again to the remnant. Scattered fugitives will become a remnant and be made into a strong nation (4.7); but nations who are assembling to destroy Israel, are, unknown to themselves, being gathered by God as sheaves to the threshing floor (4.12).

There is a prophecy of the future ruler of Israel, who, like David of old, will be chosen from Bethlehem, from the smallest of the Judah clans. The messianic hope springs again from Bethlehem[2] not as king but as ruler, and not only, as other prophets tell, will he rule a

[1] See above, pp. 137ff, 179f.      [2] See above, p. 146f.

reunited Israel to which the remnant of his brethren will return (5.3ff), but in the strength of the Lord he will bring peace to the ends of the earth.

The book concludes with three short poems (7.11–13, 14–17, 18–20) forming a hymn of trust in God, who will hear and rescue his people and rebuild their walls. Their enemies will be ashamed, and come in fear to the Lord, who will forgive the remnant of his people, showing faithfulness and steadfast love as he had sworn to the patriarchs of old.

## Nahum

Nahum was probably an older contemporary of Jeremiah, belonging to the seventh century B.C. He must be dated after the sack of Thebes (3.8) by Assyria in 663 B.C., but in close association with the fall of Nineveh in 612 B.C., either when the destruction was imminent or when it had just taken place. Possibly he foretold the city's fate as early as 623 B.C., when Cyaxares the Mede attacked it. In language traditionally applied in the Near East to the mythical struggle between God and his foes, a description of the destruction of Nineveh is made illustrative of the Lord's vengeance on the guilty.

The book opens with part of an acrostic poem (1.1–9) describing in traditional terms a theophany, revealing the character of God and the effect of his appearance. This poem is in the form of a hymn, and because of this it has been suggested that Nahum was a cultic prophet and wrote the psalm to be used in the Temple for the Autumn New Year feast immediately following the fall of Nineveh in 612 B.C.[1] But it must be remembered that the acrostic form is a literary device used in Wisdom writings.

A battle-poem follows, and in vivid staccato language, striking imagery, and terse fine poetry there is a graphic, brilliant description of the capture of Nineveh:

> Woe to the whole bloody city
> Full of lying and plunder
> That cannot make off with its prey.
> Hark to the whips, to the rumbling of wheels!
> Horses are prancing, chariots leaping,
> Cavalry charging.
> Swords flash like flames and spears as the lightning.
> There's abundance of slain, a mass of dead bodies—
> There's no end of dead bodies—
> Men stumble on bodies. (3.1ff)

[1] A. Haldar, *Studies in the Book of Nahum* (1946).

The description closes with the refrain, found elsewhere in the book (2.13), and often in Jeremiah and Ezekiel, "Look, I am against you! says the Lord of Hosts". It is also of interest that the preface to this stirring battle-poem is a cry of victory over a foe about to be defeated (1.15, RSV; 2.1, Hebrew), but is used by Second-Isaiah (40 and 52) to herald the approach of the victorious Lord as king: "Behold upon the mountains the feet of him who brings good tidings!" This preface is immediately followed by a command, surprising to find in a pre-exilic prophetic book, "Keep your feasts, O Judah, fulfil your vows, for never again shall the wicked come against you, he is utterly cut off." Here too it must be remembered that Wisdom writers emphasized that vows once made must be kept. "Pay what you vow. It is better that you should not vow than that you should vow and not pay" (Eccles. 5.4f).

There is a great contrast in tone between Nahum and earlier prophets.[1] As well as calling for Temple observances, Nahum utters a great cry of exultation over the fall of a national foe. He may be one of the nationalist prophets whom Jeremiah condemned. It is easy to see that the two men would oppose each other. Nahum was convinced that Nineveh was doomed because of her treatment of Jerusalem. Jeremiah was convinced that Jerusalem was doomed because of the sins of the Jewish people.

## Habakkuk

At the beginning of his book, Habakkuk is called "the prophet" (1.1; 3.1). Only Haggai and Zechariah are like him in this, and the Hebrew word for prophet, *nabi*, is the title Amos emphatically rejects. The title is made more significant by two facts; that in the Apocryphal legend "Bel and the Dragon"[2] Habakkuk is called a Levite, and that the psalm that closes the book of Habakkuk is supplied with musical instruction for singing by the choir (3.1, 9, 13, 19). The psalm was clearly used in Temple worship, and Habakkuk may well have been a "cult" prophet, part of the Temple personnel. "Bel and the Dragon" regards him as living c. 539 B.C., just before the rise of Cyrus and the defeat of the Babylonians (Chaldaeans, 1.6). He would therefore be later than Jeremiah.

In the first section (1–2, 5) there is a dialogue, a frank exchange between himself and God, initiated by the prophet, reflecting the

[1] H. M. Chadwick, *Growth of Literature* II (1932–40), p. 730.
[2] In LXX. Cf. S. R. Driver, *Century Bible*, Minor Prophets, Vol. II, p. 50.

same outspoken attitude as we found in the book of Jeremiah. The
prophet complains that he is surrounded by violence and injustice, a
state of affairs that God is allowing to go unchecked. God replies that
he is establishing the Chaldaeans[1] to punish these crimes. First-
Isaiah (10.5) had said that Assyria was the rod of God's anger,
Jeremiah (27.6) believed that the Babylonians were sent by God and
that Judah should surrender to them. For neither First-Isaiah nor
Jeremiah, apparently, did God's use of a foreign heathen nation
present any moral problem. But Habakkuk seems to go deeper. He
knew the reputation of Babylon as a bitter, hasty people (1.6), dread-
ful, terrible, and proud (1.7), like an eagle swift to devour (1.8), going
beyond all bounds, "guilty men, whose own might is their god!"
(1.11). Habakkuk asks whether God is not making crime and violence
worse by using such a wicked nation to destroy Judah, who, with all
her faults, is more righteous (1.13). Can the means really be justified
by the end?

For a time, like Jeremiah, he received no reply from God. But in
complete confidence he went off alone to await God's revealing vision,
and he was answered:

> Write the vision;
>     make it plain upon tablets
>     so he who runs may read it.
> For still the vision awaits its time;
>     it hastens to the end—it will not lie.
> If it seem slow, wait for it;
>     it will surely come, it will not delay. (2.2f)

There are no visual details of this "vision"; but a new insight is
revealed to the prophet in words that become his distinctive teaching.
No time-table can be drawn up for God's fulfilment of his purpose.
Such men as Jeremiah are likely to be impatient, and in thinking about
the future they foreshorten God's time; but in God's plan character
determines destiny: "Behold, he who is not upright is filled with
pride,[2] but the righteous man lives by his faithfulness' (2.4). There is
in the excesses of the Babylonian tyrant the germ of self-destruction,
just as in the faithfulness of the righteous there is the principle of life.
Faithfulness is here in contrast to the puffed-up pride of the Chaldaeans, and suggests humble trust in God. Perhaps here too (cf. Isa.
7.9) the word has not lost all connection with its primitive Hebrew

---

[1] The participle "rousing", RSV, does not necessarily imply that God is
only now about to call them up; cf. the perfect "Thou hast ordained" (1.12).
[2] Hebrew, "puffed up". RSV, "shall fail".

root, and still implies something of the surrendered yet active dependence of an infant being suckled by its mother.[1] Such trustful standing before God enabled Abraham to be treated as righteous, as having fulfilled his obligations to God. Paul, quoting this passage (Rom. 1.17; Gal. 3.11). uses the Greek word *pistis*, faith, a word which equally with the Hebrew contains both passive and active implication, and suggests a similar contrast to puffed-up pride and self-glorification, a contrast further emphasized in the Epistle to the Ephesians: "By grace you have been saved through faith; and this is not your own doing, it is the gift of God" (2.8).[2]

In the second section of the book (Hab. 2.5–20), five Woes against the wicked give flagrant examples of what the prophet means by puffed-up pride. He condemns wine, ambition, and the ruthless lust for power (2.5–8), building a dynasty on greed, "to set his nest on high". He condemns building cities on violence (2.12ff), savage triumph over men (2.15ff), and the senselessness of trusting in dumb idols (2.18f). In contrast to these dumb things, the prophet exclaims that it is man who should be dumb in the presence of the Lord:

> The Lord is in his holy temple;
> Hush, all the earth before him! (2.20)

In the poem of faith that concludes the book, the poet entreats the help and mercy of God (3.2), describing God's advent which brings trembling and dread, but also the deep confidence that enables the prophet to wait hopefully for God when trouble and massive invasion overwhelm the land. It is this humble, confident trust that gives him the power in the midst of famine and disaster to rejoice in the Lord and joy in the God who delivers him. There is a sudden leap beyond doubts about the justice of God and the suffering of the righteous to a friendship that makes God himself and God alone the reward of his life. That is what Habakkuk means by faith and faithfulness.

## Zephaniah

Another contemporary of Jeremiah, probably older and prophesying only in the reign of Josiah (639–08) was Zephaniah, whose long

---

[1] See pp. 149f. The Hebrew word is passive in form, but may have an active nuance.

[2] LXX Hab. 2.5 has the personal pronoun "My faith", as though it is an attribute of God not of man. Paul omits "my". In Heb. 10.38 "my" is transferred to "righteous one", and the contrast to faith is "shrinking back" a word also applicable to a baby that refuses to be suckled.

pedigree suggests that he was a royal prince, the great-great-grandson
of Hezekiah.[1] Mention of the Assyrian empire and of Nineveh as still
standing suggests that the prophet was a contemporary of Nahum.
There is no hint of the reform of Josiah in 621 B.C. (2 Kings 22f) or
from 631–21 B.C. (2 Chron. 34) apart from the phrase "remnant of
Baal" (1.4).[2] Far from suggesting any religious reform, the book
reflects a high degree of religious syncretism in Judah and Jerusalem
(1.5, 9), intrigue and corruption among court officials and princes, and
practical atheism among merchants and traders, who say that though
God may exist, he gives no evidence of it; he does neither good nor
evil (1.12).

But the Lord is about to take action. Using the same phrase as
Habakkuk (2.20) the prophet says, "Hush before the Lord! for the
Day of the Lord is near" (1.7). In the teaching of Amos, the popular
idea of the Day as a day for Israel's vengeance on her foes, became a
day for God's judgement on Israel because of her sins, and Zephaniah
follows this teaching. In the coming universal catastrophe consuming
man and beast, birds and fish, Judah and Jerusalem will not escape
(1.2ff). Using other imagery, Zephaniah proclaims that God has
invited all nations of the earth to his sacrificial feast (1.7), implying
that Judah will be the slaughtered victim. To the terrors of the Day
will be added the new dread of war. In words that in their Latin translation inspired the great hymn of Thomas of Celano (c. A.D. 1250),
*Dies irae, dies illa*, Zephaniah cries:

> A day of wrath is that day,
>     a day of distress and anguish,
>   a day of ruin and devastation,
>     a day of darkness and gloom
>   a day of clouds and thick darkness,
>     a day of trumpet blast and battle cry . . .

It is clear that the threat (1.18) is still, as in 1.4, directed particularly
against Judah, for the universal catastrophe to the whole "earth"
(1.2, 3) is limited to the "land".[3]

---

[1] Because his father's name was Cushi, A. Bentzen (op. cit. II, p. 153)
suggests that he was an Ethiopian Temple slave and *nabi*, familiar with
Temple cultic language.

[2] Here the Greek version has "name of Baal", which agrees more closely
with the parallel phrase "the name of the idolatrous priests", a term used for
the priests of the golden calves (Hos. 10.5) and the priests of the high places
destroyed by Josiah (2 Kings 23.5).

[3] RSV obscures this by translating two different Hebrew words by the one
English word "earth".

The prophet turns from his judgement on Judah and Jerusalem to appeal to the humble and meek of the land (2.3), in words comparable to those of Amos, to seek the Lord, to seek righteousness and humility. Perhaps they may be hidden on the day of God's wrath—the "perhaps" too probably derives from Amos,[1] and is echoed in one of the most haunting lines of the medieval hymn when it speaks of the Day *cum vix iustus sit securus*—a Day when scarcely may the righteous man be safe. Zephaniah proclaims that all the foreign nations, both the neighbours of Judah and distant Egypt and Nineveh, will be destroyed. He describes Nineveh, in words Second-Isaiah (47.8) uses of Babylon, as the joyous city dwelling securely, saying in her heart, I am, and there is none beside me (2.15).

In the final section the prophet turns again to condemn Judah, her princes, judges, prophets, and priests in terms used by Jeremiah, Ezekiel, and Habakkuk. Foreign nations have been destroyed by God so that Judah may learn to fear him (3.6f); but it has been all to no avail, and God makes his final promise to the humble and poor who will be left in Jerusalem when the proudly exultant ones are taken into captivity (3.11f). Zion and Jerusalem, addressed as Israel, is told to sing and rejoice, for the Lord has taken away the judgements against her. In her midst is the King of Israel, strikingly equated with the Lord, the mighty warrior (3.15; cf. Isa. 41.21; 42.13). The promise seems to be to those left in Jerusalem after the Babylonian destruction; they were despised by Ezekiel, and called "bad figs" by Jeremiah, but later were offered comfort by Second-Isaiah (40.1).

God's promise through Zephaniah unites all who at present cannot share the joy of the religious festival—both the remnant in ruined Jerusalem and the exiles in foreign Babylon—in the vision of one restored people whose shame will be turned into praise. Here from a prophet in the devastated land there first sounds the note of hope that swelled to a mighty chorus fifty or sixty years later in Second-Isaiah. From a deep sense of sin, and the necessity for judgement and discipline, comes Zephaniah's conviction that humble piety alone can survive the Great Judgement Day. Such humility is basic to all morality and true religion.

## Haggai and Zechariah

Haggai and Zechariah, towards the end of the sixth century, lived under the shadow of the teaching of Jeremiah, whose influence still

[1] See above, pp. 232f.

persisted. Assyrian and Babylonian empires had vanished, and some exiled Jews had been encouraged by the Persian Cyrus to return home, with help towards building their Temple and reinstituting their national and religious life. But the popular religious confidence of the nation had been undermined by Jeremiah's stern emphatic pronouncement of God's doom on the city of Jerusalem, the Davidic dynasty, and the Temple. First-Isaiah's lofty preaching that the place where God dwelt was inviolable had lent strength to the popular belief that the buildings themselves were a magic talisman on which the people could rely for safety, and now their ruins, like those of Shiloh in the time of Jeremiah (Jer. 7.12), were a constant reminder of a creed that had proved illusory. Even the wonderful visions of Second-Isaiah seemed to have foundered on those ruins. After all, there had been no triumphal homeward march of an exiled host returning under their divine king. The ruins still silently testified that God's ban was not lifted, and exiles were slow to take a new risk.

But in a less spectacular way, round Jerusalem itself a new movement had begun. People were building private houses, and Haggai urged the priority of the Lord's house (1.4, 9). Shortly afterwards, Zechariah emphatically reiterated that the Lord was returning to Jerusalem with compassion. He would again comfort Zion and again choose Jerusalem (1.16f).[1] Moreover, for two years there had been fierce rebellions against Darius among the subject peoples of the Persian empire. Hopes of national independence were beginning to stir, and this must have been particularly so in Judah when Zerubbabel, the Davidic prince, received the Persian appointment as governor. Zerubbabel's grandfather, Jehoiachin, had spent thirty-seven years in a Babylonian prison before he was released at the age of fifty-five in 560 B.C. (2 Kings 25.27). Haggai called Zerubbabel God's chosen one, his servant, the signet ring of the Davidic dynasty that God had put back on his finger (2.23), despite the fact that Jeremiah (22.24) had declared that God had taken the signet ring off, and that none of Jehoiachin's offspring should "succeed in sitting on the throne of David and ruling again in Judah".

Meanwhile, the people were continually postponing the rebuilding of the Temple, which, according to the teaching of Jeremiah and Ezekiel, God himself had destroyed. Sixteen years before Haggai, Sheshbazzar had laid its foundations (Ezra 5.16), and the old stone

---

[1] Zechariah picks up First-Isaiah's words in reference to the Northern kingdom (14.1), Second-Isaiah's call to comfort Jerusalem, and Ezekiel's picture of the glory returning to Zion.

altar had been set up again in its place (3.3). At about the same time, however, another voice was reaffirming the belief of pre-exilic prophets that the Temple building was unnecessary (Isa. 66.1). Definitely it was not a first priority in expenditure for the struggling new community round Jerusalem (Hag. 1.2).

But in 520 B.C. there was drought and famine, which Haggai said was due to neglecting to build a dwelling-place for God. A start must be made at once. Three weeks later all the people began work on the Temple site, led by Zerubbabel and Joshua,[1] and despite discouragement from those who drew unfavourable comparisons with the glories of Solomon's Temple. Three months later the foundations were laid, and Haggai promised the economic situation would change as God poured out blessing.

There is an interesting account of Haggai sending for an oracle from the priests on the day the foundations were laid (2.10ff), probably the same occasion as is recorded in Ezra (4.1ff). Adversaries of Judah, native people (4.4, people of the land) offered to help in the building, "for we worship your God as you do, and we have been sacrificing to him ever since the days of Esar-haddon king of Assyria who brought us here". The priestly oracle was required to pronounce on the problem whether contamination from ritual uncleanness was stronger than holiness, and when it was declared that uncleanness infected holy things, the prophet rejected the proffered help, decreeing, in a way that suggests the offer had come from the Samaritan remnant of the Northern kingdom, "So is it with this people and with this nation before me, says the Lord, and so with every work of their hands; and what they offer there is unclean" (2.14). This rejection was probably one factor that caused the bitter enmity between Jews and Samaritans, still strong in the first century A.D. (John 4.9). Zechariah's vision (3.1ff), concerned with Joshua's fitness to officiate as priest, may be part of the same Samaritan problem. For some reason Joshua was regarded as unclean, wearing filthy garments—perhaps he had been in the unclean land of captivity, or perhaps he had officiated with Northerners at Bethel before the Jewish community was formed again around Jerusalem. Zechariah declared Joshua was a brand plucked from the burning (3.2; cf. Amos 4.11). God himself had forgiven his sin and clothed him in high-priestly robes.

Zechariah, like Haggai a *nabi*, was consulted about the keeping of national fasts (Zech. 7). Nearly two years after the Temple foundations

[1] Grandson of the high priest slain by the Babylonians in 586 B.C.

were laid and about two years before the building was completed and consecrated, a deputation came from Bethel to inquire whether the fasts that had been kept there since 586 B.C. should still be kept. Apparently they had fasted four times a year.[1] The prophetic oracle pronounced that these fasts "shall be to the house of Judah seasons of joy and gladness, and cheerful feasts" (8.19). Many peoples and strong nations will come to worship Israel's God, having heard that God is with them. The prophet here tactfully ignored the problem whether Bethel, which had been for seventy years the centre of national worship, or Jerusalem, which Jeremiah and Ezekiel had regarded as destroyed by God, was to be the one central sanctuary where God's name would dwell.

But in a parallel passage (7.8—8.16) this problem is answered clearly. First, the ethical teaching of earlier prophets is repeated: "Render true judgements, show kindness and mercy each to his brother, do not oppress the widow, the fatherless, the sojourner or the poor"—and it is taken even further: "let none of you devise evil against his brother in your heart" (cf. Mic. 2.1). It was failure to meet these demands of God that had caused the disasters commemorated in the fasts. Then, in strong, emphatic language (8.1ff) Zechariah proclaims that the Lord is zealous for Jerusalem. He is returning to dwell there, and the city will be renamed the City of Truth or Faithfulness (cf. Isa. 1.26). The despised remnant will be brought back for a long and prosperous life (cf. Isa. 65.20) and the old covenant formula will be repeated, My people, Your God. Finally, he reminds his hearers of the words of the prophet (Hag. 2.15f) when the Temple foundations were laid. Since then three evils have vanished—unemployment, fear of war, and internal strife (8.10). God's promise of peace is renewed. Judah need not fear, for God is purposing good towards her, and once again God's requirements are repeated as moral, not ritual, acts: "These are the things that you shall do: Speak the truth to one another, render in your gates judgements that are true and make for peace, do not devise evil in your hearts against one another, and love no false oath, for all these things I hate, says the Lord" (8.16f). It is of interest that neither in Haggai nor in Zechariah is there any hint that the prophet thinks of reinstituting the sacrificial cult. To both pro-

---

[1] In the fifth month for the destruction of Jerusalem in 586 B.C., in the seventh month for the murder of Gedaliah (2 Kings 25.8, 25; Jer. 41.1ff). Zechariah (8.18ff) mentions two more fasts, in the fourth month when the walls of Jerusalem were breached (Jer. 39.2) and in the tenth month when the siege began (2 Kings 25.1).

phets, as to First-Isaiah and Second-Isaiah, the Temple is the place where God dwells (Hag. 1.8; Zech. 1.16).

The book of Zechariah opens with a reference back to former prophets and repeats their call to repentance. Often to Zechariah, as to them, came direct revelation, prefaced with the phrase, "The word of the Lord came, saying"—in reply to the Bethel deputation (7.4), and also with reference to Zerubbabel's completion of the Temple building. Most of his teaching, however, is given as autobiography in the form of eight night-visions, whose imagery, like Haggai's parable, needs to be interpreted. These are imaginative pictures, not perceptions like those of Jeremiah, where natural phenomena become vehicles of revelation. Clearly they speak to a contemporary situation, and there is a reason why the prophet uses this oblique visionary form. When Ezekiel talked of Gog and Magog he was living in territory controlled by foreigners, and perhaps he had to be cautious. The same was true of the writer of the Book of Daniel and of John the Divine, who used some of the same visionary symbols when writing from his island prison of Patmos. We do not know whether Zechariah found the same precautions necessary, or whether he thought it the best way to obtain a hearing.

The visions are interpreted to Zechariah by a messenger;[1] but often the interpretation is not sufficiently clear for us to be sure of the meaning in detail. The first vision indicates that the world revolution which might give Judah freedom, and which Haggai had expected, would not now take place; "behold, all the earth remains at rest" (1.11). The messenger was afraid that God's wrath still burnt against Jerusalem even after seventy years of her ruin; but the Lord's gracious reply and the second vision showed that he was about to send his agent to destroy the Persian empire. God's four smiths would destroy the horns or power of the four corners of the world.

In the third vision (2) the messenger prevents a young man, probably Zerubbabel, from measuring Jerusalem to build its walls. Knowing that rebuilding the city walls would inevitably rouse opposition (Ezra 4.13), the messenger claims that God would be the wall of the city, would dwell within her, and would defend her. Both Haggai (2.5) and Zechariah (4.6) stress the need to rely on the spirit of God, not on military power.

The fourth vision concerns Joshua's fitness to officiate as high priest, and the fifth deals with the relationship between him and

---

[1] It is probably wiser to translate the Hebrew for this "interpreter" by the colourless word messenger, rather than import the idea of angel.

Zerubbabel. A golden lampstand has seven bowls for oil and wicks, giving great light and security, and is fed direct with oil from two olive trees representing Joshua and Zerubbabel. It is upon co-opera-tion between these civil and religious heads of the community that security will rest. The double, equal rule of the two anointed, priest and prince, is stressed (4.11ff; 6.13).

The sixth and seventh visions answer a major religious problem of the exilic age: how to prevent unforgiven sins accruing until once again God would have to destroy the whole nation, and how assurance of forgiveness can be given. A flying scroll (5.1ff) bearing punish-ments for sins is to enter the house of every individual sinner (cf. Ezek. 18), and a box containing a woman representing wickedness or guilt of the whole nation is flown by two women with stork-like wings to Babylon.[1] All the nation's past guilt has been expiated in Babylon (cf. Isa. 40.1f) and left there, and in future every individual sinner will be punished only for his own sins.

The last vision (6.1f) shows God's chariots going out from his presence to the four corners of the world to prevent any power again rising up against his people.

Interspersed among the visions are references to crowns, silver and gold, brought by the returned exiles (6.10) intended for Joshua, or perhaps originally for Zerubbabel who, Haggai (2.23) had predicted, was to be the Davidic ruler, and to whom Zechariah seems to refer as Branch or Shoot (3.8; 6.12), the name used by First-Isaiah (4.2)[2] which had become a symbol of the messianic ruler (Isa. 11.1; Jer.23.5; 33.15). Possibly there was strife between Joshua and Zerubbabel (Zech. 6.13), and perhaps Zerubbabel took literally the prophecy and the crown so that he—and perhaps Joshua too—was removed by the Persians; for neither of them is mentioned in the story of the dedica-tion of the new Temple (Ezra 6.16ff).

To both Haggai and Zechariah is given the hope of an imminent change in the fortunes of Israel. God is shaking the nations, and from widespread unrest there will accrue to Jerusalem new wealth and power (Hag. 2.7). To Zechariah, as to Second-Isaiah, is given the promise that all obstacles, however great, will be removed (Zech. 4.7; cf. Isa. 40.4). Isaiah of Jerusalem had prophesied that God would make Jerusalem secure by laying a sure foundation stone (Isa. 28.16) and Zechariah pictures Israel crying, Grace, grace, as the stone is laid. But his vision breaks through national boundaries. Jerusalem is

---

[1] Shinar, RSV, 5.11; cf. Gen. 11.2; Isa. 11.11.
[2] See above, p. 141.

still to be the centre of God's kingdom, for there he will dwell, but Judah's name will be no longer a byword of cursing among the nations (Zech. 8.13); like Abraham's name, it will be used for blessing by all peoples (Gen. 12.3). Whenever a Jew living in the far countries returns to Jerusalem, "ten men from nations of every tongue" will accompany him, saying, "Let us go with you, for we have heard that God is with you" (Zech. 8.23; cf. Isa. 44.4f). The early prophecy made to Judah alone, of the coming of Immanuel, will be given wider significance to many peoples and strong nations (cf. Mic. 4.3).

## Second-Zechariah (9—14) and Malachi

The prophetic literature ends with three small books, each beginning with the words "The burden (RSV oracle) of the word of the Lord" (Zech. 9.1; 12.1; Mal. 1.1). Two of these books have been bound up with the book of Zechariah as chapters 9—11 and 12—14, and the third appears separately under the anonymous title Malachi—my messenger.[1]

### SECOND ZECHARIAH

The first book prophesies the restoration of the Jewish kingdom through the Lord's defeat of surrounding peoples, and through the remnant's acceptance of Judaism and its food laws (9.7). Zion's king, just, delivered, and lowly will ride into Jerusalem,[2] weapons of war will be taken away, and the king will rule in peace over the realm promised to Abraham and ruled by Solomon. Prisoners will return to Zion and will be given a double portion (9.12; cf. Isa. 61.7). The people have been misled by teraphim, diviners, and dreamers (10.2); but God, having punished the false shepherds, calls on the prophet himself to act as Shepherd. In response, the prophet takes two staffs for his task, Pleasantness and Covenant Bonds; but the people reject him, the Good Shepherd, insulting him by offering him a paltry sum as payment.[3] Many conjectures have been made to explain the haunting symbolism of these chapters. Much of the phraseology clearly refers back to early prophets, especially to First-Isaiah and Hosea. The chapters form a link between the Old Testament and the New, and were clearly a living tradition in the first century A.D., made use of by Jesus or the Gospel writers.

[1] LXX has *Malacho*, his messenger.
[2] Matt. 21.5 quotes Zech. 9.9.
[3] Zech. 11.12ff (cf. RSV marg.) referred to in Matt. 27.9 as from Jeremiah.

The next little book continues the prophecy of Jerusalem's deliverance and wonderful future, and the metaphor of the shepherd recurs (13.7). But here again the references are obscure, especially the relationships between Jerusalem and Judah. The House of David, closely associated with the inhabitants of Jerusalem, is very important; on them will be poured a spirit of compassion and supplication (12.10), and for them will be opened a fountain to cleanse them from sin and uncleanness (13.1).

It seems that prophecy has reached a low ebb (13.2ff), for prophets are associated with the unclean spirit. Any prophet must be killed by his own family; he will be ashamed of his vision, and will no longer wear the hairy garment,[1] and like Amos will deny that he is a prophet; he will claim that the wounds on his body are not prophetic marking.

The final chapter speaks of the coming Day of the Lord, when the Lord himself will fight for and save the captured and ravished city of Jerusalem. A great earthquake will split the Mount of Olives, whereupon the Lord and all the holy ones will come, and thereafter there will be one long day; night and gloom will disappear. Echoing Ezekiel's vision of the life-giving stream flowing from the Temple, the prophet foretells that a perennial stream will flow out from Jerusalem, part towards the Dead Sea, part towards the Mediterranean, carrying fertility to the whole land. All the survivors of the nations will go up to Jerusalem year by year to worship Israel's King, the Lord of Hosts (14.16), at the Feast of Tabernacles. Those who do not go will have no rain, and will suffer terrible plague and punishment. Everything in Jerusalem will be holy, even the common cooking pots, and there will be no trader in the House of the Lord (14.21; cf. Matt. 21.12). The climax of the Day is that "the Lord will be king over all the land" and, with significant reference to Deuteronomy (6.4), "the Lord will be one and his name one" (Zech. 14.9). It is the only time that this creed is quoted in the Old Testament.

## MALACHI

It is of considerable interest that Malachi too stands in the deuteronomic tradition. In these closing verses of the prophetic literature the prophet commends the law according to the deuteronomic tradition, at Horeb and to all Israel. Evidently the compilers wish to link closely together the final book of the Law and the end of the prophetic books.

---

[1] Cf. Elijah (1 Kings 19.13, 19; 2 Kings 1.8; 2.8), and John the Baptist (Mark 1.6).

Jerusalem is the one holy cult place, and as in Deuteronomy, Levites[1] will offer to the Lord right offerings (3.3); God's covenant was with Levi: "True instruction was in his mouth, and no wrong was found on his lips. He walked with me in peace and uprightness, and he turned many from iniquity. For the lips of a priest should guard knowledge, and men should seek instruction from his mouth, for he is the messenger of the Lord of Hosts" (2.6f; cf. Deut. 33.8–11). Without using Ezekiel's word "watchman", Malachi assigns the function of guardian of souls to the Levites. Malachi's attitude to the Levites is particularly interesting because he accepts their position as in the Deuteronomic Code rather than that which we saw was assigned to them by part of the Law and by Ezekiel.[2] Probably the emphatic "you" whom he condemns (2.8), like the previous "you" (2.1), means the priests, who have degraded the Levites; they have corrupted God's covenant with Levi and given wrong guidance (Torah). The prophet associates the corruption of priesthood and cult with this degradation of Levi. His dialectic method shows him at grips with a contemporary situation, in a struggle where are revealed fresh insights into the relationships within the community of God's people. Having one Father, they should act as brothers keeping faith with one another.

Israel knows that the Lord is father and master, yet neither honours him as a son nor fears him as a servant. The priests show that they despise the Lord by offering blemished gifts they would not dare bring to the civil governor. For Malachi, institutional religion is based on the reverent fear of God. In a way unparalleled in the remainder of the Old Testament, he declares that the Gentile offering of incense and gifts is acceptable, and magnifies God's name more than the Jewish offerings in the Temple. Indeed, the Temple doors should be closed and the altar fire not kindled, for priests and people treat religious observances with boredom and contempt (1.10ff).

Their neglect of institutional religion is associated with treachery to each other, which would not have happened if they really believed that they were all sons of the one Father. Family life is ruined by marriage with women who worship other gods; there is divorce and desertion, faithlessness against "the wife of your youth . . . your companion and your wife by covenant" (2.14), and in consequence God will not accept men's offerings, and the "godly seed" of Israel is ruined. The prophet speaks of arrears of tithes and offerings as heaped up against the windows of heaven, which open outwards. God

---

[1] See above, p. 85, n. 5.    [2] See below, p. 351.

will not open them to pour out his blessing until the arrears have
been removed (3.10).

There is an ambiguous expression of the messianic hope (3.1ff),
and here there is a significant development. Malachi clearly believes
that Second-Isaiah's great prophecy is to be fulfilled, but for the one
whose way is to be prepared he employs not the personal name Lord
(*Yahweh*, Isa. 40.3), but the word lord or master, *adon*.[1] This word
appears often in the Old Testament of an earthly master or in address
to the king. First-Isaiah uses it as parallel to Lord of Hosts (1.24; 3.1,
etc), and Zechariah, who applies it to the interpreter of his visions in
parellelism with the "messenger of the Lord" (1.9ff; 4.4f; 6.4), also
uses it of God in the phrase "the lord of the whole land" (4.14; 6.5).
Malachi appears to employ this word deliberately to suggest both the
thought of God and of his representative in human form. This lord
or master is parallel with "my messenger" (3.1)[2] and with "the
messenger of the covenant in whom you delight", and the Lord of
Hosts announces his imminent coming; but to this "master" is
ascribed a phrase used of God himself, "whom you seek", and God's
dwelling is called his—the master's—Temple. Malachi makes no suggestion of a Davidic messianic prince. He is hinting at a supernatural
figure, but with this are associated two other ideas: first, Levi (or the
Levites as the true priesthood) is called the messenger of the Lord of
Hosts (2.7), and second, Elijah the prophet will return. Malachi
closely associates Elijah with Moses (cf. Matt. 17.3); both were given
a special revelation by God and both disappeared from human sight
in God's company (Deut. 34.1; 2 Kings 2.9ff).[3] In words that occur in
Joel (2.31) the Lord declares that "before the great and terrible day of
the Lord comes" (Mal. 4.5), Elijah the prophet will come and recon-
cile fathers and children. For Malachi, reconciliation in family life
assumes a place of unexpected significance in preparation for the
coming of God. Just as the new religious life is to be preceded by the
purifying and cleansing of Levites, so the new community of those
who fear the Lord appears to rest on purified family life.

On this final Day of reckoning, God's justice will be vindicated for
all to see. The problem of the suffering of the innocent and prosperity
of the wicked, a problem of Jeremiah's personal life, confronts
Malachi on a broader scale, affecting the whole of institutional
religion. The people are saying openly that it is a useless waste of

---

[1] RSV marks the distinction by using Lord and LORD, but here for the first
should have used simply "lord".

[2] Cf. also Isa. 42.19; 44.26.          [3] See below, p. 281.

time and money to worship the Lord and to bring him offerings. Micah and Zephaniah had preached that salvation was to the humble ones who feared the Lord; but the people refute this from their own experience with "Blessed are the arrogant"; they say that evildoers not only prosper, but, when they put God to the test, they escape (3.15). The unshaken faith with which Malachi answers them is basic to the religion of the whole Bible. Despite all appearances to the contrary, there will be a Day when the distinction between the wicked and those who fear the Lord will be made clear. The arrogant will be as stubble; but those who fear the Lord, a closely-knit community, recognizing the same claims and standards, their names written in God's book of remembrance, will become again the Lord's peculiar treasure;[1] the sun of righteousness[2] will rise for them with healing in its wings, and a new day will dawn.

All prophetic teaching is God-centred, and it is typical of this that the teaching of the final prophetic book comes through an anonymous figure of whom no personal details are recorded. And this God at its centre is timeless. Patriarchal traditions of God's attitude to Jacob and Esau still apply to the contemporary fortunes of Israel and Edom. Details of priestly ritual regarded as absolute regulations are enforced by the prophet by the dialectic of question and answer to show their reasonableness. The age-old law of Moses is still relevant, and the great prophet Elijah, who fought the disruptive effects of Jezebel's foreign worship and her breaches of basic moral commandments, will come again to inaugurate a new kingdom of reconciliation.

Lines reaching far back into the past extend also into the unseen future, not to some arbitrary conclusion or "end", but to the joy of God's abiding presence in his Temple amid his people. It is not eschatology but continuity.

[1] 3.17; cf. Exod. 19.5; Deut. 7.6.
[2] Righteousness like the sun. Perhaps the metaphor is taken from the Egyptian worship of the sun disc.

# PART III

# WRITINGS

The third section of the Hebrew Old Testament is called Writings, and like Law and Prophets it contains five main groupings of material —Psalms, Wisdom books, Megilloth (five short scrolls used at Jewish festivals), Daniel, and the historical writings of the Chronicler. From the standpoint of the religion of the Old Testament, the first of these groups is the most comprehensive, and presents a compendium of the public and private devotion of Israel through much of its history.

# 13 The Psalms

## Arrangement

To begin with what lies before us in the book of Psalms in its present form, there is clear evidence that the whole work has been edited and arranged from previous collections. Five smaller books each conclude with a doxology, 1–41, 42–72, 73–89, 90–106, 107–150. It is of interest that 72 ends with the words "The prayers of David, the son of Jesse, are ended" though this psalm itself is attributed to Solomon, and later in the whole Psalter other psalms occur which are called Davidic (e.g. 86). Clearly, Psalm 72 once formed the conclusion of a small, independent collection. A further distinction is that the second and third books use the general divine name for God (*Elohim*),[1] and it is significant that two psalms (14; 40, 13–17) which in the first book use "the Lord" (*Yahweh*), occur also in the second book (53; 70) with *Elohim* instead of this divine name. This fact is clearly comparable to the changing use of the divine names as we saw it in the section on the Law.[2] The man who uses the more personal and national name, Lord (*Yahweh*), has a different religious attitude or approach to the deity from that of the man who prefers the more universal term God (*Elohim*).

Many suggestions have been made to explain the change from Yahweh (as in Pss. 14; 40) to Elohim (as in 53; 70). Though it is generally recognized that the whole Psalter has been adapted for Temple worship in Jerusalem, it has been suggested that Books II and III emanated from the Northern kingdom (Bethel, Shechem, or Dan), Book I from the Southern kingdom, and Books IV and V from the Priestly circle, and their origin has been linked with the documentary theory of the origin of the law books.[3] It is clear from the duplicated

[1] 1–41 uses *Yahweh* 272 and *Elohim* 15 times.
42–72 uses *Yahweh* 30 and *Elohim* 164 times.
73–83 uses *Yahweh* 13 and *Elohim* 36 times.
84–9 uses *Yahweh* 31 and *Elohim* 7 times.
90–150 uses *Yahweh* 339 and *Elohim* only in Pss. 108 and 144. Psalm 108 is an amalgam of 57.7–11 and 60.5–12 from the Elohistic Book II.

[2] See above, p. 13, n. 1.

[3] J. A. Montgomery, *American Journal of Religion* XVI (1934), p. 192.

psalms that the Elohistic recension is secondary, and it is highly likely
that this recension was prepared for public worship in a time or place
when it was felt desirable to avoid the personal name for Israel's God
(*Yahweh*), but it is not clear what that time or place was. So far as
time is concerned, the last prophetic book, Malachi, still uses the
name *Yahweh*, and Exodus (6.2, P) gives no hint that it should not be
uttered, though a story in Leviticus (24.10–16) emphasizes the sacredness of the name.[1] In LXX, the Greek translation of the Law, "my
Lord" (*Kurios*) is substituted for it, and often in the Qumran scrolls
the Hebrew for "my Lord" is added above the divine name as though
to aid the reader. Thus it is possible that in Egypt at some time between 400 and 250 B.C. when the Greek translation was made, and in
Palestine before 100 B.C.[2] this divine name *Yahweh* ceased to be
pronounced.

It is equally possible that the different name may indicate a different place of origin. LXX was traditionally used in Egypt, and the first
psalm in Book II (42) longs for Jerusalem. The Elohistic books may
come from Jews resident away from reach of the Temple in the dia-
spora, the Babylonian exile, or even in the northern districts of the
old kingdom of Israel, where, perhaps, at least in public worship, it
was not thought advisable to utter the name. But against this suggestion it must be remembered that Psalm 48.8ff presupposes presence
in the Temple; and that where the Lord (*Yahweh*) occurs most frequently (84–150) musical directions which would show Temple usage
are rare, whereas they are frequent in Books I–III.

A further possibility is that the change reflects a different circle of
thought, rather than simply a different time or place. Many of the
Elohistic psalms are connected with the Sons of Korah (42–9; 84f;
87f), Asaph (50; 73–83), Heman (88), and Ethan (89), all usually
regarded as representing guilds of levitical singers. Also, as we shall
see, many psalms have affinities with Wisdom literature, which had
its home in the schools of the wise men rather than in the Temple
cultus. One type of Wisdom literature was particularly international
in its religious emphasis and preferred to use the general name *Elohim*
for God. Thus perhaps Books II and III were selections used in
schools of the wise men. All these suggestions are speculative, for
there do not appear to be adequate, generally accepted criteria on

[1] Cf. also Exod. 20.7; Deut. 5.11.
[2] There is still considerable difference of opinion as to the date when the
Qumran Scrolls were written. In some manuscript fragments at Qumran the
personal divine name is written in the ancient superseded script.

which to decide the date and origin of the five small collections which now comprise the Psalter.

## Relation to the Cult

It is not in dispute, however, that by far the majority of the psalms are intended to be sung. Indeed, the book of Psalms has been called an anthem book of the levitical choirs,[1] which reminds us that the poet-king David and the heads of levitical families (Heman, Asaph, Jeduthun)—singers and poets—were the chief psalmists of Old Testament tradition (1 Chron. 25.1), and suggests that psalmody may have been particularly the creation of professional Temple singers[2] to which the whole congregation would listen, perhaps responding at intervals. But clearly many psalms are not of this type, and a second common descriptive title for the whole book—the hymn-book of the Second Temple—recognizes the importance of lay hymns of praise and petition in which the whole community participated in Temple worship.[3] Wheeler Robinson wrote, "No just view of Jewish religion can be gained by anyone who does not see the Psalter written ... in parallel columns with the Book of Leviticus" and "The presence of the Psalter in the Bible and its close relation to the worship of the Temple in the post-exilic period must . . . preclude any idea that the Jewish approach to God (i.e. the priestly sacrificial cult) was unspiritual." Though many psalms may have originated in private devotion, full value must be given to references to such elements of public worship as sacrifice and altar, Zion and the house of God, and the music of worship.[4]

No one can read through the book of Psalms even rapidly and superficially without being struck by the medley of themes and differences in poetic and spiritual achievement, and here help is given by the modern emphasis on the relation between the Psalms and the public Temple worship or cult. A. F. Kirkpatrick[5] suggested that speaking broadly and generally the Psalms in Book I are personal prayers and thanksgiving, those in Books II and III are national prayers and thanksgiving, those in Books IV and V are liturgical praise and thanksgiving for general use in Temple services. A new

---

[1] H. W. Robinson, *Religious Ideas of the Old Testament* (1913), pp. 149f.
[2] Cf. Y. Kaufmann, *The Religion of Israel* (1961), p. 110.
[3] Ibid., pp. 110, 309f.
[4] H. W. Robinson, op. cit., p. 151.
[5] *The Psalms* (1921), p. lviii.

approach to Old Testament literature[1] has sought to classify it into
various forms and types, and to trace their historical changes and discover the circumstances and situations in which they originated and
were used. In his final study of the Psalter in the light of this "form-
criticism" Gunkel used five main classifications, the psalms in each of
which were considered to share a common set of thoughts expressed
in a common traditional set of conventional formulas, and to originate
from a common situation in individual or national life.

These five main categories were:

1. Hymns of Praise sung in Temple ritual, but later used without
cultic associations (e.g. 8; 100). Among these Gunkel differentiated
(a) Songs of Zion; (b) Enthronement psalms celebrating the Lord's
universal kingship (e.g. 95); (c) Songs of Deliverance.

2. Communal Laments sung at a time of some great national need (e.g.
44; 74).

3. Royal Psalms celebrating special royal occasions in the pre-exilic
monarchy such as the establishment of the Davidic dynasty (132), the
reigning king's accession (2; 110), or his wedding (45); the preparation for battle (20) and its victorious outcome (18).

4. Individual Laments, in which the psalmist in distress appeals to
God for help. Often these psalms include vows of thanksgiving made
either because God has heard the prayer and delivered the supplicant
or in the certainty that he will hear (7; 22).

5. Individual songs of thanksgiving uttered in public and probably
accompanying a sacrifice of thanksgiving (34; 116). These often
include a call to others to share in the act of gratitude.

Gunkel thought it was possible to isolate other subsidary types:
Communal Songs of thanksgiving (e.g. 124), Pilgrimage Songs (122),
Wisdom Poems (1; 127), and Liturgical Psalms developed from antiphonal, prophetical, or torah sayings (12; 75). Sometimes single
elements found in the major groups give rise to separate psalms (confession in 51, confident trust in 23), sometimes they are mingled to
form mixed psalms (e.g. 40). He concluded that most psalms in their
present form are imitations of earlier cultic poems produced and used
in a more spiritual worship than the sacrificial cult of the Temple.

[1] H. Gunkel, *Genesis* (1901); "The Poetry of the Psalms" *in Old Testament
Essays* (1927); *What Remains of the Old Testament* (1928); H. Gunkel,
J. Begrich, *Einleitung in die Psalmen* (1933).

S. Mowinckel[1] carried further Gunkel's comparison of Hebrew psalmody with that of Babylon and Ugarit as revealed by archaeology. It is generally agreed that, though the whole Psalter in its present form is a product of the post-exilic period, it contains much that dates from earlier centuries, from the worship in Solomon's Temple and even some material taken over and adapted from pre-Israelite Canaanite worship. In particular, it has been suggested that Ezrahite, patronymic of Ethan and Heman[2] denotes "native" and indicates Canaanite origin[3] and it must be pointed out that very ancient rhythms and language may still be distinguished. At this point consideration of Mowinckel's important, but conjectural, work is relevant. Using comparison with psalmody of other Near-Eastern countries, and emphasizing the cultic background of the Hebrew psalter, he constructed a picture of Old Testament annual New Year festivals and royal enthronement ritual based on supposed pre-exilic festivals. Other scholars prefer to relate many psalms to the Feast of Tabernacles and to a supposed annual ceremony at that feast of the renewal of the Covenant, which, it is claimed, continued the rites of an assumed early Israelite tribal confederacy.[4] Many years earlier, Hans Schmidt had set many psalms in the framework of a Temple ritual of trial by ordeal.

Here, as so often in scholarly research of many kinds, the general emphasis tends to reflect changing contemporary religious attitudes. The modern ecumenical movement is associated with a growing interest in the theories and practices of liturgical and ritual worship, an interest shown by the fact that worship may often be described as "cultic" or "non-cultic" without its being precisely clear what this term implies on each occasion. Perhaps too the rapid decrease in the number of monarchies in the Western world has produced as a natural reaction a tendency to investigate the origin of kingship, its religious as well as its social function, and an attempt to recover, through the thought of a divine kingship, some of the sense of security given to people by a monarchical form of leadership. Further, in an age when organized religious institutions are losing adherents, and revolt

[1] *Psalmenstudien I–IV* (1921–4), E. T., A. R. Ap-Thomas, *The Psalms in Israel's Worship* (1962); "Wisdom in the Psalms" in *The Old Testament and Modern Study* (1951), ed. H. H. Rowley.
[2] Pss. 88; 89; cf. 1 Kings 4.31. Both these are levitical names; cf. 1 Chron. 15.17ff.
[3] Cf. Hebrew in Exod. 12.19; cf. W. F. Albright, *Archaeology and the Religion of Israel* (1942).
[4] Cf. above, pp. 102f; A. Weiser, *The Psalms* (1962).

against social and moral traditions and conventions has produced a disintegrated, "cultless" community, interest turns to cult as acts observable by the senses, organized at fixed times and places, expressing religious experiences through the social community linked with priests and liturgy.[1]

It would be generally agreed that at least the majority of the psalms in their present form are cultic psalms in the sense that they were used in public worship of the post-exilic community. Clearly not all the religious songs and psalms of the Israelite people are in the Psalter, and it may be true that this selection from that larger literature was of psalms that the post-exilic community could sing in worship, thus comprising, like a revised hymn-book of any modern church, those psalms which, in their present altered form, the editors regarded as expressing the right theology for their own particular time and situation. It is to be expected that there would be extreme conservatism in religious language, especially as regards metaphorical and symbolic ways of expressing deep religious truths and spiritual realities, and that there would be reliance on ancient traditions of God's saving acts, as at the Deliverance from Egypt. These two factors would naturally tend to make the psalms stereotyped both in form and content.

The importance of the psalms in Old Testament religion is not, however, disposed of simply by pointing out their association with Temple worship. We have already referred to Mowinckel's interesting suggestion concerning the connection between the Psalter and the cult, and especially to his emphasis on the ancient enthronement psalms. Equally important is his stress on the close connection between the psalms in their present form and the schools of the wise men, where religious instruction was given to the flower of Israelite youth, including probably the future Temple singers. As we have seen, many psalms have no liturgical or musical directions (cf. 17; 25–8, and Books IV and V) and thus, like the Psalter as a whole, "cannot, without more ado, be designated song-books for the Temple worship collected for that purpose. The earlier collections came into existence among singers, but the Psalter as a whole, and even the Davidic Book I, were collected in the 'learned' circles, the scribes or the wise men, who show their interest in ancient sacred tradition and all matters of religion."[2] The sacred and inspired poetry which these men collected might serve as models of prayer and praise, find their place in Temple services, and be used in communities of those who lived like Samuel

---

[1] Cf. Quell, *Cultic Problem of the Psalms* (1931).
[2] Mowinckel, op. cit. II, p. 203.

within the Temple precincts, forerunners of communities such as were found at Qumran. The primary object was to praise God and to witness publicly to him. Even confession of sin was regarded as giving glory to God and rendering praise to him (cf. Josh. 7.19).

To the collectors, the cultic point of view seemed of minor importance. They looked on the psalms as springing from individual experience, often writ large in the life of kings, particularly of David (e.g. 51), as is shown by the headings with which they furnished them. It may even be postulated that these brief notices of historic occasions are shortened versions of fuller accounts, for example the story of Hannah's visit to the Temple, culminating in her psalm of praise and thanksgiving, and the picture of Jonah pouring forth a paean of spontaneous praise in gratitude for his return to life. Here too it may be noticed how frequently in the Former Prophets, when a momentous occasion calls forth deep emotion, it is a king who occupies the centre of the stage and utters lament or thanksgiving—David after the death of Saul and Jonathan, Hezekiah on recovery from sickness—so that the psalm springing from the event is vested with nobility, dignity, and power to speak for every man.

Such considerations serve to remind us that there can never have been hard and fast divisions within the religious and cultural life in Israel. The cult itself, it has been pointed out, belongs to the sphere of supra-personal religion and is concerned with the whole community. Though it springs from religious experience and includes individual emotion, it works effectively to create such experience anew for those who participate in it with willing minds. Though it may wither and become sterile, its power is to foster and sustain piety. When through historical circumstances the Israelite cult was largely preserved as a living force in the synagogue, the Psalter was used for instilling the traditional formulas from the past, to give rise within the community of the faithful to a living experience of divine intervention, in the present as in the past witnessing to the reality of God.

We must think therefore of the psalms as usually springing from "the spontaneous overflow of powerful feelings"[1] at the recollection of a great event of national history, or at a significant landmark in the life of an individual. What lies before us is a collection of at least five smaller collections; but we must remember that all the collecting has been done not for its own sake but with a constant aim in view—that religious experience should continue to live within the community, whether the community's natural expression of its religious life were

[1] W. Wordsworth, of poetry, in the preface to Lyrical Ballads.

the solemn ritual of Solomon's Temple or the thoughtful, contemplative worship of the later synagogues. The psalms speak from human experience of the divine, to re-create that experience within human hearts. It is this that gives the psalms their vitality, and their power to speak also to us today, and it is tantalizing to realize that if we could place them accurately in their living background, we should have a valuable key to much of Old Testament religion. But their long and complicated history, while it gives them richness and depth, makes all such attempts very hazardous.

The Psalter raises all the problems of dating that would attach to a modern hymnbook used in the religious services if records of authorship, date of composition, and history of successive modifications had been lost. Language and imagery are used that are the relics of centuries of indebtedness to the religious experiences and traditions of the various peoples who made up the Israelite nation, as well as of those who in Babylonia, Phoenicia, Canaan, and Egypt were her neighbours. It is a tribute to the faithfulness with which the tradition was preserved that competent scholars confidently date the same psalm as Davidic or Maccabean, or assert the priority of Second-Isaiah or the psalmist. Ancient forms have often been modified by later hands to make them relevant to a new age.[1] In addition, psalms that express aspirations and experiences of many separate individuals have been blended into psalms written deliberately to foster community experience as they were used in the cult; or they may be found jostling one another as separate units.

The Hebrew name for the Psalter, *tehillim*, is connected with the English Hallelujah (Praise ye the Lord), and denotes corporate shouts of joy and homage to God.[2] In a note at the end of Book II (72.20) they are called "prayers", which in Hebrew as in English can be used of personal as well as corporate address to the deity, and the word leaves open the question whether they were originally composed for public worship or were too personal to have been regularly used in this way. Some of the other words used in the titles of Psalms are of doubtful meaning. They may designate previous collections from which particular psalms were taken, such as The Precentor's or Chief Musician's, Davidic, and guilds of singers; or they may be musical or liturgical notes for the assistance of choir or congregation. Some possibly show the aim of a psalm or the purpose for which it was

---

[1] Cf. the "rude barbarian" and "God made them high or lowly, And ordered their estate", altered in contemporary English hymnbooks.
[2] Cf. Mowinckel, op. cit. II, p. 218.

used: "for thanksgiving" (100) or "for humble penance" (88, RSV Leannoth); for a reminder or memorial (38; 70); "a song at the dedication of the Temple" (30); "a song for the Sabbath" (92).[1] Psalms 120–34 have the common title "A song of ascents" (Hebrew going up) and may be a selection used on pilgrimage to the three great annual festivals[2]. Another group, 146–50 (cf. 106; 111ff; 117; 135 and at the end of 104ff; 115ff) are entitled Hallelujah, Praise ye the Lord, which may be the Precentor's call to worship or (104.35) the congregation's antiphonal response. Yet another group have been called Enthronement psalms. They contain the statement of confident trust that "The Lord reigns" or "has become King" (93.1; 96.10; 97.1; 99.1).[3] They appear to be comparable to Second-Isaiah's declaration, "Your God reigns" (52.7, omitted in parallel in Nahum 1.15; cf. also Isa. 24.23).

These "Hallelujah" and "Enthronement" psalms may, like the Psalms of Ascent, have been developed from particular annual festivals in the pre-exilic Temple at Jerusalem. In recent years there have been, as we have seen, many attempts to connect individual as well as groups of psalms with specific cultic occasions. Particularly the Enthronement psalms have been regarded as evidence of an annual festival at which the kingship of the Lord was celebrated. But as there is no direct evidence for this either in the Law or in historical records in the Former Prophets, it seems wiser to regard these psalms in their present form as the joyful expression of Israel's faith in the all-powerful rule of her God.

## The Religion of the Psalter

Jewish writers made a distinction between the "spirit of prophecy" and the "spirit of the holy Writings", and it is possible to make an equally clear distinction between the religion of the Law and the Prophets on the one side, and that of the Psalter on the other. The former may be regarded as God speaking to man, declaring his commands, the terms of his covenant, the conditions of life lived with him, and the way men must walk; the latter as men addressing God, bringing thanksgiving and petition, aspiration and confession, offering praise, and calling on all men and created things to glorify him. According to this view, the psalms would be thoughts and feelings of

---

[1] Cf. also titles in LXX to Pss. 24.1; 29.1; 48.1; 93.1; 94.1. Mowinckel, op. cit. II, p. 202.

[2] Cf. Deut. 16; Isa. 30.29.

[3] Cf. 2 Kings 9.13, Jehu reigns, or has become king.

men rather than the teaching of God, human songs and prayers, a human response to God, and while the Law and the words of the prophets reveal God's character and purposes, the psalms express what man had learned and apprehended of that revelation.

But this distinction can be carried too far. Both are inspired by the great Teacher, and both are conditioned by human understanding. The Law of Moses and the visions of prophets are God's message through human mediation; the psalms reflect the same message in the religious experience of dialogue and close companionship with God. Sometimes indeed the relationship between the two types of literature is so close that some psalms have been regarded as containing antiphonal responses between priest or cult prophet and the people (cf. 24), thus demonstrating that there was no arbitrary division between priestly and prophetic religion and that of the congregation.

Religious experience in the psalms is expressed in simple, direct language which makes it possible for us to understand and share it, and enriches our own experience. Well-loved models of prayer enable us to formulate our own. For centuries they have inspired religious experience because in them are crystallized and expressed the devotion of many earlier generations, and they present us not with homogeneous unity but with a rich catholicity. Mowinckel emphasized that most psalms are "real prayers uttered by real men of flesh and blood, praying in actual situations at a very definite period, and with a real place and function in the personal religious life and corporate worship of the Israelite-Jewish congregation".[1] Each psalm is a personal expression of praise or petition, whether written and used for individual or for corporate worship, and even in their present literary form, polished and gleaming from centuries of careful and pious use, most of them contain a complex of devotional words of thanksgiving and petition, aspiration and confession, so defying neat classification.

It is as difficult to present systematically the religion of the Psalter as that of the whole Old Testament. The psalms present Old Testament religion as a whole, and it is probably true to say that there is little that is distinctive except the unforgettable poetry in which wonderful, simple piety expresses well-known facets of the character of Israel's God. Names and titles of God are the same as we have found in the other two parts of the Old Testament. But it must always be remembered that the language is the language of poetry, not of

[1] Op. cit. I, p. 1.

systematic theology. Ideas which in philosophical theology might be summed up in such terms as omniscience, omnipresence, omnipotence, become themes of whole stanzas describing God as one who knows our thoughts before they are spoken (139.1–6), whose hand leads and right hand upholds us, though we take the wings of the morning to flee from him (139.7–12), and whose wonderful power forms the human embryo in the womb (139.13–18). The eternity of God contrasted with human transitoriness is not an abstraction but a living reality:

> Lord, thou hast been our dwelling place
>   in all generations.
> Before the mountains were brought forth
>   or ever thou hadst formed the earth and the world,
>   from everlasting to everlasting thou art God. . . .
> Thou dost sweep men away; they are like a dream,
>   like grass which is renewed in the morning:
> in the morning it flourishes and is renewed;
>   in the evening it fades and withers. (90.1–2, 5–6)

Then, as today, popular theology was expressed and instilled by hymns repeatedly sung. But the figurative, often beautiful language needs sympathetic interpretation. For instance, in the final stanza of Psalm 139 it is the psalmist's complete devotion to God, his longing for the removal of every hindrance to God's perpetual rule on earth in other men and in himself, which is expressed in terms so vividly personal that they could cause offence by giving the impression of a harsh, unforgiving spirit.

Basic in Old Testament teaching is the loathing of evil itself, a loathing regarded as divinely implanted in mankind since the first sin.[1] In the story of the Fall evil is identified with the serpent, and throughout the Old Testament the identification of sin with sinner persists. It is seen again in God's promise to curse those who treat Abraham lightly (Gen. 12.3). The "cursing psalms" (e.g. 137.7ff), like the bloodthirsty stories of the conquest of Canaan, are a particularly vivid way of expressing the faith that, as Israel is God's chosen people, he who fights Israel is fighting God. The deliverance of man by God involves the destruction of evil. In the story of the Great Doom, those on the King's left hand, who have persistently disregarded their needy Lord, their hungry, naked, and imprisoned

---

[1] See above, p. 10.

neighbours, are cursed and sent into eternal torment prepared for the devil and his angels (Matt. 25.41f). It is often true that

> There is some soul of goodness in things evil,
> Would men observingly distil it out.

But here it is envisaged that a point is reached where it is no longer possible to distil out evil from the evil-doer—they are cursed, and perish together.

In the poetry of the psalms there is no argument for the existence of God, but only a simple, confident acceptance of the fact that he is actively present in history, nature, and creation. One of our own poets said poetry should come "as naturally as leaves to a tree" or not at all,[1] and certainly there is nothing forced in the work of the psalmist. His poetry is a spontaneous flowering from the roots of his spiritual experience, and it is with the unforced delight of a good craftsman that he offers his best to God. Men are not exhorted to believe in God but to praise him, give thanks to him, and bless his glorious name. Only the fool—the irreligious man without understanding, whose whole life shows his lack of wisdom—says there is no God (14.1), and his practical atheism ignores God and the generally accepted moral standards (10.4; 94.7f).

## Praise and Thanksgiving

But for the religious man there is in his faith a force that impels him openly to acknowledge the goodness of God, his benefits and his wonderful deeds to the children of men. Praise is the natural over-flowing of appreciation and enjoyment of all that is lovely—the good, true, and beautiful, and the joy needs for its fulfilment someone who shares the appreciation, who will join in expressing praise. Ultimately, there can be no richer and deeper joy than that of men who are aware of a personal response from the object of their praise.

All these elements are found in Israel's praises in the Psalter. Spontaneously the psalmist cries:

> How lovely is thy dwelling place,
>    O Lord of hosts!
> My soul longs, yea, faints
>    for the courts of the Lord;
> my heart and flesh sing for joy
>    to the living God. (84.1-2)

or declares that it is his firm purpose to praise God:

[1] Keats, Letter to John Taylor.

I will bless the Lord at all times;
    his praise shall continually be in my mouth. (34.1)

In a psalm of outstanding beauty to which we shall draw further attention, a writer addresses himself—"O my soul", all his powers, his internal organs thought of as the seat of intellect, will, and emotion (cf. Deut. 6.5, love the Lord your God with all your heart . . . soul . . . and might), and commands his whole being to adore the holy God:

Bless the Lord, O my soul;
    and all that is within me, bless his holy name! (103.1)

More often, the psalmist uses a plural form of address and calls on others to join in praise:

O come, let us sing unto the Lord;
    let us make a joyful noise to the rock of our salvation! (95.1)

O sing to the Lord a new song;
    sing to the Lord, all the earth!
Sing to the Lord, bless his name; (96.1-2a)

The new song may be accompanied with gladness, dancing, and music on timbrel and lyre (149.3), and the final psalm of the Psalter calls for praise of the Lord in his holy place and his mighty firmament from a whole orchestra of musical instruments and everything that breathes. Throughout the Psalter resounds the ringing joy of a whole people actively participating in praise. There is clapping of hands and shouting with loud songs of joy (47.1), and responding with chorus or refrain "for his steadfast love endures for ever" (as after each of the twenty-six verses of 136, and often elsewhere).

In all these hymns of praise it is clear that human praise is a response. From God came the initial act that began the growth of religious experience which came to be expressed in praise. By word or deed God made known his presence, his permanent attitude of "steadfast love", "loving kinship" which proved that his choice of Israel and his covenant relationship still stood. Turning once more to Psalm 103, we find these deeds of God are summed up as "all his benefits" (v. 2). This Hebrew noun can be used of weaning a child and ripening fruit, of dealing fully and adequately with someone. Praise springs from the recollection of the many acts making up the long, slow process by which God brought man to maturity. The psalmist here goes on to enumerate the benefits using, as does Second-Isaiah, the literary device of active participles to link God's past and present acts in one continuous whole. All through his life and still today he finds the Lord is the one forgiving the stain that comes from wandering off the right road, healing physical disease, like a near kinsman rescuing man's life from the grave, crowning or surrounding him with steadfast love and affection tender as a mother's.[1]

Then the psalmist's praise moves out from his own experience of God's personal help to God's habitual dealings with all men (103.6). The Lord does loyal acts of righteousness that show him to be true to his character and to his obligations to needy men, giving judgement to all who are wronged. All this is characteristic of the Lord, and steadfast love, righteousness, and judgement as we have found them in the Law and Prophets stand out in the praises of the Psalter. But often the emphasis on judgement has, as here, a particular shade of meaning. God's "judgement" is the righting of wrongs. He comes as champion of the oppressed.[2] He is the powerful judge to whom the wronged plaintiff never supplicates in vain. The proud and wicked fear God's judgement, but the poor and humble long for it, and rejoice at the thought of its coming:

> Let the heavens be glad, and let the earth rejoice; . . .
>   before the Lord, for he comes,
>   for he comes to judge the earth.
> He will judge the world with righteousness
>   and the peoples with his truth. (96.11ff)

Steadfast love and righteous acts link the Lord expressly to Israel his people. Righting wrongs is a more universal thought; wrongs are the legal crimes of deceit, defrauding, violence, and the oppression of a foreign invading conqueror.

## The Use of Traditions

Though it is nowhere stated that enslaved Israel was "wronged" by the Egyptians, it is to the traditional story of that Deliverance that the psalmist turns for illustration of God's self-revelation of his character. Again he emphasizes by the verbal forms he uses that the same God who revealed himself in the historic past is active today. "He made known" is the imperfect or frequentative tense, and may be translated "would, or used to, make known". The traditional words that spring to the psalmist's mind are found also in Exodus (33.13).

---

[1] Cf. J. N. Schofield, *Introducing Old Testament Theology*, p. 100.
[2] Cf. C. S. Lewis, *Reflections on the Psalms* (1958), pp. 15ff.

He used to make known his ways to Moses,
  To the Israelites his terrible, ruthless deeds (RSV his acts). (103.7)

And he reminds his hearers of the thrilling words with which, in the
climax of that theophany, the Lord revealed himself to Moses (Exod.
34.6):

> Tenderly affectioned and gracious is the Lord,
>   slow in anger and abounding in steadfast love.
> Not perpetually does he take legal action
>   nor for ever keep watching.[1] (103.8f)

The same gracious, forgiving picture of God fills the remainder of
the psalm.

Then the psalmist recalls the story of Creation and the destructive
Flood[2] as he draws a clear comparison between man's frailty and
temporariness and the permanence of the steadfast love of the Lord,
whose throne is in the heavens and whose rule is universal, so that he
deserves the praise of all created things.

A similar pattern based on the use of traditions is found in other
hymns of praise and thanksgiving. Sometimes the introduction calling
on all created things to praise the Lord becomes an independent
psalm (96; 148), sometimes the particular act for which praise is
offered is made into a separate psalm. Psalm 104, which once may
have formed part of 103, is an expression of wonder at the marvellous
acts of God in creation, nature, and human life. It ends with a prayer
for the permanency of God's glory, for his joy over his work, his
acceptance of the hymn, and the destruction of the wicked. In many
psalms as well as in 103 the great theme of praise is the historic event
of Deliverance from Egypt, an act which has been called the basis of
all Israel's religious experience. But this outstanding theme is not
usually isolated from the rest of Israel's history, nor from creation,
nor from God's continuing help in the present of the people or the
individual.

An example of this blending of past and present in thanksgiving is
Psalm 66. In the first part (1–12) God's past and present deliverance
of the nation is celebrated. The whole land (all the earth) is bidden
shout joyfully, bow in worship, and sing God's glory revealed in his

---

[1] Cf. F. Brown, S. R. Driver, C. Briggs, *A Hebrew and English Lexicon of
the Old Testament* (1906), p. 643 for the use of the same Hebrew root for
being on guard or imprisoning. "Anger" is not in the Hebrew text.

[2] Made from dust (Gen. 2.7). "Frame" is the word used of formation,
103.14; RSV, imagination (Gen. 6.5: 8.21).

fearful acts that make his enemies come cringing to him. An invitation is then issued to come and see the fearful, ruthless acts of the God who dried up the sea, who rules for ever and keeps watch over nations. In the third stanza (66.8ff) the psalmist calls on foreign peoples to praise "our" God for keeping "us" alive, then turning to God he narrates how God has given them "abundance" (cf. 23.5) after trials and dangers which he himself had sent. In the second part of the psalm there is an abrupt change from plural to singular, "we" becomes "I". The psalmist declares he will enter the Temple to fulfil the vows he had cried out when he was in trouble—bringing burnt offerings of fatlings, rams, bulls, and goats. Finally he bids all who fear the Lord come and listen to his recital of God's answer to his prayer, an answer which has proved his innocence, for God does not heed the prayer of one in whose heart wickedness is contemplated.

It is not possible now to separate references in this psalm to ancient history from those to more recent experience. "He turned the sea into dry land, men passed through the river on foot" suggests that the primary reference is to the Deliverance from Egypt. That "God has tested us, tried us as silver is tried" may also show a recollection of the "fiery furnace"[1] of Egypt, as an encouragement to believe that present trials too are sent by God, who rescues them that fear him. Or it is possible that the whole of this first part may be not actualizing a past tradition but giving thanks in traditional terms for a present deliverance. The "I" of the second part may be the national leader on behalf of the nation making the annual sacrifice to celebrate the Deliverance from Egypt, or paying vows made in distress before a recent delivery. The reference to "cherishing iniquity in my heart" (v. 18) seems very personal, and it is also possible that an individual in worship is recalling the nation's history as he sings a hymn of thanksgiving for a similar deliverance, paying his vows and offering animal sacrifices, which are regarded as a completely fitting act of worship.

There is no reference to personal, individual experience in a similar psalm (68), where the story of the Deliverance is related as a past event in language close to that of Deborah's Song (Judges 5). God is described as father of the fatherless, protector of widows, who gives a home to the desolate, and prosperous freedom to prisoners. The psalmist is steeped in the language and thought of Law and Prophets and the memories of ancient Temple ritual, the central motif apparently being theophanies, God's self-revelations in power, and

---

[1] Cf. Deut. 4.20; 1 Kings 8.51; Jer. 11.4, a traditional way of referring to the Egyptian slavery; used of the siege of Jerusalem (Ezek. 22.18ff).

triumphal processions. The psalm opens with reminiscence of the prayer uttered when the Ark led Israel through the wilderness (Num. 10.35), calls for a highway for God through the desert (68.4, RSV marg.), and remembers his marching from Sinai to the Kishon in thunder and storm, his entry as a great king with chariot at the head of a mighty host into his dwelling-place at Jerusalem (cf. 68.29), his festal processions into the Temple with singers, maidens with timbrels, and minstrels. Finally, the writer lifts his eyes to the God who rides through the heavens revealing his presence with a mighty sound.

This great God is the Lord "who daily bears us up" (68.19). He carries his people as a burden (cf. Isa. 46.3) and can be confidently trusted to give them strength and power. This psalmist's love of older language and metaphor appears to have led him to borrow the vivid, but revolting, words used in Canaanite myth at Ras Shamra to describe Anat, goddess of war and love, as "washing her feet in the blood of her enemies" (cf. 68.23). The psalm, like the song of Deborah and the accounts of the Conquest of the promised land, regards God as a mighty warrior constantly fighting against evil.

In some psalms, traditions of the past are used to rebuke the present sin and ingratitude of the nation. Psalm 81 in its present form opens with the call to let the sound of joy ring out to God, and to fulfil the ancient law by blowing the trumpet proclaiming the feasts of the new and the full moon. Then the voice of God is reported, recounting his deeds for Israel and pleading with the people to obey his voice and walk in his ways, so that once again he may rescue her (cf. also 95).

## Lament

But more often appreciation of God's help in the past prefaces a cry of deep distress from suffering which the psalmist cannot understand and regards as undeserved. Psalm 44 emphasizes that the mighty, saving acts of God in the past are hearsay, not personal experience: "with our ears we have heard, O God, our fathers have told us", how God drove out the heathen and gave them a land to possess. Freely the psalmist confesses it was all God's doings, his right hand and not the strength of the fathers' swords that was victorious. Even now he trusts in God, not in Israel's sword and bow.[1]

Yet inexplicably God has cast them off and disgraced them, no

[1] Cf. pp. 98f, reference to Wars of the Lord.

longer marching out with Israel's hosts. The word "cast off" occurs in the previous psalm, that of an individual whose hope in God remains firm. But in this corporate hymn no hope is expressed. God has abandoned his people though they have not forgotten him nor been disloyal to his covenant. Though it is for God's sake that they are being killed like sheep all day long, the psalm ends not with faith or hope but with a desperate cry that God will awake from his sleep, rise up and help them, setting them free for the sake of his steadfast love.

Another hymn of lament, using the same word "cast off", is Psalm 74. But here disaster has fallen long ago, all lies in ruins and the great God has given no help. The psalmist begs him to remember the congregation[1] he acquired long ago (v. 2), the tribes to whom he was kinsman, Mount Zion where he used to dwell. Now Zion is a perpetual desolation and all the sanctuaries or trysting-places[2] have been burnt. Vividly he describes the wanton destruction of the Temple by God's foes, and God's inactivity. There is no sign or token that God is acting, no prophet to bring a message of hope. God's right hand is folded in his bosom. Then suddenly the "I" of the psalmist intrudes. "Yet it is God who is my king from long ago" (74.12), and with a succession of credal statements in which "thou" is always emphatic he uses the historic traditions and the popular myths of creation to assert God's mighty power in the past, entreating that he will remember, not give the life of his defenceless people to the mob, attend to the covenant, rise up and plead for them. The outspoken language, like that of Jeremiah, reveals the psalmist's close personal relationship with the living God, who is a real part of his daily life, and from whom he expects response.

## The Suffering of the Innocent

These hymns of complaint against undeserved suffering draw some comfort from the myths and traditions of God's great power revealed in the past, but see no sign of it in the present. Bitterly they cry out against God's abandonment of his people, and end with an anguished plea for help. But the fact of innocent suffering is faced by other psalmists in a more contemplative and philosophical way. When the intense challenge to faith is over and confident trust is again enjoyed,

[1] Cf. above, p. 70; the word is used in P for the people of Israel (Num. 16.3ff).

[2] So T. K. Cheyne, *The Book of Psalms* (1888), ad loc.

they trace back the track along which they have travelled. Usually these psalms are called "wisdom psalms", and regarded as the fruit of intellectual reflection on experience by wise men, recorded to teach and inspire the faith of Israel. Such are Psalms 37, 49, and 73. In all three the basic problem is doubt as to the fairness of God's rule of the universe. In a world controlled by a righteous, all-powerful God, why does evil go unpunished and goodness unrewarded, why do the wicked prosper and the innocent suffer? We have seen how Jeremiah's faith in God was tried by his own experience. These three writers show how their doubts were dispelled.

Psalm 37 shows most clearly its "school" origin, being arranged as an acrostic in which successive sections begin with a letter of the Hebrew alphabet (cf. 119). The writer asserts quite confidently that wickedness and the wicked will wither like green herbs, but the Lord will support those who trust in him. The good will inherit the earth and receive at the end the reward of peace (37.29, 37). Psalm 49 is clearly teaching wisdom and setting the answer to the same problem to music (49.4). Its theme is that death comes alike to all, rich and poor, wise and foolish, and wealth cannot purchase exemption from the common fate of all men. There is therefore no need for the righteous to be afraid when the powerful persecute him (49.5), nor when men become wealthy. Death puts an inevitable end to human power and wealth. But "the upright shall have dominion over them in the morning" (49.14, RSV marg.). Though no man can pay God sufficient to ransom his life from the grave (49.7), the psalmist believes, "Yet God will ransom my life from the power of Sheol, for he will take me."[1]

The third psalm that makes the suffering of the innocent its theme also ends with the belief that God will "take" the psalmist, but is more explicit in reliance on personal fellowship with God:

> But as for me, I am continually with thee,
>    thou hast grasped me with thy right hand.
> With thy counsel thou hast led me
>    and thou wilt take me afterwards gloriously. . . .
> Though flesh and heart perish
>    God is the rock of my heart . . .
> Those that are far from God perish. . . .
> But as for me, the nearness of God is my good (73.23ff).

But in this psalm, the writer's pilgrimage to faith is peculiarly his own, and it would certainly be true to say that he is recollecting in

[1] See below, p. 281. RSV translates the word as "receive" (49.15; 73.24).

tranquillity the deep emotion that arose from his personal suffering. He reaches a depth and wealth or spiritual experience unsurpassed anywhere in the Old Testament. He begins by citing without comment a statement of Israel's traditional faith:

> Surely God is good to Israel
> to those who are pure in heart. (73.1, RSV marg.),

and then he relates his own experience with strong emphasis on "I" (cf. 73.2, 22f, 28) in contrast to Israel and the pure in heart. His struggle rose from envy of the peace and welfare of the arrogant and wicked, whom he vividly describes. Their lives are full of pride, violence, malice, and oppression:

> They set their mouth against the heavens,
> and their tongue struts through the earth (73.9).

With atheistic sarcasm they ask how it is possible to believe that "God knows, the Most High has knowledge". In contrast to their prosperity, despite his struggle to keep his heart clean and his hands innocent, the writer has been under the stroke of God all day and chastened every morning. He could not even share his troubles lest he should be treacherous to—perhaps shake the faith of—"the generation of thy children", possibly young people, who did believe in God. His faith returned when in the sanctuary he was able to take a longer view and perceive the outcome of the life of the wicked. Then he confessed that bitterness had made him as stupid and ignorant as an animal. He had not realized the value of the outcome of his own life, nor, through all his suffering, taken into account the continual presence of God, his guidance, and the fact that though man's earthly powers might fail, God was his rock and portion. It is typical of the general attitude to praise in the Psalter that this psalmist should conclude with the discovery that, now he has made his refuge in the Lord God, he can witness to all God's works.

## The Afterlife

Consideration of the psalmists' attitude to innocent suffering raises the related problem of their view of death and the afterlife. It used to be emphasized by scholarly opinion that the idea of a future life for the individual was hardly reached within the Old Testament;[1] but a careful survey of burial customs, and hints by some Old Testament

---

[1] H. W. Robinson, *The Religious Ideas of the Old Testament*, (1913), p. 91.

writers that it might be possible for some men to escape the lifeless existence of Sheol (the underworld) and be "taken" by God[1] show that this view should be modified. Just as today there is a wide diversity of opinions on the subject, so in the Old Testament there is no one uniform view, even though the documents were often thoroughly revised by editors. This is particularly true of the Psalms, where we may expect to find not only conflicting opinions of different individuals but also that any one individual psalmist, writing out of his changing experiences, might at one time express despair and at another time in his devotional life move towards the greatest heights of spiritual confidence. At the same time it must be remembered that the psalmist is moving within the circle of stable Hebrew religious ideas, and reflecting varying shades of opinion found elsewhere in the Old Testament.

In the Law and Prophets interesting hints remain, enabling us to discover how in some sections of Hebrew thought men moved towards a more satisfying concept of life after death. The writer in Genesis differentiates Enoch from other patriarchs, all of whom died, by saying: "He walked with God and was not, for God took him" (Gen. 5.24). The word "take"[2] used here, which we have already noted in Psalms 49 and 73, occurs also in stories of Elijah, who pleaded with God to "take" him (RSV "take away", 1 Kings 19.4), and whom the prophets said God would take (2 Kings 2.3, 5, 9f). It is interesting that it is used of the Servant of the Lord (Isa. 53.8).[3]

Some of these passages may be understood to refer to God's healing and saving from premature death, but clearly not all of them can. The belief that Elijah was taken up (2 Kings 2.11) and remained alive so that he could be expected to come again before the great and terrible Day of the Lord (Mal. 4.5) must be linked with the belief expressed in Amos (9.2):

> Though they dig into Sheol,
>   from there shall my hand take them;
> though they climb up to heaven,
>   from there I will bring them down.

In either place, they were still under God's control. The same belief is very clear in Hosea. When God is declaring his wrath against Israel, he summons the powers of death against them:

---

[1] Cf. J. N. Schofield, *Archaeology and the Afterlife* (1951), and literature there cited.

[2] See above, p. 10.         [3] Cf. also Jer. 15.15; Jonah 4.3; Job. 1.21.

> Shall I ransom them from the power of Sheol?
>   Shall I redeem them from Death?
> O Death, where are your plagues?
>   O Sheol, where is your destruction?
> Compassion is hid from my eyes. (Hos. 13.14)

This belief that God is supreme throughout the universe, that he is not shut out from the realm of death, is basic to the faith of the writer of Psalm 139:

> If I ascend to heaven, thou art there!
> If I make my bed in Sheol, thou art there!
> If I take the wings of the morning
>   and dwell in the uttermost parts of the sea,
> even there thy hand shall lead me
>   and thy right hand shall hold me. (8ff)

Reliance on God's ultimate power in man's extremity is clear too in Psalm 23 in its latest revised translation:

> Yea, though I walk through the darkest valley I will fear no evil:
> for thou art with me, thy rod and thy staff comfort me.
>
> *(The Revised Psalter,* v. 4)

Frequently in the Psalter we may trace the teaching of the Law. It was man's disobedience that "brought death into the world, and all our woe". God created man by his word, moulded him from clay, breathed his own breath into him. Life and health come from God, and man lives in utter dependence upon him:

> When thou hidest thy face, they are dismayed;
>   When thou takest away their breath, they die
>   and return to their dust.
> When thou sendest forth thy Spirit
>   they are created. (104.29f)

In complete contrast to the everlasting glory of God, man is only transitory. The psalmist feeling himself under the wrath of God makes no attempt to gloss over the inevitability of death:

> Hear my prayer, O Lord . . .
> For I am thy passing guest,
>   a sojourner, like all my fathers.
> Look away from me, that I may know gladness,
>   before I depart and be no more! (39.12f)

and when he gives thanks for deliverance it is in a spirit of humility:

> As for me, I am poor and needy,
> but the Lord takes thought for me. (40.17)

It is man's duty as well as his joy to praise God as long as his life lasts; "I will sing to the Lord during my life; I will praise my God while I still am" (104.33), and he knows no higher bliss than to "dwell in the house of the Lord" all his days (27.4). In complete contrast, the psalmist in imminent dread of death cries out:

> Do the shades rise up to praise thee?
> Is thy steadfast love declared in the grave? (88.10f)

God rules everywhere, but in the lifeless existence of the underworld when he has withdrawn from men his spirit they return to their dust and have no knowledge of his presence, and the silence of the grave is felt as peculiarly terrible:

> If the Lord had not been my help
> my soul would soon have dwelt in the land of silence. (94.17)

In particular, the wicked are threatened with the terrors of the death that is to be their portion. The Lord, who will never permit the righteous to be moved, will cast the wicked down into the lowest pit, and they will not live out half their days (55.22f).

Just as the psalmist emphasizes the loving-kindness of God, so he emphasizes that God's purpose is that man should live and enjoy fellowship with him. God sustains man's strength throughout his life, so that his youth is renewed like the eagle's (103.5). As in the Law it is tragic that grey hairs should go down in sorrow to the grave, so in the Psalms there is fullness of joy in a long life lived out to witness to God's goodness:

> I have been young, and now am old;
> yet I have not seen the righteous forsaken
> or his children begging bread. (37.25)

and the psalmist prays that we may "rejoice and be glad all our days". It is right that men should delight in seeing the work of their hands established (90.14, 17), and it is a wholesome and natural joy that ageing man takes in his children and in looking forward to the generations that in the purpose of God will succeed him:

> Let this be recorded for a generation to come,
> so that a people yet unborn may praise the Lord:
> The children of thy servants shall dwell secure;
> their posterity shall be established before thee. (102.18, 28)

Though individual man is transitory, the people of God is more enduring. Indeed, in the thought of the psalmist the death as well as the life of the righteous is completely different from that of the wicked. To die with those fitting accompaniments of old age, "honour, love, obedience, troops of friends", to die in peace, was a sign of God's blessing. It was like a shock of ripe corn garnered at harvest time. A life lived in the favour and presence of God had completeness and might be thought of as rounded off by death.

There are, however, some psalms which contain a suggestion that experience of fellowship with God in this life may be so strong that, like love to the writer of the Song of Songs (8.6), it is stronger than death. The writer of Psalm 16 knows the joy of living in the presence of God, a joy he perhaps glimpsed in the worship of the sanctuary, and is confident that

> Thou dost not give me up to Sheol
> or let thy godly one see the Pit.
> Thou dost show me the path of life;
> in thy presence is fullness of joy. (16.10f)

The words may imply that he has been rescued from premature death; but clearly the psalmist here does not contemplate any end to the protective presence of God. He has insight into a conception of life as quality, not quantity, not length of days but a type of life lived in nearness to God. The writer of the Fourth Gospel makes such a concept explicit—eternal life is a new way of living which begins here, and in which death is only an incident. Possibly the tradition of Enoch's "taking" was in the mind of the psalmist. Walking in fellowship with God causes his soul to rejoice and his body to dwell secure. Similarly the closing verse of Psalm 17, "As for me, in righteousness I shall behold thy face; I shall be satisfied when I awake with the vision of thy form", suggests that when he enters the unknown afterworld the writer looks forward to receiving a vision of God such as was vouchsafed to Moses the great leader (Num. 12.8). Recognition of the everlasting quality of fellowship with God is implicit elsewhere:

> For with thee is the fountain of life;
> in thy light do we see light. (36.9)

and one psalmist declares that God has set him in his presence for ever (41.12). It has been well said that "in converse with God the saint found the fullness and certainty of life; the highest and most endurable joy conceivable to him was in the access to God he ex-

perienced in the sanctuary . . . the loftiest hope for his own future took
the form of an anticipation of the continuance of that access".[1] But
clearly the psalmist is sometimes struggling to express a hope of
access to God beyond anything that has hitherto been known to him,
and it is in Psalm 73 that faith reaches its highest peak:

<blockquote>afterward thou wilt take me to glory.</blockquote>

[1] S. D. F. Salmond, *Christian Doctrine of Immortality* (1901), p. 199.

# 14 The Religion of the Wise: Introduction

The books included in the Wisdom literature are Proverbs, Ecclesiastes, Job, and some of the Psalms.[1] Within the Old Testament itself the Wisdom tradition has evidently a very long history, going back to the practical knowledge gained from experience in family and tribal life, emerging into history as one of the splendours of Solomon's court, and developing into a finished, cultured philosophy of life which aimed at commending the religion of Israel both to fellow-Israelites, especially to youth, and to non-Jews. Here we shall confine ourselves in the main to the Old Testament canonical writings with a glance at Ecclesiasticus and The Wisdom of Solomon. We shall look at the standards of conduct advocated by the wise men in Proverbs and Ecclesiasticus, and we shall consider one of the most interesting books in the whole Old Testament, the Book of Job, as showing how they faced our most baffling religious problems. Ecclesiastes, which reflects their attitude to life, is in the Hebrew Bible one of the Megilloth, and, with The Wisdom of Solomon, will be treated in Chapter 17.

## International Wisdom

Whereas when we consider the Law and the Prophets and the bulk of the Psalms we are dealing with what was peculiarly the Hebrew genius within the people of Israel, when we come to the Wisdom literature we have to reckon with the same genius open and responsive to influences from the outside world. It is only since about 1920 that scholars have realized the extent to which the thought of Israel's

[1] 1; 19.7–14; 32.8–11; 34.11–23; 37; 49; 73; 94.8–23; 111; 112; 119; 128; 133. Outside the Old Testament are Ecclesiasticus or The Wisdom of ben Sirach; The Wisdom of Solomon; 1 Esdras; Tobit; Baruch; The Letters of Aristeas; 4 Maccabees; Pirke Aboth or Sayings of the Jewish Fathers; and in Christian literature the Epistle of James, and the Didache or Teaching of the Twelve Apostles.

wise men was affected by foreign influences, and that Hebrew Wisdom literature is part of a world literature that can be studied in the written remains of Babylon and Egypt as well as of Greece. Egyptian Wisdom writings go back to the third millennium B.C. Texts written on inside walls of pyramids and later on coffins have been combined to form the "Book of the Dead". The aim of the writers was the moral and cultural training of younger men at court who aspired to official positions. They gave prudential advice on how to obtain preferment, and reflective assessments, often pessimistic, of the meaning of life. Sometimes they show disdain for the ignorant and the manual worker, though there were sages who fought against this tendency. In the main, Israelite Wisdom was, however, democratic and free from class-consciousness, though there is some evidence of class-consciousness in Ecclesiasticus.

In Babylonia there were books of Proverbs which, like the Old Testament, used "My son" as a form of address, and there were longer dialogues such as the one known as the Babylonian Job.

There is considerable difference of opinion as to the extent of Greek influence, some scholars finding in Israelite Wisdom traces of the influence of Greek gnomic poetry of the sixth century B.C. and of Stoic and Epicurean philosophers. Where the spirit of inquiry or of doubt is obvious they would link it with the Greeks, as also the doctrine of the "mean", the moderation taught in Ecclesiastes. But these views can be taken too far. The doctrine of moderation in Hebrew thought is ancient, for men were warned against attracting God's attention to themselves either by giving hospitality to a prophet (1 Kings 17.18) or by speaking during a plague (Amos 6.10). Probably we should agree with Cheyne that during the Greek period there was a fertilization of the intellectual soil by new ideas throughout the Jewish world. Many Jews migrated to Egypt where they were exposed to Greek influence. Further, Alexander the Great brought Persian as well as Greek influences into Palestine, and as in Babylonia first Ea, then Nabu, was god of wisdom, so in Persia wisdom was a chief divine attribute, distinguished from human wisdom.[1]

Study has shown common features in all the Wisdom literature of the Near East from the Nile to the Tigris. Cheyne[2] described Hebrew Wisdom as the link between the most exceptional revelation of Old

---

[1] O. Loretz, Qoheleth und der Alte Orient, (1964), cited in Concilium, December, 1965), pp. 68ff, finds Mesopotamian influence paramount rather than Greek or Egyptian.

[2] T. K. Cheyne, Job and Solomon (1887).

Testament prophecy and the best moral and intellectual attainments of other nations. Scribes were wise men, and outside Israel wisdom often includes some knowledge of the mysteries of the gods as well as an understanding of practical conduct necessary to bring prosperity and happiness. Though sometimes personal divine names are used, there is a monotheistic tendency to describe the deity as "god" or "the god". All the wise men inculcated the study of wisdom, duty to parents and superiors, respect for property, generosity, peacefulness, contentment, purity, temperance, truthfulness, and justice. They showed the folly and wickedness of disobedience, strife, pride, arrogance, sloth, and meddlesomeness. The quality of character portrayed was high and the concept of the good citizen the same in all the Wisdom literature in Egypt, Babylonia, and Israel. Sins of the flesh were condemned, but there was equally condemnation of the sins of the spirit.

## Hebrew Wisdom

Israel knew of the existence of this wider Wisdom literature, and that wisdom was international rather than national. Her own wisdom was regarded as belonging to the same general category. Solomon's wisdom excelled that of the children of the east, and the biblical writer thought it worthwhile to name some of these lesser rivals (1 Kings, 4.31). Hezekiah's scribe, Shebna, has a foreign name. First-Isaiah knew how the Egyptians trusted in wisdom, and he knew of the sages who were court counsellors (19.11ff). We hear of Edomite (Obad. 8; Jer. 49.7), and Babylonian Wisdom (Jer. 50.35). Ezekiel (28.2–5) says that the prince of Tyre was wiser than Daniel. Balaam, Job and his friends, and Lemuel and Agur in the Book of Proverbs are all represented as non-Jews. It is not surprising that early Israelite Wisdom literature has little interest in national beliefs and forms of worship, but stresses that morality is binding on all men, its observance essential if man is to go unpunished.

In early Hebrew thought wisdom was regarded as the source of ability and common sense, producing very much the same effect as the Spirit of God. Often it came through dreams, as to Joseph (Gen. 37; 41.33). It was the name for the technical skill of the builders of the the Tabernacle (Exod. 35.35). But its outstanding traditional exponent was Solomon, who shows that element of shrewdness in his practical sagacity—illustrated by the story of the two women with one baby (1 Kings 3.28)—which remained a characteristic of Hebrew

Wisdom. Another outcome of his wisdom is academic and scientific, his listing of trees "from the cedar that is in Lebanon to the hyssop that grows out of the wall", and his speaking of beasts, birds, reptiles, and fish. In complete dependence he had prayed to God for wisdom, and his prayer had been granted: "God gave Solomon wisdom and understanding beyond measure, and largeness of mind like the sand on the seashore" (4.29–33). Also characteristic was an element, possibly utilitarian and conservative, opposed to the radical innovations of the prophets, though it seems evident that the prophets themselves were influenced by, and lent additional emphasis to, the tradititional moral and religious teaching of early, perhaps oral wisdom.[1] After the exile, when the flow of prophecy had ceased, wise men became mediators and interpreters of the prophets, almost taking their place and enforcing their teaching.

Scholars have differentiated earlier canonical wisdom from a later type seen in some of the psalms and in writings outside the canon. In the former, the wise men do not form a separate class and all who seek wisdom can find it. There is no appeal to scripture, but strong emphasis on religious motives as the basis of ethics and social behaviour. The fact of God is unchallenged and his judgement and control of destiny always accepted, as also the fact of human sin and failure (Prov. 20.9). A good character and moral qualities are believed to grow from wisdom; but the frankly utilitarian approach is a great limitation to morality. Moral instructions are often enforced by reference to God as creator or maker of man (14.31; 17.5). There is, however, little interest in theological speculation or principles of cosmic order. The starting-point of the teaching of these wise men was the form of religion that had filtered through to the masses and had become an accepted part of their background. God is just and righteous, rewards and punishes men for their conduct, and intervenes to give good fortune as the reward for right living, though excuses are made for the prosperity of evil people. Unlike Egyptian Wisdom, the early Hebrew form limits its outlook to this life, taking no account of a life after death. In later wisdom, however, the Jew has shown his capacity to assimilate and incorporate in Israelite religion the elements he borrowed from outside. Wisdom becomes part of the Hebrew national religious tradition, Israel alone has true wisdom, here identified with the Mosaic code, the wise man is now the scribe who teaches the Law, and the superiority of Jewish wisdom is emphasized (Apocalypse of Baruch, 3.23f).

[1] H. W. Wolff, op. cit.

This development in the Wisdom tradition is reflected in the description of the wise man. In Babylonia and Egypt wise men and priests were often linked together. The priest might be called a wise man, though usually the wise man and the writer of proverbs had no interest in magic or in cultic rites. But more often wise men were rulers, important state officials who held responsible positions and instructed their successors. There were, however, regular scribal schools in Mesopotamia and Egypt where writing, wisdom, manners, and ethics were taught, by scribes and teachers who were professional wise men.

All these elements are found in Israel too (Deut. 4.6). Moses chose wise men as officials (1.13); Joshua (34.9) as well as Solomon possessed wisdom; but there was also the wise woman of Tekoa (2 Sam. 14.2). David had scribes among his court officials (2 Sam. 8.17). Shaphan the scribe was a Temple official (2 Kings 22.3), Ezra was both priest and scribe. There was a city in south Palestine called Kirjath Sepher (town of books) or Sopher (of scribes, Josh. 15.16) perhaps suggesting that it housed a school of scribes, especially as apparently the same place was also called Kirjath-sannah (town of the palm leaf, a common writing material, 15.49). An interesting story of another wise woman who saved her home town, Abel (2 Sam. 20.16f), suggests that various towns vied with each other, as do universities today, in their reputation for wisdom, Teman (Jer. 49.7) as well as Tekoa receiving special mention.

In Israel the wise ranked as national leaders with prophets, priests, and prince. In the eighth century First-Isaiah (29.11ff) laments that the vision of God has become like a book that is sealed to those who can read as it is to those who cannot, worship is lip service, reverence for God is "a commandment of men learned by rote". Therefore the wisdom of the wise will perish, and God himself will intervene so that the deaf may hear, the blind see, and the meek and poor find new joy in the Holy One of Israel. Jeremiah (8.7ff) a century and a half later is equally scathing to those who say, "We are the wise men, we have the Lord's revelation", whereas in reality the false pen of the scribes has written lies. The wise men will be ashamed and dismayed because they have rejected the word of the Lord—and what wisdom can there be apart from that? The Lord forbids the wise man to glory in his wisdom, the mighty in his might, or the rich in his riches. "Let him that glories glory in this, that he has shrewdness which enables him to know me, that I am the Lord who act with loving kindness, judgement, and loyalty in the land, and these are the things I delight in"

(9.23f). Jeremiah's opponents, whose slander and deadly snares awakened in him such revengeful prayers, regarded themselves as standing with prophet, priest, and wise man against him: "Then said they, Come, let us devise devices against Jeremiah, for instruction shall not perish from the priest, nor counsel from the wise, nor the word from the prophet" (18.18). Their antagonism suggests that the wise were not enthusiastic for reform, and that much of their prudential counsel was irreligious, showing a shrewd wit and sharp tongue, then as now not always welcomed by faithful prophet and priest. But no single description can be trusted to be adequate for them all. Job (15.18) suggests that wisdom is a living, ancient tradition heard and repeated from the fathers, so being a conservative element. The Deuteronomist shows no hostility to the wise men, nor does he treat them as in any way a separate class (1.15; 16.19).[1]

## The Wise Men

It has been suggested that the wise men were occupying themselves with the life of the individual in its everyday setting, seeking to distil, from the particular thought of Israel, principles which both in morals and religion should be universal and applicable wherever men live. Thus the truths taught by the prophets before the downfall of the State were now applied by wise men to the individual, not the nation. H. W. Robinson[2] emphasizes this individualism: "We may define the wisdom of Israel as the discipline whereby was taught the application of prophetic truth to the individual life in the light of experience." Another writer[3] also stressed interest in religious individuality. Whereas to prophet and lawgiver it was the community as a whole that mattered, the wise men took into account individual welfare and happiness in family and community, studying particularly all the great motives of human conduct, gratitude, friendship, love, hate, wealth, and renown. This emphasis on the individual has even been used to date the Book of Proverbs after the teaching of Jeremiah and Ezekiel.[4]

But it may be doubted whether the book of Proverbs and proverbial literature in general is individualistic in the usual sense of the word.

[1] If this is from the Northern kingdom, it perhaps indicates that professional wisdom, and wise men as a class were better known in the south.
[2] *Inspiration and Revelation in the Old Testament* (1946), p. 241.
[3] O. S. Rankin, *Israel's Wisdom Literature* (1936), pp. 353ff.
[4] Cf. R. H. Pfeiffer, *Zeitschrift für A.T. Wissenschaft* (1926), pp. 13ff.

UL

The essence of a proverb is that it applies within a whole community. It includes in its sweep all rolling stones, all people who live in glass houses, and is concerned with them in relation to, and as part of, the community. In the Wisdom literature, as elsewhere in the Old Testament, there is no thought that the individual man, even the religious one, is sufficient unto himself apart from his people.

These men were practical teachers with an intimate knowledge of human life, in living contact with ordinary folk, and having the power to express sensible counsel in forceful language using concrete terms, a power characteristic of Hebrew thought. Hence they use the terms "Son", "Father", "Mother", there is vivid contrast between the live dog and the dead lion, the wise and the fool are spoken of rather than wisdom or folly except when these latter are personified. Then Wisdom becomes not an abstract idea but an attractive woman with beauty and nobility, as living a figure as Babylon, the fallen queen in Isaiah 47. The function of counsellor is frequently assigned to the wise man, who is concerned with his fellow men not as separate individuals but as "members of the family of Israel, the people of God".[1]

The chief interest of the wise men was in teaching their fellows and the youth of the nation how to live happy, healthy, moral, and prosperous lives, and their teaching can be summed up as consecrated common sense in daily life. It has been said that their ideal is expressed in Psalm 1.1f:

> O how happy is the man
> Who walks not in the counsel of the disloyal,
> Nor stands about with those who miss the mark,
> Nor sits in the company of scoffers.
> But in the revelation of the Lord is his delight
> And in his revelation he meditates day and night.

They recognized: however, as one of them said, "He who devotes himself to the Law is filled with it, but the profane man stumbles therein." Some men can start their religious pilgrimage with the Bible despite all its difficulties, some do not possess the necessary religious attitude that might be described as "devoting" themselves to it, an attitude that enables them to accept the presuppositions that make the Bible intelligible. Frankly sceptical and agnostic, many of them would like to believe but have not "the willing suspension of disbelief"; religious assertions appear unreal or unproved, God, the afterlife, the spiritual

[1] A. B. Davidson, Job, *Encyclopedia Britannica*, 9th edn.

world, are speculation or wishful thinking. The wise men tried to help such men as these by approaching theology from common human experience, not from the dogma of divine revelation. Themselves endowed with critical, questioning minds, they were often at variance with prophet and priest. Unlike the writers of the popular stories in the Law and Former Prophets, they began as good teachers with the things everyone knew in daily life, and attempted to lead from this to religious truth. They were middlemen, between the inspired religious leaders and the ordinary Israelite, and their approach may be called horizontal rather than vertical.[1] Jesus, son of Sirach, author of Ecclesiasticus, may be regarded as a typical, cultured wise man at the beginning of the second century B.C. He was a teacher who had his own "house of instruction", where he invited the unlearned to lodge (Ecclus. 51.23) just as Wisdom (Prov. 9.3ff) invites men to her house. He had seen many things in foreign lands, trying both good and bad—reminding us that knowledge of foreign countries is shown also by the prophets, another indication that the wise men shared their learning and must not be marked off as a completely isolated class in Israel. Often he had been in grave danger, but had been saved by his wisdom (Ecclus. 34.12ff). Slander and a deceitful tongue had met him, and wicked devices had brought him in peril of his life (51.2f). His own picture of an ideal scribe (39.1–11) seems to describe him well. He was a man of leisure, fond of feasts, giving careful rules for behaviour; a family man, strict in discipline, wise in family lore, and worrying over family affairs. His grandson, who at some time after 135 B.C. translated the book into Greek, tells us: "My grandfather, Jesus, having given himself greatly to the reading of the Law and the Prophets and the other books of our fathers, and having acquired sufficient familiarity with them, was also himself led to take a part in writing something appertaining to instruction and wisdom, in order that those who are lovers of learning and instructed in these things might so much the more progress by a manner of life in accordance with the Law." A younger contemporary of Jesus ben Sirach, who wrote the book of Daniel in its present form, praised such men: "And those who are wise shall shine like the brightness of the firmament; and those who turn many to righteousness, like the stars for ever and ever" (12.3). Here the word for "wise" is the same as is used of Eve's temptation (Gen. 3.6), the emphasis being on shrewdness, worldly wisdom, perhaps the quality required of religious teachers by Jesus of Nazareth—wise as serpents.

[1] J. N. Schofield, *Introducing Old Testament Theology*, p. 23.

By the second century, the wise man had vanished and in his place we find the wise scribe. But he had left a legacy of preaching the gospel to the poor, taking religion and morals into the street and market place, and had attempted to bring wisdom to dwell with men, to make men's homes pure and loving, their business just, their pleasures clean, their human relationships generous.

To the prophet the will of God came through his life and conscience, and came with the proclamation, "Thus says the Lord". The priest possessed a body of law given by God through Moses and had material means of obtaining oracles. Wise men like prophets appealed to experience, but unlike prophets claimed no special inspiration. Yet that they gained respect and veneration is evident from the fact that in the Hebrew Bible many psalms, Proverbs, Job, and Ecclesiastes have gained a place as inspired writings:

> The fruit of the righteous is a tree of life,
> and the wise man is one who captures souls. (Prov. 11.30)

# 15 The Religion of the Wise: The Standard of Conduct

## *The Form of the Book of Proverbs*

The Book of Proverbs has been called a carefully prepared handbook of practical religion. Its aim is to present a high standard of conduct, though, as we have seen, this is not theocentric. Its method is to present "sensible" conduct as that which leads to prosperity and happiness, rather than "right" conduct based on law and Decalogue or "good" conduct accepting the will of God through the prophetic word. Like the Psalter, it contains five main sections, and each is marked by a separate title.

Chapters 1—9, "The Proverbs of Solomon, son of David king of Israel", appears intended as introduction to the whole book, and is usually regarded as its latest part. Much of it is devoted to an exhortation to respond to the call of Wisdom, portrayed as a good and beautiful woman, attractive, friendly, interested in everyone, and able to save men from the seductive allurements of an adulterous female called Folly.

10—22.16 is also called "Proverbs of Solomon", and consists of independent sayings, many of them duplicated, of two parallel lines often in strong contrast:

> A wise son makes a glad father,
>> but a foolish son is a sorrow to his mother.
>> (10.1; cf. 15.20).

22.17—24 are "Words of the Wise", longer than the sayings of the previous section and usually containing two couplets, the second giving a reason for the first:

> Do not withhold discipline from a child;
>> if you beat him, he will not die:
> When you beat him with the rod
>> you will save his life from Sheol. (23.13f)

In this section there are very close parallels with the Egyptian book of wisdom known as the Book of Amenemope. There are also parallels with another book known throughout the ancient Near East, found among the remains of the Jewish colony that lived at Yeb in Upper Egypt in the fifth century B.C., and called the Proverbs of Ahikar. In this book the proverb quoted above occurs as "Withhold not thy son from the rod if thou canst not keep him from wickedness. If I smite thee, my son, thou shalt not die, but if I leave thee to thine own heart thou shalt not live."

25—29 has the interesting title, "These also are the Proverbs of Solomon which the men of Hezekiah king of Judah copied." They are short sayings comparable to those in chapters 10—22.

30—31. This final section consists of three groups of sayings: the Words of Agur, which include some of the most agnostic and sceptical statements in the whole book, and number sayings perhaps originally associated with riddles; a fragment called the "words of king Lemuel taught him by his mother" and warning him against bad women and strong drink; and in contrast the final acrostic poem in praise of a virtuous woman, revealing a high ideal of womanhood and home life—a "pure religion breathing household laws".

Many of the sayings drive home truth by a straightforward analogy: it is as senseless to tie a stone in a sling as to give honour to a fool (26.8). Some of these short pithy sayings doubtless sprang from experience and observation of life, were accepted as proverbs, as brief statements of truth that could scarcely be more strikingly expressed, and were preserved by years of oral transmission so that they became the "distilled wisdom of ages". Sometimes they were extended into longer parables:

> Over the field of the slothful I passed,
> And by the vineyard of the man who lacks heart for his work;
> And lo, it was all overgrown with thorns,
> Its face was covered with weeds,
> And its stone wall overthrown.
> As I gazed I took good heed.
> I saw and received instruction,
> A little sleep, a little slumber,
> A little folding of the hands to rest;
> In comes a highwayman—thy poverty,
> And thy want like an armed man. (24.30ff; cf. 6.10f)

Truth might also be taught by riddles to which proverbs provided the answers, and some such form seems to lie behind

My son, eat honey, for it is good,
and the drippings of the honeycomb are sweet to your taste,
Know that wisdom is such to your soul. (24.13f)

There seems a likeness here to the riddle asked of Samson (Judges 14.
18) "What is sweeter than honey?", to which the appropriate answer
at a wedding feast would be "love", but in this context is "wisdom".

A well-established and ancient form of teaching was by the use of
numbers, and the prophecies of Amos in the eighth century show that
it was a form with which he was well acquainted: "For three transgressions, yea for four, I will not keep back punishment" (Amos 1.3).
It is found also in Proverbs:

These three things are not satisfied,
Four say not, Enough.
Sheol, and a barren womb,
Earth not satisfied with water,
And fire saith not, Enough. (30.15f)

A more religious usage is seen in Proverbs 6.16–19:

These six the Lord hates
seven are abominations to him;
haughty eyes, a lying tongue,
and hands shedding innocent blood,
feet hurrying to run into mischief,
a false witness breathing out lies,
and one spreading discord among brethren.

While many of the proverbs must have a long history and go back
to oral, folk wisdom, others doubtless emanated from sophisticated
minds that could coin epigrams—"what oft was thought, but ne'er
so well expressed". Indeed, it has been claimed[1] that no aphorisms in
the Book of Proverbs are popular, folk sayings, but all are reflective
and academic in tone, and must be regarded as the products of
schools of moralists in a period of high moral culture. Certainly much
of the collection has the high epigrammatic finish that would be
expected if the proverbs were current in a circle of lively and intelligent minds; but to say this is not to venture into the field of dating, or
to pass judgement on separate proverbs. Clearly some of the writings
are longer and more elaborate, such as the praise of wisdom (Prov. 8).
Clearly too some of the duplicates reflect different milieux from which
the proverbs came. Perhaps a town dweller thought it was better to
dwell in a corner of an attic than with a nagging woman in a big house

[1] C. H. Toy, *Proverbs* (1899), p. xi.

(21.9), while a countryman would prefer to dwell alone in the desert (21.19). Many proverbs could be quoted to show the great variety of experience reflected in the book and to prove that they were drawn from many walks of life. A more significant variation on two forms of the same proverb occurs when one saying runs:

> The teaching of the wise is a fountain of life,
> Turning aside from the snares of death. (13.14)

but another has:

> Reverence (RSV fear) for the Lord is a fountain of life. (14.27)

Similarly, two distinct attitudes may be traced even in chapters 1—9, which are regarded as the latest part of the book. The usual motive for avoiding evil is wordly wisdom and common sense:

> My son, when sinners entice you, consent not.
> If they say, Go with us, let us lurk for blood,
> Let us ambush the innocent without cause . . .
> My son, go not the way they go,
> Keep your foot from their paths,
> For their feet run to evil,
> They hasten to shed blood.
> Surely in vain is the net spread
> In the sight of those who can fly.
> These men for their own blood are lurking,
> They ambush their own lives.
> So are the ways of all who are greedy for gain
> It takes away the life of those who get it. (1.10ff)

But there is another attitude that regards wisdom as firmly linked with reverence for the Lord. It is those who have despised this reverence who reject the counsels of wisdom and will meet with distress and anguish (1.27ff).

Yet despite the wide variety of proverbial wisdom, none of the proverbs quoted in other parts of the Old Testament occurs in this book. Historians and prophets used proverbs, and others occur in the Psalms, yet though there are duplicates within the Book of Proverbs itself and the selection was made from such a wide range of experience, not one of those other proverbs has found a place in it. Samson was credited with a proverbial saying with a country background, "If you had not ploughed with my heifer, you would not have learned my secret" (Judges 14.18). David, who may have been a coiner of epigrams, appears to have been a father worthy of Solomon, who was credited with speaking three thousand proverbs. When closely pursued by Saul he could call to mind an ancient proverb, "From wicked people wickedness goes out" (1 Sam. 24.13). Hosea the Northern prophet speaks of sowing wind and reaping storms (8.7), ploughing evil and reaping disaster (10.13). Using simple comparison he says, Like people like priest (4.9), and Ezekiel uses a proverb of similar form, Like mother like daughter (16.44). Ezekiel quotes other proverbs—Days tarry and every vision fades (12.22) and with Jeremiah says, The fathers have eaten sour grapes and the children's teeth are set on edge (18.2; cf. Jer. 31.29). A psalmist uses an agricultural proverb, "Sow in tears, reap in joy" (126.5). Why are none of these sayings quoted in the Book of Proverbs? Do they belong to a a different age, or to a different circle of thought? It is difficult to date the book; but most scholars consider that in its present form it belongs to the late post-exilic age, perhaps as late as the Hellenistic period, though much of the material used in it may be very ancient. It seems probable that Proverbs sprang from a more secular, cosmopolitan background than that which gave rise to Israel's Law and Prophets.

## Its Attitude to Judaism

The book peculiarly lacks interest in Jewish national hopes or racial consciousness, and gives no hint that duty to one's fellow men may be affected by such considerations. Except in the titles where Solomon is called king of Israel and Hezekiah king of Judah—information that would appear unnecessary if the book was intended simply for readers who knew the nation's history—there is no mention of Israel or its usual synonyms. There is no reference to such basic religious ideas as the Day of the Lord, the Covenant,[1] the Law,[2] priesthood, Zion, the Messiah, the Davidic kingship, election, my people, the chosen people, the contrast between Jew and Gentile and between the worship of the Lord and other gods. Clearly there is contact with other Old Testament writings. It is promised, as in the Psalter, that the upright will inherit the earth (2.21). The deuteronomic command to bind the words of the Law on hand and forehead may be compared with the advice to bind on heart and neck the instruction of parents

[1] In Prov. 2.17, the parallelism suggests a marriage covenant, not the Covenant at Sinai.
[2] Law (*torah*) is that of a mother (1.8); a father (3.1) of wisdom (7.2) or the wise (13.14). The Law of God may be referred to (28.4, 9; 29.18).

(6.20f) and the teaching of the wise (7.3). The difference becomes even clearer when the motive for thanksgiving at harvest is merely the lively expectation of favours to come:

> Give honour to the Lord from your substance
> and from the first fruit of all your increase;
> so shall your barns be filled with plenty
> and your presses burst with new wine. (3.9f)

This is not the joy in harvest taught by the Deuteronomist.

It has been maintained that the institutions and peculiar ideas of the religion of Israel are omitted because they were taken for granted.[1] However this may be, there is no tendency to propagate the religious institutions of Judaism, a fact that is all the more striking if the book received its final form in the third and second centuries B.C., when the Jews developed so strongly their stress on the peculiar treasure of Israel. But it is doubtful whether at any period in the religious history of Israel there was an absence of the national hopes and aspirations so prominent in the prophets, and, if the wise men do not allude to them, it is not because these hopes are dead, but because another direction of thought absorbed them.

However closely or loosely the writers of the Book of Proverbs were attached to Judaism, their explicit approach was from man's experience rather than from institutional religion. It was cosmopolitan, ignoring the boundaries of religion and of race, of secular and holy. The Wisdom they portrayed made her voice heard by all humanity, her delight was with all the sons of men (8.4, 31). The gulf between Israel and the outsider was ignored, and the appeal was not to dogma or to the language of organized religion, but was on the level where all men are one—the universal level of common human experience.

All this presents a clear contrast to the later book of Ecclesiasticus, where it seems that an attempt is made to redress the balance in favour of Judaism. This book might be interpreted as an effort to revive the national heritage within the Jewish people, scattered as they were and exposed to foreign influences. Clearly it venerates wisdom, but this is regarded as the gift of God and may be equated with the Law. The writer is interested in the externals of religion—robes and ritual, and there are many references to the history of Israel (16.8; 44—51). As in other Jewish writings of this late post-exilic period, there is considerable stress on the importance of the Law and the Covenant. All the gifts of wisdom are comprised in the

[1] Cf. W. O. E. Oesterley, *The Book of Proverbs* (1929), pp. xviif.

Book of the Covenant of God Most High, the Law which Moses commanded as a heritage for the assemblies of Jacob (24.23); converse with the wise is comparable to converse in the Law of the Lord (9.15); taking hold of the Law enables a man to find wisdom (15.1; 19.20); the good scribe meditates in the Law of the Most High (39.1); a sinner is one who rejects the Law (41.8) and a godless woman shall be his portion (26.23). It is as though the cry is being uttered, "Back to the Law!" as the basis of national existence and freedom.

Yet the fundamental attitudes of the wise man are to be seen in both Proverbs and Ecclesiasticus. It is the audience, the environment, and the aim that are different. Both are representative of the same living tradition.

## Reverence for the Lord

The editor responsible for the present arrangement intended that 1—9 should be regarded as the prologue to the whole work, giving its purpose and the way it should be interpreted. If the chapters are an addition, he must have been a wise man convinced that religious truth is valid and important, and can be offered even to a rational, cultured outlook on life as a deep basis for reason and ethics. Having attributed the work to King Solomon, he stated his aim that men should know wisdom and instruction, perhaps in distinction from a prophetic aim that they should know the Lord. But the close link with religion is clear in the motto—Reverence for the Lord is the beginning (the same Hebrew word as Gen. 1.1), or perhaps firstfruits (Prov. 3.9), of knowledge; the stupid[1] despise wisdom and instruction (1.7). Indeed, it is almost as though the whole book were an exposition of God's requirements (Mic. 6.8)—acts of justice, deeds of mercy, living in the presence of one greater than oneself to whom one is committed as a bride to her husband. The phrase "reverence for the Lord" occurs often in the Wisdom literature and is a basic requirement of one type of wise man.

Although, as we have seen, Proverbs contains no references to Israel's history nor to distinctive Israelite religious ideas, yet Israel's personal name for the deity, translated as The Lord, is used much more often throughout than the general divine name, God, suggesting that the writers regarded themselves as within the circle of Israel's revealed religion and as propagating it. It is personal monotheism

---

[1] Perhaps "thick-headed" or sluggish. Cf. Brown, Driver, Briggs, op. cit., p. 17, col. 1, of a liquid that thickens.

without argument or dogma. In 1—9 this name occurs often, five times in the phrase "reverence (fear, RSV) for the Lord". Men can choose this reverence just as they can love knowledge (1.29). If they seek wisdom, they understand reverence for the Lord and find knowledge of God (2.5). Reverence for the Lord makes men hate evil and pride (8.13) and it is the beginning of wisdom (9.10).[1] In the second section, where the phrase occurs eight times, the value of this reverence is clearly attested from ordinary human experience. It gives long life (10.27), and confidence that one's children will have a place of refuge (14.26). As we have seen, it is a fountain of life enabling men to depart from the snares of death (14.27), while in another duplicate it is compared with, and has the same efficacy as, righteousness:

> Better is a little with reverence for the Lord (righteousness, 16.8)
> than great treasure and trouble with it. (15.16)

As man's steadfast love and faithfulness atone for sin, so reverence for the Lord turns men from evil (16.6). It gives the kind of satisfaction in life that enables a man to sleep without fear of evil (19.23), and when it accompanies humility there are granted three great gifts prized by the wise and elsewhere regarded as the gift of wisdom—riches, honour, and life (22.4). In the third section of the book (23.17), daily reverence for the Lord is the antidote to being jealous of sinners, reminding us of the attitude in the Wisdom psalms. It must be stressed that the phrase "reverence for the Lord" does not suggest fright, but the humble respect and awe of which man is conscious when in the presence of someone much greater than himself. The Lord is a loving Father who corrects his son (3.11f). Quite clearly, humility or reverence is a basic attitude inculcated by these wise men.

When they use the name "Lord" they are picturing their God as real and personal. He is the giver of Wisdom (2.6), forming her before creation (8.22) and sending her out into street and market-place seeking to save men from folly. So close is their association of Wisdom with the Lord, that the beautiful eulogy of Wisdom (3.13–18) occurs in the context of a chapter where the Lord is so named nine times, and the connection is equally close in chapter 8. Always the Lord is the God presented by the Law and the Prophets, one who is directly concerned with men:

---

[1] "Beginning" here is a different Hebrew word from that in 1.7. In Ps. 111.10 words from both verses are combined.

> Trust in the Lord with all your heart
> and lean not on your own understanding.
> In all your ways acknowledge him,
> and he will make plain your paths. (3.5f)

To him the perverse man is an abomination and his curse is on the house of the wicked (3.32f). All men's ways are known to him (5.21). Always there is the emphasis on the presence and interest of God in the affairs of daily life, and there breathes a simple, almost naive faith which speaks across the centuries to us today:

> The Lord will not suffer the soul of the righteous to famish,
> but he thrusts away the desire of the wicked. (10.3)

Those who trust the Lord are happy (16.20), understand all (RSV "it", 28.5) and are safe (29.25). With the prophets it is asserted that the Lord abominates lying lips, perverse hearts, evil devices, the way of the wicked and their sacrifices, and false balances. He takes pleasure in good men, fair dealing, and the prayer of the upright, and when a man's ways please the Lord he makes even his enemies to be at peace with him (16.7). His counsels alone stand, whatever man's plans or devices (19.21; 21.30). So near is the Lord that man's breath is the Lord's lamp entering and searching the innermost recesses of the life and body (20.27), an analogy perhaps for what we mean by "conscience". The Lord's judgement is altogether different from the favour of a ruler (29.26). Vengeance may be safely left to the Lord (20.22), and it is wrong to retaliate (24.29). Sometimes the motive is not high:

> Rejoice not when your enemy falls
> nor let your heart be glad when he is overthrown,
> lest the Lord see it and it displeases him
> and he turns away his wrath from him. (24.17f)

Sometimes the motive is not clear:

> If your enemy is hungry, give him bread to eat,
> if he is thirsty, give him water to drink;
> for you will heap coals of fire on his head,
> and the Lord will reward you. (25.21f)

This stamp of orthodox Old Testament religion is clearly imparted by whoever was responsible for the final form of the book, who must have preserved this characterization of the Lord and perhaps even enhanced it. In the same way, despite the low position theoretically held by women in Judaism,[1] the practice reflected in Proverbs gives them the high standing already noted in the Decalogue and the Prophets.[2] That there was practical monogamy is seen in the way father and mother are so often bracketed together, suggesting a life partnership (10.1, etc.). Outshining all the beauty of the virtuous woman of chapter 31 is her reverence for the Lord, available to her just as much as to the wise or simple man:

> Charm is deceitful and beauty vain.
> A woman that reverences the Lord, she shall be praised.

By this statement, what might be otherwise regarded as a "religion-less" picture of a virtuous wife has been brought into relationship with the personal God of Israel, and it is of interest here that the Greek version merely has:

> Charm is deceitful and beauty vain.
> A woman of intelligence, she shall be praised.

It is probably with the same aim in view that "Next-of-kin" (RSV Redeemer) appears as substitute for the "might of the moon" in what seems to be a quotation from the Wisdom of Amenemope (Prov. 23.10f).[3] The identical phrase "Their Next-of-kin is strong" is found in Jeremiah (50.34), and this title for the Lord is used often by Second-Isaiah.

Thus, in the Book of Proverbs there is commended as the supreme good in Judaism a personal relationship with Israel's God, a religion learned from the instruction of parents and wise teachers and tested by one's own experience, rather than an institutional religion of corporate acts of worship and ritual based on doctrines revealed in the history of the nation, its law, and its prophets. From this institutional religion, however, the wise man takes the word "abomination"[4] and uses it for his own purpose when he catalogues those practical ways of life that are hateful to the Lord and prevent man's personal relationship to him. Seven sins are thus described (6.16–19; cf. 26.25). The

---

[1] Women could be bought and sold, be divorced but not divorce a bad husband, a husband could take many wives.

[2] See above, p. 50, n. 2. Whatever the explanation, it is noticeable that though in the Book of Proverbs there is a rational estimate of woman as man's equal partner, in Ecclesiasticus, where wisdom is again linked with institutional religion and nationalism, the estimate is considerably lower (25.16; 2 .27; 9.1–9; 42.9–14).

[3] Cf. W. O. E. Oesterley, op. cit., p. 1.

[4] See above, p. 57, n. 1. Cf. Deut. 25.13ff, where "abomination" is applied ethically.

wise men commended the ethical idealism of the Prophets and the Law as giving moral standards superior to those of their heathen neighbours. They taught that to prosper it was not necessary to throw morals overboard. The common-sense morality of the wise preserved respect and affection for Judaism among many ordinary people whom the Levites could not touch.

A striking omission in the religion of Proverbs is any reference to the mercy or steadfast love of the Lord. In the Prophets this is the basis of the covenant relationship, and in Psalms the ground of man's plea for forgiveness. In Proverbs the emphasis lies on justice and righteousness, and steadfast love is mentioned only as a human quality. That this omission was regarded as strange is seen in the fact that it is remedied in Ecclesiasticus, where there is a new stress on the covenant relationship and the width of God's mercy:

> The mercy of a man is on his neighbour,
> But the mercy of the Lord is on all flesh. (Ecclus. 18.13)

God's mercy is as great as his righteousness, and the Deliverance from Egypt as the initial act of divine mercy looms as large in Ecclesiasticus as in the teaching of the Prophets; but this emphasis on divine mercy springs from a deep recognition of human frailty not seen so clearly in Proverbs. In Ecclesiasticus, man's hope is ultimately in the divine grace and goodness, not in reason, independence, or understanding.

Perhaps it is because Proverbs is not so aware of the frailty of all flesh that it is so outspoken about those it calls fools. The simpleton can be taught by seeing the scorner punished or hearing the wise instructed (Prov. 21.11; 19.25), but, if he has no desire for knowledge, he must be urged to it (8.5; 9.4); he may be easily enticed into a fatal act (1.32) by listening to the allurements of the harlot, Folly (7.7; 9.16); he lacks the power to make judgements, believing every word he is told (14.15), and having no foresight (22.3; 27.12). There is a worse fool, stupid and obstinate, hating knowledge (1.22), who will not learn (18.2), boasting in evil and proclaiming it (10.23; 12.23). His tongue pours out folly (15.2; cf. 14) and he brings sorrow to his parents. Some fools are morally bad, despising a father's instruction (1.7; 15.5), meddlesome (20.3), proud (14.3), and always right in their own eyes (12.15). Their foolishness is incurable (27.22). Worst of all is the scoffer, arrogant (21.24), delighting in scorn (1.22), abusing those who try to correct him (9.7), never willing to listen nor to associate with the wise. He is dangerous, setting a city aflame

(29.8), bringing strife (22.10), and earning the Lord's scorn (3.34). Perhaps the wise men had to face definite hostility when they taught in the market-place, and learned that it may be useless to correct fools, and perhaps also they found that those who are supplied with the opportunity of learning are not always those really capable of it (17.16). Yet all fools are not hopeless. Early response may save a fool from his folly (9.6).

As there is no reference to the mercy of God, there is no mention of his forgiveness of human sin. It is the righteous act that delivers from death (10.2; 11.4), love is the covering for all sins (10.12), and by steadfast love and faithfulness iniquity is purged and atonement is made (16.6). Sacrifices are mentioned only in a derogatory way. The sacrifice of the wicked is an abomination to the Lord, and is even worse when brought with an evil intention (15.8; 21.27); the peace offerings and vows mentioned in 7.14 would clearly be regarded as sacrifices of the wicked. A dry morsel with quietness is better than a houseful of sacrifices with strife (17.1) and in words that may reflect Samuel's famous comparison of obedience and sacrifice (1 Sam. 15.22) and Micah's dictum (6.8) we are told:

> To do a righteous act and justice
> is chosen by the Lord more than sacrifice. (Prov. 21.3)

This estimate of the relative value of sacrifice is retained in Ecclesiasticus. The Most High has no pleasure in the offerings of the ungodly neither is he pacified for sins by the multitude of sacrifices (Ecclus. 34.19). But there is much more interest in ritual. Priests are to be reverenced, honoured, and given their portion of trespass offerings, heave offerings, and right sacrifices (7.29ff) and wisdom is compared with the smoke of incense in the tabernacle (24.15).

## The Figure of Wisdom

But the religion of Proverbs is not completely cold and detached, for there is warmth and tenderness in the remarkable personification of Wisdom. She calls to men, even fools, in street and market-place, sends out her maidens to seek and invite them to her home to share her bread and wine (Prov. 9.3f). But she issues a stern warning against those who disregard her stretched-out hand. She is portrayed as vividly as Second-Isaiah's personifications of Babylon (Isa. 47), Zion (49.14ff), and the Word (55.11). The fact that the Hebrew word for wisdom is feminine makes her almost a sublimation of the female element in deity, standing for mercy and loving-kindness. She was the first of God's creation alongside him "when he marked out the foundations of the earth" (Prov. 8.29),[1] and associated with him in all subsequent creation. In her God takes constant delight. She has a message for men that is concerned with truth, righteousness, and knowledge. She is the source of all right conduct. But she is the Lord's gift and his creation, and there is no challenge to monotheism. Though often the language suggests personality, she is not another divine being. She is God's wisdom, an attribute of God (Prov. 3.19; 8.22). This attitude to wisdom goes far beyond utilitarianism (8.10; cf. 16.16), though it is true that to those who seek her she gives riches, honour, and righteousness (8.18; RSV "prosperity"). To her man responds, and some of the psalmist's longing for, and joy in, God finds expression in this response.

Always it is to the Lord that prayer is made, and the Lord who abominates the sacrifice and the prayer (28.9) of the wicked delights in the prayer of the upright (15.8).

In both Proverbs and Ecclesiasticus the whole setting of life appears to be thought of as in this world. There are many references to the tree of life (Prov. 3.18; cf. Gen. 2.9) and the fountain of life (10.11), and there is the statement that man's hope shall not be cut off (23.18); but these are probably figurative expressions for long life in this world. The same may be true of other verses in which scholars have found the hope of immortality expressed in the contrast between the fate of the wicked and of the righteous, who have an "everlasting foundation" (10.25) and will be delivered from death in the day of catastrophe (11.4).[2] In Ecclesiasticus, though there is no clear refer- ence to resurrection or immortality, the thought of Elijah's return (cf. Mal. 4.5) is taken up:

> Blessed are they that saw thee,
> and they that have been beautified with love.
> For we also shall live. (Ecclus. 48.11)

The writer makes it clear that he regards man's hope as lying in his children and his good name when he declares:

---

[1] See above, p. 5.

[2] The clearest reference in Proverbs to life after death is "the righteous has hope in his death" (14.32); but the text is doubtful and the Greek version has "integrity" instead of "death".

WL

Their bodies were buried in peace,
and their name liveth to all generations. (Ecclus. 44.14)

The value of Proverbs in the Canon is that it brings into the realm of religion the whole range of human life, and particularly man's probing intelligence as an activity of God's wisdom implanted in him.[1] It has been well said that the theology of the Wisdom writers is Creation theology.[2] Wisdom was God's first creation, and "delighted" in the habitable world and the sons of men. In the Creation stories man has high dignity; he is made in the image of God and given dominion over all living things (Gen. 1.26). Divine delight in man's intelligent response, his ability to work with his Maker, gleams through the more popular story of the great Creator bringing each new species to man "to see what he would call them" (2.19). Peculiar to the religion of the Wise when compared with Priestly and Prophetic religion is this emphasis on man's dignity, in which his intelligent ability marks him out as separate from other creatures, but makes him dependent on the Creator in whose image he is made. Nothing could be further from Swinburne's agnostic humanism

Glory to man in the highest,
For man is the master of things.

It was God who made him "little less than God" and crowned him with glory and honour, putting all things under his feet (Ps. 8), and as daily he goes forth to his labour until the evening amid all the various evidences of God's creative power he exclaims:

O Lord, how manifold are thy works!
In wisdom hast thou made them all. (104.24)

[1] See above, p. 289.
[2] W. Zimmerli, *Scottish Journal of Theology* 17, (1964), pp. 146–58.

# 16 The Religion of the Wise: The Experience of Suffering

## The Prologue to the Book of Job

The Book of Job perhaps more than any other book has been held to illustrate the truth of Augustine's famous saying that the New Testament is latent in the Old, and the Old Testament is patent in the New. But we need to be warned against reading back into the book truths revealed in the New Testament, and to be reminded that Job is part of the Wisdom literature of the Jews, and aims at finding a meaning in experience that helps men in the practical tasks of daily living, rather than at constructing a comprehensive philosophical system.

The compiler of Proverbs was not an abstract thinker. In his use of the personal name for God and his whole approach to life there is something of the simple "Jesus" type of Christianity. Reverence for the Lord is the chief thing about the right attitude to life, and prosperity is its reward. Evil and suffering present no problem, for the prosperity of the wicked is illusory, and the suffering of the wise may be the refining of metal in the furnace. Ecclesiastes springs from much more sophisticated experience of life, with much less knowledge of the religious experience of fellowship with God. Facing the disillusionments of life, it tries to answer the question: Is life worth living? The simple outlook of Proverbs is rejected; there is no proof that God treats differently the righteous and the wicked, the wise and the fool. The same chance comes to both and death is their end. The worth of life depends on its purpose, and neither wealth nor wisdom is worth striving for. Job goes much deeper. It starts from a religion that is quite as personal as the simple naivety of Proverbs, though the personal name for God occurs only in the prologue,[1] but has a deeper basis in thought and experience. It is integral to the story that calamity, suffering, and the loss of loved ones is an experience Job felt on his pulses, and from many angles the book attempts to face the problem.

[1] And 12.9, but see commentaries ad loc.

The basis of Job is probably an ancient folk-tale now lost, the story of a good man who endured intense and undeserved suffering. We know the similar Babylonian story of a sufferer, and in the excavations at Sultantepe in 1951 more of that story was discovered on Assyrian tablets from the seventh century B.C. Dr Albright[1] says that the name Job is found on Egyptian lists of Palestinian chieftains of about 2000 and 1400 B.C. Ezekiel (14.14) mentions him with Noah and Daniel as the three greatest righteous men of antiquity. Noah we know from Genesis; Daniel in the Ras Shamra tablets is a Canaanite figure.[2] Job figured in very old west Semitic tradition, probably as an outstandingly wealthy and righteous man, and in later Christian tradition he has become proverbial for patient endurance (Jas. 5.11). In the Book of Job he is regarded as perfect and upright, and like the ideal wise man he has reverence for God and turns from evil; in his perfection he resembles Noah. The simple belief of Proverbs that it pays to be good is wonderfully illustrated by his life. He is blessed with seven sons and three daughters, and is the wealthiest, most respected man of the whole Near East. He does not flout the institutions of religion, but offers sacrifices to atone for sins perhaps thoughtlessly committed by his children, who appear to have drifted away from organized religion—and his wife can hardly be thought of as sharing his wisdom or reverence.

Suddenly the blows of misfortune fall on him. War, lightning, and tempest rob him of all his wealth and bereave him of his children. With dramatic vividness one messenger follows another in rapid succession announcing disaster, and Job mourns his children, worships the Lord, and says, "Naked I came from my mother's womb, and naked shall I return; the Lord gave, and the Lord has taken away; blessed be the name of the Lord" (Job 1.20f). He still eschews evil and remains wise.[3] But his misfortunes have not ended. The health which Ecclesiasticus says is better than all gold (30.14ff) is taken from him, and alone on his ash-heap he scrapes his suppurating flesh. His wife, who has stood by him through the loss of wealth and children, is surprised that he still maintains that he is perfect and suggests it is better to curse God and die. To Job that would be renouncing wisdom, acting like a foolish woman, and sinning with his lips; "Shall we receive good at the hand of God and not evil?" (Job 2.10). All experience comes from the one God, who forms light and

---

[1] *From Stone Age to Christianity.*

[2] In Jubilees Daniel is father-in-law of Enoch.

[3] He does not attribute "folly" (RSV "wrong") to God.

creates darkness, makes good and creates evil (Isa. 45.7); man must accept life as it comes to him, even though it brings pain that is worse than death (cf. Ecclus. 30.17). So Job accepts it all without revolt against God or loss of faith in him. He neither understands it nor seeks to understand. It is from the hand of God.

With fine dramatic skill the writer presents two other scenes in this first act or prologue. Unknown to Job, before each of his great misfortunes there has been a gathering in the throne-room of the Lord. All the divine servants of God present themselves at court, among them the Rover, the Satan who goes to and fro in the earth so that he can make his report—adversely—on what he sees. There is humour in the description of the Satan and in God's proud question to him about Job: Have you noticed Job? The Satan's reply is one often made by the man in the street: Job's reverence is purely utilitarian, he does it for what he gets out of it. There is no pure goodness even in a man like Job. The Lord cannot but accept his servant's challenge and permit suffering, so that Job may set an example of worship independent of outward circumstances. All Job's possessions, and later his health, are placed in the power of the Satan to test the truth of his sneer: Does Job reverence God for nought? We watch the Satan go out from the presence of the Lord before the curtain rises on each successive scene of Job's desolation.

The prologue gives one answer to the problem of unmerited suffering. God allows Job to suffer in order to prove that there are men who will reverence him though they lose everything. Agur had feared riches lest it caused a man to deny God (Prov. 30.9). Ecclesiastes recognized that wealth does not necessarily reward wisdom (2.18f). God does not mind taking possessions from a man, and here Job is presented as a wise man of great wealth, who is stripped of all material prosperity yet neither sins nor charges God with folly (Job 1.22). So perfect is he that God counts him sufficiently trustworthy to undergo intense physical suffering as a test of the intrinsic nature of man's worship, and at the end, free from all bitterness, he repeats the great lesson, the refrain of all Wisdom literature, "Reverence for the Lord, that is wisdom, and to depart from evil is understanding" (28.28). The story has been compared with the poem at the end of the book of Habakkuk:

> Though the fig tree does not blossom
> and no fruit on the vines,
> the work on the olive has failed,
> and fields yield no food,

cut off from the fold is the flock,
and no cattle in the stalls;
then I indeed in the Lord will exalt,
I will rejoice in the God who delivers me. (3.17ff)

and with the reply of the three Jewish youths to Nebuchadrezzar:
"Our God whom we serve is able to deliver us. . . . But if not, be it
known to you, O king, that we will not serve your gods" (Dan. 3.17).
It has even been regarded as revealing a meaning of the cry of desolation from the cross, when Jesus, stripped of his fellowship with
God, his most precious possession, in complete trust committed
himself into the hands of his Father.

But it is going too far to read such depths into the prologue. This is
clearly based on the belief that man must accept good and evil from
the hand of the one God, and "serve him for nought". There is no
hint in the final chapter that Job had been filling a strange and
tremendous destiny, nor is any use made in the epilogue of such a
theory, and the whole poetic drama following the prologue has other
themes.

It has often been pointed out that the book portrays the attitude to
suffering of two kinds of religious persons—the best religious man,
Job, and his orthodox religious friends. They all accept the fact that
suffering comes from the Creator and Ruler of the universe; but the
friends have escaped with whole skins and their theorizing and self-
righteousness are blatant. They are condemned for folly—the strongest condemnation known to Wisdom literature, to which the book
belongs. Even the most respectable religious people may be "fools",
and the wise man, Job, knows that there is no easy answer to his
problem.

Certainly Job cries out continually to know why God should be
"moved against him to destroy him without cause" (2.3); but this
does not mean that the philosophical problem why the innocent
suffer is really the theme of the whole work, nor that the book intends
to propound a theology of the meaning of suffering. Indeed, most
writers who regard this as the purpose of the book would agree that
"apart from airing the problem, the debate proves comparatively
fruitless, and God himself is finally introduced to remind Job that,
just as the wonders of the physical world leave man with much he
cannot understand, so he must not expect to find a complete answer to
so urgent and personal a problem as unmerited suffering".[1]

But the friends are condemned for their theorizing, and perhaps it

[1] *The Bible Today* (1960), p. 48.

is better to interpret the book in terms of an actual experience of suffering. Interest focuses not on why the innocent suffer—this is accepted as a fact of life. Concern is with the wise man's reaction to the experience. It is helpful to remember that in the nature of things suffering was an inescapable theme of Old Testament thought. Jeremiah had been occupied with the dark problem of the suffering of the faithful in Israel, and his own betrayal and rejection. Ezekiel talks of Noah, Daniel, and Job as the three most righteous men—of Noah, whose righteousness had saved his sons (Gen. 7.1, 13), whereas in the Job story no righteousness of Job could save his sons and daughters. So not even the sacrifices of the Temple nor anyone's righteousness had been able to save Israel's sons from the death of exile. It was a time when those who escaped the suffering of exile might easily fall into self-righteousness (Ezek. 33.24f; Deut. 9.4); and a time too when many innocent perished. Such suffering was sometimes regarded as a process of divine refining—a belief closely associated with the theme of Job. Proverbs (17.3) says that, as gold is refined in the furnace, so the Lord tries hearts, and Job himself exclaims that after his testing he will "come forth as gold" (Job 23.10). How closely these ideas in the Wisdom literature reflect the climate of opinion during and after the exile is seen in the words spoken through Second-Isaiah (48.10):

> Behold, I have refined you, but not like silver:
> I have tried you in the furnace of affliction.[1]

The same God governed the sufferings of both the people and the individual:

> When he hides his face, who can behold him,
> whether it be a nation or a man? (Job 34.29)

and Elihu goes on to assert that there is more than one possible answer to the problem of innocent suffering:

> Whether for correction, or for his land,
> or for love, he causes it to happen. (37.13)

This is what the writer of Job is concerned with—what the wise man does when it is to him that suffering happens. Meditation gave him the insight that no man, not even Job, can be righteous before God, for "the imagination of man's heart is evil from his youth" (Gen. 8.21), and the more a man asserts his righteousness, the nearer he gets

---

[1] "Furnace" is used of the suffering in Egypt, see above, p. 276, n. 1.

to self-righteousness, which needs to be brought to self-humiliation by a vision of God himself. This is vital to the book of Job, and equally vital is the fact of God and the surprise and thrill of his intervention, a thrill that is integral to the Old Testament experience of theophany, whether to Moses (Exod. 34.6) or to Second-Isaiah (40.10). Job might have said with George Macdonald:

> My how or when thou wilt not heed
> But come down thine own secret stair,
> That thou mayest answer all my need,
> Yea, every bygone prayer.

There is an element of discovery and release when Job realizes that his personal kingdom of pain does not embrace the universe. The Holy One is in the midst again, but has come not to destroy. As he was beside Jeremiah as a dread warrior,[1] so he is beside Job, and leads him out to look around him. Personal experience lies here, "whether it be a nation or a man", and Second-Isaiah's picture of the bereaved widow and mother, Zion, lifting up her downcast eyes to see her children come streaming home, offers a parallel to the epilogue of Job.

Finally, when we recognize that the book is part of the Jewish Wisdom literature, we shall not expect to find in it theories about calamity and loss, nor the reason why the innocent suffer in a world governed by a loving, almighty God, but the much more practical and existentialist discussion of the wise man's attitude to such suffering when it becomes a fact of experience for him or his nation. The book will not lose in depth for us if we do not attempt to find in it what we think a discussion of the suffering of a righteous man ought to contain.

## The Three Cycles of Speeches

The second act in the drama shows the arrival of three friends of Job to comfort him, their mantles rent, dust on their heads, and weeping. There are three cycles of speeches, and in each cycle there is a speech by each friend and Job's reply. It is noteworthy that Job makes no complaint, nor seeks a meaning for what has happened, nor does any problem arise for him till the friends arrive. No loss or misfortune has moved him from his rock-like faith in the Lord. They sat down with him seven days and nights gazing silently at the afflicted man, and even Job's endurance broke; then we get the sudden transition from

[1] See above, pp. 185f.

patient sufferer to impatient rebel. Job opened his mouth, cursed the day he was born, and prayed impatiently for death in words Dean Swift always used on his birthday. Rebelliously he asks why God keeps alive a man who wishes so badly to die. From the sequel it is clear that what caused the outburst was that the religious friends did not believe in Job. It was his friends that caused Job's deepest suffering, his spiritual agony. They doubted his integrity. Accepting the orthodox dogma that rewards and punishments invariably followed goodness and sin, they were sure that despite all appearances Job had sinned. The description of Job's illness (2.7) uses words found in Deuteronomy (28.35, 59) and shows the author's intention to suggest that it was orthodox of the friends to assume that Job was under God's curse. The conflict arises because of the attitude of these representatives of dogmatic religious theory, and the intensity of Job's struggle makes it probable that it was from the agony of personal experience that he faced their theorizing. We should notice the skill with which the writer makes Job exaggerate in his outburst, giving a hint that he is in danger of being self-centred, of being in need of a vision to lift him out of himself. But this does not destroy the overall impression that we are meant to conclude that there is something wrong with religious teaching which sparks off such an outburst from a good man.

Eliphaz (4—5), the first of the friends, roused by Job's lack of reverence for God, with kindly dignity suggests that the comfort Job has so often given others should help him now, and his own integrity should give him hope. Categorically he states that the innocent do not perish, and men reap what they sow (4.7f). He does not speak from his own experience, he has had a special revelation like Elijah's.[1] He claims that in a vision he heard a voice saying: Can a mortal be more just than God, or a man more pure than his Maker? Seek God, lay your case before him. In beautiful language he pleads with Job to submit to the chastening of the Almighty so that all the joys of life may be restored. True wisdom would acknowledge man's sinfulness, remember that suffering was God's loving discipline (4.17–21; 5.17f), and cease to rely on one's own human power (5.12ff). There is a graciousness and piety in the speech that should not be allowed to mask the fact that Eliphaz is not speaking out of his own experience nor with sympathetic insight into Job's condition and Job's needs. He is repeating as though they were a proved fact of his own experience the dogmatic principles which were fundamental tenets of Israelite religion, that sin and suffering belong together. The pre-exilic

[1] Cf. the same Hebrew phrase (Job. 4.16; 1 Kings 19.12).

prophets had stimulated men's conscience to discover and repent of the sins that were bringing disaster, the deuteronomic writer had modified the uncompromising doctrine that a perfect and upright man would never fall into disaster by recalling the possibility that God tests men as he tested Abraham (Gen. 22), or that he disciplines and chastens them (Judges 2.13ff). So Eliphaz, assuming that Job was not a wilful sinner, suggests that his misfortunes come from the loving hand of a Father, purifying him from unintentional and unrecognized sins, to which all men are liable.

Job's reply (6.8) is a pathetic plea for mercy to the pitiless God who will not even kill him to save him further suffering. His friends have failed him when he needed them most, when he cried out in agony they offered not help but dogma and reproof. In the intensity of his woe, his words to God are a parody of Psalm 8.4:

> What is man that you should magnify him
> And set your heart on him,
> That you should visit him every morning,
> And test him every moment! (Job 7.17)

This second outburst shocks Bildad, who is even more emphatic than Eliphaz. God does not cast away a perfect man (8.20), nor does he pervert justice (8.3). Bildad has need of no special revelation; his wisdom relies on reason and the knowledge of past tradition (8.8), which, he finds, prove that God unfailingly punishes evil. He will reward Job if he is perfect, but if not, as his children perished for their sins, so will Job perish. Job (9—10) admits the greatness of God revealed in traditions of creation; but to him all this shows God as cruel and terrifying, breaking him with a tempest and multiplying his wounds without cause, slaying suddenly with plague, and jeering at the calamity of the innocent (9.17, 23). Man cannot be just before God because he can never lay his cause before him; there is no arbiter to lay his hand upon them both. If only God would cease to terrorize him, he would speak to him unafraid (9.33f). God had created him, he knows and foresees all, and must have made him in order to enjoy the brutal pleasure of destroying him.

Zophar, the most dogmatic of the three, picks up Job's plea that he might meet and speak to God:

> Oh that God would speak
> and open his lips against you,
> showing you the secrets of wisdom
> and its wonderful working. (11.5f)

Then, turning on Job, he declares that God forgets most of his iniquities:

> Can you find out the depths of God,
>   or search to the end the Almighty?
> Height of heaven! What can you do?
> Depths of Sheol! What can you know? (11.7f)

If Job will repent, God will forgive, and Job will be able to lie down and none will make him afraid. Eliphaz had appealed to his own special revelation from God, Bildad to the well-known traditions of the past. Zophar needs neither. He is his own oracle and knows everything.

Job (12—14) in his longest speech against these friends, flares out against their claims to superior knowledge:

> No doubt you are the people,
>   and wisdom will die with you.
> But I too have understanding. (12.2f)

Every living soul lies in the control of God, yet the perfect man is a laughing-stock and the tents of the wicked prosper. Then from the false wisdom of his friends—forgers of lies, worthless physicians (13.4)—he turns to the God he had known from his experience before trouble came, and, knowing his own innocence, he pleads with God to speak to him before he is swallowed up by death. As a soldier waits patiently, however long his period of duty, if he knows his relief is coming (14.14), so Job will wait if he knows that God will call. He will reply to God's call, and God will desire the one that he himself has made.

In the second cycle of speeches the friends have abandoned hope of making Job repent. Eliphaz (15) rebukes him for conceit, Bildad (18) in vivid pictures paints the fate of the wicked, Zophar (20) stresses the brevity of the triumphant joy of the wicked and godless. Job, wearied by the repeated dogmas of his miserable comforters, breaks down again in bitter complaint against the God who has leapt on him like a wild beast, broken him to pieces like a powerful bully, though there was no violence in his hand and his prayer was pure (16.17). As Abel's uncovered blood had cried for vengeance, so would his blood cry, but to whom! Would God who is destroying him become the avenger of blood? But now as he sinks nearer the grave comes the certainty that God is there, that God himself has overthrown him (19.6), and, though he is forsaken by everyone, his friends have no pity, he can leave no written record, yet the God who has shown his presence by his tortures is alive and acts as his next-of-kin. He himself will see God and know him, as the great prophet of the exile[1] had known him, as his avenging kinsman. He will hear his vindication (19.25).

At the end of the first cycle of speeches, Job had finally reasserted his knowledge of his own innocence. At the end of the second, he had realized that the fact of his sufferings proved there was a living God who in the end would vindicate him. He was enabled to accept in a new way the two facts of experience: that the wicked do prosper, and yet that God avenges his slaughtered saints.

The text of the third cycle of speeches is confused. Eliphaz (22) accuses Job of acting like those wicked men who, he claims, prosper, believing God does not see. He makes his final appeal to Job to repent. But Job no longer hears him; his thoughts are on God, how to find him. He is searching for God, but he is fearful:

> I am troubled at his presence,
>    when I consider, I am afraid of him. (23.15)

Again he emphatically states the facts of experience, that evil and oppression go unpunished. There is a defiant acceptance of the fact:

> And if it be not so, who will prove me a liar,
>    and make my speech worth nothing? (24.25)

However great his fear of God, he will not pretend a faith contrary to the facts of experience. That is the way God works, that is a revelation of the God he is searching for. Bildad (25) asks again how can a man be just before almighty God. Job (26.1—27.6) emphatically declares that, however great God may be, he, Job, will never be forced into pretence or deceit:

> Till I die I will not put away my integrity from me,
> My righteousness I will hold fast, I will not let it go. (27.6)

What appears to be part of Zophar's final speech (27.7–23) is followed by the poem on wisdom (28). Some have suggested this is out of place in the dialogue, especially as Job in the following three chapters (29—31) returns to his complaints in a long speech. But perhaps the writer preferred to let the curtain descend as Zophar rehearses his wearisome orthodox beliefs that sin and punishment belong together, without any reply from Job. Then a speaker comes

---

[1] See above, pp. 157f.

forward to pose the question that has been roused in the mind of every listener:

> Where shall wisdom be found,
> and where is the place of understanding? (28.12)

Despite all his marvellous powers, inventions, and discoveries,

> Man knows not the price thereof,
> Neither is it found in the land of the living.
> The deep says, It is not in me,
> The sea says, It is not with me.
> It cannot be got for treasure,
> Nor is silver to be weighed out for its purchase. (28.13-15)

The question is posed again (v. 20) followed by the assertion that wisdom is unattainable by men. The Book of Proverbs may have claimed (8.3f) that she stands by the city gates, offering herself to all who respond. Ecclesiasticus can believe that she is poured out on all men (Ecclus. 1.10) and has found her dwelling in Jerusalem. But the writer of Job states that God alone knows where she dwells (cf. Enoch 44; 94.5) and man cannot grasp divine wisdom, which is beyond his reach. But, and this is the message of all the Wisdom writers and the real key to the book of Job, God has said to man:

> Behold, reverence for the Lord, that is wisdom,
> and to depart from evil is understanding. (28.28)

This chapter, like the heavenly scenes in the prologue, may be intended as hidden from Job. The listener was told the secret of the cause of Job's suffering, and is now given the wise man's answer to the problems raised in the dialogue of Job with his friends. So the way is prepared for the second half of the book, culminating in the appearance of God himself.

As Job had ignored the final speech of Eliphaz, so he ignores Zophar. When Eliphaz spoke, Job had already turned towards God to search for him. As Zophar speaks, Job's thoughts return to the old happy days, before God's curse fell on him. In vivid contrast (29; 30) he paints two pictures of his life and makes his last wonderful confession of innocence. It begins by refuting concrete accusations made in Eliphaz's final speech (22.6ff); but there is a new spirit in Job's reply. He is more detached, almost as though he were alone on the stage speaking his thoughts in a soliloquy, oblivious of "friends" or of God, and trying calmly like an ideal wise man to appraise the actual facts of his experience. God's providence had been as obvious as the presence of his own children. The respect of all who knew him had attested his integrity, his conformity to the national ideals,[1] and his reputation for generous helpfulness to the needy and wronged. Now all is different. God has clearly withdrawn his protection and approval; there is no respect from even the vilest men. For a moment the old attitude of complaint against God returns; but afterwards he moves to a calmer self-examination against a long-accepted and well-known standard. Except for the crime of seducing a virgin, which to him was unthinkable, there is no statement of innocence but a series of "If I have", followed by a plea that appropriate punishment may fall on him. The standard represents the height of moral conduct, and suddenly breaks off in a longing for a clear statement of the indictment against him and an answer from the Almighty (31.35).

Divine wisdom is beyond man's finding; but clearly Job states the facts of his own experience, the one thing of which he is sure and to which he holds fast. It was that which had disproved the orthodox assertions of his friends. At the beginning of his troubles nothing could move him from his rocklike faith that all in life comes from the hand of God, and throughout the dialogue he had not been entirely hopeless in so far as he had held to the belief in God as Creator and Ruler. The common ground between him and his friends had been the old belief that somehow God rules in moral justice. At the end of the first cycle of speeches he declared God would intervene against the deceit of his friends (13); he invoked God's just retribution, and expected to be mocked because he accepted the fact of the prosperity of the wicked (21.3). He is suffering because of his sense of injustice, believing as he does that a blameless man like himself cannot fall into disaster. Continually he protests his innocence, and the more his friends insist on God's justice, goodness, and power, the more he revolts against their whole theology and wisdom. Sometimes suffering may be neither the result of sin nor discipline, and to the end Job maintains his right before the Almighty:

> Oh that I had one to hear me!
> Look, here is my mark—let the Almighty answer me
> and the book that my adversary has written. (31.35f)

His cry was that God would speak to him, and despite his calamity and the doctrine of suffering and sin, would show that he was innocent. There is no expression of the height of faith of Psalm 73 (23ff)

[1] 29.13, the blessing of Jacob; cf. Deut. 26.5; "An Aramaean about to perish (RSV wandering) was my father".

that fellowship with God is its own reward. The spiritual tension caused by Job's belief that he is suffering unjustly and yet God is just, is retained throughout the dialogue except at the end where, in the chapter on wisdom (Job 28) and later in the divine speeches, thought is centred on God's wisdom and power rather than his justice.

## Elihu's Speech

After Job's confession of innocence, quite unexpectedly a fourth friend, Elihu, is introduced, in a short prose passage comparable to the prologue and epilogue, and makes a long speech (32—37). Job's friends had ceased to answer him because he was righteous in his own eyes. Elihu is angry with Job because he justified himself rather than God, and is angry with the friends because, though they could find no answer, they condemned Job. He is much younger, claiming that

> It is not the great that are wise,
>      nor the aged that understand judgement. (32.9)

but unlike the speaker of chapter 28 (20f) he believes

> There is a spirit in man,
>      and the breath of the Almighty gives them understanding. (32.8)

God speaks to men in various ways:

> In a dream, in a vision of the night
>      when deep sleep falls on men
>      in slumbering on their beds
>      then he opens the ears of men. (33.15f)

or there is an intervention, and a messenger, one of the thousand, comes and shows man what is right, pleads for him, and he is saved from destruction (33.23). Yet Job has added rebellion to his sin, multiplying words against God (34.37). Then he pleads with Job to think of God rather than of himself:

> Look to the heavens and see,
>      Behold the skies that are higher than you.
> If you have sinned, what do you do against him? . . .
> If you are righteous, what do you give him,
>      or what does he receive from you? (35.5f)

and he moves on to picture the greatness of God and his unknowable, unsearchable power (36.26f); he calls on Job to praise him (36.24).

This whole speech is usually regarded as a later addition, because no mention is made of Elihu among the three friends in either prologue or epilogue (42.9), neither Job nor the Lord answers him, and his arrival and departure are sudden. But if we take the book as it stands, his speech is clearly intended as a curtain-raiser for God's appearance. Elihu is the forerunner of the Lord, and does not take sides with either Job or his friends. Dramatically he calls attention to the first visible signs that God is about to appear:

> But now men cannot see light—
> bright it is in the heavens
> as when a wind has passed by and made them clear.
> From the north comes golden splendour
> around God, terrible in majesty,
> The Almighty, whom men cannot find. (37.21f)

Job's problem has been self-centredness, self-pity, and self-righteousness, and his friends have advocated self-examination; now comes a demand for self-abasement, for humility, that third element in the prophetic requirements (Mic. 6.8) so strongly stressed in the Wisdom literature as reverence for the Lord, leading to the final stage of self-surrender. Job needed the new vision of God. The first point of attack from Eliphaz had been on Job's attempt to justify himself before God, and the book shows that health does not return till he ceases to be completely absorbed in himself. Elihu continues the move in the wisdom chapter (28.23) away from human wisdom to divine, and asserts that wisdom does not come even from human experience: it is the gift of the divine spirit in man (32.8). Elihu himself claims that his counsel springs from God's special revelation to him, and uses technical words used by the prophets. Yet, just as the dogmas of the three friends could not help Job, so ultimately it was no use for Elihu to tell him about the greatness of God. Only a personal vision of God makes a man say, "Depart from me, O Lord, for I am a sinful man."

## The Advent of God

Suddenly out of the storm God speaks to Job, and takes him out into the "picture gallery" of his world. For the first time in Hebrew thought nature is looked at objectively, not as serving man's purpose (38.26). At the vision of God, Job replies:

> Behold, I am of small account, what shall I answer you?
> I lay my hand on my mouth.

> Once I have spoken, I will not answer,
> Yea twice, but I will not proceed further (40.4f.).

The Lord's second speech begins with the question the friends had asked: Will you condemn me that you may be justified? (40.8). He declares his own power over creation and over the proud and the wicked, and Job cries:

> I heard of you with the hearing of the ear (cf. Ps. 44.1),
> but now my eye sees you,
> wherefore I abhor myself
> and repent in dust and ashes. (42.5f)

The prose epilogue has been regarded as unnecessary and out of keeping with the spiritual heights of the poem. But like the accounts of the bodily resurrection of Jesus, it is a concrete way of expressing God's approval and God's vindication. The whole book of Job must be allowed to make its impact as a unit. Clearly the book has gradually grown to its present form; but prologue and epilogue, the chapter on wisdom, and Elihu's speech all make their necessary contribution to the rich spiritual value of the whole.

At the end of the story, Job's friends must offer their sacrifices to the Lord, go to Job, whom God accepts, and ask him to pray for them that God may not deal with them according to their folly. And when Job, purged from all bitterness, had prayed for his friends who had despitefully used him, God restored the fortunes of Job.

# 17 The Megilloth

In the present form of the Hebrew Bible the five books following Job are known as the Megilloth or Scrolls, which became[1] part of Jewish liturgy, being read at annual festivals:

The Song of Songs on the eighth day of Passover

Ruth at the Feast of Weeks or Pentecost

Lamentations on the anniversary of the destruction of Jerusalem on the Ninth Ab

Ecclesiastes at the Feast of Tabernacles

Esther at Purim, a feast not mentioned in the pentateuchal calendars

## The Song of Songs

The link of the Song of Songs with Passover probably reflects the Jewish traditional reason for its retention among the sacred books of the Old Testament—that it was an allegory of the Lord's love for his people. The eighth day of Passover was the final day of the festival that commemorated the Deliverance from Egypt, and God's choice of Israel as his people brought about a relationship which in the prophets was thought of in terms of marriage and human love.

The songs are clearly love poems arranged in the form of a dialogue between a youth and a maiden. As the beauty of nature is described (2.11ff; 6.11), so the delight of each in the beauty of the other's body is expressed with complete frankness (4.1–7; 5.10–16). There is no agreement as to the origin and purpose of the collection of poems. They may have been love songs, wedding songs, a dramatic expression of the relation of Solomon, a maiden and her country lover, or in part the remains of sacred marriage liturgies in the widespread fertility rituals of the Near East.[2] For any of these purposes the language of human love would be used, and it is clear that these songs celebrate

[1] There are conflicting views as to the date.
[2] Cf. H. H. Rowley, *The Servant of the Lord* (1952), pp. 189ff.

the dignity and purity of human love.[1] That in the Old Testament man is essentially a unity of body and spirit, and that this recognition makes for wholesomeness in religion, needs to be remembered, together with the implications of Blake's words: "Man has no body apart from his soul, for what we call body is but that part of the soul discerned by the five senses." Human love in marriage at its highest finds expression in the Song:

> Many waters cannot quench love,
> neither can floods drown it.
> If a man offered for love
> all the wealth of his house
> it would be utterly scorned. (8.7)

It is important that in Old Testament religion it was not felt necessary to find another word, one not used in the language of marriage and friendship, to express the intimate love between God and his people. It is not without significance that the feminine personification of Wisdom, these love-songs, and the idyll of Ruth's love for her mother-in-law, Naomi, all find a place among the sacred books of the Jewish people and the Christian Church. Both Jewish and Christian traditions have interpreted the poems as an allegory of the close relationship between God and his people or his Church. There echo through the book words and phrases reminiscent of Old Testament beliefs in God's intimate care for his people and their land, and his joy in their response. But this allegorical application of the poems must not be allowed to obscure the fact that the experience of human love between bride and bridegroom, husband and wife, can open human life to an appreciation and understanding of the intensity of God's love, and the bliss of seeking and finding him.

## Ruth

That the book of Ruth should have been used at the Feast of Weeks is understandable. As we saw, this was an agricultural feast, celebrating all the joy of harvest seven weeks after the first corn was cut (Deut.

---

[1] Cf. E. J. Young, *An Introduction to the Old Testament* (1949), p. 237; D. Bonhoeffer, *Letters and Papers from Prison* (1967), p. 162: "Even the Bible can find room for the Song of Songs, and one could hardly have a more passionate and sensual love than is there portrayed. It is a good thing that that book is included in the Bible as a protest against those who believe that Christianity stands for restraint of passion (is there any example of such restraint anywhere in the Old Testament?)"

16.9ff). The book of Ruth depicts scenes in the corn-harvest fields.

In the English version of the Old Testament, in a similar way to Esther and Job it is treated as an historical book, and because of its opening verse was naturally placed after Judges, telling a story of the parents of David's grandfather. It stresses that his ancestry went back to Ruth, a Moabite woman who had married a Jewish refugee from Bethlehem and who, when he died, returned with her mother-in-law to her husband's kinsfolk. It breathes a spirit of international tolerance very different from the exclusive nationalism in Deuteronomy (23.3f), Nehemiah (13.1f), and Esther. It is a beautiful expression of family "piety", Ruth's loyalty to her mother-in-law and Boaz' loyalty to his obligations, both leading to the marriage from which sprang Israel's great king.

From a religious standpoint, it is important as an illustration of one meaning of the concept "next-of-kin" or "redeemer", used by Second-Isaiah as a title for the Lord.[1] He was not only an avenger of blood on a murderer (Num. 35.19), but, as we also see from the Law (Lev. 25.25), had more general functions within the family circle. He must buy back a kinsman who had been enslaved or was in need, and land which was in danger of being sold out of the family. He must also raise an heir to a woman whose husband had died childless. All these usages confirm that the word derives from time-honoured social and family custom, and that we rob it of its true warmth and living power if we consider it as merely a legal term of the later law-courts.

Compared with the intensity of the Song of Songs, it is family loyalty and gentle affection that furnish the background of the religion of the Book of Ruth. It is another approach to religion, very clear, very definite, and perhaps from a feminine milieu, reminding us of the atmosphere of some of the stories of Rebecca and Rachel. There is disregard of national barriers matching the wide sympathies of the Book of Jonah, a woman's calm acceptance of the facts of life (Ruth 1.12f), and simple, unquestioning faith in the presence and guidance of the Lord. He has afflicted Naomi, he feeds his people and makes her return possible, he will deal kindly with Orpah and find a home for her in Moab, he will guide Ruth and Naomi at every step in their behaviour when they return. It is fitting that the blessing of the elders on Ruth and Boaz has become a traditional Jewish wedding benediction, and the story told by a mother to her children would nourish faith in the Lord's working.

[1] See above, pp. 157f.

The Gospel of Matthew (1.5, 16) emphasizes to the Christian Church that from the union of Ruth and Boaz sprang not only a king, "the sweet psalmist of Israel" (2 Sam. 23.1), but Jesus "who is called the Christ". It is a family tree where

Un roi chantait en bas, en haut mourait un dieu[1]

## Lamentations

In Jewish tradition[2] this book was associated with Jeremiah as in the English version of the Old Testament, but in the Hebrew Bible it is a scroll appointed to be read at the anniversary of the fall of Jerusalem in 586 B.C. It consists of five poems, all of which are probably communal, not individual laments, although in places the first person singular appears. Four of the five have the artificial literary device of an acrostic, with successive verses or groups of verses beginning with a letter of the Hebrew alphabet, and the fifth, though not an acrostic, has twenty-two verses, the total number of the Hebrew letters. Despite this form, the book has a passionate description of the suffering of people and city, and should be read with sympathetic attention before the vengeful spirit in certain psalms is hastily condemned.[3] There is a strongly expressed belief that all the disaster and misery come from the Lord (1.15) and that his actions are amply justified by the sins of the whole nation, especially its prophets and priests (4.13f; cf. 2.9). The confessions of sin have become for Christian as well as for Jew a model of penitent prayer. The destruction is entirely the Lord's work; there is no suggestion that the enemy or his gods have shown their power.

In the final poem the people's hopelessness is expressed in a reference to that proverb which both Jeremiah (31.29) and Ezekiel (18.2) had contested:

Our fathers sinned and are no more,
and we bear their iniquities. (Lam. 5.7)

Throughout the book there is a constant cry for help, and in the third poem there is strongly expressed the hope and faith that come, as in the opening verses of Psalm 73, from remembering the past traditions of the Lord's action for Israel:

It is of the Lord's loving kindnesses that we are not cut off,
that his compassions do not end; they are new every morning.
(3.22; cf. RSV marg.)

[1] Victor Hugo, Booz Endormi.    [2] Baba Bathra 15ᵃ.
[3] Cf. H. H. Rowley, Worship in Ancient Israel (1967), p. 268.

It is amazing that these poems that mourn sickening horrors, cruelty, and disaster also reach the height of trust that exclaims, "Great is thy faithfulness", and asserts:

> The Lord is good to those who wait for him,
>     to the soul that seeks him.
> It is good that one should wait quietly
>     for the salvation of the Lord. (3.25f)

## Ecclesiastes
## The Religion of the Wise
## Their Attitude to Life

The general attitude to life in the Wisdom literature may be described as realistic. The wise man encourages no illusions in himself. But the realism of Proverbs and Ecclesiasticus is very different from that of Ecclesiastes. Proverbs in many ways mediates some of the teaching of the great prophets of Israel, and accepts the belief that the Lord reigns, can be depended on to act consistently with his character and purpose revealed in history, so that his government of the universe is rational and moral. Facts of experience might force men to modify a rigid doctrine that the wicked are always punished and the righteous rewarded, but in general there is a firm belief that goodness pays and morality is worth while. Just as the Law and the Prophets showed in the record of the past history of the nation how calamity followed sin, so the writers of Proverbs believed that this was proved in man's experience, and developed a conception of the moral character of God. Lingering fears that God might be irrational, or act capriciously because of jealousy or revenge, were overcome, together with any idea that life might be directed by fate or blind chance. Ultimately the basis of their cheerful attitude to life was the faith that God can be relied on to act rightly and that man, despite all his limitations, can understand sufficient of God's character and purposes to co-operate with him.

As to questions about man's limitations themselves, these are scarcely raised in Proverbs, and it is these very questions with which Ecclesiastes is overwhelmingly concerned — the mortality of man and the inscrutability of God. It is scarcely surprising that his attitude has been called pessimistic, and out of harmony with the rest of the canon.

Clearly, the book belongs to the Wisdom literature, and needs to be considered in order to complete the picture presented in Proverbs and the Book of Job.[1] In the Hebrew Bible, however, it is one of the Megilloth, scrolls traditionally read at annual Jewish festivals. It is significant that Ecclesiastes was read at the Feast of Tabernacles, the great joy feast.[2]

Basic to this work is the Old Testament belief in God; but unlike Proverbs Ecclesiastes never uses for him the personal name the Lord (*Yahweh*), nor passes beyond the fact of God's existence to the belief that he is the "rewarder of them that diligently seek him". There is no personal experience of God, nor the belief that he is just and merciful.

Equally basic is the view that man is a creature dependent on the Creator, whose knowledge and purpose is secret and hidden from him. Proverbs shows the same belief:

> All the ways of a man may be clean in his own eyes,
> but the Lord weighs the spirit. (Prov. 16.2)

> There is a way that seems right to a man,
> but the end is death. (16.25)

> It is the glory of God to conceal a thing (25.2)

But the problem to Ecclesiastes is whether man knows enough of the will of God for happiness. No conclusion is drawn that man should be satisfied with committing his work to the Lord (Prov. 16.3). Wisdom is not man's secular possession but a hidden divine intelligence he can never discover, and at this impasse Ecclesiastes knows despair.

Belief in the omnipotence of God, too, is basic in the Wisdom literature, but whereas in Proverbs this thought supports the idea of the orderliness of creation:

> The Lord by wisdom founded the earth,
> by understanding he established the heavens. (3.19)

in Ecclesiastes as in Job it leads to the thought of God's inscrutability. Divine wisdom cannot be obtained nor the divine purpose understood; man has no capacity to bridge the gap between himself and the great God. Neither of these writers was willing to fall back on an irrational, unverifiable faith in the goodness of God. A similar pessimism appears in the sceptical queries of Agur (Prov. 30.3f):

> I have not learned wisdom,
> nor have I knowledge of holy things.
> Who has ascended into heaven and descended?
> Who gathered the wind in his fists?

---

[1] See above, p. 309.

[2] Cf. R. Gordis, *Koheleth, the Man and his World* (1955), p. 121.

> Who bound the waters in his garment?
> Who established all the ends of the earth?
> What is his name? What is his son's name?

But here vain inquiry about God concludes with an orthodox statement that his every word proves true, and the twofold request:

> Give me neither poverty nor riches,
> feed me with my portion of bread,
> lest I be full and deny, and say, Who is the Lord?
> or lest I be poor and steal,
> and profane the name of my God.

In Ecclesiastes too statements of orthodox Judaism sometimes stand out against the general attitude of "not proven", and some scholars believe that passages have been interpolated to make the book safe for the youth of Israel to read. Others claim that the book is a carefully thought-out answer to the question: Is life worth living? Within it they discern a critical speculative mind, showing that all man's goods and possessions—all he has and knows and does—bring no satisfaction; this is a revolt against the orthodox teaching in Wisdom literature that worldly success is worth living for, and is like the standpoint of Jesus, who pictured the wealthy man pulling down his barns to build bigger as a fool, forgetting he could take none of his possessions with him at death (Luke 12.20). They further discern a practical and ethical spirit, commending as at least a relative good the cheerful enjoyment of work and life. But whatever truth there may be in these views, it may be fairly said that even Ecclesiastes 12.11–14, which is regarded as an addition to redress the scepticism of the book, has very little real faith which might serve to turn the author into a pillar of an orthodoxy he had tried and found wanting. There is a unity of temper throughout the work that does not conflict with the assumption that it has one author.

Clearly there are references to historical events within the experience of the author and his audience, if only we could interpret them aright. We hear of the old foolish king who would receive no instruction though he had been born poor and went from prison to the throne, the youth who stood in his stead (4.13ff), the woe of the land whose king is a child and whose nobles feast in the morning, contrasted with the happiness of the land whose king is a freeman and whose nobles feast at the proper time for strength and not drunkenness (10.16f). There are practical notes of caution that would fit a dictator's rule in any age: Curse not the king, no, not in your thought, for a bird will carry the sound (10.20). These sayings have been the happy hunting ground of those who would date the book; but the final test is not whether the words fit a particular time or place, but the far more difficult proof that they fit no other.

There is general agreement that whatever the date of Ecclesiastes, in its present form the book meets the situation in Palestine during the Hellenistic period, towards the last two centuries before the Christian era. Gradually new ideals penetrated Judaism, dominated its life, and challenged its stable, traditional ways of thought. The political freedom of the democratic Greek city state had brought mental freedom, the spirit of inquiry untrammelled by traditions; but no basis for morality, other than belief in God, had been discovered to satisfy ordinary intelligent men. The eternal why of youth facing all the customs of social life, the sanctions of moral life, and the dogmas of religion, had found no reason for moral idealism, without which no civilization can endure. Belief in the destiny of the people of God and in the particular responsibility of its members was now largely irrelevant to the general life and problems of the young. The value of the book of Ecclesiastes lies in his completely fresh approach to this complex situation.

It is probably helpful to clear our minds of the usual implications of the word "Preacher". This is certainly not a man with a gospel he is bound to declare—rather we may think of a skilled teacher who has much contact with the young. They are critical, questioning, sceptical —but so is he, and in answer to any of the problems they raise he will use his fund of proverbial lore and personal experience. In so far as he feels a moral responsibility for them, it is that they shall go from him more equipped with truth than they were when they came. But what he gives them are just flashes of truth, sometimes contradictory. He is not trying to present systematic philosophy, he tells them what life has taught him.

By a stroke of genius, he puts his judgement on life into the mouth of Solomon, who was able to have everything the world could offer. He was very wise, and decided to see if he could find satisfaction in pleasure, but found it was useless (2.2). He turned to the creative work available to him—building houses, laying out grounds, gathering slaves and treasure, hiring singers—and took pleasure in it all, yet knew it was no lasting satisfaction (2.10f). He considered how precious was wisdom: "The wise man has eyes in his head, but the fool walks in darkness." But as soon as he said it, he remembered that in spite of all his wisdom he would die and be forgotten, just as if he had been a fool

(2.15). He remembered that all his parks and palaces he must leave to another, and decided that all man's efforts are vexation and vanity.

Looking back on it all, he came to the conclusion that he had been happiest when he was busy with his work (2.24), and, in so far as there is religion in Ecclesiastes, this is an important part of the contribution he brings. He teaches that among all the gifts and possessions given to man by God, the most vital is man's power of enjoying them: "Every man also to whom God has given wealth and possessions and power to enjoy them, and to accept his lot and find enjoyment in his toil— this is the gift of God" (5.19). Time and again he points out the folly of striving for more than one can enjoy—"to one's own hurt"—or for the motive of envy, getting more than other people. To him the Creator has put man into this world with power to act and to acquire (Deut. 8.18), but within him he has placed as a most precious gift that of power to enjoy. It is in line with God's plan for the world that the happiest man is one "occupied, with joy in his heart" (5.20). It is a considerable contribution the Preacher makes, even though there are many things that do not come into his teaching at all.

At the beginning of his work, he sets a poem which might be summed up in Christina Rossetti's words, "Passing away, says the world, passing away". Everything is endlessly repeated, with a sameness in change:

> A generation goes, and a generation comes,
> but the earth remains for ever. (1.4)

This is not the faith of Second-Isaiah in the word of God, or the experience of comfort in his everlastingness. Yet God is real. What he does endures for ever and cannot be altered: "God has made it so, in order that men should fear before him" (3.14). God made everything beautiful in its time, but within men's hearts has set something that is hidden (RSV eternity) so that they cannot understand his doings (3.11; 11.5). The inscrutable omnipotence of God and man's frail nothingness must never be forgotten. "The race is not to the swift, nor the battle to the strong, nor bread to the wise, nor riches to the intelligent, nor favour to the men of skill; but time and chance happen to them all" (9.11). Man must accept his limitations, there is no point in struggling against life; "he is not able to dispute with one that is stronger than he" (6.10). It is wise and prudent to reverence God and to remember that it is dangerous to play with religion (5.1-8).

Watch your step when you go to the house of God, for to draw nigh to hear is better than to offer the sacrifice of fools, for they do not know that they are doing evil. Be not rash with your mouth and let not your heart be rash to utter a word before God; for God is in heaven and you upon earth, therefore let your words be few. . . . If you make a vow do not delay to fulfil it, for God has no pleasure in fools. . . . It is better not to make vows than to vow and not pay. (cf. Deut. 23.21)

To anyone to whom God is present in daily life this is realistic common sense. It is a useful corrective to any tendency to take religion lightly or casually, to run into pious platitudes, or to promise in word or hymn what one has no intention of fulfilling.

Ecclesiastes has a keen sense of man's avarice. Man's appetite for money grows by what it feeds on: "He who loves money will not be satisfied with money, nor he who loves wealth with gain" (5.10). This greed for riches blinds man's eyes to the fact, so clearly seen by the Preacher, that he can only hold them for a limited time and then must leave them to another—and who knows whether the heir will be a wise man or a fool (2.19). He is equally sensitive to the oppression and injustice man practises on man: "Behold the tears of the oppressed! and they had no one to comfort them" (4.1). This is all judged against his belief that God has ordained that men should live happily together. The money-grabber knows no real happiness, the oppressed would be happier if he had never been born. Further than this he does not go, but that he relates it to God's plan should not be forgotten.

Speaking from his own experience, he remarks that it is useless for a man to think that he can escape from God's plan by turning to know wickedness and folly with a suitable woman. Instead of finding freedom he will find her heart to be snares and nets, and her hands fetters (7.26), and again would be happier if he were dead. He reflects that he himself found one good man among a thousand, but never a good woman. Perhaps he speaks to a young bridegroom whom he regards as more fortunate than himself when he says, "Go, eat your bread with enjoyment . . . for God has already approved what you do . . . . Enjoy life with the wife whom you love. . . . Whatever your hand finds to do, do it with your might; for there is no work or thought or knowledge or wisdom in Sheol, to which you are going" (9.7ff).

Over it all broods his obsession with "man's sad mortality". Perhaps early in life he had faced death at close quarters and made a kind of peace with it, so that ever after life's values were completely different, and the concrete way in which he expressed this truth is that it is better to go to the house of mourning than to the house of feasting (7.2ff). He had no belief that there was any life after death to redress the inequalities of this life, "folly in high places" and "slaves on horses" (10.6f), and is not willing to accept the hypothesis of the immortality of the soul. Using the creation story of Genesis 2 he says: "All go to one place; all are from the dust, and all turn to dust again. Who knows whether the spirit of man goes upward and the spirit of the beast goes down to the earth?" (3.20f). One fate comes to all, righteous and wicked, good and evil, clean and unclean, to him who sacrifices and to him who does not sacrifice (9.2). There is hope for one who is still alive, and it is better to be a living dog than a dead lion (9.4). Nor can there be any reliance on the memory of a good man persisting: "For of the wise man as of the fool there is no enduring remembrance" (2.16).

It is in the beautiful closing chapter that the acceptance of mortality appears not as pessimism but as sober realism. "Remember your Creator in the days of your youth", he says, perhaps the only sound and indisputable counsel that age can give to inexperience. He goes on to paint a haunting picture of inevitable old age when the faculties are dimmed and desire fails, man is closed in on himself and the power of enjoying all God's good gifts diminishes. While the young possess the power of enjoyment to the full, let them remember the presence of God in all their daily life, for happiness and fulfilment are here alone.

Perhaps the greatest contribution of Ecclesiastes is that he has little to do with the earthbound materialistic view of rewards and punishments which the teaching of the prophets not only failed to break, but had helped to fasten on to religion. He opened the way for a belief that virtue—happiness in living according to God's plan—is its own reward. The happiness of giving to others rather than of receiving for oneself he does not mention, which is certainly a glaring lack. But we can be grateful that this subtle and lovely work finds its place in the canon, because it begins from the place where there stand many ordinary people to whom God is a memory from childhood teaching, who sees and judges all, but with whom man can have no contact, and from whom he can expect no help. Ecclesiastes is doing what organized religion, then as now, finds so difficult, speaking of what in his own experience are the sober facts of life to make people stop and think.

## Esther

It has been said of the books of Esther and Daniel that a favourite theme in the narrative books of the Old Testament is the presentation, in legendary fashion, of the marvellous success of the Jews against heathen who sought their hurt (Esth. 8.11, 13).[1] We have seen this tendency in the stories of the "Wars of the Lord" in the Law and Former Prophets. But there victory was attributed to the Lord, his name was in the battle-cry, and the fear of him fell on Israel's enemies. Here in Esther there is no mention of any divine being, the battle-cry is only in the name of the human Jewish leader, and it is the fear of the Jews that falls on the foe. Only the refusal to plunder the massacred Gentiles is reminiscent of the early ban on booty. The strong anti-Gentile feeling also remains, and a joy in the sudden reversal of fortunes, understandable in a people who every year uttered its terrible memories of anguish and defeat in Lamentations, and its prayers for the Lord's vengeance on cruel oppressors.

It is usually believed that the Feast of Purim commanded in the Book of Esther originated as a secular feast, probably incorporating mythological elements of conflicts between Near-Eastern deities, but whatever its origin, its celebration among the Jews two weeks before the spring equinox would inevitably increase the joy at the national Deliverance from Egypt commemorated so soon afterwards at Passover. Elements in the book that shock should serve to remind us that it is as important to understand religious traditions aright as it is to have them at all, and that this is true of all world faiths. The Jewish faith was based on the tradition of God's Deliverance of his people and his conquest of their foes; but there was a deeper spiritual element in that faith, revealing the character of their God, whose moral demands on his people were absolute. He was the only God, transcending nationalism, whose aim was the salvation of all men, and whose almighty power could not be exploited for their own advantage by the cleverness of any nation or people. We look in vain for recognition of this faith in the book of Esther.

Although there is no mention of God, there is an oblique reference to a providence in Mordecai's words to Esther: Who knows whether you have not come to the kingdom for such a time as this? and there is, too, faith that in some way God's people will be preserved: relief and deliverance will arise from another quarter (4.14) if she keeps silence.

The book may have arisen from a persecution that attempted to annihilate a Jewish minority. In the Book of Lamentations, recognition of mutual hatred between Jew and Gentile is modified by acknowledgement that disobedience to God's commands had made people and city abhorrent (Lam. 1.8, RSV filthy), even though, as

[1] H. Schultz, *Old Testament Theology* (E.T. 1895), Vol. II, p. 17.

with Jeremiah's prayer,[1] the cry for vengeance on enemies persists. Perhaps the reason that the book of Esther, despite its colourful features, has a sombre, saddening effect, is that here this mutual hatred is so frankly and unreservedly accepted.

[1] See above, p. 184.

# 18 Apocalyptic Religion: Daniel

Apocalyptic literature, as the Greek word from which this name comes shows, is concerned with the revelation and interpretation of hidden or secret things. It is most clearly represented in the Old Testament by the book of Daniel, and in the New Testament by the Revelation of John. It had clear distinguishing features.

1. It was written in the names of great figures of the past, such as Enoch, and Daniel who is previously mentioned by Ezekiel (14.14; 28.3). It was written as though the revelation of the secrets had been made long ago to them, and any history from that assumed setting is given as prophecy of the future. Daniel the hero is supposed to have lived 606–535 B.C. (Dan. 1.1; 10.1). Often it is possible to date the actual writing of an apocalyptic book exactly by the place where these "predictions" cease to be historically accurate because they really are predictions. Daniel (11.45) predicted that the death of Antiochus Epiphanes would take place in Palestine. Actually he died in Persia in 168 B.C. Much of the rest of this chapter is thought by scholars to be an account of events in the mid-second century B.C., and to be contemporaneous with the writer of the Book of Daniel.[1]

2. It was concerned with eschatology or the knowledge of the Last Things, the final end of this age. It envisaged a clear-cut division between this age and the age to come.

3. It was not concerned primarily with individuals nor with Israel as a nation, but had a universal outlook in which the veil between the present age and the next, between earth and heaven, was pulled aside. The conflict between good and evil was represented as being fought out on a cosmic stage, rather than among men and nations on this earth. It spoke of victory won by the direct intervention of God from above (7.13f), resurrection and life beyond the grave. Heavenly figures, angels and archangels associated with earthly nations and empires, and God himself were seen in vision. But the coming events

[1] Cf. H. H. Rowley, *Darius the Mede and the Four World Empires* (1935); E. R. Bevan, *Jerusalem under the High Priests* (1904).

were not told clearly for all to understand. The language was cryptic, human protagonists were represented by animals, and divine by human, and there were fantastic visions and numerical symbolism. The secrets still remained sealed (12.9); but sufficient understanding was imparted to give courage to endure and the comfort of knowing that the end purposed by God was certain and imminent.

## Its Relationship to Prophetic Religion

Apocalypse was the outcome of a religious movement in late post-exilic Judaism, but it had its roots deep down in Hebrew prophecy. We have already noticed traces of it in the books of Isaiah (24—27; 33), Ezekiel, who has been called the father of apocalypse (38f), and Zechariah (9—14). Although it appears to be the form into which Old Testament prophecy flowed after the end of the canonical prophets, it is significant that in the Hebrew text Daniel is placed not as in the English Bible with the prophetic books, after Ezekiel and before the Book of the Twelve, but in the Writings, so that it is associated with the religion of the wise, the annual festivals, and the "paradigm" history[1] with which the Hebrew Bible concludes. This difference in placing is reflected in the discussions between scholars as to Daniel's relationship to prophetic religion. Some[2] stress the links between the two, others[3] the differences. We have seen that the purpose of prophecy was to reveal God and his judgement, not the future. Certainly there was much prediction in prophecy, warnings, or hopes of the inevitable outcome of God's judgement or blessing. But in prophetic prediction the contingent element was continually stressed —a bad man or nation could repent, a good one sin, and the Lord too might "repent".[4] Apocalypse is given wholly as prediction. Its theory was that the books are secret information given long before the contemporary events, and that these are the prelude to the imminent catastrophic end of this age. This end was preordained and is unalterable.

But of course this clear-cut distinction needs to be modified as to both apocalyptic and prophetic religion. Daniel has the practical aim of giving comfort and hope to a persecuted people facing life in this world, and of encouraging them to be loyal in spite of oppression. Though they are killed, their reward will come: "And many of those

---

[1] Esther, Ezra, Nehemiah, Chronicles. See above, p. 96.
[2] Cf. O. Procksch, op. cit., pp. 401ff; H. H. Rowley, *The Relevance of Apocalyptic* (1944).
[3] Cf. von Rad, op. cit. II, p. 303.　　　　[4] See above, pp. 116f.

who sleep in the dust of the earth shall awake, some to everlasting life, and some to shame and everlasting contempt" (12.2). On the other hand, the possibility of repentance—the "Perhaps" of Amos (5.15)—when rejected by the people, can lead to the message that God will not pass that way again and the "End" is coming.

Prophetic religion was set in biography or autobiography, it started from actual contemporaneous happenings which showed the present to be a time of crisis. In the past were all God's saving acts for Israel, and different prophets emphasized the importance of different acts—the creation of the universe and of Israel, God's choice of the patriarchs, the Deliverance from Egypt, giving the law-book through Moses, the gift of the land, the establishment of the Davidic monarchy and of the Temple on Zion. The national traditions of the past, the present response of the nation to God, the future fortunes of the people, were a unity inextricably bound together. The Book of Daniel, however, like the Wisdom religion, for the most part does not speak explicitly of the traditions of the saving history. In the forefront are the ways of thought of general Near-Eastern cosmology. The sweep of world history, four empires (2.38ff) or four beasts (7.2ff), is its unity, and the saving event concerns the living last generation, upon whom the final event is about to break. But the great exception to this statement is Daniel's prayer (9.3–19),[1] where the final event is pictured as the last great saving act of God for his people, and the language is that of a man steeped in the pentateuchal stories. Calamity has befallen Israel as just punishment for her disregard of the Lord's voice constantly heard through his servants the prophets, disobedience has brought on her the curse written in the Mosaic covenant,[2] the Lord God is addressed as the one who brought his people out of Egypt. In the present form of the book of Daniel, this prayer provides a valuable link between prophetic and apocalyptic religion.

Nor would it be just to deny to prophetic religion all trace of imagery usually termed apocalyptic. In fact, some features now in prophetic pictures of the Day of the Lord are missing from Daniel— —the great cosmic battles (Zeph. 1.15f; Ezek. 38f) and the fate of the sun, moon, and stars (Isa. 13.9ff)—though in his vision of the beasts from the great sea (Dan. 7.2f) he probably alludes to the creation story and God's fight with the mythical sea-monster. So overwhelming is the prophets' sense of human sin that it is sometimes possible to present prophetic religion as depicting a cosmic, titanic

---

[1] Cf. N. Porteous, *Daniel* (1965), pp. 135ff.

[2] There may be a reference to pentateuchal dietary laws in Dan. 1.8.

struggle between the sovereignty of God and the rebellion of man which must end in "definitive discontinuity of history and its dissolution in a new aeon",[1] a belief to which Eichrodt gives the name eschatology, remarking that this element effectively lifts the whole prophetic concept of history out of the dualism of perpetual struggle. It is true that the prophets' certainty of the presence and power of God, the reality of Israel's sin, and the terrifying imminence of God's judgement gave their message vital urgency. Israel's repeated sin had broken her intimacy with God.

The prophets, however, did not envisage total destruction, an end of history and this world, and an absolutely new beginning, a rolling-up of the map of the universe as in the eschatology of the later apocalyptists. To the prophets, the power of God guaranteed the ultimate fulfilment of his purpose for Israel and the world. The plan did not have to be discarded and a new start made. The new covenant, the new heart, the new creation would spring from the old, and Second-Isaiah declared he could see what was new beginning to sprout (43.19). Always there was a remnant that became the nucleus of the new world-order. There was not a new creation from nothing, but a succession of rescues of the righteous. The same pattern of God's activity was seen running through all the stories of the saving history—the Flood, Sodom, the staying of slaughter at Sinai when Moses rejected God's offer that he alone should be the remnant, the belief in some remnant however small, and even the basket of good figs. It was never absolute destruction that would show that God's plan had been defeated, but absolute confidence in the creator God who was bringing his plan for humanity to a victorious conclusion in this world. It is doubtful whether, to the prophets in general, their overwhelming sense of the reality of God made an impassable gulf between this age and the age to come as it did to the later apocalyptists.[2] God's promise guaranteed an enduring order of existence in this world. The new movement forward caused by the power of God did not in the prophetic vision point beyond history, but beyond the present into the emerging future of a purged people and a world made new.

Such a viewpoint was not possible for Daniel, who had to come to terms with the new and actual situation, bewildering as it was. Israel had been removed from "the glorious land" (Dan. 11.41) and somehow had to find in God's purpose a kingdom not of this world. The

---

[1] "eines endgültigen Abbruchs der Geschichte und ihrer Aufhebung in einem neuen Aeon" (op. cit., p. 385).

[2] Eichrodt, op. cit., p. 390.

seedtime of the nation's past had to issue in a wider harvest, and the process was puzzling and painful. They had now been placed by God as a scattered people living under the shadow of great empires. Not for them were decisions of politics, not even whether to seek alliance with Egypt or Assyria or wait for the guidance of the Lord. To Daniel came the vision that despite all appearances God was ever on the throne, not that he had come new to his kingdom, nor that he would show his power by actively intervening on the side of Israel as a political entity. He was enthroned with everlasting dominion, his kingdom enduring from generation to generation (4.34). Nothing was more sure than that he would not finally allow the pride of an emperor to stand in place of his own glory. While Nebuchadnezzar was boasting of his greatness just after he had received Daniel's warning (4.30), he would be driven from men to eat grass like an ox. Belshazzar the Chaldean would die on the very night that he and his concubines drank wine from the vessels of the Temple. Meanwhile it was for "youths without blemish, handsome and skilful in all wisdom" (1.4) to wait in quiet obedience and be careful not to defile themselves, ready to die rather than to be disloyal to the God who looked on them as his own (3.17). Further, when Daniel, like a true wise man, offered counsel to Nebuchadnezzar, his brave words are in keeping with the early prophetic teaching: "break off your sins by practising righteousness and your iniquities by showing mercy to the oppressed, that there may perhaps be a lengthening of your tranquillity" (4.27; cf. Amos 5.15). It is helpful to notice how Daniel's meditation on what had been learned in centuries of experience of the people with their God is still bearing fruit in the counsel of this Old Testament apocalyptist. There is no real break.

As a contrast between the prophet and the apocalyptist, it should, however, be noticed that there is no suggestion in the prophetic writings of information to be kept secret. When First-Isaiah (8.16) sealed up his testimonies among his disciples, it was because they had been publicly delivered and rejected; the writing and sealing was to preserve them for the future to prove the truth of the prophetic inspiration. It is this historic act, however, which is taken up into the imagery of Daniel and the Book of Revelation in the New Testament when they write of seals and sealings. The concept of secret information is, as we have seen, basic to the apocalyptic approach. The apocalyptists studied the prophetic books, and where it appeared that prophecy had not been fulfilled or was capable of a secondary interpretation, they gave it a new meaning. Daniel (9.2) reinterpreted

Jeremiah's prophecy (25.11; 29.10) that the Babylonian captivity would last seventy years. The seventy years were to be seventy weeks of years (Dan. 9.24; cf. Lev. 25.8), or 490 years divided into three periods of 70 weeks = 49 years, 62 weeks = 434 years, and one week = 7 years. Scholars do not agree about the starting-point or significance of these dates.[1] As with so much of the symbolism of apocalypse, the clues to understanding the symbol have been lost. But to the writer's audience the significance would have been clear: God's power was sure. It was not "an intricate puzzle to test the ingenuity of the faithful". In conclusion it may be remarked that the fascination of numbers, not words, may have enticed some devout people, both Jews and Christians, away from serving the best interests of the religion they would wish to promote. What emerges from Daniel's message is the faith that God's purpose cannot fail and his power is available for men when they are at their wit's end (Ps. 107.27).

## Stories and Visions

The Book of Daniel is usually divided into two sections, 1—6 and 7—12, though it is possible that the division should be made after chapter 7, which like 2.4—6 is written in Aramaic, while the rest of the book is in Hebrew. The first section shows the flower of Jewish piety forced to challenge worldly power at its highest and on its own ground, the great Babylonian emperor in his own court, and, like the Jews in Esther, they are living a separated life though coexisting with their Gentile neighbours, sharing their general life and earning royal honours. Again, as in Esther, this separated-ness could suddenly cause hatred of the Jews (Dan. 1; 3; 6) and it is recognized that faithful obedience to God's laws may cause martyrdom (3.18). We learn too that the Jews were observing the custom of turning towards Jerusalem (1 Kings 8.38) and praying three times a day (Ps. 55.17).

But though the setting is in this world, heaven is all about them, and there are many references to God's action and the intervention of supernatural beings. It was God who brought Daniel to favour (Dan. 1.9), gave the Israelite youths knowledge and wisdom (1.17), and revealed mysteries (2.28). A great stone cut by no human hand destroyed the world empires (2.34). A figure of human appearance, later called an angel by Nebuchadnezzar (3.25), delivered the three men from the fiery furnace. "A watcher, a holy one" came down from

[1] Cf. O. Procksch, op. cit., pp. 418f; N. Porteous, op. cit., p. 140.

heaven to announce sentence on the king (4.13), and his two successors, Belshazzar and Darius, were shown by supernatural intervention
the power of God over their life and kingdom (5.5; 6.16, 27). Daniel's
visions show him that God has thousands of messengers always ready
at his bidding (7.10) and that he holds the powers of the world in
check. The visits of these messengers are similar to the type of
divine activity represented in some of the patriarchal stories, and it is
interesting that to Abraham in Ur of the Chaldees (Gen. 24.7) as to
Daniel, God was known as God of heaven (Dan. 2.18f; cf. 4.37). It
has often been remarked that Daniel may be compared with Joseph,
and Nebuchadnezzar's dream with its God-given interpretation has
features, such as interest in numbers, which make it comparable with
Pharaoh's dream.

When we pass from the stories to the dream and visions (7ff),
Daniel is writing from a standpoint where an emperor's court, pomp,
and decrees no longer frame his thinking. The supernatural is more
pronounced and the setting is the world above. Again and again it is
emphasized that the visions terrify and confuse Daniel. He falls on
his face, he has to be raised to his feet, his colour changes, he is sick,
he does not understand, he can only keep it to himself, it is some days
before he can rise and go about the king's business. The first vision
which he is granted is less restrained than the theophanies to Moses at
Sinai, or to First-Isaiah and Ezekiel—the Ancient of Days has rai-
ment white as snow (7.9f), hair like pure wool, a throne of fiery flames
with wheels of fire. Power too becomes more explicit in the figure of
this almighty God, universal judge, ruler of an everlasting kingdom,
giving power to whom he will, whether it be a heavenly "Son of Man"
(7.13)[1] or the saints of the Most High (7.22). The passive forms of
verbs (7.4, 6) give the same hint of a power controlling the empires of
this world as we have seen in Esther.

In the second vision it is helpful to notice, after this overpowering
impact of the Ancient of Days, how Daniel is concerned with the
problem of humanity, of man. The interpretation of the ram and the
goat (8.20f) is in human form. These empires are, as it were, men who
are carried away with the impulse and power of beasts. A man's voice
between the banks of the river calls to Gabriel[2] and Daniel is addressed, as is Ezekiel, as "son of man", human being.

Following these two visions received under Belshazzar is recorded

[1] Cf. J. A. Emerton, *Journal of Theological Studies* (N.F. ix, 1958), pp.
224ff.
[2] In Enoch 9 Gabriel is one of the archangels.

an experience after the emperor's well-merited death. Daniel had been studying "the books" (9.2). We are not told what these books were; there follows an explicit reference to Jeremiah, and there are elsewhere many allusions to the visions of Ezekiel, so that clearly there were books of Law and Prophets which had for Daniel the status that we should call canonical, as containing the word of God. He had been concerned to discover whether Jeremiah's prophecy of seventy years had relevance to his own age, that there would be an end to the present suffering. As seventy years had relevance to the Babylonian exile, had it also relevance to the anguish of his own day? His great prayer to God was neither that he should be saved from disbelief, nor that he should be able to work out the meaning as an arithmetical, predicted calculation. Impressed by the appalling sin and folly of the past, as Josiah when the lawbook was discovered in the Temple, he "prayed to the Lord and made confession", addressing God as the Lord, as righteous, great, and fearful, keeping covenant and steadfast love with those who love him and keep his commandments (9.4). He remembered the desolate sanctuary (9.11–17) and was reminded of the hoped-for prince (or leader) and anointed one (9.25f). He based his whole plea not on the people's righteousness but on God's great mercy (9.18). How deeply he meditated on God's word in "the books" emerges in the fact that, when he felt himself trembling and powerless after the next vision, the words of comfort that came to him were invigorating, as earlier the same words had been to Joshua the son of Nun: "Be strong and of good courage" (Josh. 1.6; Dan. 10.19).

While Daniel was still making his great prayer, at the time of the evening sacrifice the man Gabriel came to him in swift flight, bringing the assurance that he was "greatly beloved" (9.23; 10.11, 19), and so might understand Jeremiah's prophecy as meaning that the punishment on Israel was to have an appointed end. God still was supreme, "and in the immediate future God's transcendent power would manifest itself on his people's behalf".[1]

The spiritual sympathy between Daniel and Ezekiel emerges very clearly in the next vision, received at the bank of the Tigris. The linen-clothed, supernatural figure, his body translucent as beryl (10.6), again assured Daniel that from the moment he tried to understand and humbled himself before God, God had listened to him. Contemporary history is outlined in plain, not cryptic language (ch. 11), and the end is foretold that God will bring about through

[1] N. Porteous, op. cit., p. 134.

Michael. The naming of angelic figures occurs only here in the Old Testament. Michael is called one of the chief of princes, your prince, and the great prince who stands over your people (10.13, 21; 12.1). He had been delayed in coming to answer Daniel's prayer for three weeks (the time of Daniel's fasting) because "withstood by the prince of Persia" (10.13). This curious concept seems to rest on a belief that angels were appointed guardian spirits of every nation, and Michael was Israel's angel.[1] Possibly the idea has associations with the deuteronomic suggestion (Deut. 4.19f; cf. 29.26) that different gods were given to different nations and the Lord was Israel's God. God's answer to Daniel's prayer had gone out at the beginning of the three weeks' fasting (cf. Dan. 9.23), but his messenger had been delayed—an interesting explanation of apparently unanswered prayer!

## Resurrection

A most vital element in this book is the explicit statement that the dead will rise. "Many" of those who sleep in the dust of the earth will awake (12.2), and among them will be both good and bad. With this statement must be contrasted the universal concept of the Great Judgement Day in the "little apocalypse" of Isaiah 24—27, which we have already noticed.[2] There death itself is to be destroyed: "He will swallow up death for ever, and the Lord God will wipe away tears from all faces" (Isa. 25.8). In both books there is a clear distinction between the fate of the wicked and the good. But in Isaiah 24—27 there is no resurrection for the wicked; they will not live, they are shades, they will not arise (26.14). But:

> Thy dead shall live, their bodies shall rise.
> O dwellers in the dust, awake and sing for joy! (26.19)

Perhaps this has proved to be our most precious heritage from apocalyptic, the faith in the ultimate, invincible, living power of goodness, and trust in an almighty God; death is no longer regarded as the last line of all. It has been suggested that "the saints of the Most High" (7.22, 25) may have been the name given by the writer to the righteous Israelites who would be raised from the dust and shine like stars.

---

[1] Cf. Matt. 18.10, their angels, of the children.
[2] See above, p. 141.

## Son of Man and Messianic Prince

The most enigmatic figures in the book in view of later developments in apocalyptic and in the New Testament are the "one like a son of man" (7.13), and the Messiah, the prince (leader) (9.25), who will be cut off before the city and sanctuary are destroyed by the people of "another prince" (9.26). To an Aramaic reader, the words "son of man" would certainly suggest a human form (cf. 8.17; Ezek. 2.1), but the "clouds of heaven" would link him with the theophanies of the Old Testament and the way in which God himself appeared to men or visited the holy shrines in the wilderness. Thus, whatever myths or ritual lie behind the phrase, for Daniel it represents a transcendent, heavenly figure in human form, as by him all divine figures are presented. But to this divine "son of man" is given "dominion and glory and kingdom, that all peoples, nations, and languages should serve him; his dominion is an everlasting dominion which shall not pass away, and his kingdom one that shall not be destroyed" (Dan. 7.14).

The anointed prince or Messiah-prince is perhaps more difficult to interpret (9. 25f). Both terms are applied elsewhere in the Old Testament to David, who is called Leader (2 Sam. 5.2; Isa. 55.4) and Anointed (2 Sam. 23.1). In Solomon's Temple-prayer (2 Chron. 6.5f, 42) both terms are used of David. Here in Daniel the words are usually thought to refer to the High Priest Onias III, deposed by Antiochus Epiphanes. In the Old Testament, the word Messiah is not used as a technical term for the ideal leader in the new age. It is used of kings, high priests, prophets, and Cyrus, and is used often, but always without any ideal reference except possibly in Psalm 2, which speaks of people and ruler conspiring against God and his anointed. Here in Daniel it seems to signify an ideal ruler who would lead the people into the Kingdom of God. He had been killed before it began. Probably this verse in Daniel must be connected with the equally cryptic reference to one who has been pierced (Zech. 12.10).

This book, written at the end of the Old Testament period, or more accurately in what used to be called the silent period between Malachi and Matthew, is important for our study of Old Testament religion. It is a vigorous call to fellow-Jews to be loyal to their faith at a time when powerful forces were making a supreme attempt to destroy their religion. Many had forsaken the holy covenant, seduced

by flattery; the Temple was desolate, the daily sacrifices had ceased
(11.31). But many others had willingly accepted martyrdom rather
than deny their past traditions and the God who through so many
centuries had shown his love and saving power to the nation. They
had fallen by sword and flames, captivity and plunder (11.33). With
understanding of the vision of Second-Isaiah (53) the writer speaks of
the vicarious death of some of Israel's finest sons—the wise who gave
them understanding—who died to refine, cleanse, and make white
"many who join themselves to them by flattery" (11.35). Though he
believed that these martyrs would receive "little help" and that their
leader would perish, nothing shakes the writer's own deep faith that
God does and will intervene. Daniel's imagery has been called static
and lifeless. It is static in the same way as great stained-glass windows
in a cathedral may be called static; light pours through in myriad
streams and colours upon the faithful who contemplate them. The
message of the Book of Daniel is that God's power is supreme in the
present which he relates as future, and though the end of suffering is
not yet, it has been appointed by God. It is sure and near.

The anguished cry "How long?" that had rung so often from the
homes and shrines, folk-lore and liturgy of the past (cf. Pss. 74.10;
79.5; 80.4) is echoed again in this book (Dan. 8.13; 12.6), but it is
answered as before by confident certainty of God's victory (Ps. 79.13).
Daniel asserts that the Most High rules the kingdom of men (Dan.
4.17).

# 19 The Religion of the Chronicler

As at the end of the Law in the book of Deuteronomy, so at the end of the Writings in the work of the Chronicler, there is a reconstruction, a rewriting of the old national and religious traditions from another standpoint. Ezra and Nehemiah with the two books of Chronicles, which end the Hebrew Bible, are all regarded by scholars as the Chronicler's work; but theories differ considerably as to when this work was written and where.[1] Usually it is thought to have been written between 400 and 300 B.C. and to have been based on the books of Samuel and Kings, but where similarities occur there is evidence to suggest that the deuteronomic editor of Samuel and Kings, and perhaps the first writer of Chronicles, were independently using common sources.[2]

In the Hebrew canon, Ezra and Nehemiah are placed before Chronicles, but in the English versions Chronicles is put first, and it is thought this must have been the original sequence. Ezra and Nehemiah continue the story of Israel from the event at which 2 Chronicles ends, and a connection is made by a duplication of the last two verses of Chronicles and the first two verses of Ezra. In Ezra and Nehemiah[3] we are given the historical background of the prophecies of Haggai and Zechariah, who are mentioned together in the book of Ezra (5.1; 6.14). 1 and 2 Chronicles cover the same period as the Law and the Former Prophets, from the creation of Adam to the end of the Jewish monarchy in 586 B.C., but with neither the additional history of the subsequent appointment of Gedaliah as governor and his murder, nor the release of Jehoiachin in Babylon in 567 B.C. after thirty years in captivity (2 Kings 25.22–30).

[1] A. Lods, *The Prophets and the Rise of Judaism* (1937), p. 299, dates it after Ecclesiasticus.

[2] Cf. C. F. Burney, *Notes on the Hebrew Text of the Books of Kings* (1903), pp. 28ff, where a comparison of 1 Kings 3 with 2 Chron. 1 shows that the latter is without the deuteronomic additions in Kings. Minor differences between Chronicles and Kings suggest that each editor was perhaps separately translating from an Aramaic source.

[3] Nehemiah is usually dated in 444 and Ezra in 397 B.C.

## David and the Levites

The history from Adam to the death of Saul is given in the form of genealogies in which Adam the first man is linked with the people of Israel, just as Second-Isaiah linked creation with the Creator's choice of Israel—"stretching out the heavens, and laying the foundations of the earth, and saying to Zion, 'You are my people' " (Isa. 51.16). The selective genealogical tables carry the line through David and the kings of Judah (1 Chron. 3.16) to the descendants of the captured king Jehoiachin.[1] At the end of the genealogies (1 Chron. 10) an account is given of the death of Saul and his three sons, after which the interest centres on David and the act in which "all Israel" gathered to Hebron to make him king, saying that they were his "bone and flesh" and the Lord had ordained it. David's early struggles, and later his sin with Bathsheba, are not mentioned, the motive perhaps being not to whitewash his character but to fit with the theological status which the Davidic dynasty had acquired in the Chronicler's own time (cf. Isa. 55.3f and many psalms). It was probably for this motive too that the continuation of his genealogy was recorded as though God's promise might be fulfilled in a new Davidic monarchy. But it is clearly stated that the promise is conditional on obedience to God's commands, statutes, and ordinances (2 Chron. 7.17f). The omission in Nathan's prophecy of the statement that Solomon will be punished for sin (2 Sam. 7.14; cf. 1 Chron. 17.13) thus does not seem to be significant.[2] But the Lord's "promise" to David (1 Kings 9.5) becomes his "covenant" (2 Chron. 7.18; cf. 21.7), and what in Kings is the throne of David or of Israel (1 Kings 1.35; 10.9) becomes in Chronicles the throne of the Lord or the throne of the kingdom of the Lord (1 Chron. 29.23; 28.5).

David's first act as king, after he had captured Jerusalem, was to attempt to bring the Ark, neglected since the days of Saul, to Jerusalem. A tent shrine was built for it there (15.1) and preparations were begun for the building of a permanent Temple, whose purpose was to house it. The pattern of the building was made known to him "in

---

[1] Also a selective list of apparently eight generations, not always carried through eldest sons and so possibly covering up to two hundred years. This would bring its date to c. 397 B.C.

[2] Against von Rad, "Das Geschichtsbild des chronistischen Werkes", *Beitrage zur Wissenschaft von Alten und Neuen Testaments* (1930), pp. 119ff.

writing from the hand of the Lord concerning it" (28.19), and David is credited with the establishment of public worship under the levitical families (23ff). As a warrior he had shed blood (28.3), so although he could make all preparations for the Temple building, his son Solomon, "who will sit on the throne of the kingdom of the Lord" after David, had to do the building.

The Ark was clearly an essential element in the cultus, and when, after sacrifices had been offered, it was brought into the newly-built Temple and songs of praise and thanksgiving were raised, the house of the Lord was filled with a cloud and "the glory of the Lord filled the house of God" (2 Chron. 5.14). The Lord had chosen the Temple for himself as a house of sacrifice, and had entered it with the Ark. But again God's promise was conditional: "if my people who are called by my name humble themselves, and pray and seek my face, and turn from their wicked ways, then I will hear from heaven, and will forgive their sin and heal their land" (7.14).

With the Ark, Levites also were important for Davidic religion in Jerusalem. They are mentioned as distinct from the sons of Aaron (1 Chron. 15.4) and from Zadok and Abiathar the priests (15.11), they retained the duty of carrying the Ark (15.15), and because the Lord helped them, they offered sacrifices (15.26). David appointed them to minister before the Ark in the tent (16.4). But another function of the Levites came to the fore when the Ark had been finally brought to Jerusalem and there was no further need for it to be carried (cf. 2 Chron. 35.3). The Chronicler emphasizes that they had the very important task of bringing to remembrance the wonderful works of the Lord (1 Chron. 16.12; cf. titles to Pss. 38; 70) and it was their duty to invoke, thank, and praise the Lord the God of Israel with psalms and harps[1] under the leadership of Asaph's cymbals (1 Chron. 16.4). Temple singers and musicians are not mentioned in the Law, although Deuteronomy, as well as Amos (5.23; 8.10) and First-Isaiah (30.29; cf. 38.20), stresses the great joy of festivals. In Chronicles, however, singing gains in significance because it is stated that sacrifices were accompanied by songs: "And when the burnt offering began, the song to the Lord began also, and the trumpets accompanied by the instruments of David king of Israel" (2 Chron. 29.27; cf. 23.18). There seems to be a reference to the content of these songs when the function of these singers is associated with prophecy (1 Chron. 25.1) and one levitical musician is called the king's seer (25.5). Indeed, the whole arrangement of the Temple music is said to have been under

[1] See above, p. 73.

the direction of David, Gad the king's seer, and Nathan the prophet (2 Chron. 29.25). It is interesting to notice that in the Chronicler's account of Josiah's covenant, Levites stand in the place of prophets (cf. 2 Kings 23.2; 2 Chron. 34.30).

We have seen (p. 255 above) that a comparison of Malachi (3.3) with Ezekiel (44.10–14) shows that the position of Levites in the post-exilic period is far from clear. In the lists of returning exiles (Ezra 2.40; Neh. 7.43) only seventy-four Levites are mentioned as having returned with Zerubbabel compared with 4,289 priests, and when Ezra called for volunteers to return with him (perhaps 120 years later) there were no Levites until thirty-eight were specially invited (Ezra 8.18f). Sometimes in Ezra and Nehemiah singers are differentiated from Levites, as also are gatekeepers (Neh. 11.19), but usually they are included with them. Levites were also in charge of Temple business (11.16) and the regulating and measuring of offerings (1 Chron. 23.29). It is possible that at some period all these officials became part of an inclusive levitical guild (cf. 9.14–34).

A ritual function normally reserved for priests (2 Chron. 29.34)—a function which in the priestly code had been carried out by laymen (Lev. 1.6)—was taken over by Levites when there was a shortage of priests, and they prepared animals for sacrifice, "for the Levites were more upright in heart than the priests in sanctifying themselves". How important to the Chronicler were all duties connected with sacrifice is seen in the fact that to him even the pre-exilic custom by which the king offered sacrifice was no longer acceptable, and Uzziah's leprosy is accounted for by his usurping the priestly privilege (2 Chron. 26.16ff). The importance of the Passover too was emphasized in the post-exilic period. Hezekiah is said to have used it as an occasion to invite all Israel, north and south, to a united festival at Jerusalem in the second instead of the first month, as allowed by the law (30.2; cf. Num. 9.9–13), to allow time for priests and people to sanctify themselves. But even so, many had not sanctified themselves, so "the Levites had to kill the Passover lamb for everyone who was not clean" (2 Chron. 30.17) and Hezekiah prayed for the pardon of those who ate the passover otherwise than as prescribed. At Josiah's Passover also (35) the Levites killed the Passover animals and the priests sprinkled the blood.[1]

Levites also appear to have taken over from the elders (Deut. 1.13ff; cf. 16.18) the position of officers and judges (1 Chron. 23.4). They remained teachers (Neh. 8.7; cf. Deut. 33.10) though they may have

---

[1] Cf. Ezra 6.20, where the killing is shared by priests and Levites.

shared this function with priests (2 Chron. 35.3; cf. 15.3). Basically, however, the Chronicler links together David as the one who planned the Temple which housed the Ark, and the Levites who ministered before the Ark.[1]

## Moses and the Law

But there appears to be running through the books of the Chronicles another thread whose interest centres on Moses, the Law, the tabernacle, and the priests.[2] It was Moses rather than David who had commanded that Aaron and his sons should offer sacrifices and that the Levites should serve in the tabernacle (1 Chron. 6.48ff) and should carry the Ark (15.15). The tabernacle that Moses made in the wilderness where oracles were obtained (21.29) remained as a separate shrine at the high place at Gibeon even after the Ark had been installed at the Jerusalem tent (2 Chron. 1.3f), and there the older altar of burnt offering remained. There Solomon (1.6), as well as Zadok with the priests, had offered daily sacrifices morning and evening while the Levites led the thanksgiving in music (1 Chron. 16.39f). Solomon's prosperity depended on his observing the statutes and ordinances given by the Lord through Moses (22.13; cf. 2 Chron. 25.4). The Ark had its importance because in it were the two tablets of stone that Moses had placed there when the covenant was made at the Deliverance from Egypt. It was Moses too who had fixed the festivals and the amount of sacrificial offerings (8.13; 24.6,9). The law of Moses was observed at the Passover in Hezekiah's reign when priests sprinkled on the altar the blood they had received from the Levites (30.16; cf. 35.6, 12). The law given through Moses is often mentioned (33.8; 34.14) and even the regulations for the division of the people at the Passover are ascribed to Moses (35.6).

To this strand of tradition, David's importance lay in his kingship over all Israel, his bringing the Ark to Jerusalem, and his concern for the Temple.[3] It would appear unnecessary for David to be given by God a pattern for the Temple building (1 Chron. 28.11f, 18f), since Moses had already been given one of the tabernacle (or "dwelling place") and all its fittings (Exod. 25.9, P). The Levites had carried the tabernacle and its fittings, but when under David the people were given

[1] See above, p. 85, n. 4.
[2] Cf. J. N. Schofield, *The Religious Background of the Bible*, pp. 171f.
[3] Cf. W. Rudolph, *Chronikbüches* (1955).

rest, this duty was no longer necessary and they were able to wait on the sons of Aaron for the service of the house of the Lord (1 Chron. 23.25f, 28).

The relationship between these two strands is not clear, for in them seem to mingle many features from the separate neat theoretical patterns constructed by scholars. David and the Temple should clearly belong in a Jerusalem tradition, together with the belief that the Ark was housed there in the pre-exilic period; but from the Jerusalem tradition seen in Ezekiel it is clear that the importance of Levites is greatly reduced by his distinction between the Zadokite priesthood and the inferior Levites. In Deuteronomy,[1] however, where the tradition of Moses and the Law is supreme, priests and Levites appear to be used as coextensive terms—all priests Levites and all Levites priests. But in the Chronicler's handling of the tradition of Moses and the Law, the smaller group of Levites descended from Zadok is replaced by the wider group of those descended from Aaron, the descendants of Moses also being reckoned as Levites (23.14). Possibly, after the Ark, Temple, and Davidic monarchy had been destroyed by the Babylonians, and the hoped-for Davidic revival had suffered, perhaps by the death of Zerubbabel, all these would recede into the background, while the traditions of Moses and the Law, as acceptable to both Northern[2] and Southern remnants would grow in importance. It is possible that there was a struggle for supremacy within the priesthood after the fall of Jerusalem, and that various compromises were attempted between Northern and Southern traditions. The outcome seems to have been that more levitical families were recognized as of priestly status than merely the Zadokites who would have been approved by Ezekiel; some of the other Levites may have returned to secular occupations (Neh. 13.10), or joined the ranks of the wise and teachers. Repeated attempts have been made to resolve the confusion in the traditions on a chronological basis; but to the present writer it appears that the Deuteronomist and the Chronicler are not far apart and are grappling with a contemporaneous situation in the early post-exilic period.[3] It is generally recognized that Deuteronomy is of Northern origin. The Chronicler in these two strands may preserve and mingle a Jerusalem and a Northern tradition.

[1] See above, p. 85, n. 5.
[2] N.B. The connection of Moses with Dan (Judges 19.30).
[3] See above, p. 124 n. 1. "Deuteronomist" and "Chronicler" are here regarded as each representing a group or a school of writers.

## The Work of Ezra and Nehemiah

The books of Ezra and Nehemiah seem to be based on actual memoirs reused by a chronicler to write, as did the Former Prophets, paradigmatic rather than pragamatic history.[1] Despite the present order of the two books, it is usually believed that Nehemiah preceded Ezra. The story begins with the return of the first exiles from Babylon at the beginning of the reign of Cyrus (536 B.C.), led by Sheshbazzar "the prince of Judah" ("lifted-up one" as in Ezekiel) whom Cyrus made governor (Ezra 5.14). The opening words of Cyrus' decree fulfil the prophecy of Second-Isaiah that Cyrus would acknowledge the Lord (*Yahweh*) and would ascribe his victories to him; but the use of technical Hebrew words suggests that the decree as presented in Ezra was at least rewritten by a Jew. It is interesting too that there is a stress on Jerusalem, in that the Lord is described as "the Lord God of Israel, that is the God who is in Jerusalem" (1.3), as though it may have been necessary to assert this supreme claim against any suggestion from any other section of Israel that he might have made any other place his dwelling. Sheshbazzar laid the foundations for the Temple at Jerusalem (5.16); but it was not completed till the sixth year of Darius (6.15), twenty years after the first return.

Meanwhile the prophets Haggai and Zechariah had been working in Jerusalem from 520 B.C. under Joshua the High Priest and Zerubbabel the governor, a grandson of Jehoiachin the Judaean king taken into exile in 597 B.C. The altar for burnt offerings was built and set on its base for the celebration of the autumn Feast of Tabernacles, because they were terrified of their heathen neighbours (3.2ff). Two months later (Hag. 2.18) or seven months later (Ezra 3.8ff) the foundations were (again?) laid.[2] What is claimed to be the edict of Cyrus confirmed by Darius is given in Ezra (6.3), and the book also records the rejected offer of help with the building from adversaries of Judah (4.2f) who had worshipped Israel's God since the days of Esarhaddon (680–669 B.C.).[3]

Ezra is given a long genealogy linking him with Aaron as a true

---

[1] See above, p. 96. Note also that the records are chronologically out of order. Ezra 1.1 is 536, 2.2 is 520 B.C., but Ezra 4 is very confused.

[2] Misplacement and confusion are seen in 4.23f where a letter of Artaxerxes I (began to reign 464 B.C.) caused the building to cease till 520 B.C., nearly sixty years earlier.

[3] Cf. above, p. 249.

priest.[1] He is described as a priest (7.11) and a scribe skilled in the law of Moses (7.6) who had studied the law to keep it and teach it (7.10). He was sent to inquire about Judah and Jerusalem, according to the book of the law which he carried with him.[2] Though he was offered an armed escort for his company and the rich Temple treasure they carried, he refused because he was trusting in the Lord. Ezra's mission of inquiry was jeopardized because exiles who returned with him, or perhaps with earlier leaders, were marrying non-Israelite women (9.1, 4). Ezra seems to have had no authority to deal with this matter, but after fasting and a prayer of confession a commission was set up to investigate, and after three months ordered the annulling of 113 proved mixed marriages, involving seventeen priests, ten Levites and eighty-six laymen (10.44). But it is noticeable that in any case there were Elamites, who were foreigners, among the returned exiles (8.7).

The rest of Ezra's work is related in the book of Nehemiah.[3] At the Feast of Tabernacles Ezra read "the book of the law of Moses which the Lord had given to Israel" (Neh. 8.1) in accord with the command in Deuteronomy (31.10). It is not stated that this was the law book brought back from Babylon by Ezra; but the manner of the reading is carefully described. A wooden pulpit was made for him to stand on, with six men on his right and seven on his left.[4] The book was opened before the people, who stood up. Then Ezra blessed the Lord and all the people responded with Amen, lifted their hands, bowed their heads to the ground, and worshipped the Lord. Ezra read from early morning till midday throughout the seven days of the Feast, while men—possibly Levites—"helped the people to understand", reading from the book with interpretation (RSV marg.) and giving the sense, so that the people understood the reading (Neh. 8.7f). This possibly implies that the reading was translated into the vernacular Aramaic. It is stated that Nehemiah was present with Ezra (but this fact is not mentioned in the parallel Greek version).

It is also recorded that the custom of dwelling in booths during the festival was revived. The secular and religious heads of the people (probably including those who had been left in Palestine), while studying the law book with Ezra, found what is described as "the

---

[1] With Ezra 7.1ff cf. 1 Chron. 6.50f and the longer genealogy in 6.3ff.

[2] Cf. J. N. Schofield, op. cit., pp. 168ff.

[3] In the Greek version of 1 Esdras 9.37ff, the account follows immediately on Ezra 10.

[4] In 1 Esdras 9.43f these numbers are reversed.

law that the Lord had commanded by Moses" (8.14). This law, no longer extant in the form quoted here, is reflected in Leviticus (23.42). As it is emphasized that it was the returned exiles who dwelt in the booths, possibly this was a modification of the practice of Babylonian Jewry which Ezra accepted. It is further related that Ezra led one of the musical processions round the walls when they were dedicated (Neh. 12.36).

The Greek version (RSV marg., 9.6) says that a fortnight after the feast Ezra made a long prayer confessing the sins of Israel from the beginning of its history, which he traced back to creation. The covenant at the end of the prayer, made by princes, Levites, and priests, and the people, was sealed by Nehemiah. Probably levitical helpers drew up both prayer and covenant, but whoever was responsible, the terms of the covenant reflect religious conditions in Palestine more than seventy years after the rebuilding of the Temple. It was necessary to promise that there should be no intermarriage (10.30; cf. 9.2), and no trading on the Sabbath or holy days. The sabbatical year required in Deuteronomy (15.1ff) would be observed. An annual poll tax of $\frac{1}{3}$ shekel would be paid to provide the service of the Temple (Neh. 10.32f). Lots were cast among priests, Levites, and people for providing wood for the altar fire. Firstfruits of land and trees, cattle and children, were to be given to the priests at the Temple, and a tithe of corn, wine, and oil was to be given to the Levites, who themselves were to give a tithe of this tithe to the priests. The house of God was not to be neglected.

The intention of the compiler is apparently to suggest that Nehemiah arrived in Jerusalem thirteen years after Ezra (Ezra 7.7; cf. Neh. 2.1).[1] His first purpose was to build the wall of Jerusalem to give security to the community there. Again we are given a clear picture of religious conditions at the time of his return. Social injustice and political exaction, comparable to conditions in the eighth and seventh centuries B.C., had caused countrymen to mortgage their property and to sell themselves and their children into serfdom. Prophets and the prophetess could be hired for political purposes (6.12ff) to prophesy against the will of God.

Nehemiah was governor for a period of twelve years (5.14), but remained only until the wall was rebuilt, when, handing over charge

---

[1] Most scholars reverse the order by putting Nehemiah's arrival in the twentieth year of Artaxerxes I, 444 B.C., and Ezra's in the seventh year of Artaxerxes II, 397 B.C. For literature cf. H. H. Rowley, *The Servant of the Lord* (1952), p. 129.

of Jerusalem, he returned to his duties in Persia. When he came back (13.6) at the end of this period, he found that many of the laws must be re-enacted. Tobiah, an Ammonite who had opposed him, had become allied to the High Priest and had been given a room in the Temple itself (13.5; cf. Deut. 23.3ff), tithes had not been given to the Levites, the Sabbath was not observed, intermarriage had produced a generation of children who could not speak Hebrew, and even the High Priest's son had married a daughter of the Horonite governor of the province, who had also opposed Nehemiah twelve years earlier.

## Special Features

Certain general tendencies stand out in the religion of the Chronicler. There seems to be a preference to speak of God (*Elohim*) rather than the Lord (*Yahweh*); the Temple is sometimes referred to as "the house of God" in contexts where elsewhere it is called "the house of the Lord" (cf. 2 Chron. 4.11, etc.).[1] Even the Ark is similarly referred to (1 Chron. 13.14) and offerings are made before God (16.1). In the story of the naming of Baal-perazim, David's words, "The Lord has broken through" (2 Sam. 5.20), are given as "God has broken through" (1 Chron. 14.11; cf. RSV marg.), perhaps making even clearer the distinction between the Lord and the Baal. It was God who appeared to Solomon at the high place at Gibeon (2 Chron. 1.7; cf. the Lord, 1 Kings 3.5); here, however, the Chronicler is more consistent in his usage than the writer of Kings, and may represent more closely the original source.

Even more significant is the dissociation of the Lord from the cause of evil. The Chronicler wrote: "Satan stood up against Israel and incited David to number Israel" (1 Chron. 21.1); but the parallel passage (2 Sam. 24.1) has: "Again the anger of the Lord was kindled against Israel, and he incited David against them, saying, Go, number Israel and Judah."

There is too an even sharper distinction between Israel's God and the gods of the heathen (2 Chron. 32.19), who are only the work of men's hands. The schismatic priests of the Northern Kingdom are here called priests of "no gods" (13.9). Israel's God is creator and owner of heaven and earth (2.12; 1 Chron. 29.11), he stirs up the spirit of the Assyrian king (5.26) and the anger of the Philistines

[1] Cf. von Rad, op. cit.

(2 Chron. 21.16). Words from his mouth come to Josiah through Pharaoh Necho of Egypt (35.22). This is explicit monotheism.

Firmly the writer believed in rewards and punishments in this life as demonstrating the righteousness of God, and often he appears to have adjusted facts from his sources to conform with his theory (cf. 25.20 with 2 Kings 14.11). As in the stories of the Wars of the Lord in the Former Prophets, the most important factor in battle was reliance on God. However great the opposing forces, God would give victory to those who trusted in him, and the Chronicler's watchword, like First-Isaiah's, was Trust (or believe) in the Lord. Jehoshaphat's message to the people was: "Believe in the Lord your God and you will be established; believe his prophets, and you will succeed" (2 Chron. 20.20), and as the singers went out before the army, after a Levite had uttered an oracle (20.14), it was the Lord who set an ambush, routing the foe. Similarly, even a small Syrian army could defeat the very great army of Israel "because they had forsaken the Lord, the God of their fathers" (24.24).

With all the intensity of his monotheism and his belief in the righteousness of God, there is a narrowness in the outlook of the Chronicler. He uses "all Israel" far more frequently than Deuteronomy,[1] but he means by "all Israel" simply the small worshipping community around Jerusalem and anyone who joins them. There is a sense in which he is the first real sectarian, with all a sectarian's strength and weakness. The primacy of Jerusalem is now finally established. The great words choice and covenant are limited to David, the Levites, and Zion, and when Davidic hopes fade, faith finds its focus in Moses.

The Law delivered through Moses remains basic to the religion of the Old Testament.

[1] Cf. D. W. Thomas (ed.), *Essays and Studies presented to S. A. Cook* (1948), pp. 25ff.

# Conclusion

The Chronicler began by tracing the connection between Adam and the history of his own people, a small remnant of Israel in the Southern kingdom. God, who created Adam, chose Israel—this is, in outline, the story of the whole Old Testament. The Old Testament portrays God as the unseen Almighty Creator coming into the world and time from eternity and outer space, speaking words that impose order upon universal chaos, creating human beings in his own image and giving them authority over all that he made. It recognizes man's failure, rebellion against his Creator, jealousy and murder of his brother, and the utter corruption that brought inevitable destruction.

But God did not abandon the world that he had made, his garden where he had walked with man when the evening breeze blew. He remained intimately interested in human existence, showing his presence by calling Abraham whom he could reckon as loyal, and founding a people. He established times, places, and rites by which they could gain access to him, parents and priests through whom they could approach him, and prophets through whom he could proclaim the word that revealed his will, created new hearts and a new world.

As the Hebrew Old Testament closes (2 Chron. 36), we are given a realistic picture of a proud, rebellious Israelite king, with the chief of his priests and all his people, polluting the dwelling-place God had set for himself to dwell in their midst, mocking his messengers, despising his word. Inevitable destruction fulfilled the prophetic word. But still the Lord remained in the midst, and stirred up the spirit of another man from the East: "Thus says Cyrus king of Persia, The Lord, the God of heaven, has given me all the kingdoms of the earth, and he has charged me to build him a house at Jerusalem, which is in Judah" (36.23).

The inspired inheritors of the ancient Old Testament traditions, through whose hands the book comes to us, are not presenting the stirring up of Cyrus as the end of the story. It is another significant moment[1] in the continuing, struggling dialogue that makes up the

[1] See above, p. 28.

experience of the people with their God, a moment when again man realizes that the God who, he fears, has forgotten him (Isa. 40.27) has been allowing him to mature, to come of age, but has never abandoned his concern for his divine plan. There is a pool of light, man has emerged from the tangled undergrowth of frustration into a clearing, and the dialogue can be followed as a history of these significant moments.[1] Especially is this so when the experience is both revealing and shattering, when it is not Cyrus who breaks into the clearing as an unconscious agent of God's plan, but a great figure of Israel's story, one of the people of God aware that for the moment the "eternal light" is focused on him among all mankind. Such a one might say:

> There are hours when there seems no past or future,
> Only a present moment of pointed light
> When you want to burn.[2]

For us who come after, perhaps the thought is more easily expressed in terms of the weaving of a vivid thread through a tartan pattern. With careful seeking it can always be found, but sometimes it is hidden, overlaid by other colours, while at other times it stands out boldly for all to see. The God of whom the heathen said, "He hides himself" (Isa. 45.15),[3] has revealed himself once more.

There are hints[4] that the Old Testament is again establishing its position as central to Theology. Dietrich Bonhoeffer[5] in his prison cell recorded his realization that much of his comfort and strength came through the Old Testament, and today many seekers after God would echo his judgement. Forced to put his thought into very few words, he drew a distinction between salvation-myth and the history of redemption; he found it of vital importance that man in the Old Testament is redeemed for life on earth—in the land promised to the people of God. Today the "land" is the world. It is as true as ever that the world must be saved, it must not be "prematurely written off".

In recent centuries, growing scientific knowledge has increasingly pushed God out to the fringes of human existence as an unnecessary explanation of the unknown. But today necessity has new pressures

---

[1] For this notion of *Lichtungsgeschichte*, see J. M. Robinson, "The Historicality of Biblical Language" in *The Old Testament and Christian Faith*, ed. B. W. Anderson

[2] T. S. Eliot, *Family Reunion*.                    [3] See above, p. 155.

[4] Cf. E. Käsemann and W. Zimmerli in *New Century* (30 January 1960), p. 75.

[5] Op. cit., pp. 103, 156f, 185f.

and man new problems. Man in his need for guidance and "meaning" is being pushed to the point where his very restlesssness may toss him to the breast of God.[1] The presence of the living God of Abraham, Moses, the prophets, the psalmists, and Job is, in our contemporary history, still confronting us with the indispensability of reverence for the highest, moral requirements, and the stark prophetic "either . . . or" of life or death.

What theologians have been accustomed to call sin, and the Hebrews called wandering, missing the mark, rebellion, guilt, may still be purged by turning to the God of the Bible in repentance, faith, and the security of quiet, confident trust.

[1] G. Herbert, *"The Pulley"*.

# INDEXES

# Index of Names

# Index of Subjects

# Index of Biblical References